Developing Java™ Servlets

James Goodwill

SAMS

A Division of Macmillan Computer Publishing
201 West 103rd St., Indianapolis, Indiana, 46290 USA

DEVELOPING JAVA™ SERVLETS

Copyright ©1999 by Sams Publishing

International Standard Book Number: 0-672-31600-5

Library of Congress Catalog Card Number: 99-62246

Printed in the United States of America

First Printing: June 1999

01   00   99   4   3

Interpretation of the printing code: the rightmost double-digit number is the year of the book's printing; the rightmost single-digit, the number of the book's printing. For example, a printing code of 99-1 shows that the first printing of the book occurred in 1999.

Composed in Function Condensed, A Garamond and MCP Digital by Macmillan Computer Publishing

Trademarks

Warning and Disclaimer

EXECUTIVE EDITOR
Tim Ryan

ACQUISITIONS EDITOR
Steve Anglin

DEVELOPMENT EDITOR
Tiffany Taylor

MANAGING EDITOR
Jodi Jensen

PROJECT EDITOR
Tonya Simpson

COPY EDITOR
Rhonda Tinch-Mize

INDEXER
Erika Millen

PROOFREADER
Eddie Lushbaugh
Linda Morris

TECHNICAL EDITOR
Chris Seguin

TEAM COORDINATOR
Karen Opal

INTERIOR DESIGNER
Anne Jones

COVER DESIGNER
Anne Jones

COPY WRITER
Eric Borgert

LAYOUT TECHNICIANS
Brian Borders
Susan Geiselman
Liz Johnston
Mark Walchle

OVERVIEW

CONTENTS

ABOUT THE AUTHOR

James Goodwill is a professional consultant with extensive experience in telecommunications and Internet-related applications. He has been focusing his efforts on the design and development of e-commerce applications for several years. He is a senior software engineer and principal at Oak Mountain Technologies, Inc., located in Denver, Colorado. James can be reached at goodwill@oakmountaintech.com.

DEDICATION

To Christy and Abby.

ACKNOWLEDGMENTS

Before I get started thanking those close to home, I need to thank the people who made this book what it is. They are the people who took my words and molded and shaped them into something that I hope will help you become an effective servlet developer. I would like to thank Steve Anglin, my Acquisitions Editor, who answered all my questions and resolved any issues that came up. I would like to thank Tim Ryan, my Executive Editor, for his continuing flow of feedback and constructive criticism. I would especially like to thank Tiffany Taylor for her excellent editing. She really added a lot of good advice. I would like to thank Chris Seguin for his great technical comments and recommendations. I would also like to thank Rhonda Tinch-Mize and Tonya Simpson for making several catches during their copy editing. Each and every person made this the book what it is.

I would like to thank the folks at LiveSoftware for all their support when I ran into questions about Jrun. Edwin Smith was especially helpful with quick responses to all my questions.

On a closer note, I would first like to thank Steve Wilkinson of Tsunami Consulting for saving me when he agreed to pick up Chapters 9 and 14. There was no way under my deadline that I could have completed those chapters myself. He not only finished the chapters, he also did a great job with two very complicated subjects. His name might not be on the book as an author, but without him, the book would not have been completed.

I would also like to thank Chuck Nelson for his insightful comments at the very beginning of this process. He really helped me find my voice.

Finally, the most important contributors to this book are my wife, Christy, and our daughter, Abby. They supported me throughout the entire book, with complete understanding. They listened to me complain and took care of things when I disappeared into the office. With their support, I can do anything.

TELL US WHAT YOU THINK!

As the reader of this book, *you* are our most important critic and commentator. We value your opinion and want to know what we're doing right, what we could do better, what areas you'd like to see us publish in, and any other words of wisdom you're willing to pass our way.

As an Executive Editor for Sams Publishing, I welcome your comments. You can fax, email, or write me directly to let me know what you did or didn't like about this book—as well as what we can do to make our books stronger.

Please note that I cannot help you with technical problems related to the topic of this book, and that due to the high volume of mail I receive, I might not be able to reply to every message.

When you write, please be sure to include this book's title and author as well as your name and phone or fax number. I will carefully review your comments and share them with the author and editors who worked on the book.

Fax: (317) 581-4770
Email: java@mcp.com
Mail: Tim Ryan
         Executive Editor
         Sams Publishing
         201 W. 103rd Street
         Indianapolis, IN 46290 USA

INTRODUCTION

HOW THIS BOOK IS ORGANIZED

Before you begin reading this book, you might want to take a look at its basic structure. This should help you outline your reading plan if you choose not to read the book from cover to cover. This introduction gives you an overview of what each chapter covers.

Chapter 1, "Servlet Overview and Architecture"

Chapter 1 lays the foundation for the rest of the book. It discusses what servlets are and some practical applications. It also covers the basics of the Java Servlet Architecture.

Chapter 2, "Configuring the Development Environment"

Chapter 2 discusses what you will need to begin your servlet development project. It also covers some basic administrative tasks of two of the more popular servlet engines: Sun's Java Web Server and Live Software's JRun.

Chapter 3, "Servlet Basics"

Chapter 3 starts to take a real look at what servlets are and how they work. It covers the life cycle of a servlet and pulls apart a basic servlet to examine all the pieces.

Chapter 4, "Servlets and HTML"

Chapter 4 discusses how HTML form data is retrieved by a servlet. It also covers the creation of a simple HTML object library.

Chapter 5, "Server-Side Includes"

Chapter 5 covers server-side includes. It defines server-side includes and discusses their syntax. It discusses how to parse initialization parameters. It also describes how to create a server-side include.

Chapter 6, "Servlet Chaining"

Chapter 6 covers servlet chaining. It describes what servlet chains are and some practical uses for them. It gives examples of how to invoke a servlet chain. It also describes a practical example of using servlet chaining.

Chapter 7, "HTTP Tunneling"

Chapter 7 covers HTTP tunneling. It provides a definition of HTTP tunneling and describes object serialization, which is required in tunneling. It describes the creation of a tunneling client and server and gives a practical tunneling example. It also covers some of the pros and cons of applet-to-servlet communications.

Chapter 8, "Servlets and the JDBC"

Chapter 8 discusses how servlets can use the JDBC to interact with relational databases. It gives a basic introduction to the JDBC and then combines the technology with servlets. It also discusses a technique used to communicate between servlets.

Chapter 9, "Servlets and Object Databases"

Chapter 9 discusses how servlets can leverage object database technologies. It defines what an object database is, and it discusses how to use one of the more popular object databases, ObjectStore PSE Pro.

Chapter 10, "ServletBeans"

Chapter 10 covers servlet beans. It defines what a servlet bean is and how to create one. It shows you how to package, install, and invoke a servlet bean. Finally, it shows you how to create a practical servlet bean.

Chapter 11, "JavaServer Pages"

Chapter 11 describes a very new technology called JavaServer Pages (JSP). It provides a definition of JSP and describes the different JSP parts and their syntax.

Chapter 12, "Servlet Sessions"

Chapter 12 covers session management in servlets. It describes several different techniques used to manage sessions. It also describes the session management functionality that is built into the servlet SDK.

Chapter 13, "Security"

Chapter 13 describes security issues that you face when deploying an application to the Internet. It covers the most popular security techniques. It also describes some of each technique's pros and cons.

Chapter 14, "Servlets as Distributed Object Clients"

Chapter 14 discusses the use of servlets as distributed object clients. It provides an introduction to distributed computing and looks at two distributed object technologies: RMI and CORBA. It also provides practical examples for each of the described methods.

Chapter 15, "The Online Catalog"

Chapter 15 wraps everything up with a practical Web application. It takes you from requirements to usage of an online video store.

Appendix A, "The javax.servlet Package"

Appendix A describes the core package of the servlet SDK: the javax.servlet package. It discusses each interface and class and provides an object model, showing each element's place in the package.

Appendix B, "The javax.servlet.http Package"

Appendix B covers the HTTP protocol specific package of the servlet SDK. It discusses each interface and class and provides an object model showing each element's place in the package.

SERVLET OVERVIEW AND ARCHITECTURE

IN THIS CHAPTER

MOVEMENT TO SERVER-SIDE JAVA

When the Java language was first introduced by Sun Microsystems Inc., its purpose was to embed greater interactivity into Web pages. Java has accomplished this through the use of applets. Applets add functionality to Web pages, but because of compatibility and bandwidth issues, businesses have started moving to server-side Java.

Java applets are programs that are embedded directly into Web pages. When a browser loads a Web page, which contains a reference to an applet, the applet byte-code is downloaded to the client box and executed by the browser. This is fine for very thin clients, but as your applets grow in size, the download times becomes unacceptable. Applets are also faced with compatibility problems. In order to run an applet, you must have a compatible browser. If your customer does not have a compatible browser, he will not be presented with the proper content. These issues have forced businesses to take a look at server-side Java.

Server-side Java solves the problems that applets face. When the code is being executed on the server side, there are no issues with browser compatibility or long download times. The Java application on the server only sends the client small packets of information that it can understand. Java servlets are one of the options for server-side Java development.

WHAT IS A JAVA SERVLET?

I have worked on several applications that have been deployed to the Internet. CGI was really great at first, but after porting and maintaining three different sets of code that had the same functionality, I couldn't take it anymore. And then along came Java servlets. Servlets are generic extensions to Java-enabled servers. Their most common use is to extend Web servers, providing a very secure, portable, and easy-to-use replacement for CGI. A servlet is a dynamically loaded module that services requests from a Web server. It runs entirely inside the Java Virtual Machine. Because the servlet is running on the server side, it does not depend on browser compatibility. Figure 1.1 graphically depicts the execution of a Java servlet.

FIGURE 1.1
Execution of a Java servlet.

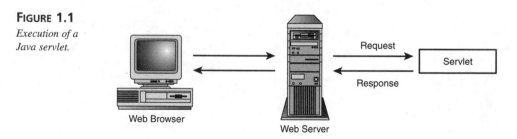

PRACTICAL APPLICATIONS FOR JAVA SERVLETS

Servlets can be used for any number of Web-related applications. When you start using servlets, you will find more practical applications for them. The following are three examples that I believe are some of the most important:

- Developing e-commerce "store fronts" will become one of the most common uses for Java servlets. A servlet can build an online catalog based on the contents of a database. It can then present this catalog to the customer using dynamic HTML. The customer will choose the items to be ordered, enter the shipping and billing information, and then submit the data to a servlet. When the servlet receives the posted data, it will process the orders and place them in the database for fulfillment. Every one of these processes can easily be implemented using Java servlets.

- Servlets can be used to deploy Web sites that open up large legacy systems on the Internet. Many companies have massive amounts of data stored on large mainframe systems. These businesses do not want to re-architect their systems, so they choose to provide inexpensive Web interfaces into them. Because you have the entire JDK at your disposal and security provided by the Web server, you can use servlets to interface into these systems using anything from TCP/IP to CORBA.

- When developing a distributed object application that will be deployed to the Web, you run into access issues. If you choose to use applets in your client browser, you are only able to open a connection to the originating server, which might be behind a firewall. Getting through a firewall using RMI is a very common problem. If servlets are employed, you can tunnel through the firewall using a servlet technology called HTTPTunneling. This enables the applet to access objects that can be running almost anywhere on the network.

These are just a few examples of the power and practicality of using Java servlets. Servlets are very viable options for most Web applications.

JAVA SERVLET ALTERNATIVES

There are alternatives to using Java servlets. You can use CGI, proprietary server APIs, server-side JavaScript, or even Microsoft's Active Server Pages. All these are viable solutions, but they each have their own set of problems.

Common Gateway Interface

The Common Gateway Interface (CGI) is one of the most common server-side solutions used to develop Web applications. A CGI application is an independent module that receives requests from a Web server. The application processes the data it receives and sends it back to the server, typically as HTML. The server then sends the data to the browser. CGI has become a standard that is used by most of today's Web servers. Figure 1.2 shows the interaction between the browser, Web server, and CGI application when you implement this type of solution.

FIGURE 1.2

The interaction of a CGI solution.

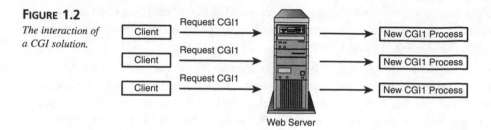

Although CGI is a widely used solution to dynamic Web development, it is also a very problematic solution. The following are some of the most common problems with CGI:

- A Web server creates a new process every time it receives a CGI request. This results in the loss of response time because the server must create and initialize a new address space for every process. You can also face the problem of running out of processes. Most servers are configured to run a limited number of processes. If the server runs out, it will not be able to handle the client's requests.

- Although CGI code can be implemented in almost any language, the most common platform-independent language is Perl. Although Perl is very powerful at processing text, it requires the server to start a new interpreter for every request. This takes longer than starting compiled code and still eats up available processes and resources.

- Additionally, CGI runs in a completely separate process from the Web server. If a client submits a request to a CGI program that terminates before responding to the Web server, the browser has no way of knowing what happened. It just sits there waiting for a response until it times out.

Proprietary APIs

Many Web servers include APIs that extend their functionality. The most common examples include Netscape's NSAPI, Microsoft's ISAPI, and O'Reilly's Website API called WSAPI. The problem with these solutions is that they are proprietary. You cannot decide to change servers without porting your code. These APIs are also developed using languages like C or C++ that can contain memory leaks or core dumps that can crash the Web server.

> **NOTE**
>
> Version 2.0 of O'Reilly's WSAPI includes a technology called FaultGaurd that is supposed to help prevent server failures due to programming errors.

Server-Side JavaScript

Server-side JavaScript is another solution for implementing dynamic Web sites. It lets you embed JavaScript into precompiled HTML pages. By precompiling the Web pages you improve performance, but the only servers that implement server-side JavaScript is Netscape's Enterprise and FastTrack servers. This again ties you to a particular vendor.

Microsoft's Active Server Pages

Microsoft has developed its own solution to the problem of dynamic Web content with Active Server Pages. Like Server-Side JavaScript, ASP is also embedded into HTML pages, but it is not precompiled. It is again similar to Server-Side JavaScript in that it is tied to a particular Web server, specifically Microsoft's Internet Information Server. Some third-party products implement ASP, but you must purchase them separately at additional costs.

REASONS TO USE JAVA SERVLETS

Java servlets are one of the most exciting new technologies I have had the opportunity to work with. Servlets are efficient, persistent, portable, robust, extensible, secure, and they are receiving widespread acceptance. If you use them only to replace CGI, you will have saved yourself a lot of time and headache. Servlets solve many of the common problems you run into when using CGI, and they prove to have a clear advantage over many of the other alternatives.

Efficient

A servlet's initialization code is executed only the first time the Web server loads it. After the servlet is loaded, handling new requests is only a matter of calling a service method. This is a much more efficient technique than loading a completely new executable with every request.

Persistent

Servlets can maintain state between requests. When a servlet is loaded, it stays resident in memory while serving incoming requests. A simple example of this would be a Vector that holds a list of categories used in an online catalog. When the servlet is initialized, it queries the database for a list of categories and stores these categories in a Vector. As it services requests, the servlet accesses the Vector that holds the categories instead of querying the database again. Taking advantage of the persistent characteristics of servlets can improve your applications performance drastically.

Portable

Servlets are developed using Java; therefore, they are portable. This enables servlets to be moved to a new operating system without changing the source. You can take code that was compiled on a Windows NT platform and move it to a Solaris box without making any changes.

Robust

Because servlets are developed with access to the entire JDK, they are very powerful and robust solutions. Java provides a very well-defined exception hierarchy for error handling. It has a garbage collector to prevent problems with memory leaks. In addition, it includes a very large class library that includes network support, file support, database access, distributed object components, security, and many other classes.

Extensible

Another advantage servlets gain by being developed in an object-oriented language like Java is they can be extended and polymorphed into new objects that better suit your needs. A good example of this is an online catalog. You might want to display the same catalog search tool at the top of every dynamic page throughout your Web site. You definitely don't want to add this code to every one of your servlets. So, you implement a base servlet that builds and initializes the search tool and then extend it to display transaction-specific responses.

Secure

Servlets run on the server side, inheriting the security provided by the Web server. Servlets can also take advantage of the Java Security Manager.

Widespread Acceptance

Because of all there is to be gained from using Java servlets, they are being widely accepted. Vendors are providing servlet support in two main forms. The first form is servers that have built-in support for servlets, and the second is by using third-party add-ons. Tables 1.1 and 1.2 list the vendors and their associated products.

TABLE 1.1 SERVERS WITH BUILT-IN SERVLET SUPPORT

Product	Vendor
Acme.Serve	Acme Java Software
Apache Web Server	Apache
Domino Go Web Server	Lotus
Dynamo Application Server	ATG
Enterprise Server	Netscape
Enterprise Server	KonaSoft
Internet Connection Server	IBM
iTP Web Server	Tandem
Java Web Server	Sun Microsystems
Jetty	Mort Bay
Jigsaw Server	World Wide Web Consortium
NetForge	Novocode
ServletFactory	Early Morning Software
Sun Web Server	Sun Microsystems
Tengah Application Server	WebLogic
Visual Age WebRunner Toolkit	IBM
WEASAL	Web Easy
WebCore	Paralogic
Website Professional	O'Reilly
Zeus Web Server	Zeus Technology

TABLE 1.2 THIRD-PARTY ADD-ONS WITH SERVLET SUPPORT

Product	Vendor
WAICoolRunner	Gefion Software
JRun	Live Software
ServletExec	New Atlanta
Servlet CGI Development Kit	Unicom
WebSphere Application Server	IBM

THE JAVA SERVLET ARCHITECTURE

Two packages make up the servlet architecture: the `javax.servlet` and `javax.servlet.http`. The `javax.servlet` package contains the generic interfaces and classes that are implemented and extended by all servlets. The `java.servlet.http` package contains the classes that are extended when creating HTTP-specific servlets. An example of this would be a simple servlet that responds using HTML.

At the heart of this architecture is the interface `javax.servlet.Servlet`. It provides the framework for all servlets. The `Servlet` interface defines five methods. The three most important are the `init()` method that initializes a servlet, the `service()` method that receives and responds to client requests, and the `destroy()` method that performs cleanup. All servlets must implement this interface, either directly or through inheritance. It is a very clean object-oriented approach that makes it very easy to extend. Figure 1.3 is an object model that gives you a very high-level view of the servlet framework.

FIGURE 1.3

A high-level object model of the servlet framework.

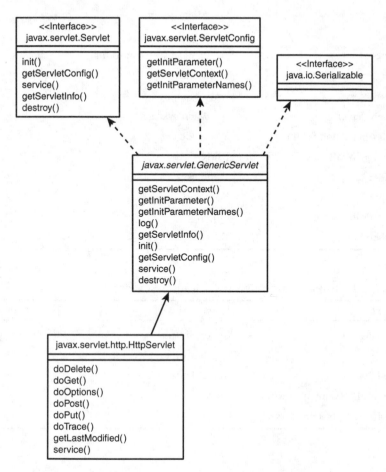

GenericServlet and HttpServlet

The two main classes are the `GenericServlet` and `HttpServlet` classes. The `HttpServlet` class is extended from `GenericServlet`. When you are developing your own servlets, you will most likely be extending one of these two classes. Java servlets do not have a `main()` method, which is why all servlets must implement the `javax.servlet.Servlet` interface. Every time a server receives a request that points to a servlet, it calls that servlet's `service()` method.

If you decide to extend the `GenericServlet` class, you must implement the `service()` method. The `GenericServlet.service()` method has been defined as an abstract method in order to force you to follow this framework. The `service()` method prototype is defined as follows:

```
public abstract void service(ServletRequest req,
ServletResponse res) throws ServletException, IOException;
```

The two objects that the `service()` method receives are `ServletRequest` and `ServletResponse`. The `ServletRequest` object holds the information that is being sent to the servlet, whereas the `ServletResponse` object is where you place the data you want to send back to the server. Figure 1.4 diagrams the flow of a `GenericServlet` request.

FIGURE 1.4

A GenericServlet request.

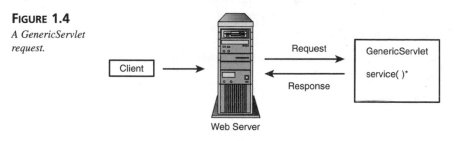

* abstract method

Unlike the `GenericServlet`, when you extend `HttpServlet`, you don't usually implement the `service()` method. The `HttpServlet` class has already implemented it for you. The following is the prototype:

```
protected void service(HttpServletRequest req, HttpServletResponse resp)
throws ServletException, IOException;
```

When the `HttpServlet.service()` method is invoked, it reads the method type stored in the request and determines which method to invoke based on this value. These are the methods that you will want to override. If the method type is GET, it will call `doGet()`. If the method type is POST, it will call `doPost()`. There are five other method types; they are discussed in Chapter 3, "Servlet Basics." All these methods have the same parameter list as the `service()` method. You might have noticed the different request/response types in the parameter list of the `HttpServlet` versus the `GenericServlet` class. The `HttpServletRequest` and

`HttpServletResponse` classes are just extensions of `ServletRequest` and `ServletResponse` with HTTP-specific information stored in them. Figure 1.5 diagrams the flow of a `HttpServlet` request.

FIGURE 1.5
An HttpServlet request.

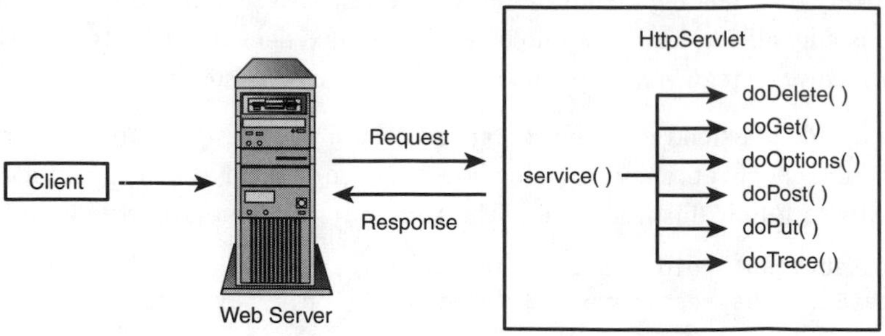

SUMMARY

In this chapter, you learned about Java servlet basics, practical applications for servlets, servlet alternatives, reasons to use servlets over the alternatives, and the basic architecture of servlets. At this point, you should have a high-level understanding of the flow of a servlet request and what objects are involved.

In the next chapter, we are going to cover what you need to create Java servlets and which Web servers support Java servlets.

CONFIGURING THE DEVELOPMENT ENVIRONMENT

IN THIS CHAPTER

SERVLET REQUIREMENTS

To begin a development effort using Java servlets, you will need to decide what tools you will use to both write and run your servlets.

You will need only a minimal set of tools to actually write Java servlets. The two most important requirements are the Java Development Kit (JDK), currently on version 2.0, and the Java Servlet Development Kit (JSDK), also on version 2.0. Both of these development kits can be downloaded from the JavaSoft home page at http://www.javasoft.com with no cost.

> **NOTE**
>
> Currently the Java Web server's JRE only supports JDK 1.1.6; therefore, we will be doing all our sample development using this version of the JDK.

There are many other third-party products you can purchase. Currently the two most popular are Inprise JBuilder 2.0 and Symantec Visual Café 3.0. Although neither of these products is necessary to write Java servlets, they might improve your development cycle.

The only items you will need to run a Java servlet is a server that supports Server-Side Java and a client to make a request. In Chapter 1, "Servlet Overview and Architecture," there is a list of Java-enabled server products. I will be discussing Sun's Java Web Server and Live Software's JRun in the next section. Our client requests will be made using a Web browser.

The two Java-enabled server products that will be focused on are Sun's Java Web Server and Live Software's JRun. You can find evaluation versions of these products on the companies' Web sites at http://www.javasoft.com and http://www.livesoftware.com, respectively. Both are very easy to use and administer. This section is only going to cover specific areas of these products that you must understand while reading this book. The areas you will study are administration and internals. Several aspects of these products are beyond the scope of this book. You can find further documentation on Sun's and Live Software's respective Web sites.

JAVA WEB SERVER

Sun's Java Web Server was the first to implement Server-Side Java. It is a richly featured commercial-quality product based on a service framework. This framework is a set of classes for implementing protocol-specific services, which use multiple threads to process requests from clients. We will be extending these services using Java servlets. The service we will focus on is the Web Service, an HTTP protocol specific service.

> **NOTE**
>
> You might have trouble starting the Java Web server on a Windows platform if the `<server_root>` has spaces in its path.

Administration

The Java Web Server Administration Tool has been implemented as an applet; therefore, you will need a Java-enabled Web browser to perform any administration tasks. The following sections explain step by step the administration tasks you will need during your reading of this book.

Logging in to the Administration Tool

To log in to the Administration Tool, point your Web browser to the administration port of the server where Java Web Server is running. The default administration port is 9090.Figure 2.1 shows the login screen for the server running on my local box.

FIGURE 2.1

The Java Web Server login screen.

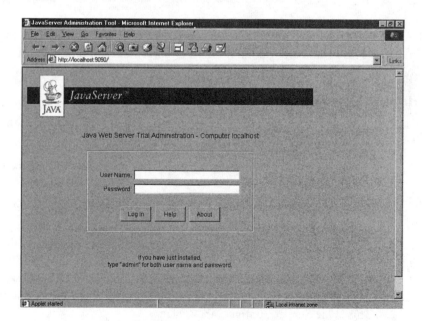

Next, enter the user name and password. The default for both is `admin`. If you successfully log in, you should see the Manage Servers and Services screen. Figure 2.2 shows the Manage Servers and Services screen after logging in.

FIGURE 2.2

The Manage Servers and Services screen.

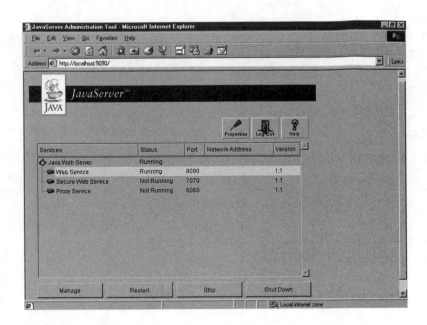

The Manage Servers and Services screen shows all the services that are currently installed on this server. This is the starting point for most of our administration tasks. The service we will be concentrating on will be the Web Service.

Adding a Servlet

To add a servlet to the Web Service, you need to first log in to the Administration Tool, as described in the previous section, and then implement the following:

1. Select Web Service and click the Manage button. You should see a screen similar to the one in Figure 2.3.

2. Click the Servlets button and select Add. You should now see the Add a New Servlet screen. Figure 2.4 shows the Add a New Servlet screen and its options.

3. Enter the name you want to reference your servlet with and then enter the class file of the actual servlet. For this example, I used the servlet `HelloWorld`. Make sure that the class file is in the `servlets` directory of the Java Web Server. After you have done this, click the Add button. If you were successful, you should see a screen similar to Figure 2.5. This is the Servlet Configuration screen.

4. You should now see the name of your servlet in the tree control on the left side of the page. If you do not see the Servlet Configuration screen, find your servlet and select it. The following list details the options available for each servlet:

FIGURE 2.3

The Web Service screen.

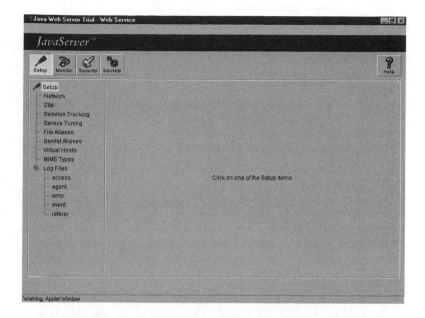

2

CONFIGURING THE
DEVELOPMENT
ENVIRONMENT

FIGURE 2.4

The Add a New Servlet screen.

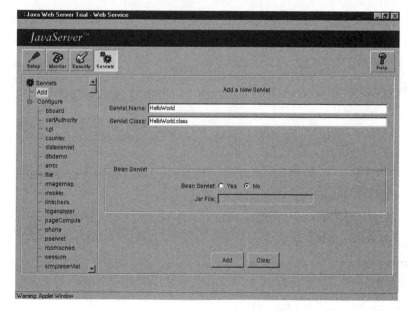

FIGURE 2.5

The Servlet Configuration screen.

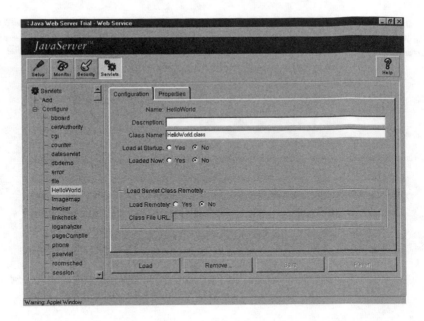

- Name—The unique name of the servlet. This name must be unique to the service.

- Description—A text string that describes the servlet. This field is optional.

- Class Name—The name of the class file of the servlet. If the servlet is part of a package, the package must also be referenced. For example, if the servlet `TestServlet` was part of package `TestPackage`, the class name would be `TestPackage.TestServlet`.

- Load at Startup—If this option is selected, the servlet will be loaded when the server starts.

- Loaded Now—If this option is selected, the servlet is currently loaded.

- Load Remotely—If this option is selected, the servlet is loaded from a remote location.

- Class File URL—This is the URL that points to the class file of the remote servlet.

At this point, you do not need to make any further changes. In later chapters, you will select different options on this screen.

Setting Up a Servlet Alias

Servlet aliases are used as shortcuts to commonly used servlets with lengthy names. They are also used to force a particular servlet to be executed when a file extension pattern is recognized.

To set up a servlet alias, go to the Manage Servers and Services screen and select SServlet Aliases. You should see a list of the current servlet aliases (see Figure 2.6).

FIGURE 2.6

The Servlet Alias screen.

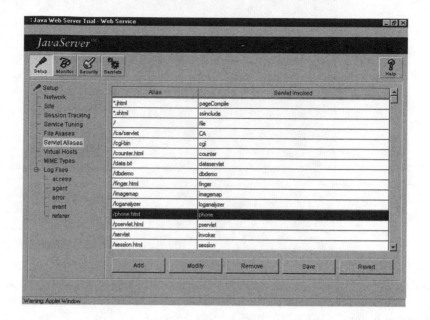

Select the Add button. Enter the alias for your servlet and the name of the servlet to be invoked. After you have entered these, click the Save button. You should now see your servlet alias in the list.

Setting Up a Servlet Chain

There are two steps involved in setting up a servlet chain. You must first enable servlet chaining for the service. Then you must actually define the servlet chain.

Enabling Servlet Chaining

To enable servlet chaining, go to the Manage Servers and Services screen, select Site, and then choose the Options tab. You should see the Site Options screen (see Figure 2.7).

Next, select Enabled for Servlet Chains and then click the Save Button.

Defining the Servlet Chain

There are two common ways to define a servlet chain. The first is to create an alias. The second is to tell the server to send all output of a specific content type to a particular servlet.

Figure 2.7

The Site Options screen.

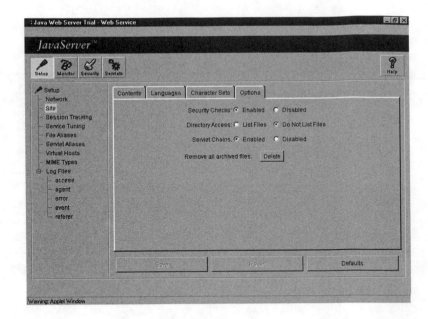

To define a servlet chain using an alias, you follow the same steps involved in setting up an alias. The only difference is you provide a comma-delimited list of servlets to be invoked instead of a single servlet. These servlets will be invoked in order according to their appearance in the list.

When you want to define a servlet chain based on a particular content type, you must go through a little more trouble. There is currently no GUI tool to perform this function. You must edit the `mimeservlets.properties` file by hand. This file is located in the `<server_root>`/properties/server/javawebserver/webpageservice/ directory. The following entry in this file tells the server to pass all responses with the Content-Type header of `java-internal/parsed-html` to the `ssinclude` servlet.

`java-internal/parsed-html=ssinclude`

We will be looking at servlet chaining in more detail in Chapter 6, "Servlet Chaining."

Internals

The Java Web Server architecture is based on a service framework, which makes it very flexible. The server takes advantage of this flexibility by partitioning its work between several internal servlets.

File Servlet

The `file` servlet is responsible for the standard document serving functionality of the Java Web Server. It includes caching mechanics to improve response times for frequently accessed documents. The `file` servlet also recognizes file extensions that are to be parsed by the `ssinclude` servlet.

Invoker Servlet

The `invoker` servlet invokes servlets that are explicitly requested by name.

Server Side Include Servlet

The `ssinclude` servlet services documents with the .shtml extension. When the server serves a file with this extension, the file is passed to this servlet for parsing. The `Server Side Include` servlet searches this file for the `<SERVLET>` tag. When it finds this tag, it loads and invokes the referenced servlet. The output of the invoked servlet is then merged with the original document and sent to the client.

Admin Servlet

The `admin` servlet services all administration requests received from the GUI Administration Tool.

CGI Servlet

This servlet acts as a replacement for the CGI 1.1 interface. The `cgi` servlet allows any program that uses the CGI 1.1 standard to function under Java Web Server.

Imagemap Servlet

The `imagemap` servlet provides server-side imagemap functionality. It uses an extension of standard NCSA mapfiles.

JRUN

JRun is a third-party add-on that extends your current Web server, making it 100 percent compatible with the JSDK. It is made up of native code that interfaces directly with your Web server and Java code that provides an abstraction layer between your Web server and your servlets. JRun does include a Web server, but it is mainly for development purposes.

Administration

JRun administration is accomplished by using the JRun Administration program. The JRun Administration program allows you to configure JRun from a single application.

Starting the Administration Tool

To start JRun's Administration program, under a Windows platform, double-click the Administration icon in your JRun Servlet Engine folder. You can start the Administration program under all platforms by executing the startadmin script found in the /jsm-default/ directory. Figure 2.8 shows the JRun Service Settings screen, which is the opening screen of the JRun Administration Program.

FIGURE 2.8

The JRun Service Settings screen.

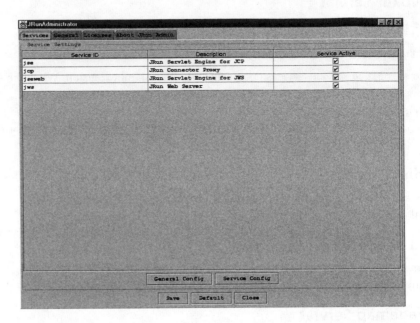

We will be doing all our administration from the JRun Servlet Engine Service Config screen. To open the Service Config screen, perform the following steps:

1. First, open the JRun Service Settings screen as previously described.
2. Next, select the jseweb service ID, and click the Service Config button. You should now see the Service Config screen, as depicted in Figure 2.9. This is the starting point for all the following administrative tasks.

Adding a Servlet

JRun does not include an administration function for adding a servlet. All you must do is copy the servlet to the /servlets directory.

FIGURE 2.9
*The Service
Config screen.*

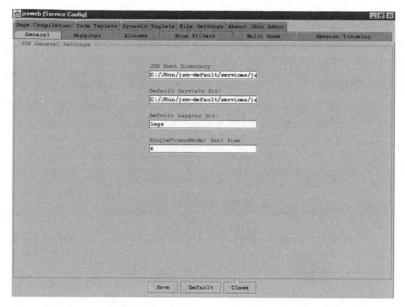

Setting Up a Servlet Alias

To set up a servlet alias, select the Aliases tab on the Service Config screen. This should display a Servlet Alias Settings page similar to the one in Figure 2.10.

FIGURE 2.10
*The Servlet Alias
Settings page.*

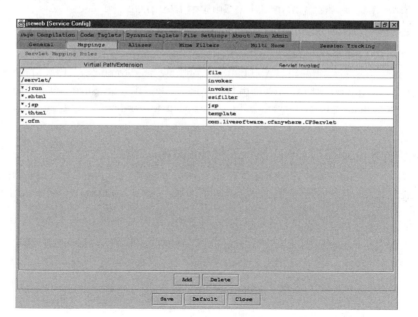

The following list describes each of the settings available to a servlet alias:

- Name—The name of the alias that represents your servlet. It should not contain spaces or special characters.
- Class Name—The fully qualified class name of your servlet.
- Init Arguments—An option list of tag/value pairs to be passed to the servlet.
- Pre-Load—This option specifies whether the servlet should be loaded at startup.

NOTE

A servlet must have an alias associated with it to be loaded at startup.

Now click the Add button. At a minimum, you should enter the servlet name and class name. To complete your change, click the Save button.

Setting Up a Servlet Chain

There are two ways to set up a servlet chain using JRun. The first is to define a mapping. The second is by creating a new mime-type filter.

Defining a Servlet Chain Using Servlet Mapping

To create a servlet chain using servlet mapping, first select the Mappings tab on the Service Config screen. This should display the Servlet Mapping Rules page, as seen in Figure 2.11.

The next step is to press the Add button. You now need to enter a virtual path/extension and a comma-delimited list of servlets to be invoked, and click the Save button. Now, whenever a request is made for the new virtual path or extension, the comma-delimited list of servlets will be invoked.

Defining a Servlet Chain Using a Mime-Type Filter

Mime-type–based servlet chaining is similar to servlet mapping. The only difference is that instead of explicitly mapping a name to a servlet chain, you specify a particular mime-type that triggers a servlet chain.

FIGURE 2.11

The Servlet Mapping Rules page.

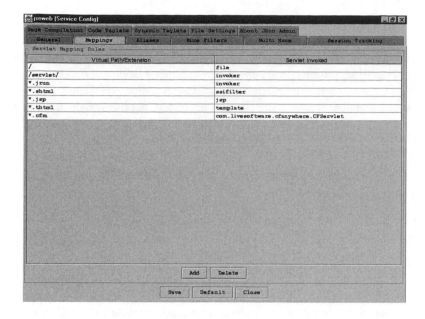

To define a mime-type filter, select the Mime Filters tab on the Service Config screen. This should display the Mime-Type Filter Settings page, as seen in Figure 2.12.

FIGURE 2.12

The Session Persistence Settings page.

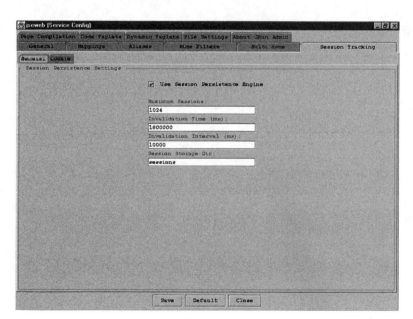

Next, click the Add button and enter the mime-type and servlets to be invoked. To complete the changes, click the Save button. Now when a request of that particular mime-type is received, the servlet chain you specified will be invoked. The current entry shows a mime-type of text-html being filtered through the `UpperCaseFilter` and `LowerCaseFilter` servlets. You probably wouldn't want to actually implement this behavior unless you want to capitalize all your responses and then convert them again to lowercase, but this is only an example.

Enabling Servlet Session Tracking

To enable servlet session tracking, select the Session Tracking tab on the Service Config screen and then select Use Session Persistence Engine. Figure 2.13 shows the Session Persistence Settings page.

Use Session Persistence Engine should be enabled by default. If it is not, select it and then click the Save button.

Internals

JRun is also based on a service framework. It includes several internal servlets that are similar to the Java Web Server's internal servlets. The most notable are the `File` servlet, the `Invoker` servlet, and the `Server Side Include` servlet. Each of these servlets behaves much like their counterparts in the Java Web Server.

FIGURE 2.13

The Session Persistence Settings page.

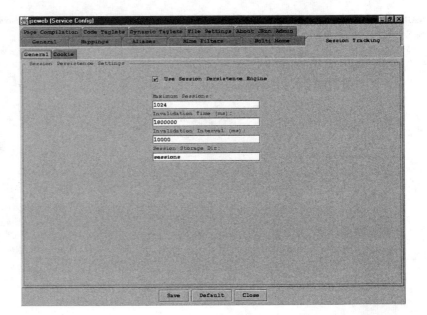

SUMMARY

In this chapter, I discussed what is required when you are going to be developing and deploying Java servlets. You should now be able to gather all the necessary tools to begin your Java servlet project.

We also took a look at the Java Web Server and JRun servers. In the following chapters, I will be referencing the Java Web Server as our server product.

This chapter is meant as a reference for later chapters. You should be able to look back at the administration steps performed here and substitute your specific options without much difficulty.

The next chapter discusses the servlet life cycle. You will also start to look at the pieces of a servlet and where they fit into the servlet framework.

SERVLET BASICS

IN THIS CHAPTER

Developing Java Servlets

THE LIFE CYCLE OF A SERVLET

The life cycle of a Java servlet is a very simple object-oriented design. A servlet is constructed and initialized. It then services zero or more requests until the service that it extends shuts down. At this point, the servlet is destroyed and garbage is collected. This design explains why servlets are such a good replacement for CGI. The servlet is loaded only once and it stays resident in memory while servicing requests.

The interface that declares this framework is the `javax.servlet.Servlet` interface. The `Servlet` interface defines the life cycle methods. These methods are the `init()`, the `service()`, and the `destroy()` methods.

init()

The `init()` method is where the servlet's life begins. It is called by the server immediately after the servlet is instantiated. It is called only once. In the `init()` method, the servlet creates and initializes the resources that it will be using while handling requests. The `init()` method's signature is defined as follows:

```
public void init(ServletConfig config) throws ServletException;
```

The `init()` method takes a `ServletConfig` object as a parameter. You should save this object so that it can be referenced later. The most common way of doing this is to have the `init()` method call `super.init()`, passing it the `ServletConfig` object.

You will also notice that the `init()` method can throw a `ServletException`. If, for some reason, the servlet cannot initialize the resources necessary to handle requests, the `init()` method should throw a `ServletException`.

service()

The `service()` method handles all requests sent by a client. It cannot start servicing requests until the `init()` method has been executed. You will not usually implement this method directly, unless you extend the `GenericServlet` abstract class.

The most common implementation of the `service()` method is in the `HttpServlet` class. The `HttpServlet` class implements the `Servlet` interface by extending `GenericServlet`. Its service() method supports standard HTTP/1.1 requests by determining the request type and calling the appropriate method. The signature of the `service()` method is shown in the following:

```
public void service(ServletRequest req, ServletResponse res)
throws ServletException, IOException;
```

The `service()` method implements a request and response paradigm. The `ServletRequest` object contains information about the service request, encapsulating information provided by the client. The `ServletResponse` object contains the information returned to the client.

destroy()

This method signifies the end of a servlet's life. When a service is being shut down, it calls the servlet's `destroy()` method. This is where any resources that were created in the `init()` method should be cleaned up. If you have an open database connection, you should close it here. This is also a good place to save any persistent information that will be used the next time the servlet is loaded. The signature of `destroy()` is very simple, but I have displayed it as follows just to complete the picture:

```
public void destroy();
```

A BASIC SERVLET

In this section, we are going to look at building and running a very basic servlet. Its purpose will be to service a request and respond with the request method used by the client. We will take a quick look at the servlet's source code, the steps involved in compiling and installing the servlet, and the HTML necessary to invoke the servlet.

The BasicServlet Source

Listing 3.1 contains the source code for this example. You can find the following source listing on this book's Web site. If you have the time, it is probably best if you type the first few examples yourself. This will help you become familiar with the basic parts of servlets. As you type or browse over this listing, feel free to look up the referenced classes in Appendix A, "Servlet API."

LISTING 3.1 BASICSERVLET.JAVA DISPLAYS THE REQUEST METHOD USED BY THE CLIENT

```
import javax.servlet.*;
import javax.servlet.http.*;
import java.io.*;
import java.util.*;

public class BasicServlet extends HttpServlet {

  public void init(ServletConfig config)
    throws ServletException {

    // Always pass the ServletConfig object to the super class
```

continues

LISTING 3.1   CONTINUED

```java
    super.init(config);
  }

  //Process the HTTP Get request
  public void doGet(HttpServletRequest request,
    HttpServletResponse response)
    throws ServletException, IOException {

    response.setContentType("text/html");
    PrintWriter out = response.getWriter();

    out.println("<html>");
    out.println("<head><title>BasicServlet</title></head>");
    out.println("<body>");

    // Prints the REQUEST_METHOD sent by the client
    out.println("Your request method was " + request.getMethod()
      + "\n");

    out.println("</body></html>");
    out.close();
  }

  //Process the HTTP Post request
  public void doPost(HttpServletRequest request,
    HttpServletResponse response)
    throws ServletException, IOException {

    response.setContentType("text/html");
    PrintWriter out = response.getWriter();

    out.println("<html>");
    out.println("<head><title>BasicServlet</title></head>");
    out.println("<body>");

// Prints the REQUEST_METHOD sent by the client
    out.println("Your request method was " + request.getMethod()
      + "\n");

    out.println("</body></html>");
    out.close();
  }
```

```
//Get Servlet information
  public String getServletInfo() {

    return "BasicServlet Information";
  }
}
```

Building and Installing the BasicServlet

There are two steps that you need to complete to run your newly created servlet. The first step is to compile the servlet code. The second is to install the servlet in a place where the Java Web Server can find it.

To compile the servlet, you will need to make sure the Servlet SDK is on your CLASSPATH. If you installed the Java Web Server, you can find the JSDK classes in the lib/jws.jar file.

There are two steps involved when installing a new servlet. The first is to place the BasicServlet.class file on the Java Web Server's CLASSPATH. The easiest way to do this is to move the class file into the server's /servlet directory.

The next step is to add the servlet to the Web service. To do this, follow the steps for "Adding a Servlet" in Chapter 2 within the "Java Web Server" section. Use BasicServlet for the servlet name and BasicServlet.class for the servlet class.

The HTML Required to Invoke the Servlet

This servlet implements both the doGet() and the doPost() methods. Therefore, there are two ways to invoke this servlet.

The first is to just reference the servlet by name in the URL. The following URL will execute the servlet on my server:

http://localhost:8080/servlet/BasicServlet

Using this method defaults the request method to GET, which will invoke the servlet's doGet() method.

The second way to invoke the servlet is to create an HTML page that will send a request to the servlet using the POST method. This will invoke the servlet's doPost() method. Listing 3.2 shows the HTML listing to complete this task.

```
<HTML>
<HEAD>
<TITLE>
BasicServlet
</TITLE>
</HEAD>
<BODY>

<FORM
  ACTION=http://localhost:8080/servlet/BasicServlet
  METHOD=POST>

  <BR><BR>
  press Submit Query to launch servlet BasicServlet
  <BR><BR>
  <INPUT TYPE=submit>
  <INPUT TYPE=reset>
</FORM>

</BODY>
</HTML>
```

When you invoke the servlet using either of these methods, the results should be similar to Figure 3.1. The only notable difference should be the request method returned.

DISSECTING THE BASICSERVLET

Now that you have the BasicServlet installed and running, let's take a closer look at each of its integral parts. We will examine the location where the servlet fits into the framework, the methods that the servlet implements, and the objects being used by the servlet.

Where Does the BasicServlet Fit into the Servlet Framework?

The first thing we are going to look at is where the BasicServlet fits into the servlet framework. This servlet extends the HttpServlet class. The HttpServlet class is an abstract class that simplifies writing HTTP servlets. It extends the GenericServlet class and provides the functionality for handling HTTP protocol-specific requests. The BasicServlet overrides four of its inherited methods. Figure 3.2 shows where the BasicServlet fits into this hierarchy.

FIGURE 3.1
The BasicServlet HTML response page.

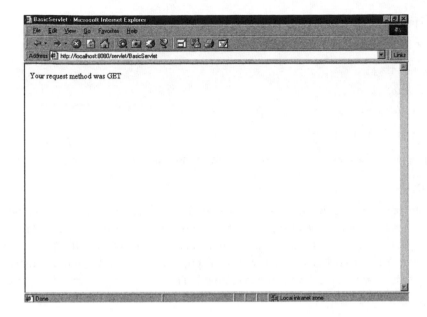

FIGURE 3.2
The BasicServlet depicted in the framework.

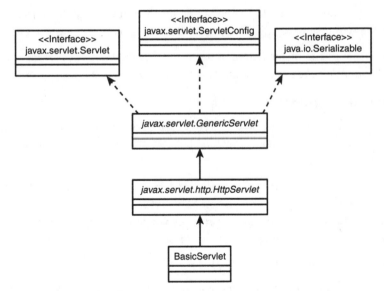

The Methods Overridden by the BasicServlet

The following four methods are overridden by the `BasicServlet`:

- `init()`
- `doGet()`
- `doPost()`
- `getServletInfo()`

Let's take a look at each of these methods in more detail.

init()

The `BasicServlet` defines a very simple implementation of the `init()` method. It takes the `ServletConfig` object that is passed to it and passes it to its parent's `init()` method, which stores the object for later use. The parent that actually holds on to the `ServletConfig` object is the `GenericServlet`. The `GenericServlet` provides your servlet, through inheritance, with methods to access the `ServletConfig` object. The code that performs this action follows:

```
super.init(config);
```

This is a very important step. If you do not do this, you must hold the `ServletConfig` object yourself. We will discuss the significance of the `ServletConfig` object in later chapters.

Also notice that this implementation of the `init()` method does not create any resources. This is why the `BasicServlet` does not implement a `destroy()` method.

doGet() and doPost()

The `BasicServlet`'s `doGet()` and `doPost()` methods are identical. The only difference is the requests they service. The `doGet()` method handles GET requests, and the `doPost()` method handles POST requests.

Both methods receive `HttpServletRequest` and `HttpServletResponse` objects. These objects encapsulate the request/response paradigm. The `HttpServletRequest` contains information sent from the client, and the `HttpServletResponse` contains the information that will be sent back to the client. The first executed line of these methods is listed as follows:

```
response.setContentType("text/html");
```

This method sets the content type for the response. You can set this response property only once. You must set this property before you can begin writing to a `Writer` or an `OutputStream`. In our example, we are using a `PrintWriter` and setting the response type to `"text/html"`.

The next thing to do is get the `PrintWriter`. This is accomplished by calling the `ServletRequest`'s `getWriter()` method. This is done in the following line of code:

```
PrintWriter out = response.getWriter();
```

Now you have a reference to an object that will allow you to write HTML text that will be sent back to the client in the `HttpServletResponse` object. The next few lines of code show how this is done:

```
out.println("<html>");
out.println("<head><title>BasicServlet</title></head>");
out.println("<body>");

// Prints the REMOTE_ADDR sent by the client in the request
out.println("Your request method was " + request.getMethod()
    + "\n");

out.println("</body></html>");
out.close();
```

This is a very straightforward method of sending HTML text back to the client. You simply pass to the `PrintWriter`'s `println()` method the HTML text you want included in the response and close the stream. The only thing that you might have a question about is the following few lines:

```
// Prints the REMOTE_ADDR sent by the client in the request
out.println("Your request method was " + request.getMethod()
    + "\n");
```

This takes advantage of the information sent from the client. It calls the `HttpServletRequest`'s `getMethod()` method, which returns the HTTP method with which the request was made. The `HttpServletRequest` object holds HTTP-protocol specific header information. The following list shows the information contained in the `HttpServletRequest` object:

- `getAuthType()`—Returns the authentication scheme of this request
- `getCookies()`—Returns the arrayof cookies found in this request
- `getDateHeader(String)`—Returns the value of the date header field found in this request
- `getHeader(String)`—Returns the value of a specific header field in this request
- `getHeaderNames()`—Returns an enumeration containing the header names for this request
- `getIntHeader(String)`—Finds the header field in the request and converts it to an integer
- `getMethod()`—Returns the HTTP method with which this request was made; for example, either the `POST` or `GET` method
- `getPathInfo()`—Returns any optional extra path information following the servlet path of this request's URI, but immediately preceding its query string

- `getPathTranslated()`—Returns any optional extra path information following the servlet path of this request's URI, but immediately preceding its query string, and translates it to a real path

- `getQueryString()`—Returns any query string that is part of the HTTP request URI; this is the same `QUERY_STRING` used in CGI applications

- `getRemoteUser()`—Returns the name of the user making this request, if it is available

- `getRequestedSessionId()`—Returns the session ID contained in this request

- `getRequestedURI()`—Returns the part of this request's URI that is to the left of any query string

- `getServletPath()`—Returns the part of this request's URL that points to the servlet that is being invoked

- `getSession(boolean)`—Returns the current session associated with this request

- `isRequestedSessionIdFromCookie()`—Returns `True` if the session ID specified by this request came in as a cookie, otherwise it returns `False`

- `isRequestedSessionIdFromURL()`—Returns `True` if the session ID specified by this request came in as part of the URL, otherwise it returns `False`

- `isRequestedSessionIdValid()`—Determines whether this request is associated with a session that is valid in the current session context

As you have noticed, the `HttpServletRequest` object provides access to quite a bit of information. As we proceed, you will begin to make real use of this information. We will also be looking at the information it provides through inheritance.

getServletInfo()

The `getServletInfo()` method is like the applet's `getAppletInfo()` method. It can be used to provide version, copyright, author, and any other information about itself.

SUMMARY

In this chapter, we were finally able to start examining some servlet code. We looked at the servlet life cycle and the steps necessary to build, install, and invoke a servlet. We also dissected a basic servlet, which gave us a view of each integral part of a servlet.

You should now be able to create, build, and install your own servlets. You should also have a basic understanding of the servlet life cycle and where your servlets will fit into the Java Servlet framework.

In the next chapter we are going to learn how to retrieve form data in a servlet. We are also going to build an HTML object package that we will be using in future servlet development.

SERVLETS AND HTML

IN THIS CHAPTER

RETRIEVING FORM DATA IN A SERVLET

You will now learn how servlets retrieve information from the client. Servlets most commonly receive data from both POST and GET requests. The methods used to retrieve this data are the same in either case.

The three methods used to retrieve request parameters are the ServletRequest's getParameterNames(), getParameter(), and getParameterValues(). Their signatures are listed as follows:

```
public Enumeration ServletRequest.getParameterNames();
public String ServletRequest.getParameter(String name);
public String[] ServletRequest.getParameterValues(String name);
```

getParameterNames() returns the parameter names for the request as an enumeration of strings, or an empty enumeration if there are no parameters. It is used as a supporting method to getParameter(). When you have the enumerated list of parameter names, you can iterate over them, calling getParameter() with each name in the list.

The getParameter() method returns a string containing the single value of the specified parameter, or null if the parameter is not contained in the request. This method should be used only if you are sure the request contains only one value for the parameter. If the parameter has multiple values, you should use getParameterValues().

getParameterValues() returns the values of the specified parameter as an array of strings, or null if the named parameter does not exist in the request.

Now, take a look at a servlet that services a POST request. The servlet in Listing 4.1 retrieves the parameters sent to it and returns the parameters and their values to the client.

LISTING 4.1   EXAMPLE0401.JAVA DISPLAYS ALL PARAMETER/VALUE PAIRS IN A REQUEST

```
import javax.servlet.*;
import javax.servlet.http.*;
import java.io.*;
import java.util.*;

public class Example0401 extends HttpServlet {

  public void init(ServletConfig config)
    throws ServletException {

    // Always pass the ServletConfig object to the super class
    super.init(config);
  }
```

```
//Process the HTTP Get request
  public void doGet(HttpServletRequest request,
    HttpServletResponse response)
    throws ServletException, IOException {

    doPost(request, response);
  }

  //Process the HTTP Post request
  public void doPost(HttpServletRequest request,
    HttpServletResponse response)
    throws ServletException, IOException {

    response.setContentType("text/html");
    PrintWriter out = response.getWriter();
    out.println("<html>");
    out.println("<head><title>Example0401</title></head>");
    out.println("<body>");

    // Get all the parameter names
    Enumeration parameters = request.getParameterNames();
    String param = null;

    // Interate over the names, getting the parameters
    while ( parameters.hasMoreElements() ) {

      param = (String)parameters.nextElement();
      out.println("<BOLD>" + param +
        " : " + request.getParameter(param) +
        "</BOLD><BR>");
    }

    out.println("</body></html>");
    out.close();
  }
//Get Servlet information

  public String getServletInfo() {

    return "Example0401 Information";
  }
}
```

As you look over this servlet, notice that it services both GET and POST requests. You can invoke the Example0401 servlet by encoding a URL string or by using a form. The HTML source, implemented to invoke the servlet using the POST method, appears in Listing 4.2.

LISTING 4.2   EXAMPLE0401.HTML DISPLAYS THE HTML REQUIRED TO INVOKE THE SERVLET USING THE POST METHOD

```
<HTML>
<HEAD>
<TITLE>
Chapter 4 Example 01
</TITLE>
</HEAD>
<BODY>

<FORM ACTION=http://localhost:8080/servlet/Example0401
     METHOD=POST>

<TABLE STYLE="HEIGHT: 173px; WIDTH: 242px">
<TR>
    <TD>Last Name:</TD>
    <TD><INPUT NAME="Last Name" ALIGN="left" SIZE="15"></TD>
</TR>
<TR>
    <TD>First Name:</TD>
    <TD>
      <INPUT ALIGN=left NAME="First Name" SIZE=15> </TD>
</TR>
<TR>
    <TD>Age:</TD>
    <TD>
      <INPUT ALIGN=left NAME=Age SIZE=2> </TD>
</TR>
<TR>
    <TD>SSN:</TD>
    <TD>
      <INPUT ALIGN=left NAME=SSN SIZE=11> </TD>
</TR>
<TR>
    <TD>DOB:</TD>
    <TD>
      <INPUT ALIGN=left NAME=DOB SIZE=8> </TD>
</TR>
<TR>
    <TD>Username:</TD>
    <TD>
      <INPUT ALIGN=left NAME=Username> </TD>
```

```
    </TR>
    <TR>
        <TD>Password:</TD>
        <TD>
    <INPUT ALIGN=left NAME=Password SIZE=8 type=password> 
    </TD>
    </TR>
    </TABLE>
    <INPUT TYPE="submit" NAME="Submit" VALUE="Submit">
    <INPUT TYPE="reset" VALUE=Reset>
    </FORM>

    </BODY>
    </HTML>
```

After you have examined both of these listings, build and install the servlet. The next thing you will need to do is load the HTML document in your browser. The loaded page should look similar to Figure 4.1.

FIGURE 4.1
Example0401
HTML page.

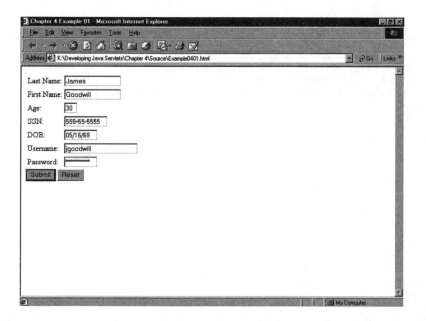

You should now complete the form and press the Submit button. The response you receive, which will of course depend on your entries, should look something like Figure 4.2.

Developing Java Servlets

FIGURE 4.2

Example0401 servlet response page.

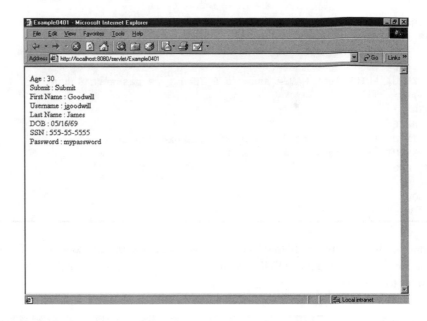

Now that you have seen what the `Example0401` servlet does, take a look at how it does it. The area you want to focus on is listed in the following:

```
// Get all the parameter names
Enumeration parameters = request.getParameterNames();
String param = null;

// Interate over the names, getting the parameters
while ( parameters.hasMoreElements() ) {

  param = (String)parameters.nextElement();
  out.println("<BOLD>" + param +
    " : " + request.getParameter(param) +
    "</BOLD><BR>");
}
```

The first executed line calls the `getParameterNames()` method for the current request. This method returns an enumerated list of parameter names. You then iterate over the `Enumeration` calling `getParameter()`, passing it each one of the parameter names, which returns the value of each request parameter. These tag/value pairs are then passed to the response writer with some HTML formatting tags. The completed response is then passed back to the client and displayed in the browser.

This example shows just how easy it is to retrieve request parameters in a servlet. Although the `Example0401` servlet works fine for most requests, it does have a flaw. When you chose to use getParameter() to retrieve your parameter values, you knew there would only be one value per request parameter. If you need to handle multiple values, you should use the getParameterValues() method discussed previously.

BUILDING A BASIC HTML OBJECT PACKAGE

In all the prior examples, you were "hand coding" HTML. It would be much easier to use an object-oriented approach. For example, if you wanted to send a table of figures to the client, you would instantiate a table object, add the data cells, and stream it to the client. This method is much simpler than trying to learn all the HTML tags necessary to do this.

In this section, you are going to create a package that encapsulates HTML. You will first create a base class in which all your HTML objects will inherit. You will then define the requirements and create the individual objects. The source code for each object is included in this section and can also be found at this book's Web site. This is not an all-inclusive list of HTML objects, but it does define a framework for future extension. At the end of this section, you will put these objects to work with a sample servlet.

The HTMLObject

The first class I would like to create is the HTMLObject. It is the root class of your HTML package. The following lists some of the requirements for your root class:

Requirements for HTMLObject

Must be a container for other HTMLObjects

Must contain a single method for streaming HTML text

Must be able to set the objects alignment

Now that I have defined the requirements, you can create the HTMLObject class. Listing 4.3 contains the source for the HTMLObject class.

LISTING 4.3   HTMLOBJECT.JAVA DISPLAYS THE SOURCE FOR THE HTMLOBJECT CLASS

```
package HTML;

import java.util.Vector;

public abstract class HTMLObject{

    // Vector used to hold other HTMLObjects
    protected Vector htmlObjects = null;

    // Static Alignment values
```

continues

LISTING 4.3   CONTINUED

```java
public static final int LEFT = 0;
public static final int CENTER = 1;
public static final int RIGHT = 2;

// Set the objects initial alignment to LEFT
private int alignment = LEFT;

// This abstract method forces all derived classes to
// implement the toHTML() method.  The toHTML() method
// should return the HTML String necessary to
// display this object in its current state.
public abstract String toHTML();

private String backgroundColor = null;

// Constructor
public HTMLObject() {

  // Default size of HTMLObject vector
  htmlObjects = new Vector(5);
}

// Add a HTMLObject
public void addObject( HTMLObject value) {

  if ( value != null ) {

    htmlObjects.addElement(value);
  }
}

// Remove a HTMLObject, if the element is removed
// successfully, returns true
public boolean removeObject( HTMLObject value) {

  if ( value != null ) {

    return htmlObjects.removeElement(value);
  }
  return false;
}

// Set the Objects Background Color
public void setBackgroundColor( String value) {
```

```
    if ( value != null ) {

      backgroundColor = value;
    }
  }

  // Get the Objects Background Color
  public String getBackgroundColor() {

    return backgroundColor;
  }

  // Set the object's Alignment
  public void setAlignment(int value) {

    if ( value >= LEFT && value <= RIGHT ) {

      alignment = value;
    }
  }

  // Get the object's Alignment
  public int getAlignment() {

    return alignment;
  }
}
```

HTMLDocument

The HTMLDocument object will be the outermost container; its code appears in Listing 4.4. It will, like all your HTML objects, be derived from HTMLObject. Most servlets will create an HTMLDocument and add other HTMLObjects to it. The requirements for an HTMLDocument are listed as follows:

HTMLDocument Requirements

Must be able to set the Title

Must be able to set the Background Image

Must be able to set the Background Color

Must be able to set the Text Color

Must be able to set the Link Color

Must be able to set the Visited Link Color

Must be able to set the Active Link Color

4

LISTING 4.4   HTMLDocument.java DISPLAYS THE SOURCE FOR THE HTMLDocument CLASS

```java
package HTML;

public class HTMLDocument extends HTMLObject {

    private String title = null;
    private String backgroundImage = null;
    private String backgroundColor = null;
    private String textColor = null;
    private String linkColor = null;
    private String vlink = null;
    private String alink = null;

    // Default Constructor
    public HTMLDocument() {

    }

    // Constructor with title
    public HTMLDocument(String value) {

      if ( value != null ) {

        title = value;
      }
    }

    // Set the document Title
    public void setTitle(String value) {

      if ( value != null ) {

        title = value;
      }
    }

    // Get the document Title
    public String getTitle() {

      return title;
    }

    // Set the document Background Image
    public void setBackgroundImage(String value) {
```

```
  if ( value != null ) {

    backgroundImage = value;
  }
}

// Get the document Background Image
public String getBackgroundImage() {

  return backgroundImage;
}

// Set the document Background Color
public void setBackgroundColor( String value) {

  if ( value != null ) {

    backgroundColor = value;
  }
}

// Get the document Background Color
public String getBackgroundColor() {

  return backgroundColor;
}

// Set the document Text Color
public void setTextColor(String value) {

  if ( value != null ) {

    textColor = value;
  }
}

// Get the document Text Color
public String getTextColor() {

  return textColor;
}

// Set the document Link Color
public void setLinkColor(String value) {
```

4

continues

LISTING 4.4   CONTINUED

```
   if ( value != null ) {

     linkColor = value;
   }
 }

 // Get the document Link Color
 public String getLinkColor() {

   return linkColor;
 }

 // Set the document Visited Link Color
 public void setVLinkColor(String value) {

   if ( value != null ) {

     vlink = value;
   }
 }

 // Get the document Visited Link Color
 public String getVLinkColor() {

   return vlink;
 }

 // Set the document Active Link Color
 public void setALinkColor(String value) {

   if ( value != null ) {

     alink = value;
   }
 }

 // Get the document Active Link Color
 public String getALinkColor() {

   return alink;
 }

 // Return String containing the HTML formatted document
 public String toHTML() {
```

```java
StringBuffer document = new StringBuffer("<html><head>\n");
document.append("<title>");
if ( title != null ) {

  document.append(title);
}
document.append("</title></head>\n\n<body ");

if ( backgroundImage != null ) {

  document.append("BACKGROUND=\"" +
    backgroundImage + "\" ");
}
String color = getBackgroundColor();
if ( color != null ) {

  document.append("BGCOLOR=\"" + color +
    "\" ");
}
String textColor = getTextColor();
if ( textColor != null ) {

  document.append("TEXT=\"" + textColor +
    "\" ");
}
if ( linkColor != null ) {

  document.append("LINK=\"" + linkColor +
    "\" ");
}
if ( vlink != null ) {

  document.append("VLINK=\"" + vlink + "\" ");
}
if ( alink != null ) {

  document.append("ALINK=\"" + alink + "\" ");
}
document.append(">\n");

// Iterate through all objects in the htmlObjects Vector
for ( int x = 0; x < htmlObjects.size(); x ++ ) {

  try {

    document.append(
```

continues

LISTING 4.4   CONTINUED

```
              ((HTMLObject)htmlObjects.elementAt(x)).toHTML() +
              "\n");
     }
     catch (ArrayIndexOutOfBoundsException ex) {

        // This will only log the error to stderr
        System.err.println(ex.getMessage());
     }
     catch (Exception ex) {

        // This will only log the error to stderr
        System.err.println(ex.getMessage());
     }
   }

   // Then close the document
   document.append("\n</body>\n</html>\n");

   return document.toString();
  }
}
```

HTMLText

The HTMLText object will be used to display simple HTML text. Listing 4.5 contains the code for this object. Its requirements are listed in the following:

HTMLText Requirements

Must be able to set the Text to be displayed

Must be able to turn BOLD on/off

Must be able to turn ITALICS on/off

Must be able to turn UNDERLINE on/off

Must be able to turn CENTER on/off

Must be able to turn PREFORMATTED on/off

LISTING 4.5   HTMLTEXT.JAVA DISPLAYS THE SOURCE FOR THE HTMLTEXT CLASS

```
package HTML;

public class HTMLText extends HTMLObject {

    private String text = new String("");
    private boolean bold = false;
```

```java
private boolean italic = false;
private boolean underline = false;
private boolean center = false;
private boolean preformatted = false;

// Default Contructor
public HTMLText() {

}

// Constructor initialized with Text value
public HTMLText(String value) {

  if ( value != null ) {

    text = value;
  }
}

// Set the text value
public void setText(String value) {

  if ( value != null ) {

    text = value;
  }
}

// Get the current text value
public String getText() {

  return text;
}

// Set Text Bold to true/false
public void setBold(boolean value) {

  bold = value;
}

// Returns True if Bold is on
public boolean isBold() {

  return bold;
}
```

continues

LISTING 4.5   CONTINUED

```java
// Set Text Italic to true/false
public void setItalic( boolean value) {

  italic = value;
}

// Returns True if Italic is on
public boolean isItalic() {

  return italic;
}

// Set Text Underline to true/false
public void setUnderline( boolean value) {

  underline = value;
}

// Returns True if Underline is on
public boolean isUnderline() {

  return underline;
}

// Set Text Center to true/false
public void setCenter( boolean value) {

  center = value;
}

// Returns True if Center is on
public boolean isCenter() {

  return center;
}

// Set Text Preformatted to true/false
public void setPreformatted( boolean value) {

  preformatted = value;
}
```

```
// Returns True if Preformatted is on
public boolean isPreformatted() {

   return preformatted;
}

// Return String containing the HTML formatted Text
public String toHTML() {

   StringBuffer html = new StringBuffer(text);

   if ( isBold() ) {

     html.insert(0, "<B>");
     html.append("</B>");
   }

   if ( isItalic() ) {

     html.insert(0, "<I>");
     html.append("</I>");
   }

   if ( isUnderline() ) {

     html.insert(0, "<U>");
     html.append("</U>");
   }

   if ( isCenter() ) {

     html.insert(0, "<CENTER>");
     html.append("</CENTER>");
   }

   if ( isPreformatted() ) {

     html.insert(0, "<PRE>");
     html.append("</PRE>");
   }
   return html.toString();
  }
}
```

HTMLHeading

The HTMLHeading object will be used to display a simple HTML heading. Its code appears in Listing 4.6, and its requirements are as follows:

HTMLHeading Requirements

Must be able to set the Heading Text to be displayed

Must be able to set the Heading Level

LISTING 4.6 HTMLHEADING.JAVA DISPLAYS THE SOURCE FOR THE HTMLHEADING CLASS

```java
package HTML;

public class HTMLHeading extends HTMLObject {

    private String text = null;

    public static final int H1 = 1;
    public static final int H2 = 2;
    public static final int H3 = 3;
    public static final int H4 = 4;
    public static final int H5 = 5;
    public static final int H6 = 6;
    private int heading = H1;

    // Constructor that initializes Heading Level to H1
    public HTMLHeading() {

    }

    // Constructor that sets the initial Heading Text and Level
    public HTMLHeading(String txt,  int head) {

      if ( txt != null ) {

        text = txt;
      }

      if ( head >= H1 && head <= H6 ) {

        heading = head;
      }
    }

    // Set Heading Text
```

```
public void setText( String value) {

  if ( value != null ) {

    text = value;
  }
}

// Get Heading Text
public String getText() {

  return text;
}

// Set Heading Level
public void setHeadingLevel( int value) {

  if ( value >= H1 && value <= H6 ) {

    heading = value;
  }
}

// Get Heading Level
public int getHeadingLevel() {

  return heading;
}

// Return String containing the HTML formatted Heading
public String toHTML() {

  StringBuffer html = new StringBuffer("<H" + heading);

  switch ( getAlignment() ) {

    case HTMLObject.LEFT:
      html.append(" ALIGN=\"LEFT\"");
      break;

    case HTMLObject.CENTER:
      html.append(" ALIGN=\"CENTER\"");
      break;

    case HTMLObject.RIGHT:
      html.append(" ALIGN=\"RIGHT\"");
```

4

SERVLETS AND
HTML

continues

LISTING 4.6   CONTINUED

```
      break;
    }
    html.append(">");
    if ( text != null ) {

      html.append(text);
    }
    html.append("</H" + heading + ">");

    return html.toString();
  }
}
```

HTMLLineBreak

The HTMLLineBreak class is a simple class that creates a string containing the HTML tag necessary to display a line break. There are no special requirements. The class's code is shown in Listing 4.7.

LISTING 4.7   HTMLLINEBREAK.JAVA DISPLAYS THE SOURCE FOR THE HTMLLINEBREAK CLASS

```
package HTML;

public class HTMLLineBreak extends HTMLObject {

    // Default Constructor
    public HTMLLineBreak() {
    }

    // Return String containing the HTML formatted Line Break
    public String toHTML() {

      return new String("<BR>");
    }
}
```

HTMLHorizontalRule

The HTMLHorizontalRule class is a simple class that creates a string containing the HTML tag necessary to display a horizontal rule. There are no special requirements. The class's code appears in Listing 4.8.

LISTING 4.8   HTMLHORIZONTALRULE.JAVA DISPLAYS THE SOURCE FOR THE
HTMLHORIZONTALRULE CLASS

```
package HTML;

public class HTMLHorizontalRule extends HTMLObject {

    // Default Constructor
    public HTMLHorizontalRule() {
    }

    // Return String containing the HTML formatted Horizontal Rule
    public String toHTML() {

      return new String("<HR>");
    }
}
```

HTMLParagraph

The HTMLParagraph class is a simple class that creates a string containing the HTML tag necessary to display a paragraph. There are no special requirements. The class's code is shown in Listing 4.9.

LISTING 4.9   HTMLPARAGRAPH.JAVA DISPLAYS THE SOURCE FOR THE HTMLPARAGRAPH CLASS

```
package HTML;

public class HTMLParagraph extends HTMLObject {

    // Default Constructor
    public HTMLParagraph() {
    }

    // Return String containing the HTML formatted Paragraph
    public String toHTML() {

      return new String("<P>");;;
    }
}
```

HTMLImage

The HTMLImage class encapsulates the HTML code necessary to display an image. The requirements for an HTMLImage are listed as follows, and its code appears in Listing 4.10.

4

**SERVLETS AND
HTML**

Must be able to set the location of the image to be displayed

Must be able to set the alternate text to be displayed, if the image can't be displayed

LISTING 4.10   HTMLIMAGE.JAVA DISPLAYS THE SOURCE FOR THE HTMLIMAGE CLASS

```java
package HTML;

public class HTMLImage extends HTMLObject {

    private String image = null;
    private String text = null;

    // Default Constructor
    HTMLImage() {

    }

    // Constructor with initial image and alternate text
    public HTMLImage(String image_string, String text_string) {

      if ( image_string != null ) {

        image = image_string;
      }
      if ( text_string != null ) {

        text = text_string;
      }
    }

    // Set the image location
    public void setImage(String value) {

      if ( value != null ) {

        image = value;
      }
    }

    // Get the image location
    public String getImage() {

      return image;
    }
```

```
    // Set the alternate text
    public void setText( String value) {

      if ( value != null ) {

        text = value;
      }
    }

    // Get the alternate text
    public String getText() {

      return text;
    }

    // Return String containing the HTML formatted Image
    public String toHTML() {

      StringBuffer html = new StringBuffer("<img src=\"");

      if ( image != null ) {

        html.append(image);
      }
      html.append("\" alt=\"");
      if ( text != null ) {

        html.append(text);
      }
      html.append("\">");

      return html.toString();
    }
}
```

HTMLLink

The HTMLLink class encapsulates the HTML code necessary for an HTML link to a document. The requirements for an HTMLLink are listed as follows, and its code is shown in Listing 4.11.

HTMLLink Requirements

Must be able to set the HREF of the targeted link

Must be able to add a HTMLObject that anchors to the link

LISTING 4.11   HTMLLINK.JAVA DISPLAYS THE SOURCE FOR THE HTMLLINK CLASS

```java
package HTML;

public class HTMLLink extends HTMLObject {

    private String href = null;

    // Default Constructor
    public HTMLLink() {
    }

    // Constructor with initial href and HTMLObject
    public HTMLLink(String href_string,  HTMLObject object) {

      if ( href_string != null ) {

        href = href_string;
      }
      if ( object != null ) {

        addObject(object);
      }
    }

    // Set the HREF
    public void setHREF(String value) {

      if ( value != null ) {

        href = value;
      }
    }

    // Get the HREF
    public String getHREF() {

      return href;
    }

    // Return String containing the HTML formatted Line Break
    public String toHTML() {

      StringBuffer html = new StringBuffer("<a href=\"");

      if ( href != null ) {
```

```
            System.err.println("HREF is an empty string.");
        }
        html.append(href + "\">");

        // Iterate through the htmlObjects Vector
        for ( int x = 0; x < htmlObjects.size(); x ++ ) {

            try {

                html.append(
                    ((HTMLObject)htmlObjects.elementAt(x)).toHTML()
                    + "\n");
            }
            catch (ArrayIndexOutOfBoundsException ex) {

                // This will only log the error to stderr
                System.err.println(ex.getMessage());
            }
        }
        html.append("</a>");

        return html.toString();
    }
}
```

HTMLList

The HTMLList class encapsulates the HTML code necessary to display an HTML list. The requirements for this class are listed as follows. The class's code appears in Listing 4.12.

HTMLList Requirements

Must be able to set the type of list

Must be able to add HTMLObjects to the list

LISTING 4.12   HTMLLIST.JAVA DISPLAYS THE SOURCE FOR THE HTMLLIST CLASS

```
package HTML;

public class HTMLList extends HTMLObject {

    // Initial list type
    private int listType = UL;
```

continues

4

LISTING 4.12   CONTINUED

```java
// List Types
public static final int UL = 0;
public static final int OL = 1;
public static final int MENU = 2;
public static final int DIR = 3;

// Default Constructor
public HTMLList() {

}

// Constructor with initial list type value
public HTMLList(int value) {

  // set to initial safe value
  listType = UL;

  if ( value >= UL && value <= DIR ) {

    listType = value;
  }
}

// Set the list type
public void setListType(int value) {

  if ( value >= UL && value <= DIR ) {

    listType = value;
  }
}

// Get the list type
public int getListType() {

  return listType;
}

// Return String containing the HTML formatted Line Break
public String toHTML() {

  StringBuffer html = new StringBuffer("\n");

  // Iterate through the htmlObjects Vector
```

```
for ( int x = 0; x < htmlObjects.size(); x ++ ) {

  try {

    html.append("<LI>" +
        ((HTMLObject)htmlObjects.elementAt(x)).toHTML()
        + "\n");
  }
  catch (ArrayIndexOutOfBoundsException ex) {

    // This will only log the error to stderr
    System.err.println(ex.getMessage());
  }
}
if ( listType == UL ) {

  html.insert(0, "<UL>");
  html.append("</UL>");
}
else if ( listType == OL ) {

  html.insert(0, "<OL>");
  html.append("</OL>");
}
else if ( listType == MENU ) {

  html.insert(0, "<MENU>");
  html.append("</MENU>");
}
else {

  html.insert(0, "<DIR>");
  html.append("</DIR>");
}
return html.toString();
  }
}
```

HTMLTableCell

The HTMLTableCell object encapsulates the HTML code necessary to display a cell in an HTML table. Its code appears in Listing 4.13. It supports both DATA and HEADING cell types. The HTMLTableCell is a supporting object for the HTMLTableRow object. The following are the requirements for an HTMLTableCell:

HTMLTableCell Requirements

Must be able to set the type of the cell

Must be able to set the COLSPAN of the cell

Must be able to control vertical and horizontal alignment

Must be able to add HTMLObjects to the list

LISTING 4.13   HTMLTABLECELL.JAVA DISPLAYS THE SOURCE FOR THE HTMLTABLECELL CLASS

```java
package HTML;

public class HTMLTableCell extends HTMLObject {

    private int horizontal = LEFT;
    private int vertical = MIDDLE;
    private int type = DATA;
    private int colspan = 1;
    public static final int TOP = 3;
    public static final int MIDDLE = 4;
    public static final int BOTTOM = 5;
    public static final int HEADING = 6;
    public static final int DATA = 7;

    // Default Constructor
    public HTMLTableCell() {

    }

    // Constructor with initial Cell Type
    public HTMLTableCell(int cell_type) {

      type = cell_type;
    }

    // Set the number of columns the cell spans
    public void setColspan(int value) {

      if ( value > 0 ) {

        colspan = value;
      }
    }

    // Get the number of columns the cell spans
    public int getColspan() {
```

```
    return colspan;
}

// Set the cell's horizontal alignment
public void setHorizontalAlign( int value) {

  horizontal = value;
}

// Get the cell's horizontal alignment
public int getHorizontalAlign() {

  return horizontal;
}

// Set the cell's vertical alignment
public void setVerticalAlign( int value) {

  if ( value >= TOP && value <= BOTTOM ) {

    vertical = value;
  }
}

// Get the cell's vertical alignment
public int getVerticalAlign() {

  return vertical;
}

// Return String containing the HTML formatted Table Cell
public String toHTML() {

  StringBuffer html = new StringBuffer("");
  String tag = null;
  String valign = null;
  String align = null;

  // Determine Alignment
  switch ( vertical ) {

    case TOP:
      valign = "TOP";
      break;

    case MIDDLE:
```

4

SERVLETS AND
HTML

continues

LISTING 4.13   CONTINUED

```
      valign = "MIDDLE";
      break;

    default:
      valign = "BOTTOM";
      break;
  }

  switch ( horizontal ) {

    case LEFT:
      align = "LEFT";
      break;

    case CENTER:
      align = "CENTER";
      break;

    default:
      align = "RIGHT";
      break;
  }

  if ( type == DATA ) {

    tag = new String("TD");
  }
  else {

    tag = new String("TH");
  }
  html.append("<" + tag + " VALIGN=" + valign +
    " ALIGN=" + align);
  html.append(" COLSPAN=" + colspan + ">");

  // iterate through the objectVector
  for ( int x = 0; x < htmlObjects.size(); x ++ ) {

    try {

      html.append(
        ((HTMLObject)htmlObjects.elementAt(x)).toHTML());
    }
    catch (ArrayIndexOutOfBoundsException ex) {
```

```
          // This will only log the error to stderr
          System.err.println(ex.getMessage());
        }
        catch (Exception ex) {

          // This will only log the error to stderr
          System.err.println(ex.getMessage());
        }
      }
      // close the cell
      html.append("</" + tag + ">");

      return html.toString();
    }
}
```

HTMLTableRow

The HTMLTableRow object supports the HTMLTable object discussed in the next section. The class's code is shown in Listing 4.14. It contains a collection HTMLTableCells. When the HTMLTableRow object is constructed and the HTMLTableCells have been added, you add it to the HTMLTable. The requirements for the HTMLTableRow object are simple. You must be able to add HTMLTableCell objects to the HTMLTableRow.

LISTING 4.14   HTMLTABLEROW.JAVA DISPLAYS THE SOURCE FOR THE HTMLTABLEROW CLASS

```
package HTML;

public class HTMLTableRow extends HTMLObject {

    // Default Constructor
    public HTMLTableRow() {

    }

    // Return String containing the HTML formatted Text
    public String toHTML() {

      StringBuffer html = new StringBuffer("<TR>";

      // Iterate through the cells
      for ( int x = 0; x < htmlObjects.size(); x ++ ) {

        try {
```

continues

4

LISTING 4.14   CONTINUED

```
            html.append(((HTMLObject)htmlObjects.elementAt(x)).toHTML());
        }
        catch (ArrayIndexOutOfBoundsException ex) {

            System.err.println(ex.getMessage());
        }
        catch (Exception ex) {

            // This will only log the error to stderr
            System.err.println(ex.getMessage());
        }
    }

    // close the Table Row
    html.append("</TR>\n");

    return html.toString();
    }
}
```

HTMLTable

The `HTMLTable` object is a little more complicated than the previous listings, as you can see in Listing 4.15. This object depends on table rows and cells. It is a container of `HTMLTableRows`, which is a container of `HTMLTableCells`. To create an `HTMLTable` the following requirements must be met:

HTMLTable Requirements

Must be able to set the caption of the Table

Must be able to set the Table Border

Must be able to set the Cell Spacing

Must be able to set the Cell Padding

Must be able to set the Table Width by percentage and by pixel

LISTING 4.15   HTMLTABLE.JAVA DISPLAYS THE SOURCE FOR THE HTMLTABLE CLASS

```
package HTML;

public class HTMLTable extends HTMLObject {

    private HTMLObject caption = null;
```

```
private int width = 0;
private int border = 0;
private int cellspacing = -1;
private int cellpadding = -1;
private boolean percentage_width = true;

// Default Constructor
public HTMLTable() {

}

// Set the caption of the table
public void setCaption(HTMLObject value) {

  if ( value != null ) {

    caption = value;
  }
}

// Get the caption of the table
public HTMLObject getCaption() {

  return caption;
}

// Set the Table Border
public void setBorder(int value) {

  if ( value > -1 ) {

    border = value;
  }
}

// Get the Table Border
public int getBorder() {

  return border;
}

// Set the Cell Spacing
public void setCellSpacing(int value) {

  if ( value >= 0 ) {
```

continues

LISTING 4.15   CONTINUED

```
      cellspacing = value;
    }
  }

  // Get the Cell Spacing
  public int getCellSpacing() {

    return cellspacing;
  }

  // Set the Cell Padding
  public void setCellPadding(int value) {

    if ( value >= 0 ) {

      cellpadding = value;
    }
  }

  // Get the Cell Padding
  public int getCellPadding() {

    return cellpadding;
  }

  // Set the Table Width as a percentage
  public void setWidth(int value) {

    width = value;
    percentage_width = true;
  }

  // Set the Table Width in Pixels
  public void setWidthByPixel(int value) {

    width = value;
    percentage_width = false;
  }

  // Get the table width
  public int getWidth() {

    return width;
  }
```

```
// Return String containing the HTML formatted Table
public String toHTML() {

  StringBuffer html = new StringBuffer("<TABLE");

  if ( width > 0 ) {

    html.append(" WIDTH=" + width);
    if ( percentage_width ) {

      html.append("% ");
    }
    else {

      html.append(" ");
    }
  }
  if ( border > -1 ) {

    html.append(" BORDER=" + border);
  }

  if ( cellspacing > -1 ) {

    html.append(" CELLSPACING=" + cellspacing);
  }

  if ( cellpadding > -1 ) {

    html.append(" CELLPADDING=" + cellpadding);
  }

  String color = getBackgroundColor();
  if ( color != null ) {

    html.append(" BGCOLOR=\"" + color + "\" ");
  }
  // Close the TABLE tag
  html.append(">\n");

  // Add the CAPTION
  if ( caption != null ) {

    html.append("\n<CAPTION>" + caption.toHTML()
      + "</CAPTION>\n");
```

continues

LISTING 4.15   CONTINUED

```
    }

    // Iterate through the rows
    for ( int x = 0; x < htmlObjects.size(); x ++ ) {

      try {

        html.append((
          (HTMLObject)htmlObjects.elementAt(x)).toHTML() +
          "\n");
      }
      catch (ArrayIndexOutOfBoundsException ex) {

        System.err.println(ex.getMessage());
      }
      catch (Exception ex) {

        // This will be logged to stderr
        System.err.println(ex.getMessage());
      }
    }

    // close the table
    html.append("\n</TABLE>");

    return html.toString();
  }
}
```

HTMLInput

The `HTMLInput` object is the root object for all HTML input objects. Its code appears in Listing 4.16. It is the supporting object for the `HTMLForm` object. The minimum requirements for an `HTMLInput` object are listed in the following:

HTMLInput Requirements

Must be able to set the type of the `INPUT` object

Must be able to set the name of the `INPUT` object

Must be able to specify additional attributes for specialized input type

LISTING 4.16   HTMLINPUT.JAVA DISPLAYS THE SOURCE FOR THE HTMLINPUT CLASS

```java
package HTML;

public class HTMLInput extends HTMLObject {

    protected String type = null;
    protected String name = null;
    protected String input_value = null;
    protected String attributes = null;

    // Default Constructor
    public HTMLInput() {
    }

    // Set the Input Type
    protected void setType(String value) {

      if ( value != null ) {

        type = value;
      }
    }

    // Get the Input Type
    public String getType() {

      return type;
    }

    // Set the Input Name
    public void setName(String value) {

      if ( value != null ) {

        name = value;
      }
    }

    // Get the Input Name
    public String getName() {

      return name;
    }

    // Set the value of the Input Object
```

4

SERVLETS AND
HTML

continues

LISTING 4.16 CONTINUED

```java
public void setValue(String value) {

  if ( value != null ) {

    input_value = value;
  }
}

// Get the value of the Input Object
public String getValue() {

  return input_value;
}

// Set the additional attributes string
// This will be used to specialize an input type
protected void setAttributes(String value) {

  if ( value != null ) {

    attributes = value;
  }
}

// Get the additional attributes string
public String getAttributes() {

  return attributes;
}

// Return String containing the HTML formatted Input
public String toHTML() {

  StringBuffer html = new StringBuffer("<INPUT TYPE=\"");

  if ( type != null ) {

    html.append(type);
  }

  html.append("\" NAME=\"");

  if ( name != null ) {
```

```
        html.append(name);
    }

    html.append("\" ");

    // Add the VALUE
    if ( input_value != null ) {

        html.append(" VALUE=\"" + input_value + "\"");
    }

    // If there is any additional attributes
    if ( attributes != null ) {

        html.append(attributes);
    }
    // Ending Character
    html.append(">");

    return html.toString();
    }
}
```

Now that you have defined the base of your input objects, you must create the specialized input objects. All your input objects will inherit their TYPE, NAME, and VALUE attributes from the HTMLInput object.

The first input object you will create is the HTMLTextInput object. Its code, shown in Listing 4.17, encapsulates the functionality necessary to create an HTML text input string. Its requirements are listed as follows:

HTMLTextInput Requirements

Must be able to set the SIZE of the INPUT object

Must be able to set the MAXLENGTH of the INPUT object

LISTING 4.17   HTMLTEXTINPUT.JAVA DISPLAYS THE SOURCE FOR THE HTMLTEXTINPUT CLASS

```
package HTML;

public class HTMLTextInput extends HTMLInput {

    private int size = -1;
    private int maxlength = -1;
```

continues

LISTING 4.17   CONTINUED

```java
// Default Constructor
public HTMLTextInput() {

  // Set the Input Type
  setType("TEXT");
}

// Set the Input Size
public void setSize(int value) {

  if ( value > -1 ) {

    size = value;
  }
}

// Get the Input Size
public int getSize() {

  return size;
}

// Set the Maximum Length
public void setMaxLength(int value) {

  if ( value > -1 ) {

    maxlength = value;
  }
}

// Get the Maximum Length
public int getMaxLength() {

  return maxlength;
}

// Return String containing the HTML formatted Text Input
public String toHTML() {

  StringBuffer attribute = new StringBuffer("");

  if ( size > -1 ) {
```

```
      attribute.append(" SIZE=" + size);
    }
    if ( maxlength > -1 ) {

      attribute.append(" MAXLENGTH=" + maxlength);
    }
    setAttributes(attribute.toString());

    return super.toHTML();
  }
}
```

The next input object you will create is the HTMLPasswordInput object, as shown in Listing
4.18. The HTMLPasswordInput object contains the functionality to display a password edit box.
Its requirements are listed as follows:

HTMLPasswordInput Requirements

Must be able to set the SIZE of the INPUT object

Must be able to set the MAXLENGTH of the INPUT object

LISTING 4.18 HTMLPASSWORDINPUT.JAVA DISPLAYS THE SOURCE FOR THE
HTMLPASSWORDINPUT CLASS

```
package HTML;

public class HTMLPasswordInput extends HTMLInput {

  private int size = -1;
  private int maxlength = -1;

  // Default Constructor
  public HTMLPasswordInput() {

    // Set the Input Type
    setType("PASSWORD");
  }

  // Set the Input Size
  public void setSize(int value) {

    if ( value > -1 ) {

      size = value;
    }
```

continues

LISTING 4.18   CONTINUED

```java
  }

  // Get the Input Size
  public int getSize() {

    return size;
  }

  // Set the Maximum Length
  public void setMaxLength(int value) {

    if ( value > -1 ) {

      maxlength = value;
    }
  }

  // Get the Maximum Length
  public int getMaxLength() {

    return maxlength;
  }

// Return String containing the HTML formatted Password
  public String toHTML() {

    StringBuffer attribute = new StringBuffer("");

    if ( size > -1 ) {

      attribute.append(" SIZE=" + size);
    }
    if ( maxlength > -1 ) {

      attribute.append(" MAXLENGTH=" + maxlength);
    }
    setAttributes(attribute.toString());

    return super.toHTML();
  }

}
```

The `HTMLHiddenInput` and `HTMLCheckBoxInput` objects are very simple input objects. These objects implement the `HTML Hidden Input` and `HTML Checkbox Input` types, respectively. Their entire implementation is in the constructor. This is where they call their parent's `setType()` method with their appropriate type string. Both of the class definitions appear in Listings 4.19 and 4.20.

LISTING 4.19 HTMLHIDDENINPUT.JAVA DISPLAYS THE SOURCE FOR THE HTMLHIDDENINPUT CLASS

```
package HTML;

public class HTMLHiddenInput extends HTMLInput {

  // Default Constructor
  public HTMLHiddenInput() {

    // Set the Input Type to "HIDDEN"
    setType("HIDDEN");
  }
}
```

LISTING 4.20 HTMLCHECKBOXINPUT.JAVA DISPLAYS THE SOURCE FOR THE HTMLCHECKBOXINPUT CLASS

```
package HTML;

public class HTMLCheckBoxInput extends HTMLInput {

  // Default Constructor
  public HTMLCheckBoxInput() {

    // Set the Input Type to "CHECKBOX"
    setType("CHECKBOX");
  }
}
```

You have also created two button objects that support the `HTMLForm` object. These two buttons are `HTMLSubmitButton` and `HTMLResetButton`. These classes can be found in Listings 4.21 and 4.22, respectively.

LISTING 4.21   HTMLSUBMITBUTTON.JAVA

```
package HTML;

public class HTMLSubmitButton extends HTMLInput {

  public HTMLSubmitButton() {

    setType("SUBMIT");
  }
}
```

LISTING 4.22   HTMLRESETBUTTON.JAVA

```
package HTML;

public class HTMLResetButton extends HTMLInput {

  public HTMLResetButton() {

    setType("RESET");
  }
}
```

The final input object that you will be implementing is the HTMLRadioButtonInput object. The only additional requirement needed to create this object is the ability to set the radio button's Checked status. The source code for the HTMLRadioButtonInput object appears in Listing 4.23.

LISTING 4.23   HTMLRADIOBUTTONINPUT.JAVA DISPLAYS THE SOURCE FOR THE HTMLRADIOBUTTONINPUT CLASS

```
package HTML;

public class HTMLRadioButtonInput extends HTMLInput {

  private boolean checked = false;

  // Default Constructor
  public HTMLRadioButtonInput() {

    setType("RADIO");
  }

  // Set checked to true/false
```

```
public void setChecked(boolean value) {

  checked = value;
}

// Check to see if RadioButton is CHECKED
public boolean isChecked() {

  return checked;
}

// Return String containing the HTML formatted Radio Button
public String toHTML() {

  if ( checked ) {

    setAttributes(" CHECKED");
  }
  return super.toHTML();
}
}
```

HTMLForm

The HTMLForm object will encapsulate common HTML Form functionality. This is the object that will present the client with a user interface. It is a container for HTMLInput objects listed previously. An HTMLForm has the following requirements:

HTMLForm Requirements

Must be able to set the ACTION

Must be able to set POST/GET

Must be able to add HTMLInput objects

Listing 4.24 contains the source for the HTMLForm class.

LISTING 4.24   HTMLFORM.JAVA DISPLAYS THE SOURCE FOR THE HTMLFORM CLASS

```
package HTML;

import java.util.*;

public class HTMLForm extends HTMLObject {

    private String action = null;
```

continues

LISTING 4.24   CONTINUED

```java
private boolean post_method = false;

// Default Constructor
public HTMLForm() {

}

// Set the action
public void setAction( String value) {

  if ( value != null ) {

    action = value;
  }
}

// Get the action
public String getAction() {

  return action;
}

// Set the POST method to true/false
public void setPostMethod( boolean value) {

  post_method = value;
}

// return true if POST, otherwise false
public boolean isPostMethod() {

  return post_method;
}

// Return String containing the HTML formatted Form
public String toHTML() {

  StringBuffer html = new StringBuffer("<FORM ACTION=\"");

  if ( action != null ) {

    html.append(action);
  }
```

```java
        html.append("\"");

        // setup the method
        html.append(" METHOD=");

        if ( post_method ) {

          html.append("POST");
        }
        else {

          html.append("GET");
        }
        String color = getBackgroundColor();
        if ( color != null ) {

          html.append(" BGCOLOR=\"" + color + "\" ");
        }
        html.append(">\n");

        // adding HTMLInputs
        for ( int x = 0; x < htmlObjects.size(); x++ ) {

          try {

            html.append(
              ((HTMLObject)htmlObjects.elementAt(x)).toHTML() +
              "\n");
          }
          catch (Exception ex) {

            // Print exception to stderr
            System.err.println(ex.getMessage());
          }
        }
        html.append("\n</FORM>");
        if ( getAlignment() == CENTER ) {

          html.insert(0, "<CENTER>");
          html.append("</CENTER>");
        }
        return html.toString();
      }
    }
```

CREATING A SERVLET THAT USES THE HTML OBJECT PACKAGE

Now that you have gone through all the trouble of creating the HTML package, you can put it to good use. In this section, you are going to create a servlet that services a simple GET request and responds with a dynamically created form. The form will then be filled out by the user and submitted using the POST method. The same servlet will service the POST request and parse the parameters sent from the form. When it has finished parsing the parameters, it will place them in an HTML document and send them back to the client. Take a look at the source code in Listing 4.25.

LISTING 4.25 NEWCUSTOMERSERVLET.JAVA DISPLAYS THE SOURCE FOR THE NEWCUSTOMERSERVLET CLASS

```java
import javax.servlet.*;
import javax.servlet.http.*;
import java.io.*;
import java.util.*;

import HTML.*;

public class NewCustomerServlet extends HttpServlet {

  public void init(ServletConfig config) throws ServletException {

    super.init(config);
  }

  //Process the HTTP Get request
  public void doGet(HttpServletRequest request,
    HttpServletResponse response)
    throws ServletException, IOException {

    response.setContentType("text/html");
    PrintWriter out = response.getWriter();

    HTMLDocument document =
      new HTMLDocument("New Customer Account");

    // Create the New Customer Account Form
    HTMLForm form = new HTMLForm();
    form.setAction("/servlet/NewCustomerServlet");
    form.setPostMethod(true);
```

```
// Add the Heading
HTMLHeading heading = new HTMLHeading("Customer Account",
  HTMLHeading.H2);
heading.setAlignment(HTMLObject.CENTER);
form.addObject(heading);

// Add the Name
form.addObject(new HTMLText("Name : "));
HTMLTextInput textinput = new HTMLTextInput();
textinput.setName("name");
textinput.setSize(30);
form.addObject(textinput);
form.addObject(new HTMLLineBreak());

// Add the Email
form.addObject(new HTMLText("Email Address : "));
textinput = new HTMLTextInput();
textinput.setName("email");
textinput.setSize(30);
form.addObject(textinput);
form.addObject(new HTMLLineBreak());

// Add the Billing Address
form.addObject(new HTMLHeading("Billing Address",
  HTMLHeading.H4));

form.addObject(new HTMLText("Street : "));
textinput = new HTMLTextInput();
textinput.setName("street");
textinput.setSize(30);
form.addObject(textinput);
form.addObject(new HTMLLineBreak());

// Add the City, State, Zip

// City
form.addObject(new HTMLText("City "));
textinput = new HTMLTextInput();
textinput.setName("city");
textinput.setSize(30);
form.addObject(textinput);

// State
form.addObject(new HTMLText("State "));
textinput = new HTMLTextInput();
textinput.setName("state");
```

continues

LISTING 4.25   CONTINUED

```
    textinput.setSize(2);
    textinput.setMaxLength(2);
    form.addObject(textinput);

    // Zip
    form.addObject(new HTMLText("Zip "));
    textinput = new HTMLTextInput();
    textinput.setName("zip");
    textinput.setSize(5);
    textinput.setMaxLength(5);
    form.addObject(textinput);

    form.addObject(new HTMLLineBreak());
    form.addObject(new HTMLSubmitButton());
    form.addObject(new HTMLResetButton());

    document.addObject(form);

    // document string sent back in response
    out.println(document.toHTML());
    out.close();
  }
//Process the HTTP Post request

  public void doPost(HttpServletRequest request,
    HttpServletResponse response)
    throws ServletException, IOException {

    response.setContentType("text/html");
    PrintWriter out = response.getWriter();

    HTMLDocument document =
      new HTMLDocument("Customer Account Added");

    // Add the Heading
    HTMLHeading heading = new HTMLHeading("Account Created",
      HTMLHeading.H2);
    heading.setAlignment(HTMLObject.CENTER);
    document.addObject(heading);

    // Display the submitted request
```

```
    document.addObject(new HTMLHeading("General Info.",
      HTMLHeading.H4));

    // Parse "name" parameter
    document.addObject(new HTMLText("Name : " +
      request.getParameter("name")));
    document.addObject(new HTMLLineBreak());

    // Parse "email" parameter
    document.addObject(new HTMLText("Email Address : " +
      request.getParameter("email")));

    document.addObject(new HTMLHeading("Billing Address",
      HTMLHeading.H4));

    // Parse "street" parameter
    document.addObject(new HTMLText(
      request.getParameter("street")));
    document.addObject(new HTMLLineBreak());

    // Parse "city", "state", and "zip" parameters
    document.addObject(new HTMLText(
      request.getParameter("city") + ", "));
    document.addObject(new HTMLText(
      request.getParameter("state")));
    document.addObject(new HTMLText(" "
      + request.getParameter("zip")));

    // document string sent back in response
    out.println(document.toHTML());
    out.close();
  }
//Get Servlet information

  public String getServletInfo() {
    return "NewCustomerServlet Information";
  }
}
```

When you have compiled and installed the servlet, you will need to invoke it. To invoke the servlet, open the URL http://youserver/servlet/NewCustomerServlet. You should see a form similar to the one in Figure 4.3.

Figure 4.3

The NewCustomer-Servlet form.

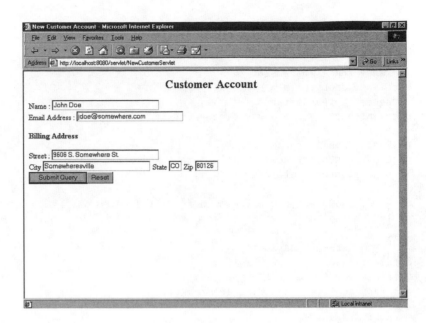

You should now fill out the form and press the Submit Query button. The response you receive should be similar to Figure 4.4.

Figure 4.4

The NewCustomer-Servlet response page.

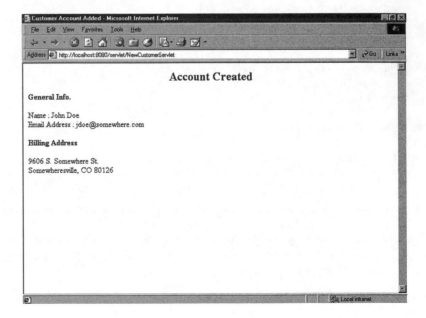

This servlet is a very good example of building dynamic forms and parsing the request sent by the form. As you look at the source code, notice that the NewCustomerServlet implements both the doGet() and the doPost() methods. It uses the first method to build the form and the later method to parse the form inputs. This example shows just how versatile servlets can be.

SUMMARY

This chapter covered a lot of information. You looked at how servlets parse request parameters. You also created an HTML package that encapsulates basic HTML. At this point, you should feel comfortable with how servlets receive information from the client. You should also have an in-depth understanding of how to use the HTML package you created. You will be using it throughout the rest of the book.

In the next chapter you are going to take a look at the JSDK's version of server-side includes. You will be examining their syntax and how to create your own server-side includes.

SERVER-SIDE INCLUDES

CHAPTER

5

IN THIS CHAPTER

WHAT IS A SERVER-SIDE INCLUDE?

A server-side include enables you to embed a Java servlet within an HTML document. The tags used are extensions to the HTML language. You place them in a file with a .shtml extension, which tells the server that the document contains a server-side include. The server recognizes the file extension and passes it to the internal servlet `ssinclude`. This servlet parses the document executing the referenced servlet code inline. The results are then merged with the original HTML document and passed back to the client.

This functionality is made possible by servlet aliasing. If you open the Java Web Server administration tool to the Servlet Aliases page, you can see the alias entry *.shtml. Figure 5.1 shows this alias on the Servlet Aliases page.

FIGURE 5.1

The Servlet Aliases page.

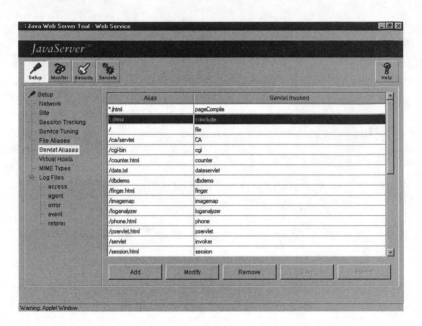

The servlet invoked by this alias is the `ssinclude` servlet mentioned previously. Server-side includes are a very good example of the power of a servlet alias.

SYNTAX OF A SERVER-SIDE INCLUDE

The syntax of a server-side include is similar to that of an applet. Listing 5.1 shows this syntax.

LISTING 5.1 SYNTAX OF A SERVER-SIDE INCLUDE

```
<SERVLET CODE=ServletName.class CODEBASE=http://localhost:8080/
INITPARAM1=init_val1
```

```
INITPARAM2=init_val2
INITPARAMN=init_valn>
<PARAM NAME=param1 VALUE=param_val1>
<PARAM NAME=param2 VALUE=param_val2>
<PARAM NAME=paramn VALUE=param_valn>
</SERVLET>
```

The syntax of a server-side include is easy to understand and flexible. Table 5.1 describes each of a server-side include's possible tags.

TABLE 1.1   SERVER-SIDE INCLUDE TAGS

Tag	Description
CODE	Name of the servlet to be executed
CODEBASE	Optional parameter; points to the location of the servlet
INITPARAM	*N* servlet initialization parameters
PARAM NAME/VALUE	*N* name/value pairs representing request parameters

PARSING INITIALIZATION PARAMETERS

Initialization parameters are very much like request parameters except initialization parameters are not part of the request. They are passed to the servlet when it is first loaded. Therefore, you have access to them in the servlet's init() method. The value of these parameters does not change until the servlet is reloaded.

Now, take a look at a servlet that parses initialization parameters. Listing 5.2 shows a servlet that parses an initialization parameter passed to it and stores it for use in later requests.

LISTING 5.2   INITPARAMETERSERVLET.JAVA SHOWS THE PARSING OF INIT PARAMETERS

```
import javax.servlet.*;
import javax.servlet.http.*;
import java.io.*;
import java.util.*;

import HTML.*;

public class InitParameterServlet extends HttpServlet {

  //Initialize global variables
  private String company_name = null;
```

continues

LISTING 5.2   CONTINUED

```java
public void init(ServletConfig config)
  throws ServletException {

  // Always pass the parent the ServletConfig
  super.init(config);

  // Parse the init parameter "company" and
  // store it in the private member company_name
  company_name = getInitParameter("company");
}

//Process the HTTP Get request
public void doGet(HttpServletRequest request,
  HttpServletResponse response)
  throws ServletException, IOException {

  response.setContentType("text/html");
  PrintWriter out = response.getWriter();

  // Use the HTMLDocument created in chapter 4
  HTMLDocument document = new HTMLDocument();

  // Add a Heading
  HTMLHeading heading = new HTMLHeading();
  heading.setAlignment(HTMLObject.CENTER);
  heading.setText("Welcome to the " +
    company_name + " Web Site");
  document.addObject(heading);

  // print the HTMLDocument's contents
  out.println(document.toHTML());
  out.close();
}

//Get Servlet information
public String getServletInfo() {
  return "InitParameterServlet Information";
}
}
```

The first thing you need to look at is the `init()` method. The line to pay attention to is listed as follows:

```java
company_name = getInitParameter("company");
```

I am passing the getInitParameter() method the string "company". This is the name of the name/value pair found in my initialization parameters. The value returned is Sams Publishing, which is stored in the private data member company_name. Listing 5.3 shows the HTML containing the server-side include necessary to invoke this servlet.

LISTING 5.3   INITPARAMETERSERVLET.SHTML INVOKES THE INITPARAMETERSERVLET

```
<HTML>
<HEAD>
<TITLE>
InitParameterServlet
</TITLE>
</HEAD>
<BODY>
        .

<SERVLET CODE=InitParameterServlet
  Company="Sams Publishing">
</SERVLET>

</BODY>
</HTML>
```

> **NOTE**
>
> Notice the actual name of the initialization parameter's name/value pair in Listing 5.3. The name Company starts with a capital C. Now look at the source in Listing 5.2. The getInitParameter() method is being passed company with a lowercase c. This is because all initialization parameter names are converted to lowercase.

The next thing you must look at is the doGet() method. It uses the previously created HTML package to create HTMLDocument and HTMLHeading objects. The heading created is a combination of the initialization parameter company, which was stored in the data member company_name, and a text string created in the doGet() method. This is a very good example of reuse. You can customize the output of the InitParameterServlet servlet by changing only the HTML that drives it.

Now go ahead and build the servlet and load the .shtml file. The output you see should look something like Figure 5.2.

FIGURE 5.2

The output of InitParameter-Servlet.

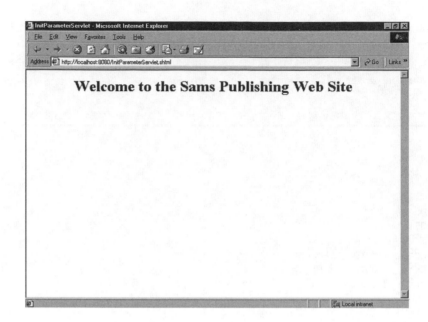

After the `.shtml` file is loaded, view the HTML source loaded in your browser. Listing 5.4 shows the browser's source.

LISTING 5.4   THE BROWSER'S SOURCE AFTER LOADING INITPARAMETERSERVLET.SHTML

```
<HTML>
<HEAD>
<TITLE>
InitParameterServlet
</TITLE>
</HEAD>
<BODY>

<html><head>
<title></title></head>

<body >
<H1 ALIGN="CENTER">Welcome to the Sams Publishing Web Site</H1>

</body>
</html>

</BODY>
</HTML>
```

The server-side include previously referenced has been replaced by the output of the InitParameterServlet servlet. This is because the output of the servlet and contents of the .shtml file have been merged into one document.

CREATING A SERVER-SIDE INCLUDE

Now that you understand what a server-side include is and how one works, you can create a practical example. The servlet you are going to create will be a basic search utility. In this example, it will reside at the top of an HTML document and service search requests. Listing 5.5 shows the source of this search servlet.

LISTING 5.5   THE SOURCE CODE FOR SEARCHSERVLET.JAVA

```
import javax.servlet.*;
import javax.servlet.http.*;
import java.io.*;
import java.util.*;

import HTML.*;

public class SearchServlet extends HttpServlet {

  //Initialize global variables
  private Integer initparam = null;

  public void init(ServletConfig config)
    throws ServletException {

    super.init(config);
  }

  public HTMLForm buildCatalogSearchForm() {

    // Instantiate the HTMLForm object
    HTMLForm search_form = new HTMLForm();

    // This is a dummy action, it is only meant as an example
    // We will connect the SearchTool to the database in
    // Chapter 8
    search_form.setAction("http://localhost:8080/servlet" +
      "/ToBeConnectedLater");

    // Set the Post method to true
    search_form.setPostMethod(true);
```

continues

LISTING 5.5 CONTINUED

```java
    try {

      // Center the Form
      search_form.setAlignment(HTMLObject.CENTER);

      // Add a HTMLTextInput
      HTMLTextInput text_input = new HTMLTextInput();
      text_input.setName("search_string");
      text_input.setSize(30);
      search_form.addObject(text_input);

      // Add a HTMLButton to Invoke the Action
HTMLSubmitButtonbutton = new HTMLSubmitButton ();
      button.setValue("Search");
      search_form.addObject(button);
    }
    catch ( Exception e ) {

      System.err.println(e.getMessage());
    }
    return search_form;
  }

  //Process the HTTP Get request
  public void doGet(HttpServletRequest request,
    HttpServletResponse response)
    throws ServletException, IOException {

    response.setContentType("text/html");
    PrintWriter out = response.getWriter();

    out.println(buildCatalogSearchForm().toHTML());
    out.close();
  }

  //Get Servlet information
  public String getServletInfo() {
    return "SearchServlet Information";
  }
}
```

There is really nothing special about a servlet that is referenced by a server-side include. The only thing different is the fact that an embedded servlet cannot set HTTP header information. This limits them to implementing either the service() or doGet() methods to service requests.

> **NOTE**
>
> The form created by the buildCatalogSearchForm() method does not include a valid ACTION. You will connect this ACTION in Chapter 8, "Servlets and the JDBC."

The next thing you must create is the HTML document with the embedded servlet reference in it. Listing 5.6 contains the HTML document with the embedded SearchServlet.

LISTING 5.6 SEARCHSERVLET.SHTML

```
<HTML>
<HEAD>
<TITLE>
The Online Catalog
</TITLE>
</HEAD>
<BODY>
<CENTER><H1>The Online Catalog</H1><CENTER>
<HR>

<SERVLET CODE=SearchServlet>
</SERVLET>

</BODY>
</HTML>
```

The file SearchServlet.shtml is loaded by the server. It is then passed to the ssinclude servlet, which parses the file and executes the servlet referenced by the following lines:

```
<SERVLET CODE=SearchServlet>
</SERVLET>
```

The output of the SearchServlet is merged with the original HTML and passed back to the client as one document. It is really very simple and easy to use. Figure 5.3 shows SearchServlet.shtml loaded in a browser.

FIGURE 5.3

SearchServlet.-
shtml.

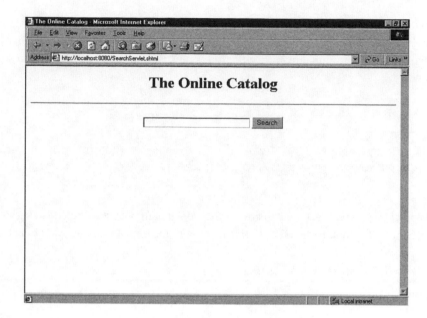

SUMMARY

In this chapter, you learned that server-side includes give you the ability to embed servlets in your HTML documents. I talked about the syntax necessary to embed a servlet into your HTML document. You learned how initialization parameters are parsed. Finally, you put a sample server-side include together.

At this point, you should feel comfortable with what server-side includes are and how to use them. You should understand how initialization parameters are used and when they are parsed. You should also be able to construct and embed your own server-side include.

In the next chapter you will learn about servlet chains. You will be looking at uses for servlet chains and how servlet chains are created and invoked.

SERVLET CHAINING

IN THIS CHAPTER

WHAT IS A SERVLET CHAIN?

Servlet chaining is a technique in which two or more servlets can cooperate in servicing a single request. It is similar to UNIX piping, where one servlet's output is piped to the next servlet's input. This progression continues down the chain until the last servlet is reached. Its output is then sent back to the client. Servlet chains are represented by a comma-separated list of individual servlets. Figure 6.1 show the flow of a servlet chain.

FIGURE 6.1
*The flow of a
servlet chain.*

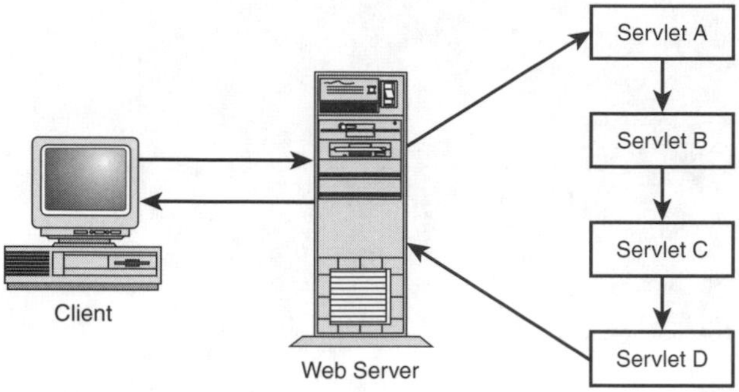

USES FOR SERVLET CHAINS

There are many uses for servlet chaining. I have listed only a few here:

- Customizing a packaged set of servlets. This can be accomplished by embedding custom tags in your HTML responses. For example, Servlet A embeds the tag <COMPANY> in its HTML response. This response is then sent to Servlet B, which parses the output from Servlet A, replacing all occurrences of the tag <COMPANY> with the company's real name. You now have HTML output tailored to the company that purchased the packaged set of servlets.

- Filtering output from other servlets. You can take the output from a servlet that performs a database query and send it to another servlet that formats the data using a previously stored customer profile.

- Translating data on international Web sites. You can have all your servlets send their output through a `language` servlet. This `language` servlet would replace all text data with the appropriate native language where the site is deployed.

INVOKING A SERVLET CHAIN

The two most popular ways to invoke a servlet chain are servlet aliasing and HTTP requests. In this section, I will provide examples of both of these methods. Before you look at these methods, take look at the two servlets that will be used in these examples.

The first servlet writes a simple text string to the response object. Listing 6.1 shows the source code for this example.

LISTING 6.1   SIMPLETEXTSERVLET.JAVA

```java
import javax.servlet.*;
import javax.servlet.http.*;
import java.io.*;
import java.util.*;

import HTML.*;

public class SimpleTextServlet extends HttpServlet {

  public void init(ServletConfig config)
    throws ServletException {

    super.init(config);
  }

  //Process the HTTP Get request
  public void doGet(HttpServletRequest request,
    HttpServletResponse response)
    throws ServletException, IOException {

    response.setContentType("text/html");
    PrintWriter out = response.getWriter();

    HTMLDocument document = new HTMLDocument("SimpleTextServlet");

    // Simple text string, can be anything
    document.addObject(new HTMLText("Hello World!"));

    out.println(document.toHTML());
    out.close();
  }

  //Get Servlet information
  public String getServletInfo() {

    return "SimpleTextServlet Information";
  }
}
```

The second servlet you are going to use is similar to the one that comes with the Java Web Server. It is the UpperCaseServlet. It takes the input from another servlet and converts all the text to uppercase. Listing 6.2 shows the source code for this servlet.

LISTING 6.2   UPPERCASESERVLET.JAVA

```java
import java.io.*;
import java.util.Enumeration;

import javax.servlet.http.*;
import javax.servlet.*;

public class UpperCaseServlet extends HttpServlet {

  public void service(HttpServletRequest request,
    HttpServletResponse response)
    throws ServletException, IOException {

    Enumeration e = request.getHeaderNames();

    while (e.hasMoreElements()) {

      // The first step is to copy and set all header
      // information passed by the previous servlet
      String header = (String)e.nextElement();
      String value = request.getHeader(header);
      response.setHeader(header, value);
    }

    // Set the responses Content-Type before getting the Writer
    response.setContentType(request.getContentType());

    PrintWriter out = response.getWriter();

    // Make sure we have the write mime type
    if (request.getContentType().startsWith("text/html")) {

      BufferedReader reader = request.getReader();
      String s;

      while ( (s = reader.readLine()) != null) {

        // Convert everything to Upper Case
        String u = s.toUpperCase();
        out.println(u);
      }
    }
    // If not write data directly to response without change
    else {
```

```
      ServletInputStream in = request.getInputStream();
       int b;

      while ( (b = in.read()) != -1 ) {

         out.write(b);
      }
    }
    out.close();
  }

  public String getServletInfo() {

    return "UpperCaseServlet";
  }
}
```

You will need to look at a couple of sections of the code. The first is shown here:

```
Enumeration e = request.getHeaderNames();

while (e.hasMoreElements()) {

  // The first step is to copy and set all header
  // information passed by the previous servlet
  String header = (String)e.nextElement();
  String value = request.getHeader(header);
  response.setHeader(header, value);
}
```

This section of code is getting all the header information from the previous servlet in the chain. It is then setting these values in the current servlet's response object. This prevents any loss of header information as execution moves down the chain.

The next section you need to look at shows how the data is read from the request object, converted into uppercase, and written to the response object. This code is as follows:

```
PrintWriter out = response.getWriter();

// Make sure we have the write mime type
if (request.getContentType().startsWith("text/html")) {

  BufferedReader reader = request.getReader();
  String s;

  while ( (s = reader.readLine()) != null) {
```

```
    // Convert everything to Upper Case
    String u = s.toUpperCase();
    out.println(u);
  }
}
```

When you have finished looking over the code, build and install both servlets. You should go ahead and run the `SimpleTextServlet`, so you can see the output before it is chained. The output should look something like Figure 6.2.

FIGURE 6.2

The output of SimpleTextServlet.

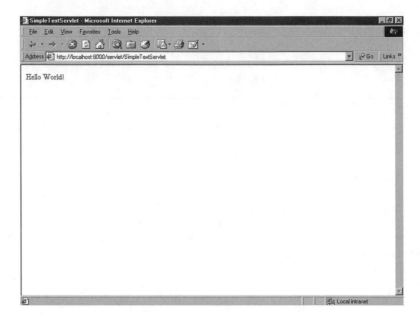

Servlet Alias

Now that you have looked at the servlet examples, I will discuss the first chaining method: servlet aliasing. Servlet aliasing allows you to set up a single alias for a comma-delimited list of servlets. Using the preceding servlets, you can set up an alias for a servlet chain in the Java Web Server's Servlet Aliases page. You need to follow the steps for adding a servlet alias in Chapter 2, "Configuring the Development Environment." Use `/simplechain` for the name of the Alias and `SimpleTextServlet,UpperCaseServlet` for the Servlet Invoked. After you have saved the new alias, the Servlet Aliases page should look similar to Figure 6.3.

FIGURE 6.3
The Servlet Aliases page.

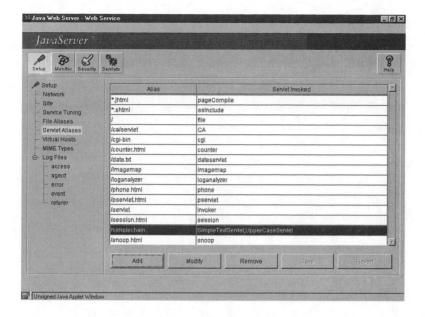

To invoke the servlet chain, open your browser to the URL `http://localhost:8080/simplechain`. This will execute the `SimpleTextServlet`'s `doGet()` method. The response from the `SimpleTextServlet` will be sent to the `UpperCaseServlet`. The `UpperCaseServlet` will convert all text received in the request to uppercase and send the results to the client. Figure 6.4 displays the results.

FIGURE 6.4
Results of the servlet chain.

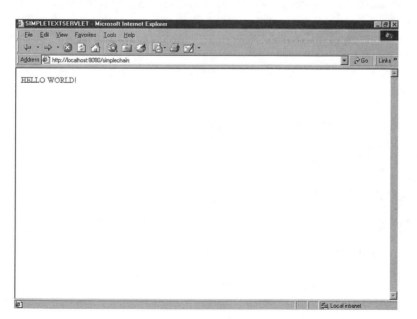

HTTP Request

The second way to invoke a servlet chain is using an HTTP request. You construct a URL string and append a comma-delimited list of servlets to the end. The example for your two servlets is as follows:

```
http://localhost:8000/servlet/SimpleTextServlet,UpperCaseServlet
```

The results should be similar to Figure 6.4.

NOTE

Currently the Java Web Server does not support the invocation of a servlet chain through an HTTP request. This functionality is supported in JRun 2.21.

A PRACTICAL EXAMPLE USING SERVLET CHAINING

You should now feel pretty comfortable with what servlet chaining is and how it works. You can cement this knowledge by creating your own practical example.

In this example, you are going to embed customized tags in your HTML documents. These tags are going to represent dynamic information you want replaced within the static HTML pages. This gives you the ability to push a standard set of documents to all your customers and have them customized on-the-fly by your servlets.

Your chain is going to consist of two servlets: the Java Web Server's internal `FileServlet` and your own `TagReplacementServlet`. The `FileServlet`, which serves all HTML files, is the first servlet in the chain. Its output will be sent to the `TagReplacementServlet`, which will parse the HTML text sent in the request object. When it finds one of your embedded tags, it will replace the tag with the appropriate customer-defined value. Listing 6.3 contains the source for the `TagReplacementServlet`.

LISTING 6.3   TAGREPLACEMENTSERVLET.JAVA

```
import javax.servlet.*;
import javax.servlet.http.*;
import java.io.*;
import java.util.*;

public class TagReplacementServlet extends HttpServlet {

  private Hashtable tag_replacements = new Hashtable(6);
```

```java
public void init(ServletConfig config)
  throws ServletException {

  super.init(config);

  // Initialize the Replace Tag/Value Pairs
  // This would normally be loaded from a database or
  // some other dynamic source

  tag_replacements.put(new String("<COMPANY_NAME>"),
    new String("The Company, Inc."));

  tag_replacements.put(new String("<LOGO>"),
    new String("<IMG SRC=\"/images/logo.gif\">"));

  tag_replacements.put(new String("<COMPANY_ADDRESS>"),
    new String("1000 Some St."));

  tag_replacements.put(new String("<CITY>"),
    new String("Somewheresville"));

  tag_replacements.put(new String("<STATE>"),
    new String("Indiana"));

  tag_replacements.put(new String("<ZIP_CODE>"),
    new String("55555"));
}

private String replaceTags(String value) {

  // Get the keys for the tag_replacements Hashtable
  Enumeration keys = tag_replacements.keys();
  int index = -1;

  while ( keys.hasMoreElements() ) {

    String tag = (String)keys.nextElement();

    // if the tag is found
    while ( (index = value.indexOf(tag)) != -1 ) {

      // Replace the tag with the appropriate value
      value = value.substring(0, index) +
        (String)tag_replacements.get(tag) +
        value.substring(index + tag.length(), value.length());
```

continues

LISTING 6.3   CONTINUED

```
    }
  }
  return value;
}

//Service the request
public void service(HttpServletRequest request,
  HttpServletResponse response)
  throws ServletException, IOException {

  Enumeration e = request.getHeaderNames();

  while (e.hasMoreElements()) {

    // The first step is to copy and set all header
    // information passed by the previous servlet
    String header = (String)e.nextElement();
    String value = request.getHeader(header);
    response.setHeader(header, value);
  }

  // Set the responses Content-Type before getting the Writer
  response.setContentType(request.getContentType());

  PrintWriter out = response.getWriter();

  // Make sure we have the write mime type
  if (request.getContentType().startsWith("text/html")) {

    BufferedReader reader = request.getReader();
    String s;
    StringBuffer buffer = new StringBuffer();

    // read each line into the buffer
    while ( (s = reader.readLine()) != null) {

      buffer.append(s + "\n");
    }
    out.println(replaceTags(buffer.toString()));
  }
  // If not write data directly to response without change
  else {
```

```
    ServletInputStream in = request.getInputStream();
    int b;

    while ( (b = in.read()) != -1 ) {

      out.write(b);
    }
  }
  out.close();
}

//Get Servlet information
public String getServletInfo() {

  return "TagReplacementServlet Information";
  }
}
```

> **NOTE**
>
> If you choose to implement a chain using the `FileServlet`, you should optimize the parsing algorithm. You might choose a unique tag that tells the parser that the page contains other replaceable tags. This would allow you to search for one tag before continuing.

The first section of code you need to examine is the `init()` method. This is where your customer-specific tag/value pairs are initialized. In this example, you are hard coding these values, but in the real world you would probably read them from a database.

The next thing you need to look at is the `service()` method. It reads all the HTML text sent in the request object and passes the buffer to the `replaceTags()` method. This is where the tag parsing is done. The `replaceTags()` method searches for your predefined tags. When it finds one, it replaces the tag with the value that matches the tag in the `tag_replacements` Hashtable. It continues to search until all tags have been replaced. Listing 6.4 shows the HTML text to be processed by the chain. It must be served by the Java Web Server in order to be processed; therefore, you should place it in the document root directory.

LISTING 6.4   CONTACT.HTML

```
<HTML>
<HEAD>
<TITLE>Contact Information</TITLE>
</HEAD>

<BODY>
<LOGO>
<HR>
<CENTER>
<COMPANY_NAME>
<BR>
<COMPANY_ADDRESS>
<BR>
<CITY>, <STATE> <ZIP_CODE>
</CENTER>
<HR>

</BODY>
</HTML>
```

Before you can execute this chain, you must define it in the Java Web Server Administration Tool. To do this, you must modify the / servlet alias. The updated entry is highlighted in Figure 6.5. You will notice that the `FileServlet` is being referenced by the name file in the Servlet Aliases page of the Administration Tool.

FIGURE 6.5

The FileServlet to TagReplacement-Servlet chain.

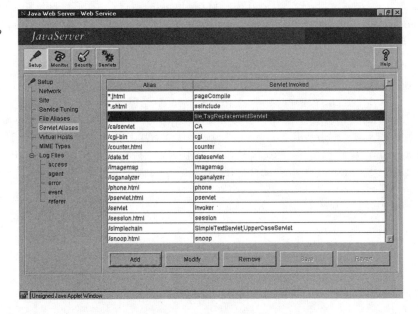

After this processing is complete, the modified text is sent back to the client for display. Figure 6.6 shows the final response.

FIGURE 6.6

The servlet chain final response.

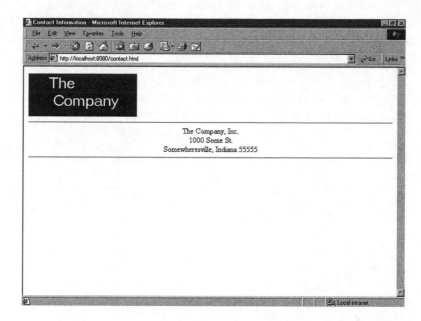

After you have executed this a few times, you should take a look at the HTML source. You can see that the tags have been replaced by their appropriate values. The modified HTML source is as follows:

```
<HTML>
<HEAD>
<TITLE>Contact Information</TITLE>
</HEAD>

<BODY>
<IMG SRC="/images/logo.gif">
<HR>
<CENTER>
The Company, Inc.
<BR>
1000 Some St.
<BR>
Somewheresville, Indiana 55555
</CENTER>
<HR>

</BODY>
</HTML>
```

SUMMARY

In this chapter, you took an in-depth look at servlet chaining. I discussed some common applications for servlet chains. You then examined servlet aliases and HTTP requests, which are common ways to invoke servlet chains. And finally, you put it all together with a practical use for a servlet chain.

In the next chapter, you will learn about HTTP tunneling. You will take an introductory look at the JDK's object serialization and where it fits into the tunneling picture. You will also look at some of the pros and cons of applet to servlet communications.

HTTP TUNNELING

IN THIS CHAPTER

WHAT IS HTTP TUNNELING?

HTTP tunneling is a method of reading and writing serialized objects using an HTTP connection. You are creating a sub-protocol inside the HTTP protocol—that is, "tunneling" inside another protocol. This relieves you from the hassles of dealing with the actual transport layer.

OBJECT SERIALIZATION

Before you can get started with HTTP tunneling, I need to discuss object serialization. Object serialization is a feature introduced in the Java Development Kit version 1.1. It allows you to create objects that are persistent across several mediums. An exceptionally convenient characteristic of serialization is that it not only serializes your object, it also unwinds and serializes all the objects that are referenced by your object.

To make an object serializable, it must implement the `Serializable` interface. This interface is found in the `java.io` package. The entire `Serializable` interface is listed as follows:

```
public interface Serializable {
    static final long serialVersionUID = 1196656838076753133L;
}
```

As you can see, there is not much to this interface. Its only purpose is to signify that an object can be serialized.

The steps involved in serializing an object are as follows:

1. Create an `OutputStream` object. This can be a stream to a file, a TCP/IP connection, or most any other target.

2. Create an `ObjectOutputStream` and pass to its constructor the `OutputStream` created in step 1.

3. Call the `ObjectOutputStream`'s `writeObject()` method and pass to it the object that implements the `Serializable` interface.

The equivalent steps involved in reading a serialized object are as follows:

1. Create an `InputStream` object that points to the location of the serialized object.

2. Create an `ObjectInputStream` and pass to its constructor the `InputStream` created in step 1.

3. Call the `ObjectInputStream`'s `readObject()` method.

4. The `readObject()` method returns an upcasted `Object` that must be downcasted to your original object's type.

Now, create a simple example that writes an object to a file and reads the same object back in. The created object will contain a vector of other objects. Listing 7.1 contains the object you will be serializing.

LISTING 7.1   STUDENTLIST.JAVA

```java
import java.io.*;
import java.util.*;

public class StudentList implements Serializable {

  // Vector holding our students
  Vector list = new Vector(6);

  // Default Constructor
  public StudentList() {
  }

  public void addStudent(String value) {

    // Add a String representing a student name
    if ( value != null ) {

      list.addElement(value);
    }
  }

  public void listStudents() {

    // Iterate over list vector, printint all Strings
    for ( int x = 0; x < list.size(); x++ ) {

      System.out.println("Student " + x + " : "
        + (String)list.elementAt(x));
    }
  }
}
```

Notice that the `StudentList` object implements the `java.io.Serializable` interface. It also contains a `Vector` of `Strings` representing student names, which are also defined as `Serializable`.

The `StudentListApplication` will be used to create, store, and retrieve the `StudentList` from persistent storage. In this example, your persistent storage is the file `file.dat`. The `StudentListApplication` is found in Listing 7.2.

LISTING 7.2   STUDENTLISTAPPLICATION.JAVA

```java
import java.io.*;

public class StudentListApplication {

  // Default Constructor
  public StudentListApplication() {

  }

  // Adds Student Names to List
  public void buildStudentList(StudentList value) {

    value.addStudent("Bob Robinson");
    value.addStudent("Steve Bobinson");
    value.addStudent("Rob Stevinson");
    value.addStudent("Todd Thompson");
    value.addStudent("Tom Toddson");
    value.addStudent("Rob Bobinson");
  }

  // Stores the Serializable StudentList to the file "file.dat"
  public void putStudentList(StudentList value) {

    try {

      // Create the ObjectOutputStream passing it the
      // FileOutputStream object that points to our
      // persistent storage.
      ObjectOutputStream os = new ObjectOutputStream(
        new FileOutputStream("file.dat"));
      // Write the StudentList to the ObjectOutputStream
      os.writeObject(value);
      os.flush();
      os.close();
    }
    catch (IOException e) {

      System.err.println(e.getMessage());
    }
  }

  public StudentList getStudentList() {

    StudentList list = null;
```

```
    try {

      // Create the ObjectInputStream passing it the
      // FileInputStream object that points to our
      // persistent storage.
      ObjectInputStream is = new ObjectInputStream(
        new FileInputStream("file.dat"));
      // Read the stored object and downcast it back to
      // a StudentList
      list = (StudentList)is.readObject();
      is.close();
    }
    catch (IOException e) {

      System.err.println(e.getMessage());
    }
    catch (ClassNotFoundException ce) {

      System.err.println(ce.getMessage());
    }
    return list;
  }

public void invoke() {

  StudentList list = new StudentList();

  buildStudentList(list);

  System.out.println("Before being serialized.");
  list.listStudents();
  putStudentList(list);

  System.out.println("After being read back in.");
  // Get the StudentList and print it out
  StudentList inList = getStudentList();
  if ( inList != null ) {

    inList.listStudents();
  }
  else {

    System.err.println("readObject failed.");
  }
  try {
```

continues

LISTING 7.2   CONTINUED

```
      System.out.println("\n Press enter to quit.");
      System.in.read();
  }
  catch (Exception e) {

    System.err.println(e.getMessage());
  }
}

public static void main(String[] args) {

  StudentListApplication studentListApplication =
    new StudentListApplication();

  studentListApplication.invoke();
  }
}
```

There are two sections of the StudentListApplication you need to look at. The first is the putStudentList() method in which the StudentList object is written to the file file.dat. This method is listed as follows:

```
// Stores the Serializable StudentList to the file "file.dat"
public void putStudentList(StudentList value) {

  try {
// Create the ObjectOutputStream passing it the
    // FileOutputStream object that points to our
    // persistent storage.
    ObjectOutputStream os = new ObjectOutputStream(
      new FileOutputStream("file.dat"));
    // Write the StudentList to the ObjectOutputStream
    os.writeObject(value);
    os.flush();
    os.close();
  }
  catch (IOException e) {

    System.err.println(e.getMessage());
  }
}
```

This method follows the exact three-step process discussed earlier. It creates the appropriate streams for writing and writes the object to persistent storage.

The second section to study is the getStudentList() method. It does the exact opposite of the putStudentList() method. One important step in this method, which is not part of its counterpart, is the downcast from an `Object` to a `StudentList`. You must do this because when the `StudentList` object was stored, it was upcasted to an `Object`. The `getStudentList()` method is listed as follows:

```
public StudentList getStudentList() {

  StudentList list = null;

  try {

    // Create the ObjectInputStream passing it the
    // FileInputStream object that points to our
    // persistent storage.
    ObjectInputStream is = new ObjectInputStream(
      new FileInputStream("file.dat"));
    // Read the stored object and downcast it back to
    // a StudentList
    list = (StudentList)is.readObject();
    is.close();
  }
  catch (IOException e) {

    System.err.println(e.getMessage());
  }
  catch (ClassNotFoundException ce) {

    System.err.println(ce.getMessage());
  }
  return list;
}
```

Build and run the application. The output should look like the following:

```
Before being serialized.
Student 0 : Bob Robinson
Student 1 : Steve Bobinson
Student 2 : Rob Stevinson
Student 3 : Todd Thompson
Student 4 : Tom Toddson
Student 5 : Rob Bobinson
After being read back in.
Student 0 : Bob Robinson
Student 1 : Steve Bobinson
Student 2 : Rob Stevinson
Student 3 : Todd Thompson
Student 4 : Tom Toddson
Student 5 : Rob Bobinson

 Press enter to quit.
```

Notice that the objects are exactly the same before and after being serialized.

CREATING AN HTTP TUNNELING CLIENT

Now that you understand Java serialization, put together an example using HTTP tunneling. The first part of this example is going to be the client. It will be a simple application that opens an HTTP connection to your servlet. It will then write the same `StudentList` object, used in the previous example, to the open connection and wait for a response. The response will be the original `StudentList` object echoed back to the client. The client can be found in Listing 7.3.

LISTING 7.3 StudentListTunnelApp.java

```java
import java.io.*;
import java.net.*;

public class StudentListTunnelApp {

  public StudentListTunnelApp() {

  }

  // Adds Student Names to List
  public void buildStudentList(StudentList value) {

    value.addStudent("Bob Robinson");
    value.addStudent("Steve Bobinson");
    value.addStudent("Rob Stevinson");
    value.addStudent("Todd Thompson");
    value.addStudent("Tom Toddson");
    value.addStudent("Rob Bobinson");
  }

  // Write the StudentList to the Connection
  public void writeStudentList(URLConnection connection,
    StudentList value) {

    try {

      // Set this to false in order to ignore caching
      connection.setUseCaches(false);

      // Set the content-type of the request
      //   application/octet-stream is used when writing
      // application specific byte size data
      connection.setRequestProperty("CONTENT_TYPE",
        "application/octet-stream");
```

```
      // Set these vales to true to use the same connection
      // for both input and output
      connection.setDoInput(true);
      connection.setDoOutput(true);

      // Create the ObjectOutputStream passing it the
      // OutputStream object.
      ObjectOutputStream os =
        new ObjectOutputStream(connection.getOutputStream());

      // Write the StudentList to the ObjectOutputStream
      System.err.println("Writing StudentList Object.");
      os.writeObject(value);
      os.flush();
      os.close();
    }
    catch (IOException e) {

      System.err.println(e.getMessage());
    }
  }

  public StudentList readStudentList(URLConnection connection)
  {

    StudentList list = null;

    try {

      // Create the ObjectInputStream passing it the
      // InputStream object from the URLConnection
      ObjectInputStream is = new ObjectInputStream(
        connection.getInputStream());

      System.err.println("Waiting for response.");

      // Read the stored object and downcast it back to
      // a StudentList
      list = (StudentList)is.readObject();
      is.close();
    }
    catch (IOException e) {

      System.err.println(e.getMessage());
    }
    catch (ClassNotFoundException ce) {
```

continues

LISTING 7.3   CONTINUED

```java
      System.err.println(ce.getMessage());
  }
  return list;
}

public void invoke() {

  try {

    StudentList list = new StudentList();

    buildStudentList(list);

    // create our URL
    URL url = new URL("http://localhost:8080" +
      "/servlet/StudentListTunnelServlet");

    // Open our URLConnection
    System.err.println("Opening Connection.");
    URLConnection con = url.openConnection();

    // Write the StudentList
    writeStudentList(con, list);

    // Get the StudentList from the response
    // and print it out.
    StudentList inList = readStudentList(con);
    if ( inList != null ) {

      System.out.println("After being read back in.");
      inList.listStudents();
    }
    else {

      System.err.println("readObject failed.");
    }

    System.out.println("\n Press enter to quit.");
    System.in.read();
  }
  catch (MalformedURLException mue) {

    System.err.println(mue.getMessage());
  }
```

```
  catch (Exception e) {

    System.err.println(e.getMessage());
  }
}

public static void main(String[] args) {

  StudentListTunnelApp studentListTunnelApp =
    new StudentListTunnelApp();
  studentListTunnelApp.invoke();
}
}
```

Take a look at exactly how the client works. You need to focus on several areas of this example. The first is creating the URL and opening the URLConnection. This section is listed as follows:

```
// create our URL
URL url = new URL("http://localhost:8080" +
  "/servlet/StudentListTunnelServlet");

// Open our URLConnection
System.err.println("Opening Connection.");
URLConnection con = url.openConnection();
```

It is a very simple procedure. It first instantiates a URL object with a String pointing to the servlet URL. It then calls the URL.openConnection() method, which returns a URLConnection object. This is the object you will be using as your communications medium. It will be passed to the writeStudentList() and readStudentList() methods. These methods are your next areas of focus.

The writeStudentList() method takes a URLConnection object and a StudentList object as parameters. This method first sets the appropriate URLConnection properties. This code is listed as follows:

```
// Set this to false in order to ignore caching
connection.setUseCaches(false);

// Set the content-type of the request
//   application/octet-stream is used when writing
// application specific byte size data
connection.setRequestProperty("CONTENT_TYPE",
  "application/octet-stream");
```

```
// Set these vales to true to use the same connection
// for both input and output
connection.setDoInput(true);
connection.setDoOutput(true);
```

These property settings are very important. The first executable line turns caching off for this request. The second is one of the more important property settings. It specifies that you will be using application-specific, byte-size data as your content type because you will be sending a binary data stream. The last two lines in this section set the doInput and doOutput connection properties to True. This makes it possible to both send and receive using the same connection.

The last section of the writeStudentList() method you are going to look at follows the same three steps discussed in the section "Object Serialization." It gets an OutputStream object from the URLConnection.getOutputStream() method. This OutputStream object is then passed to the constructor of the ObjectOutputStream, which is used to write the object to the HTTP connection. This code is listed as follows:

```
// Create the ObjectOutputStream passing it the
// OutputStream object.
ObjectOutputStream os =
  new ObjectOutputStream(connection.getOutputStream());

// Write the StudentList to the ObjectOutputStream
System.err.println("Writing StudentList Object.");
os.writeObject(value);
os.flush();
os.close();
```

The readStudentList() method is even more simple than its counterpart. It simply follows the object serialization steps for reading an object. It gets an InputStream object from the URLConnection and passes it to the constructor of the ObjectInputStream, which is then used to read the StudentList object. For your convenience, it is listed in its entirety in the following:

```
public StudentList readStudentList(URLConnection connection)
  {

    StudentList list = null;

    try {

      // Create the ObjectInputStream passing it the
      // InputStream object from the URLConnection
      ObjectInputStream is = new ObjectInputStream(
        connection.getInputStream());

      System.err.println("Waiting for response.");
```

```
      // Read the stored object and downcast it back to
      // a StudentList
      list = (StudentList)is.readObject();
      is.close();
    }
    catch (IOException e) {

      System.err.println(e.getMessage());
    }
    catch (ClassNotFoundException ce) {

      System.err.println(ce.getMessage());
    }
    return list;
  }
```

When you see how easy it is to serialize objects across an HTTP connection, or any other connection, you really have to give credit to the people who wrote these classes. They have saved all of us a lot of hassle. You will see again how easy it is in the next section, when you look at the servlet side of an HTTP tunnel.

CREATING AN HTTP TUNNELING SERVLET

Now that you have seen the client side, take a look at the server side. The servlet example will service requests from the StudentListTunnelApp. When it receives a request, it will read the StudentList object from the InputStream and send it, unchanged, back to the client. The source for the servlet is in Listing 7.4.

LISTING 7.4   STUDENTLISTTUNNELSERVLET.JAVA

```java
import javax.servlet.*;
import javax.servlet.http.*;
import java.io.*;
import java.util.*;

import StudentList;

public class StudentListTunnelServlet extends HttpServlet {

  public void init(ServletConfig config)
    throws ServletException {

    super.init(config);
  }
```

continues

LISTING 7.4   CONTINUED

```java
//Service the request
public void service(HttpServletRequest request,
  HttpServletResponse response)
  throws ServletException, IOException {

  try {

    // Create the ObjectInputStream with
    // the Request InputStream.
    ObjectInputStream ois =
      new ObjectInputStream(request.getInputStream());

    // Read the Object.  Make sure the StudentList Object
    // is in your CLASSPATH or you will receive a
    // ClassNotFoundException.
    StudentList list = (StudentList)ois.readObject();

    // The Response Begins Here
    response.setContentType("application/octet-stream");

    ObjectOutputStream oos =
      new ObjectOutputStream(response.getOutputStream());

    // Echo the object to the response
    oos.writeObject(list);
    oos.flush();
    oos.close();
  }
  catch (ClassNotFoundException cnfe) {

    System.err.println(cnfe.getMessage());
  }
}

//Get Servlet information
public String getServletInfo() {

  return "StudentListTunnelServlet Information";
}
}
```

As you can see, this is a very simple servlet. The service() method is where all the functionality is located. The StudentList objects are written and read just like they were on the client side. The same three-step process is used on both sides.

A PRACTICAL HTTP TUNNELING EXAMPLE

You are now going to put HTTP tunneling to work in a practical example. Your example will be a real-time order status tool. You will be using an applet as your client side, which will be called `OrderStatusApplet`. It will send a serializable `Order` object to the `OrderStatusServlet`. This servlet will then read the object off the wire, update the `status` attribute, and send the object back to the applet. Listing 7.5 contains the source code for the `Order` object.

LISTING 7.5   ORDER.JAVA

```java
import java.io.*;

// Notice this object implements the Serializable interface
public class Order implements Serializable {

  // This attribute holds the Order#
  private String order = new String("");
  // This attribute holds the Status of the Order
  private String status = new String("");

  // Default Constructor
  public Order() {

  }

  // Accessor used to set the Order #
  public void setOrder(String value) {

    if ( value != null ) {

      order = value;
    }
  }

  // Accessor used to get the Order #
  public String getOrder() {

    return order;
  }

  // Accessor used to set the Order Status
  public void setStatus(String value) {

    if ( value != null ) {
```

continues

LISTING 7.5 CONTINUED

```
      status = value;
    }
  }

  // Accessor used to get the Order Status
  public String getStatus() {

    return status;
  }
}
```

The Order object encapsulates the order and its status, and it will be passed between the applet and servlet.

The OrderStatusApplet

The OrderStatusApplet will leverage some of the Java Swing classes that are bundled with the JDK 1.1.6. You do not need to concern yourself with all the swing classes. The only two you need to understand are the JTextField and JTextArea classes. The JTextField will hold your order number, and the JTextArea will display the returned status. Listing 7.6 contains the source for the client applet.

LISTING 7.6 ORDERSTATUSAPPLET.JAVA

```
import java.awt.*;
import java.awt.event.*;
import java.applet.*;
import com.sun.java.swing.*;
import java.net.*;
import java.io.*;

//import com.sun.java.swing.UIManager;
public class OrderStatusApplet extends JApplet {

  boolean isStandalone = false;
  JPanel jStatusPanel = new JPanel();
  JPanel jActionPanel = new JPanel();
  GridLayout gridLayout1 = new GridLayout(1, 2);
  JButton jGetStatusButton = new JButton();
  JTextField jOrderTextField = new JTextField();
  JLabel jLabel1 = new JLabel();
  JTextArea jStatusResultTextArea = new JTextArea();
```

```java
//Get a parameter value
public String getParameter(String key, String def) {

  return isStandalone ? System.getProperty(key, def) :
    (getParameter(key) != null ? getParameter(key) : def);
}

// Default Construct
public OrderStatusApplet() {

}

//Initialize the applet
public void init() {

  try {

    jbInit();
  }
  catch (Exception e) {

    e.printStackTrace();
  }
}

//Component initialization
private void jbInit() throws Exception {

  this.setSize(400,150);
  this.getContentPane().setLayout(gridLayout1);
  jGetStatusButton.setText("Get Status");
  jGetStatusButton.addActionListener(
    new java.awt.event.ActionListener() {

      public void actionPerformed(ActionEvent e) {

        jGetStatusButton_actionPerformed(e);
    }
  });
  jLabel1.setText("Order #");
  jOrderTextField.setPreferredSize(new Dimension(50, 19));
  jStatusResultTextArea.setPreferredSize(
    new Dimension(175, 135));
  this.getContentPane().add(jActionPanel, null);
  jActionPanel.add(jLabel1, null);
  jActionPanel.add(jOrderTextField, null);
```

continues

LISTING 7.6 CONTINUED

```java
    jActionPanel.add(jGetStatusButton, null);
    this.getContentPane().add(jStatusPanel, null);
    jStatusPanel.add(jStatusResultTextArea, null);
}

//Get Applet information
public String getAppletInfo() {

    return "Applet Information";
}

//Get parameter info
public String[][] getParameterInfo() {

    return null;
}

// Write the StudentList to the Connection
public void writeOrder(URLConnection connection,
    Order value) {

    try {

        // Set this to false in order to ignore caching
        connection.setUseCaches(false);

        // Set the content-type of the request
        //   application/octet-stream is used when writing
        // application specific byte size data
        connection.setRequestProperty("CONTENT_TYPE",
            "application/octet-stream");

        // Set these vales to true to use the same connection
        // for both input and output
        connection.setDoInput(true);
        connection.setDoOutput(true);

        // Create the ObjectOutputStream passing it the
        // ByteArrayOutputStream object.
        ObjectOutputStream os =
            new ObjectOutputStream(connection.getOutputStream());

        // Write the StudentList to the ObjectOutputStream
        System.err.println("Writing Order Object.");
```

```
      os.writeObject(value);
      os.flush();
      os.close();
   }
   catch (IOException e) {

      System.err.println(e.getMessage());
   }
}

public Order readOrder(URLConnection connection)
{

   Order order = null;

   try {

      // Create the ObjectInputStream passing it the
      // InputStream object from the URLConnection
      ObjectInputStream is = new ObjectInputStream(
        connection.getInputStream());

      System.err.println("Waiting for response.");

      // Read the stored object and downcast it back to
      // a Order
      order = (Order)is.readObject();
      is.close();
   }
   catch (IOException e) {

      System.err.println(e.getMessage());
   }
   catch (ClassNotFoundException ce) {

      System.err.println(ce.getMessage());
   }
   return order;
}

void jGetStatusButton_actionPerformed(ActionEvent event) {

   try {

      // This is where the OrderStatus Transaction begins
      Order order = new Order();
```

continues

LISTING 7.6   CONTINUED

```
      order.setOrder(jOrderTextField.getText());

      // create our URL
      URL url = new URL("http://localhost:8080" +
        "/servlet/OrderStatusServlet");

      // Open our URLConnection
      System.err.println("Opening Connection.");
      URLConnection con = url.openConnection();

      // Write the Order
      writeOrder(con, order);

      // Get the Order from the response,
      // after the status has been checked, and print it out.
      Order response_order = readOrder(con);
      if ( response_order != null ) {

        // Put the status String returned from the
        // OrderStatusServlet into the jTextArea Object
        jStatusResultTextArea.setText(
          response_order.getStatus());
      }
      else {

        System.err.println("readObject failed.");
      }
    }
    catch (MalformedURLException mue) {

      System.err.println(mue.getMessage());
    }
    catch (Exception e) {

      System.err.println(e.getMessage());
    }
  }
}
```

The three areas of the applet you must focus on are the
jGetStatusButton_actionPerformed(), writeOrder(), and readOrder() methods.
These methods make up the functional areas of the applet.

The jGetStatusButton_actionPerformed() method is where the transaction is invoked. It creates an Order object, setting the order attribute to the value typed into the jOrderTextField swing component. It then opens a URL connection pointing to your OrderStatusServlet, http://localhost:8080/servlet/OrderStatusServlet. The connection and the order are then passed to the writeOrder() method.

The writeOrder() method first sets the appropriate properties of the Connection object. It then creates an ObjectOutputStream using the OutputStream of the connection. When the ObjectOutputStream is successfully created, the Order object is written to it.

When the writeOrder() method returns, the readOrder() method is called. It takes the URLConnection object passed to it and creates an ObjectInputStream. It then calls the ObjectInputStream's readObject() method, which block reads until a response object is received. This new Order object is then returned to the calling method.

The jGetStatusButton_actionPerformed() method then takes the Order object that was returned to it and calls the getStatus() method, passing the returned status to the jStatusResultTextArea's setText() method.

Compile these classes, making sure that the swingall.jar file, which contains all the swing components, is in your CLASSPATH. The HTML used to load this applet is shown in Listing 7.7.

LISTING 7.7   ORDERSTATUSAPPLET.HTML

```
<HTML>
<HEAD>
<TITLE>
Order Status Page
</TITLE>
</HEAD>
<BODY>
<APPLET
  ARCHIVE  = "swingall.jar"
  CODE     = "OrderStatusApplet.class"
  NAME     = "Order Status Applet"
  WIDTH    = 400
  HEIGHT   = 150
  HSPACE   = 0
  VSPACE   = 0
  ALIGN    = middle
>
</APPLET>
</BODY>
</HTML>
```

After you have compiled and installed the HTML and class files, you can load the `OrderStatusApplet.html` file. Figure 7.1 shows the `OrderStatusApplet` after it is loaded.

FIGURE 7.1

The `OrderStatusApplet`.

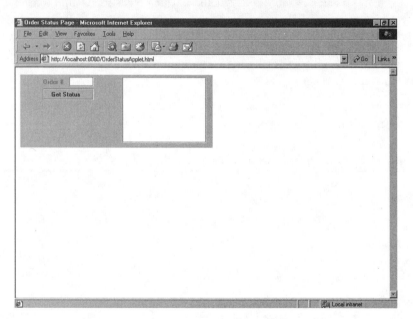

The OrderStatusServlet

The `OrderStatusServlet` services order-status requests sent by the `OrderStatusApplet`. It reads the `Order` object from the `ObjectInputStream` and passes it to the `getOrderStatus()` method. In a "real-world" application, this method would be a client to some other real-time server. It could be a CORBA client, an RMI client, or even a JDBC query to a database. For the example, it simply calls the `Order.setStatus()` method, passing it the `String` `"Your order is in transit"`. The `service()` method then writes it to the `ObjectOutputStream` to be read by the `OrderStatusApplet`. Listing 7.8 contains the source for the `OrderStatusServlet`.

LISTING 7.8   ORDERSTATUSSERVLET.JAVA

```java
import javax.servlet.*;
import javax.servlet.http.*;
import java.io.*;
import java.util.*;

public class OrderStatusServlet extends HttpServlet {

  //Initialize global variables
  public void init(ServletConfig config)
    throws ServletException {

    super.init(config);
  }

  private void getOrderStatus(Order order) {

    // This could do just about anything;
    // It could be CORBA/RMI client
    // It could be a database query, etc.
    order.setStatus("Your order is in transit.");
  }

  //Service the request
  public void service(HttpServletRequest request,
    HttpServletResponse response)
    throws ServletException, IOException {

    try {

      // Create the ObjectInputStream with
      // the Request InputStream.
      ObjectInputStream ois =
        new ObjectInputStream(request.getInputStream());

      // Read the Object.  Make sure the StudentList Object
      // is in your CLASSPATH or you will receive a
      // ClassNotFoundException.
      Order order = (Order)ois.readObject();

      getOrderStatus(order);

      // The Response Begins Here
      response.setContentType("application/octet-stream");
```

7

HTTP TUNNELING

continues

LISTING 7.8   CONTINUED

```
        ObjectOutputStream oos =
          new ObjectOutputStream(response.getOutputStream());

        // Echo the object to the response
        oos.writeObject(order);
        oos.flush();
        oos.close();
      }
      catch (ClassNotFoundException cnfe) {

        System.err.println(cnfe.getMessage());
      }
    }
//Get Servlet information

  public String getServletInfo() {
    return "OrderStatusServlet Information";
  }
}
```

NOTE

The Order.class file must be in the CLASSPATH of the Java Web Server, or the OrderStatusServlet will not be able to find it.

After you have a chance to look over the source for the OrderStatusServlet, build and install it to the Java Web Server. You then need to load the OrderStatusApplet into your browser, enter an order number, and press the Get Status button. Your results should look similar to Figure 7.2.

FIGURE 7.2

Results from
OrderStatusServlet.

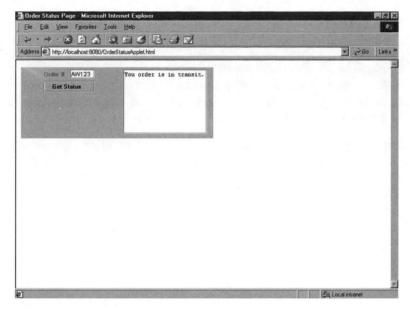

PROS AND CONS OF APPLET-TO-SERVLET COMMUNICATION

As you have seen in the previous sections, HTTP tunneling is a very simple method for applet-to-servlet communication, but it does have its own set of pros and cons. Some of the pros of using HTTP tunneling are as follows:

- It is simple to use because of the Serializable interface.
- It is very fast for lightweight objects.
- It shields you from the communications layer.
- It provides you with a method of "tunneling" through firewalls.

On the other hand, some cons of this technique are listed in the following:

- You must make sure that all your objects and nested objects implement the Serializable interface.
- Because you are opening a connection with an applet, security issues limit you to connecting only to the applet's originating server.
- When you start using larger objects or collections of objects, your throughput declines considerably.
- Because you are using an applet as a client, you must make sure that your users have a compatible browser.

SUMMARY

This chapter covered the basics of Java serialization. You created two servlets that serviced HTTP tunneling requests. You also took a look at applets and applications as HTTP tunneling clients. At this point, you should be able to create your own servlet that can service HTTP tunneling requests. You should understand how to create `Serializable` objects. You should also be able to determine when to use (or not use) an applet-to-servlet solution.

In the next chapter, you will be looking at Java's JDBC. You will first go over a basic introduction to the JDBC and then you will examine how you can leverage the JDBC in servlets.

SERVLETS AND THE JDBC

IN THIS CHAPTER

WHAT IS THE JDBC?

The JDBC is a pure Java API used to execute SQL statements. It provides a set of classes and interfaces that can be used by developers to write database applications. Basic JDBC interaction, in its simplest form, can be broken down into four steps:

1. Open a connection to the database.
2. Execute a SQL statement.
3. Process the results.
4. Close the connection to the database.

The following code fragment shows these steps in action:

```
// Step 1. Open a connection to the ODBC datasource titles.
con = DriverManager.getConnection("jdbc:odbc:titles",
    "admin", "password");

// Step 2. Execute the SQL statement.
Statement statement = con.createStatement();

ResultSet rs = statement.executeQuery("SELECT * " +
  "FROM Types");

// Step 3. Process the Results
while ( rs.next() ) {

    // get the type_id, which is an int
    System.err.println("Type ID = " + rs.getInt("type_id"));
    // get the type_name, which is a String
    System.err.println("Type Name = " + rs.getString("type_name"));
}

// Step 4. Close the Connection.
rs.close();
con.close();
```

TWO- AND THREE-TIER DATABASE ACCESS MODELS

The JDBC provides support for two- and three-tier database access models. I am going to discuss both in this section.

When you use the two-tier database access model, your Java application talks directly to the database. This is accomplished through the use of a JDBC driver, which sends commands directly to the database. The results of these commands are then sent from the database directly back to the application. Figure 8.1 shows the two-tier model.

FIGURE 8.1

The two-tier JDBC model.

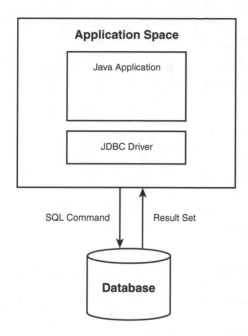

FIGURE 8.1

The two-tier JDBC model.

The three-tier model, as you might have guessed, is a little more complicated. When you use the three-tier model, your JDBC driver sends commands to a middle tier, which in turn sends commands to the database. The results of these commands are then sent back to the middle tier, which communicates them back to the application. Figure 8.2 shows the three-tier model.

8

SERVLETS AND THE JDBC

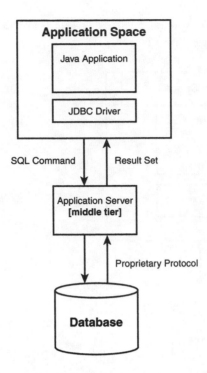

FIGURE 8.2

The three-tier JDBC model.

JDBC DRIVER TYPES

Sun has defined four JDBC driver types. Each of these types meets a different application need.

Type 1: JDBC-ODBC Bridge Plus ODBC Driver

The first type of JDBC driver is the JDBC-ODBC Bridge. This driver type is provided by Sun with the JDK 1.1 and later. It is a driver that provides JDBC access to databases through ODBC drivers. The ODBC driver must be configured on the client for the bridge to work. This driver type is commonly used for prototyping or when there is no JDBC driver available for a particular DBMS. Figure 8.3 shows the driver interaction of the JDBC-ODBC Bridge.

Type 2: Native-API Partly-Java Driver

The Native to API driver converts JDBC commands to DBMS-specific native calls. This is much like the restriction of Type 1 drivers. The client must have some binary code loaded on its machine. These drivers do have an advantage over Type 1 drivers because they interface directly with the database. Figure 8.4 show the interactions of a Type 2 driver.

FIGURE 8.3
The JDBC-ODBC Bridge.

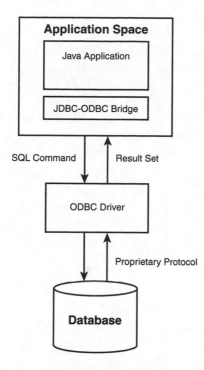

FIGURE 8.4
The Type 2 JDBC driver.

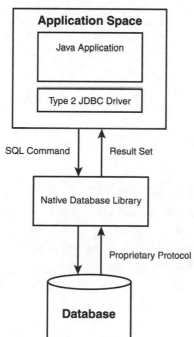

Type 3: JDBC-Net Pure Java Driver

The JDBC-Net drivers are a three-tier solution. This type of driver translates JDBC calls into a database-independent network protocol that is sent to a middleware server. This server then translates this DBMS-independent protocol into a DBMS-specific protocol, which is sent to a particular database. The results are then routed back through the middleware server and sent back to the client. This type of solution makes it possible to implement a pure Java client. It also makes it possible to swap databases without affecting the client. This is by far the most flexible JDBC solution. Figure 8.5 shows this three-tier solution.

FIGURE 8.5

The Type 3 JDBC driver.

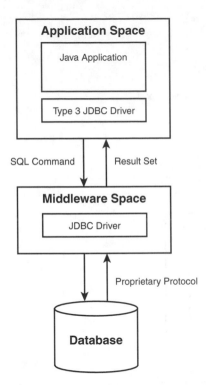

Type 4: Native-Protocol Pure Java Driver

The Type 4 drivers are pure Java drivers that communicate directly with the vendor's database. They do this by converting JDBC commands directly into the database engine's native protocol. The Type 4 driver has a very distinct advantage over all the other driver types. It has no additional translation or middleware layer, which improves performance tremendously. Figure 8.6 diagrams the communications of a Type 4 driver.

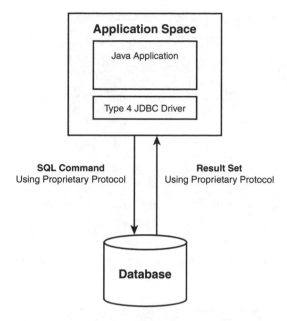

FIGURE 8.6
The Type 4 JDBC driver.

JDBC BASICS

Now that I have discussed what the JDBC is and some of its characteristics, you will start learning how to use it. In this section, I am going to discuss how to install and set up a Type 1 driver, make a connection to the database, and perform the basic SQL commands.

Installing and Setting Up a Type 1 Driver

In the JDBC examples throughout this book, you will be connecting to a Microsoft Access database using a Type 1 driver. To install the JDBC-ODBC Bridge, simply download the JDK and follow the directions for installing it. The JDBC-ODBC Bridge is included in version 1.1 and later.

The JDBC-ODBC Bridge requires no specific setup steps, but the ODBC driver does. For the examples, I assume that you are using a PC and running Win/9x or NT. If not, you will need to create your own database using the drivers supplied by your database vendor.

To configure the ODBC data source for the examples, implement the following steps:

1. Copy the database file moviecatalog.mdb, which can be found on the companion Web site, to your local drive.

2. Start the application ODBC Administrator found in the Windows Control Panel. You should see a window similar to the one in Figure 8.7.

FIGURE 8.7

The ODBC Administrator.

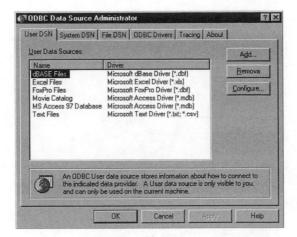

3. Select the Add button to add a new data source. Figure 8.8 shows the Create New Data Source screen.

FIGURE 8.8

The Create New Data Source screen.

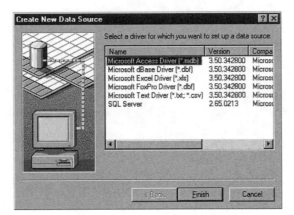

4. Select the Microsoft Access driver and click the Finish button. You should be presented with the ODBC Microsoft Access Setup screen. Figure 8.9 shows this screen.

5. Enter the string Movie Catalog as the data source name and click the database Select button. Enter the path to the location of your moviecatalog.mdb file and click OK. You should now see the ODBC Microsoft Access Setup screen with your changes displayed. Click OK to commit your changes.

6. You should now see the ODBC Data Source Administrator screen with the Movie Catalog data source in the list. Click the OK button to close this window.

FIGURE 8.9

The ODBC Microsoft Access Setup screen.

Establishing a Database Connection

The first thing you need to do when using the JDBC is establish a connection to the database. This is a two-step process. You must load the JDBC driver, and then make a connection.

Loading a JDBC driver is very simple. It takes only one line of code. In the examples, you will be using the JDBC-ODBC Bridge. The class name for this driver is `sun.jdbc.odbc.JdbcOdbcDriver`. The following code snippet shows you how to load this driver:

```
Class.forName("sun.jdbc.odbc.JdbcOdbcDriver");
```

When you call the `Class.forName()` method, it creates an instance of the driver and registers it with the `DriverManager`. This is all there is to loading a JDBC driver.

After you have the driver loaded, it is easy to make a connection. You make a call to the static method `DriverManager.getConnection()`, which returns a connection to the database. Its method signature is listed as follows:

```
public static synchronized Connection getConnection(String url,
    String user, String password) throws SQLException
```

The first parameter is the URL that points to your data source. In the case of the JDBC-ODBC Bridge it always begins with `jdbc:odbc:DataSourceName`, where `DataSourceName` is the name of the ODBC data source you set up.

The next two parameters are self-explanatory. They are the username and password associated with the database login. For the example, you will use empty strings for each. What follows is the code used to open a connection to the Movie Catalog database:

```
con = DriverManager.getConnection("jdbc:odbc:Movie Catalog",
    "", "");
```

The `Connection` object returned from the `DriverManager` is an open connection to the database. You will be using it to create JDBC statements that pass SQL statements to the database.

Performing the Basic SQL Commands

In this section, you are going to look at how to create a JDBC `Statement` object and five JDBC examples that use the `Statement`. In all the examples, you will be using the Movie Catalog database that you configured earlier.

Creating a JDBC Statement Object

To execute any SQL command using a JDBC connection, you must first create a `Statement` object. To create a `Statement`, you must call the `Connection.createStatement()` method. It returns a JDBC statement that you will use to send your SQL statements to the database. The following code snippet shows how to create a statement:

```
Statement statement = con.createStatement();
```

Creating a Table

The first thing you are going to do is create a database table that represents a list of movie titles. Currently there are two tables in the database: the Categories table and the Types table. Table 8.1 shows the composition of the Titles table.

TABLE 8.1   COMPOSITION OF THE TITLES TABLE

Field Name	Data Type
title_id	INTEGER
title_name	VARCHAR(50)
rating	VARCHAR(5)
price	FLOAT
quantity	INTEGER
type_id	INTEGER
category_id	INTEGER

The application that creates this table can be found in Listing 8.1. Notice that it follows the step-by-step process that I described earlier:

1. Opens a connection to the database.

2. Executes a SQL Statement.

3. Processes the results.

4. Closes the connection to the database.

LISTING 8.1 CREATETABLESAPP.JAVA

```java
import java.sql.*;

public class CreateTablesApp {

  public void createTables() {

    Connection con = null;

    try {

      // Load the Driver class file
      Class.forName("sun.jdbc.odbc.JdbcOdbcDriver");

      // Make a connection to the ODBC datasource Movie Catalog
      con = DriverManager.getConnection("jdbc:odbc:Movie Catalog",
        "", "");

      // Create the statement
      Statement statement = con.createStatement();

      // Use the created statement to CREATE the database table
      // Create Titles Table
      statement.executeUpdate("CREATE TABLE Titles " +
        "(title_id INTEGER, title_name VARCHAR(50), " +
        "rating VARCHAR(5), price FLOAT, quantity INTEGER, " +
        "type_id INTEGER, category_id INTEGER)");
    }
    catch (SQLException sqle) {

      System.err.println(sqle.getMessage());
    }
    catch (ClassNotFoundException cnfe) {

      System.err.println(cnfe.getMessage());
    }
    catch (Exception e) {

      System.err.println(e.getMessage());
    }
    finally {

      try {

        if ( con != null ) {
```

8

SERVLETS AND THE JDBC

continues

LISTING 8.1   CONTINUED

```
            // Close the connection no matter what
            con.close();
        }
    }
    catch (SQLException sqle) {

        System.err.println(sqle.getMessage());

    }
  }
}

  public static void main(String[] args) {

    CreateTablesApp createTablesApp = new CreateTablesApp();

    createTablesApp.createTables();
  }
}
```

The section of the listing that you want to focus on is as follows:

```
// Create the statement
Statement statement = con.createStatement();

// Use the created statement to CREATE the database table
// Create Titles Table
statement.executeUpdate("CREATE TABLE Titles " +
  "(title_id INTEGER, title_name VARCHAR(50), " +
  "rating VARCHAR(5), price FLOAT, quantity INTEGER, " +
  "type_id INTEGER, category_id INTEGER)");
```

The first statement executed creates a Statement object with the given connection. To perform the actual creation of the table, call the Statement.executeUpdate() method passing it the SQL statement to create the table. Its signature is listed as follows:

```
public int executeUpdate(String sql) throws SQLException
```

This method is used for all update type transactions. It takes a string representation of a SQL statement and returns an int. The return value is either a row count for INSERT, UPDATE, or DELETE statements, or 0 for SQL statements that return nothing, such as a CREATE.

After you have created the Titles table, the table relationships of the Movie Catalog database should look something like Figure 8.10.

FIGURE 8.10
*The Movie
Catalog tables.*

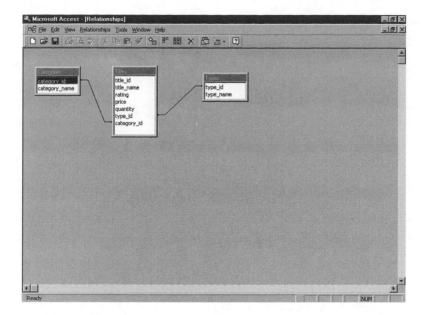

Inserting Data into a Table

Now that you have all your tables in place, you can put some data into them. Listing 8.2 show the application used to populate your database.

LISTING 8.2   INSERTDATAAPP.JAVA

```java
import java.sql.*;

public class InsertDataApp {

  public InsertDataApp() {
  }

  public void insertData() {

    Connection con = null;

    try {

      // Load the Driver class file
      Class.forName("sun.jdbc.odbc.JdbcOdbcDriver");
```

continues

LISTING 8.2   CONTINUED

```java
// Make a connection to the ODBC datasource Movie Catalog
con = DriverManager.getConnection("jdbc:odbc:Movie Catalog",
  "", "");

// Create the statement
Statement statement = con.createStatement();

// Use the created statement to INSERT DATA into
// the database tables.

// Insert Data into the Types Table
statement.executeUpdate("INSERT INTO Types " +
  "VALUES (0, 'VHS')");

statement.executeUpdate("INSERT INTO Types " +
  "VALUES (1, 'DVD')");

statement.executeUpdate("INSERT INTO Types " +
  "VALUES (2, 'Laserdisc')");

// Insert Data into the Categories Table
statement.executeUpdate("INSERT INTO Categories " +
  "VALUES (0, 'Action Adventure')");

statement.executeUpdate("INSERT INTO Categories " +
  "VALUES (1, 'Comedy')");

statement.executeUpdate("INSERT INTO Categories " +
  "VALUES (2, 'Drama')");

statement.executeUpdate("INSERT INTO Categories " +
  "VALUES (3, 'Western')");

statement.executeUpdate("INSERT INTO Categories " +
  "VALUES (4, 'Sci-Fi')");

statement.executeUpdate("INSERT INTO Categories " +
  "VALUES (5, 'Classics')");

// Insert Data into the Titles Table
statement.executeUpdate("INSERT INTO Titles " +
  "VALUES (0, 'The Adventures of Buckaroo Bonzai', " +
  "'PG', 19.95, 10, 0, 4)");
```

```
statement.executeUpdate("INSERT INTO Titles " +
    "VALUES (1, 'Saving Private Ryan', " +
    "'R', 19.95, 12, 1, 0)");

statement.executeUpdate("INSERT INTO Titles " +
    "VALUES (2, 'So I Married An Axe Murderer', " +
    "'PG', 19.95, 15, 1, 1)");

statement.executeUpdate("INSERT INTO Titles " +
    "VALUES (3, 'Happy Gilmore', " +
    "'PG', 19.95, 9, 1, 1)");

statement.executeUpdate("INSERT INTO Titles " +
    "VALUES (4, 'High Plains Drifter', " +
    "'PG', 29.95, 10, 2, 3)");

statement.executeUpdate("INSERT INTO Titles " +
    "VALUES (5, 'Cape Fear', " +
    "'NR', 6.99, 21, 0, 5)");

statement.executeUpdate("INSERT INTO Titles " +
    "VALUES (6, 'The Last Emperor', " +
    "'PG', 19.95, 12, 1, 2)");
}
catch (SQLException sqle) {

  System.err.println(sqle.getMessage());
}
catch (ClassNotFoundException cnfe) {

  System.err.println(cnfe.getMessage());
}
catch (Exception e) {

  System.err.println(e.getMessage());
}
finally {

  try {

    if ( con != null ) {

      // Close the connection no matter what
      con.close();
    }
  }
```

continues

8

SERVLETS AND THE JDBC

LISTING 8.2   CONTINUED

```
      catch (SQLException sqle) {

        System.err.println(sqle.getMessage());
      }
    }
  }

  public static void main(String[] args) {

    InsertDataApp insertDataApp = new InsertDataApp();

    insertDataApp.insertData();
  }
}
```

The InsertDataApp application uses the same executeUpdate() method you used to create the tables. You only changed the SQL string that you passed to it, using a basic SQL INSERT statement instead. You inserted data into your Types, Categories, and Titles tables, respectively. Also notice that you were able to perform all your inserts using the same Statement object. There is nothing preventing you from reusing this object instead of creating a new one for each execution.

Selecting Data from a Table

The most common SQL statement is the SELECT. It gives you the ability to look at the data stored in your tables. In the previous examples, you created and populated the Movie Catalog database. In this example, you are going to look at the data you put in these tables, and you are going to do it with a SELECT statement. Listing 8.3 contains the source for this example.

LISTING 8.3   SELECTDATAAPP.JAVA

```
import java.sql.*;
import java.io.*;

public class SelectDataApp {

  public SelectDataApp() {

  }

  public void selectData() {

    Connection con = null;
```

```
try {

  // Load the Driver class file
  Class.forName("sun.jdbc.odbc.JdbcOdbcDriver");

  // Make a connection to the ODBC datasource Movie Catalog
  con = DriverManager.getConnection("jdbc:odbc:Movie Catalog",
    "", "");

  // Create the statement
  Statement statement = con.createStatement();

  // Use the created statement to SELECT the DATA
  // FROM the Titles Table.
  ResultSet rs = statement.executeQuery("SELECT * " +
    "FROM Titles");

  // Iterate over the ResultSet
  while ( rs.next() ) {

    // get the title_name, which is a String
    System.err.println("Title Name = " + rs.getString("title_name"));
    // get the rating
    System.err.println("Title Rating = " + rs.getString("rating"));
    // get the price
    System.err.println("Title Price = " + rs.getString("price"));
    // get the quantity
    System.err.println("Title Quantity = " + rs.getString("quantity")
    ➥ + "\n");
  }
  // Close the ResultSet
  rs.close();
  System.in.read();
}
catch (IOException ioe) {

  System.err.println(ioe.getMessage());
}
catch (SQLException sqle) {

  System.err.println(sqle.getMessage());
}
catch (ClassNotFoundException cnfe) {

  System.err.println(cnfe.getMessage());
}
```

continues

LISTING 8.3   CONTINUED

```
    catch (Exception e) {

      System.err.println(e.getMessage());
    }
    finally {

      try {

        if ( con != null ) {

          // Close the connection no matter what
          con.close();
        }
      }
      catch (SQLException sqle) {

        System.err.println(sqle.getMessage());
      }
    }
  }

  public static void main(String[] args) {

    SelectDataApp selectDataApp = new SelectDataApp();

    selectDataApp.selectData();
  }
}
```

To execute a query, you use the same Statement object as you did in previous examples. You just call a different method. The method to perform a query is executeQuery(). Its signature is listed as follows:

```
public ResultSet executeQuery(String sql) throws SQLException
```

It takes a SQL string like the executeUpdate() method. The difference is that it returns a ResultSet object containing the results of the query. In the example, you passed it the string "SELECT * FROM TITLES", which returns a collection of rows resulting from the query.

After you have your ResultSet object returned from executeQuery(), you can iterate over it. The following code snippet shows how the example processes the query results:

```
// Iterate over the ResultSet
while ( rs.next() ) {

  // get the title_name, which is a String
```

```
    System.err.println("Title Name = " + rs.getString("title_name"));
    // get the rating
    System.err.println("Title Rating = " + rs.getString("rating"));
    // get the price
    System.err.println("Title Price = " + rs.getString("price"));
    // get the quantity
    System.err.println("Title Quantity = " +
    rs.getString("quantity") + "\n");
}
// Close the ResultSet
rs.close();
```

The first thing you do is call the `ResultSet.next()` method. This method returns a Boolean value indicating whether the next row in the set is valid. If it is, you can access that row using the get accessors provided by the `ResultSet` object. In the example, you use only the `getString()` method, but they all function the same except for their return type. They take a string value representing the name of the column in the table and return the type that is part of their method name. For example, `getString()` returns a `String` and `getInt()` returns an `int`. You can continue iterating over the `ResultSet` until `next()` returns `False`; at that point, you must close the `ResultSet` object. When you execute this application, the results should be similar to the following output:

```
Title Name = The Adventures of Buckaroo Bonzai
Title Rating = PG
Title Price = 19.95
Title Quantity = 10

Title Name = Saving Private Ryan
Title Rating = R
Title Price = 19.95
Title Quantity = 12

Title Name = So I Married An Axe Murderer
Title Rating = PG
Title Price = 19.95
Title Quantity = 15

Title Name = Happy Gilmore
Title Rating = PG
Title Price = 19.95
Title Quantity = 9

Title Name = High Plains Drifter
Title Rating = PG
Title Price = 29.95
Title Quantity = 10
```

```
Title Name = Cape Fear
Title Rating = NR
Title Price = 6.99
Title Quantity = 21

Title Name = The Last Emperor
Title Rating = PG
Title Price = 19.95
Title Quantity = 12
```

Updating Tables

Another SQL command you need to examine is the UPDATE statement. It looks for a matching condition and makes the specified changes if its WHERE clause is true. An example of this would be if *The Last Emperor* sold 7 copies. You would need to update its quantity to 5. The example in Listing 8.4 does just that.

LISTING 8.4   UPDATEDATAAPP.JAVA

```java
import java.sql.*;

public class UpdateDataApp {

  public UpdateDataApp() {

  }

  public void updateData() {

    Connection con = null;

    try {

      // Load the Driver class file
      Class.forName("sun.jdbc.odbc.JdbcOdbcDriver");

      // Make a connection to the ODBC datasource Movie Catalog
      con = DriverManager.getConnection("jdbc:odbc:Movie Catalog",
        "", "");

      // Create the statement
      Statement statement = con.createStatement();

      // Use the created statement to UPDATE DATA in
      // the database tables.
      // Update the Quantity of "The Last Emperor"
```

```
      statement.executeUpdate("UPDATE Titles " +
        "SET quantity = 5 " +
        "WHERE title_name = 'The Last Emperor'");
    }
    catch (SQLException sqle) {

      System.err.println(sqle.getMessage());
    }
    catch (ClassNotFoundException cnfe) {

      System.err.println(cnfe.getMessage());
    }
    catch (Exception e) {

      System.err.println(e.getMessage());
    }
    finally {

      try {

        if ( con != null ) {

          // Close the connection no matter what
          con.close();
        }
      }
      catch (SQLException sqle) {

        System.err.println(sqle.getMessage());
      }
    }
  }

  public static void main(String[] args) {

    UpdateDataApp updateDataApp = new UpdateDataApp();

    updateDataApp.updateData();
  }
}
```

If you examine the listing's executeUpdate() method, you will see the appropriate SQL string to perform the previously mentioned update. Run this application and run the example from Listing 8.3. You should see the change to the quantity value of *The Last Emperor*.

Deleting Data from a Table

The last topic for this section is deleting data from the database. It is not much different from the previous database updating functions, but it does deserve its own section.

To delete a row from a table, you again use the `executeUpdate()` method. The only change would be the SQL statement you passed to it. In the example, take *Cape Fear* off the market. It just doesn't sell as well as it had in previous years. So, put a SQL string together and substitute it into your `executeUpdate()` method. The changed call would look something like the following snippet:

```
// Use the created statement to DELETE DATA
// FROM the Titles table.
statement.executeUpdate("DELETE FROM Titles " +
  "WHERE title_name = 'Cape Fear'");
```

You can find the full application source on the Web site. The filename is DeleteDataApp.java.

After you have run this application, re-run SelectDataApp and you will see that the title *Cape Fear* is no longer in the database.

A BASIC JDBC SERVLET

In this section, you are going to connect the JDBC and servlets. You are going to take the `SearchServlet` from Chapter 5 and connect it to the `TitleListServlet`, which is a servlet that actually performs a search. The `SearchServlet` is short enough to include in this section, so it is displayed again in Listing 8.5.

LISTING 8.5   SEARCHSERVLET.JAVA

```java
import javax.servlet.*;
import javax.servlet.http.*;
import java.io.*;
import java.util.*;

import HTML.*;

public class SearchServlet extends HttpServlet {

  //Initialize global variables
  private Integer initparam = null;

  public void init(ServletConfig config)
    throws ServletException {
```

```
    super.init(config);
}

public HTMLForm buildCatalogSearchForm() {

  // Instantiate the HTMLForm object
  HTMLForm search_form = new HTMLForm();

  // The TitleListServlet will actually handle the search.
  search_form.setAction("http://localhost:8080/servlet" +
    "/TitleListServlet");

  // Set the Post method to true
  search_form.setPostMethod(true);

  try {

    // Center the Form
    search_form.setAlignment(HTMLObject.CENTER);

    // Add a HTMLTextInput
    HTMLTextInput text_input = new HTMLTextInput();
    text_input.setName("search_string");
    text_input.setSize(30);
    search_form.addObject(text_input);

    // Add a HTMLButton to Invoke the Action
    HTMLSubmitButton button = new HTMLSubmitButton();
    button.setValue("Search");
    search_form.addObject(button);
  }
  catch ( Exception e ) {

    System.err.println(e.getMessage());
  }
  return search_form;
}

//Process the HTTP Get request
public void doGet(HttpServletRequest request,
  HttpServletResponse response)
  throws ServletException, IOException {

  response.setContentType("text/html");
  PrintWriter out = response.getWriter();
```

continues

Developing Java Servlets

LISTING 8.5   CONTINUED

```
    out.println(buildCatalogSearchForm().toHTML());
    out.close();
  }

  //Get Servlet information
  public String getServletInfo() {
    return "SearchServlet Information";
  }
}
```

The only change to the SearchServlet is the value passed in the setAction() method of the search_form object. You set the form action to the URL of your TitleListServlet. The TitleListServlet is shown in Listing 8.6.

LISTING 8.6   TITLELISTSERVLET.JAVA

```
import javax.servlet.*;
import javax.servlet.http.*;
import java.io.*;
import java.util.*;
import java.sql.*;

import HTML.*;

public class TitleListServlet extends HttpServlet {

  public void init(ServletConfig config)
    throws ServletException {

    super.init(config);
  }

  //Process the HTTP Get request
  public void doGet(HttpServletRequest request,
    HttpServletResponse response)
      throws ServletException, IOException {

    doPost(request, response);
  }

  //Process the HTTP Post request
  public void doPost(HttpServletRequest request,
    HttpServletResponse response)
    throws ServletException, IOException {
```

```
// Set the response content-type
response.setContentType("text/html");
// get the Writer object
PrintWriter out = response.getWriter();
// Get the search_string parameter, passed from the
// SearchServlet.
String search_string =
  request.getParameter("search_string");

Connection con = null;

// Create the HTML Document
HTMLDocument document =
  new HTMLDocument("Title List Servlet");

try {

  // Load the Driver class file
  Class.forName("sun.jdbc.odbc.JdbcOdbcDriver");

  // Make a connection to the ODBC datasource Movie Catalog
  // In this example we are opening a connection to the
  // database with every request.
  con =
    DriverManager.getConnection("jdbc:odbc:Movie Catalog",
    "", "");

  if ( con != null ) {

    // Create the statement
    Statement statement = con.createStatement();

    // Use the created statement to SELECT the DATA
    // FROM the Titles Table.
    // In this instance we are searching for an exact match.
    // If you were to deploy this to a production site, you
    // might want to use a "LIKE" clause instead of WHERE.
    ResultSet rs = statement.executeQuery("SELECT * " +
     "FROM Titles WHERE title_name = '" +
     search_string + "'");

    // Create the Table
    HTMLTable table = new HTMLTable();
    table.setBorder(1);
```

8

SERVLETS AND THE
JDBC

continues

LISTING 8.6   CONTINUED

```java
HTMLTableRow row = null;
HTMLTableCell cell = null;

// Create the Cell Headings
row = new HTMLTableRow();

cell = new HTMLTableCell(HTMLTableCell.HEADING);
cell.addObject(new HTMLText("ID"));
row.addObject(cell);

cell = new HTMLTableCell(HTMLTableCell.HEADING);
cell.addObject(new HTMLText("Name"));
row.addObject(cell);

cell = new HTMLTableCell(HTMLTableCell.HEADING);
cell.addObject(new HTMLText("Rating"));
row.addObject(cell);

cell = new HTMLTableCell(HTMLTableCell.HEADING);
cell.addObject(new HTMLText("Price"));
row.addObject(cell);

cell = new HTMLTableCell(HTMLTableCell.HEADING);
cell.addObject(new HTMLText("Quantity"));
row.addObject(cell);

cell = new HTMLTableCell(HTMLTableCell.HEADING);
cell.addObject(new HTMLText("Type ID"));
row.addObject(cell);

cell = new HTMLTableCell(HTMLTableCell.HEADING);
cell.addObject(new HTMLText("Category ID"));
row.addObject(cell);

table.addObject(row);

// Iterate over the ResultSet
while ( rs.next() ) {

  row = new HTMLTableRow();

  // get the id, which is an int
  cell = new HTMLTableCell(HTMLTableCell.DATA);
  cell.addObject(new HTMLText(
```

```
            new Integer(rs.getInt("title_id")).toString()));
        row.addObject(cell);

        // get the name, which is a String
        cell = new HTMLTableCell(HTMLTableCell.DATA);
        cell.addObject(
          new HTMLText(rs.getString("title_name")));
        row.addObject(cell);

        // get the rating, which is a String
        cell = new HTMLTableCell(HTMLTableCell.DATA);
        cell.addObject(
          new HTMLText(rs.getString("rating")));
        row.addObject(cell);

        // get the price, which is a Float
        cell = new HTMLTableCell(HTMLTableCell.DATA);
        cell.addObject(new HTMLText(
          new Float(rs.getFloat("price")).toString()));
        row.addObject(cell);

        // get the Quantity, which is an Integer
        cell = new HTMLTableCell(HTMLTableCell.DATA);
        cell.addObject(new HTMLText(
          new Integer(rs.getInt("quantity")).toString()));
        row.addObject(cell);

        // get the Type, which is an Integer
        cell = new HTMLTableCell(HTMLTableCell.DATA);
        cell.addObject(new HTMLText(
          new Integer(rs.getInt("type_id")).toString()));
        row.addObject(cell);

        // get the Category, which is an Integer
        cell = new HTMLTableCell(HTMLTableCell.DATA);
        cell.addObject(new HTMLText(
          new Integer(rs.getInt("category_id")).toString()));
        row.addObject(cell);
        table.addObject(row);
      }
      // Close the ResultSet
      rs.close();
      document.addObject(table);
    }
  }
catch (SQLException sqle) {
```

continues

LISTING 8.6   CONTINUED

```java
      System.err.println(sqle.getMessage());
    }
    catch (ClassNotFoundException cnfe) {

      System.err.println(cnfe.getMessage());
    }
    catch (Exception e) {

      System.err.println(e.getMessage());
    }
    finally {

      try {

        if ( con != null ) {

          // Close the connection no matter what
          con.close();
        }
      }
      catch (SQLException sqle) {

        System.err.println(sqle.getMessage());
      }
    }
    out.println(document.toHTML());
    out.close();
  }

  //Get Servlet information
  public String getServletInfo() {

    return "TitleListServlet Information";
  }
}
```

All the action in the `TitleListServlet` is taking place in the `doPost()` method. It first gets the `search_string` passed in the request from the `SearchServlet`. The next steps involved are opening a connection to the database, performing a query using the `search_string`, displaying the results, and then closing the connection. This type of algorithm is very time-consuming. Opening and closing a database connection with every request is hardly an optimal solution.

Now, take a look at this servlet in action. Open the `SearchServlet.shtml` page in your browser. Enter `The Last Emperor` as the title and click the Search button. Your results should look similar to Figure 8.11. Try this several times so you can get used to the speed.

> **NOTE**
>
> You can completely skip loading the `SearchServlet.shtml` page by entering the full query string to the `TitleListServlet`, `http://localhost:8080/servlet/TitleListServlet?search_string=The Last Emperor`.

FIGURE 8.11

TitleListServlet output.

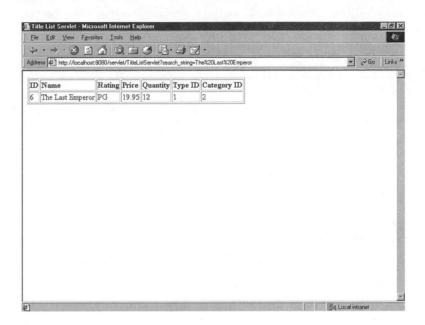

To speed up the servicing of requests, you could open the connection to the database in the `init()` method and then close it in the `destroy()` method, but you would be limited to a single connection. If you chose to do this, you would need to have your servlet implement the `SingleThreadModel` interface. This interface defines a single-thread model for servlet execution, guaranteeing that no two threads will execute concurrently the `service()` method of the implementing servlet. This would save execution time, but would limit you to servicing requests one at a time.

A JDBC CONNECTION POOL

To remedy the situation in the previous section, you are going to create a pool of connections to the database. This will give you access to a collection of already opened database connections, which will reduce the time it takes to service a request, and you can service *n* number of requests at once.

The following are the requirements for the `ConnectionPool` object:

- It must hold *n* number of open connections.
- It must be able to determine when a connection is in use.
- If *n+1* connections are requested, it must create a new connection and add it to the pool.
- When you close the pool, all connections must be released.

Now that you know what you want, look at the result. The source for the `ConnectionPool` is in Listing 8.7.

LISTING 8.7   CONNECTIONPOOL.JAVA

```
package ConnectionPool;

import java.sql.*;
import java.util.*;

public class ConnectionPool {

  // JDBC Driver Name
  private String driver = null;
  // URL of database
  private String url = null;
  // Initial number of connections.
  private int size = 0;
  // Username
  private String username = null;
  // Password
  private String password = null;
  // Vector of JDBC Connections
  private Vector pool = null;

  public ConnectionPool() {

  }

  // Set the value of the JDBC Driver
  public void setDriver(String value) {

    if ( value != null ) {

      driver = value;
    }
  }
```

```
// Get the value of the JDBC Driver
public String getDriver() {

  return driver;
}

// Set the URL Pointing to the Datasource
public void setURL(String value ) {

  if ( value != null ) {

    url = value;
  }
}

// Get the URL Pointing to the Datasource
public String getURL() {

  return url;
}

// Set the initial number of connections
public void setSize(int value) {

  if ( value > 1 ) {

    size = value;
  }
}

// Get the initial number of connections
public int getSize() {

  return size;
}

// Set the username
public void setUsername(String value) {

  if ( value != null ) {

    username = value;
  }
}
```

continues

LISTING 8.7   CONTINUED

```java
// Get the username
public String getUserName() {

  return username;
}

// Set the password
public void setPassword(String value) {

  if ( value != null ) {

    password = value;
  }
}

// Get the password
public String getPassword() {

  return password;
}

// Creates and returns a connection
private Connection createConnection() throws Exception {

  Connection con = null;

  // Create a Connection
  con = DriverManager.getConnection(url,
    username, password);

  return con;
}

// Initialize the pool
public synchronized void initializePool() throws Exception {

  // Check our initial values
  if ( driver == null ) {

    throw new Exception("No Driver Name Specified!");
  }
  if ( url == null ) {

    throw new Exception("No URL Specified!");
```

```
    }
    if ( size < 1 ) {

      throw new Exception("Pool size is less than 1!");
    }

    // Create the Connections
    try {

      // Load the Driver class file
      Class.forName(driver);

      // Create Connections based on the size member
      for ( int x = 0; x < size; x++ ) {

        System.err.println("Opening JDBC Connection " + x);

        Connection con = createConnection();

        if ( con != null ) {

          // Create a PooledConnection to encapsulate the
          // real JDBC Connection
          PooledConnection pcon = new PooledConnection(con);
          // Add the Connection to the pool
          addConnection(pcon);
        }
      }
    }
    catch (SQLException sqle) {

      System.err.println(sqle.getMessage());
    }
    catch (ClassNotFoundException cnfe) {

      System.err.println(cnfe.getMessage());
    }
    catch (Exception e) {

      System.err.println(e.getMessage());
    }
  }

  // Adds the PooledConnection to the pool
  private void addConnection(PooledConnection value) {
```

continues

LISTING 8.7   CONTINUED

```java
    // If the pool is null, create a new vector
    // with the initial size of "size"
    if ( pool == null ) {

      pool = new Vector(size);
    }
    // Add the PooledConnection Object to the vector
    pool.addElement(value);
  }

public synchronized void releaseConnection(Connection con) {

  // find the PooledConnection Object
  for ( int x = 0; x < pool.size(); x++ ) {

    PooledConnection pcon =
      (PooledConnection)pool.elementAt(x);
    // Check for correct Connection
    if ( pcon.getConnection() == con ) {

      System.err.println("Releasing Connection " + x);
      // Set its inuse attribute to false, which
      // releases it for use
      pcon.setInUse(false);
      break;
    }
  }
}

// Find an available connection
public synchronized Connection getConnection()
  throws Exception {

  PooledConnection pcon = null;

  // find a connection not in use
  for ( int x = 0; x < pool.size(); x++ ) {

    pcon = (PooledConnection)pool.elementAt(x);

    // Check to see if the Connection is in use
    if ( pcon.inUse() == false ) {

      // Mark it as in use
```

```
        pcon.setInUse(true);
        // return the JDBC Connection stored in the
        // PooledConnection object
        return pcon.getConnection();
    }
}

// Could not find a free connection,
// create and add a new one
try {

    // Create a new JDBC Connection
    Connection con = createConnection();
    // Create a new PooledConnection, passing it the JDBC
    // Connection
    pcon = new PooledConnection(con);
    // Mark the connection as in use
    pcon.setInUse(true);
    // Add the new PooledConnection object to the pool
    pool.addElement(pcon);
}
catch (Exception e) {

    System.err.println(e.getMessage());
}
// return the new Connection
return pcon.getConnection();
}

// When shutting down the pool, you need to first empty it.
public synchronized void emptyPool() {

    // Iterate over the entire pool closing the
    // JDBC Connections.
    for ( int x = 0; x < pool.size(); x++ ) {

        System.err.println("Closing JDBC Connection " + x);

        PooledConnection pcon =
            (PooledConnection)pool.elementAt(x);

        // If the PooledConnection is not in use, close it
        if ( pcon.inUse() == false ) {

            pcon.close();
        }
```

8

SERVLETS AND THE JDBC

continues

LISTING 8.7   CONTINUED

```
    else {

      // If it's still in use, sleep for 30 seconds and
      // force close.
      try {

        java.lang.Thread.sleep(30000);
        pcon.close();
      }
      catch (InterruptedException ie) {

        System.err.println(ie.getMessage());
      }
    }
  }
}
}
```

The best way to look at the ConnectionPool is to examine what it does while you learn how to use it. Take a look at the TitleListPooledServlet as an example. Its source is in Listing 8.8.

NOTE

To use the new pooled servlet, you must either change the SearchServlet to call the TitleListPooledServlet or enter the full query string to the TitleListPooledServlet,
http://localhost:8080/servlet/TitleListPooledServlet?search_string=The Last Emperor.

LISTING 8.8   TITLELISTPOOLEDSERVLET.JAVA

```java
import javax.servlet.*;
import javax.servlet.http.*;
import java.io.*;
import java.util.*;
import java.sql.*;

import HTML.*;
import ConnectionPool.*;

public class TitleListPooledServlet extends HttpServlet {

  private ConnectionPool pool = null;
```

```java
public void init(ServletConfig config)
  throws ServletException {

  super.init(config);

  // Instantiate the ConnectionPool
  pool = new ConnectionPool();

  // Set the JDBC Driver
  pool.setDriver("sun.jdbc.odbc.JdbcOdbcDriver");
  // Set the URL to the Datasource
  pool.setURL("jdbc:odbc:Movie Catalog");
  // Set the initial size of the Connection Pool
  pool.setSize(4);
  // Set the Username
  pool.setUsername("");
  // Set the Password
  pool.setPassword("");

  try {

    // Initialize the pool
    pool.initializePool();
  }
  catch (Exception e) {

    System.err.println(e.getMessage());
  }
}

//Process the HTTP Get request
public void doGet(HttpServletRequest request,
  HttpServletResponse response)
    throws ServletException, IOException {

  // If we get a GET request, pass the request/response to
  // the doPost() method
  doPost(request, response);
}

//Process the HTTP Post request
public void doPost(HttpServletRequest request,
  HttpServletResponse response)
  throws ServletException, IOException {
```

continues

LISTING 8.8   CONTINUED

```java
response.setContentType("text/html");
PrintWriter out = response.getWriter();

// Get the search_string parameter, passed from the
// SearchServlet.
String search_string =
  request.getParameter("search_string");

Connection con = null;

// Create the HTML Document
HTMLDocument document =
  new HTMLDocument("Title List Pooled Servlet");

try {

  // Get a connection from the ConnectionPool
  con = pool.getConnection();

  if ( con != null ) {

    // Create the statement
    Statement statement = con.createStatement();

    // Use the created statement to SELECT the DATA
    // FROM the Titles Table.
    // In this instance we are searching for an exact match.
    // If you were to deploy this to a production site, you
    // might want to use a "LIKE" clause instead of WHERE.
    ResultSet rs = statement.executeQuery("SELECT * " +
     "FROM Titles WHERE title_name = '" +
     search_string + "'");

    // Create the HTMLTable
    HTMLTable table = new HTMLTable();
    table.setBorder(1);

    HTMLTableRow row = null;
    HTMLTableCell cell = null;

    // Create the Cell Headings
    row = new HTMLTableRow();

    cell = new HTMLTableCell(HTMLTableCell.HEADING);
```

```
cell.addObject(new HTMLText("ID"));
row.addObject(cell);

cell = new HTMLTableCell(HTMLTableCell.HEADING);
cell.addObject(new HTMLText("Name"));
row.addObject(cell);

cell = new HTMLTableCell(HTMLTableCell.HEADING);
cell.addObject(new HTMLText("Rating"));
row.addObject(cell);

cell = new HTMLTableCell(HTMLTableCell.HEADING);
cell.addObject(new HTMLText("Price"));
row.addObject(cell);

cell = new HTMLTableCell(HTMLTableCell.HEADING);
cell.addObject(new HTMLText("Quantity"));
row.addObject(cell);

cell = new HTMLTableCell(HTMLTableCell.HEADING);
cell.addObject(new HTMLText("Type ID"));
row.addObject(cell);

cell = new HTMLTableCell(HTMLTableCell.HEADING);
cell.addObject(new HTMLText("Category ID"));
row.addObject(cell);

table.addObject(row);

// Iterate over the ResultSet
while ( rs.next() ) {

  row = new HTMLTableRow();

  // get the id, which is an int
  cell = new HTMLTableCell(HTMLTableCell.DATA);
  cell.addObject(new HTMLText(
    new Integer(rs.getInt("title_id")).toString()));
  row.addObject(cell);

  // get the name, which is a String
  cell = new HTMLTableCell(HTMLTableCell.DATA);
  cell.addObject(
    new HTMLText(rs.getString("title_name")));
  row.addObject(cell);
```

continues

LISTING 8.8   CONTINUED

```java
        // get the rating, which is a String
        cell = new HTMLTableCell(HTMLTableCell.DATA);
        cell.addObject(
          new HTMLText(rs.getString("rating")));
        row.addObject(cell);

        // get the price, which is a Float
        cell = new HTMLTableCell(HTMLTableCell.DATA);
        cell.addObject(new HTMLText(
          new Float(rs.getFloat("price")).toString()));
        row.addObject(cell);

        // get the Quantity, which is an Integer
        cell = new HTMLTableCell(HTMLTableCell.DATA);
        cell.addObject(new HTMLText(
          new Integer(rs.getInt("quantity")).toString()));
        row.addObject(cell);

        // get the Type, which is an Integer
        cell = new HTMLTableCell(HTMLTableCell.DATA);
        cell.addObject(new HTMLText(
          new Integer(rs.getInt("type_id")).toString()));
        row.addObject(cell);

        // get the Category, which is an Integer
        cell = new HTMLTableCell(HTMLTableCell.DATA);
        cell.addObject(new HTMLText(
          new Integer(rs.getInt("category_id")).toString()));
        row.addObject(cell);
        table.addObject(row);
      }
      // Close the ResultSet
      rs.close();
      document.addObject(table);
    }
  }
  catch (SQLException sqle) {

    System.err.println(sqle.getMessage());
  }
  catch (Exception e) {

    System.err.println(e.getMessage());
  }
  finally {
```

```
    // Release the connection
    pool.releaseConnection(con);
  }
  out.println(document.toHTML());
  out.close();
}

public void destroy() {

  // Empty the pool
  pool.emptyPool();
}

//Get Servlet information
public String getServletInfo() {

  return "TitleListPooledServlet Information";
  }
}
```

The first steps in using the `ConnectionPool` are to create an instance of the object and set the appropriate accessors. This is accomplished in the `init()` method of the servlet. This makes the `ConnectionPool` available to all future requests:

```
public void init(ServletConfig config)
  throws ServletException {

  super.init(config);

  // Instantiate the ConnectionPool
  pool = new ConnectionPool();

  // Set the JDBC Driver
  pool.setDriver("sun.jdbc.odbc.JdbcOdbcDriver");
  // Set the URL to the Datasource
  pool.setURL("jdbc:odbc:Movie Catalog");
  // Set the initial size of the Connection Pool
  pool.setSize(4);
  // Set the Username
  pool.setUsername("");
  // Set the Password
  pool.setPassword("");

  try {

    // Initialize the pool
```

```
    pool.initializePool();
  }
  catch (Exception e) {

    System.err.println(e.getMessage());
  }
}
```

The init() method first creates an instance of the ConnectionPool. It then sets the accessors appropriately. It sets the driver to the JDBC-ODBC Bridge, the data source URL to the Movie Catalog, and the initial number of connections to 4. The next two accessors (username and password) are set to empty strings. This is because the Microsoft Access database has no login or password.

The last executable line of the init() method initializes the ConnectionPool. This is where the ConnectionPool connections begin their life. An excerpt of the ConnectionPool. initializePool()'s method is listed as follows:

```
// Load the Driver class file
Class.forName(driver);

// Create Connections based on the size member
for ( int x = 0; x < size; x++ ) {

  System.err.println("Opening JDBC Connection " + x);

  Connection con = createConnection();

  if ( con != null ) {

    // Create a PooledConnection to encapsulate the
    // real JDBC Connection
    PooledConnection pcon = new PooledConnection(con);
    // Add the Connection the pool.
    addConnection(pcon);
  }
}
```

The initializePool() method first loads the JDBC driver. It then creates size number of Connection objects. For each Connection object created, it creates a PooledConnection object passing it the Connection in the constructor. Finally, it adds the newly create PooledConnection object to the pool.

The `PooledConnection` object simply wraps a JDBC `Connection` object in a class that holds the connection and a flag that determines whether the connection is in use. It is listed in Listing 8.9.

LISTING 8.9 POOLEDCONNECTION.JAVA

```java
package ConnectionPool;

import java.sql.*;

public class PooledConnection {

  // Real JDBC Connection
  private Connection connection = null;
  // boolean flag used to determine if connection is in use
  private boolean inuse = false;

  // Constructor that takes the passed in JDBC Connection
  // and stores it in the connection attribute.
  public PooledConnection(Connection value) {

    if ( value != null ) {

      connection = value;
    }
  }

  // Returns a reference to the JDBC Connection
  public Connection getConnection() {

    // get the JDBC Connection
    return connection;
  }

  // Set the status of the PooledConnection.
  public void setInUse(boolean value) {

    inuse = value;
  }

  // Returns the current status of the PooledConnection.
  public boolean inUse() {

    return inuse;
  }
```

continues

LISTING 8.9   CONTINUED

```
// Close the real JDBC Connection
public void close() {

  try {

    connection.close();
  }
  catch (SQLException sqle) {

    System.err.println(sqle.getMessage());
  }
}
}
```

The next part of the `TitleListPooledServlet` you need to look at is the `doPost()` method. Whereas in the `TitleListServlet` you had to load the driver and call the `DriverManager.getConnection()` method directly, here all you have to do is call the `ConnectionPool.getConnection()`, which will iterate through its vector of connections until it finds an available connection. If it cannot find an available connection, it will create one and add it to the pool. It will then mark the connection as in use and return it.

When the `doPost()` method is finished with the connection, it must return it to the pool. To do this, it calls the `ConnectionPools`'s `releaseConnection()` method, passing it the `Connection` object:

```
// Release the connection
pool.releaseConnection(con);
```

The `releaseConnection()` method searches the pool for the `Connection` object and marks it as available for use.

The last interaction the `TitleListPooledServlet` has with the `ConnectionPool` is when it shuts down. In its `destroy()` method, the servlet calls the `ConnectionPool.emptyPool()` method. This method iterates over the entire pool, closing connections until all the `Connection` objects are closed.

Now you have access to pre-opened connections to the database and can service just about any number of simultaneous requests. Try running the servlet several times to see the speed increase. You might need to add more data to your Titles table to determine a real difference.

> **NOTE**
>
> The database you use will, of course, determine the number of connections you can really have opened at once. Consult your database documentation or license agreement for this number.

INTER-SERVLET COMMUNICATIONS

In the previous section, you saw how a connection pool saves you a lot of time when servicing requests. Wouldn't it be nice if, instead of creating a `ConnectionPool` local only to one specific servlet, you could have a `ConnectionPool` that was global to all our servlets? To do this, you will need to create a servlet that can manage a `ConnectionPool` object and provide a way for other servlets to communicate with it. Listing 8.10 contains the source for a servlet that will do just this.

LISTING 8.10   CONNECTIONPOOLSERVLET.JAVA

```
package ConnectionPool;

import javax.servlet.*;
import javax.servlet.http.*;
import java.io.*;
import java.util.*;

public class ConnectionPoolServlet extends HttpServlet {

  //Initialize global variables
  public void init(ServletConfig config)
    throws ServletException {

    super.init(config);

    // Instantiate the ConnectionPool
    ConnectionPool pool = new ConnectionPool();

    try {

      // Set the JDBC Driver
      pool.setDriver("sun.jdbc.odbc.JdbcOdbcDriver");
      // Set the URL to the Datasource
      pool.setURL("jdbc:odbc:Movie Catalog");
      // Set the initial size of the Connection Pool
```

continues

LISTING 8.10   CONTINUED

```java
      pool.setSize(4);
      // Set the Username
      pool.setUsername("");
      // Set the Password
      pool.setPassword("");

      // Initialize the pool
      pool.initializePool();

      // Once the pool is Initialized, add it to the
      // Global ServletContext.  This makes it available
      // To other servlets using the same ServletContext.
      ServletContext context = getServletContext();
      context.setAttribute("CONNECTION_POOL", pool);
    }
  catch (Exception e) {

      System.err.println(e.getMessage());
    }
}

//Process the HTTP Get request
public void doGet(HttpServletRequest request,
  HttpServletResponse response)
    throws ServletException, IOException {

  // Set the response content-type
  response.setContentType("text/html");
  // get the Writer object
  PrintWriter out = response.getWriter();
  out.println("This Servlet does not service requests!");
  out.close();
}

public void destroy() {

  // Access the ServletContext using the getAttribute()
  // method, which returns a reference to the ConnectionPool.
  ServletContext context = getServletContext();
  ConnectionPool pool =
      (ConnectionPool)
      context.getAttribute("CONNECTION_POOL");

  if ( pool != null ) {
```

```
    // empty the pool
    pool.emptyPool();
    // Remove the Attribute from the ServletContext
    context.removeAttribute("CONNECTION_POOL");
  }
  else {

    System.err.println("Could not get a reference to Pool!");
  }
}

//Get Servlet information
public String getServletInfo() {

  return "ConnectionPoolServlet Information";
}
}
```

> **NOTE**
>
> In this example we are using JSDK 2.1-specific code. At the time of this writing the JSDK 2.1 is only supported by a few vendors. It should be widely supported by the time of this publication.

The two areas of the `ConnectionPoolServlet` that you need to examine are the `init()` and `destroy()` methods. The `doGet()` method is just a placeholder; it has no functionality.

The `ConnectionPoolServlet.init()` method creates the `ConnectionPool` and makes it available to the other servlets. It does this by first creating an instance of the `ConnectionPool` just like any other application would. It then takes the newly created `ConnectionPool` object and adds it to the shared `ServletContext`. It does this in the following code snippet:

```
// Once the pool is Initialized, add it to the
// Global ServletContext.  This makes it available
// To other servlets using the same ServletContext.
ServletContext context = getServletContext();
context.setAttribute("CONNECTION_POOL", pool);
```

The preceding code gets a reference to the `ServletContext`, which is shared by all servlets that live in the same `ServletContext`. It then calls the `setAttribute()` method, passing it a string that represents a key and a reference to the `ConnectionPool` object. This makes the `ConnectionPool` available to other servlets.

8

SERVLETS AND THE JDBC

The destroy() method does just the opposite. It first gets a reference to the ConnectionPool by calling the ServletContext.getAttribute() method. The signature for this method is as follows:

```
public java.lang.Object getAttribute(java.langString name)
```

It takes a string that represents the key that was used to add the object in the setAttribute() method, and returns a reference to an object. You must downcast the object back to a ConnectionPool because when it was stored in the ServletContext, it was stored as an object.

The destroy() method then empties the ConnectionPool and removes the attribute from the ServletContext using the removeAttribute() method. The destroy() method is listed in the following:

```
public void destroy() {

  // Access the ServletContext using the getAttribute()
  // method, which returns a reference to the ConnectionPool.
  ServletContext context = getServletContext();
  ConnectionPool pool =
    (ConnectionPool)
    context.getAttribute("CONNECTION_POOL");

  if ( pool != null ) {

    // empty the pool
    pool.emptyPool();
    // Remove the Attribute from the ServletContext
    context.removeAttribute("CONNECTION_POOL");
  }
  else {

    System.err.println("Could not get a reference to Pool!");
  }
}
```

NOTE

You might want to set up the ConnectionPoolServlet as a preloaded servlet. This will make sure that the connections are already available before the first request is made.

Now that you have created and understand the `ConnectionPoolServlet`, you can put it to use with another example. This example is based on the previous two servlets. It takes a search parameter from the request object and performs a database query looking for a match. There are two important changes to this servlet. The first is how it gets a connection and the second is how it releases that connection.

The `TitleListGlobalPooledServlet` gets a `Connection` object by calling the `ServletContext.getAttribute()` method, passing it the key `"CONNECTION_POOL"`, which returns a reference to the `ConnectionPool` object. It can then call the `ConnectionPool.getConnection()` method to get a JDBC connection:

```
// Get a reference to the ConnectionPool from the Global
// ServletContext
pool =(ConnectionPool)
  getServletContext().getAttribute("CONNECTION_POOL");

// Get a connection from the ConnectionPool
con = pool.getConnection();
```

When the servlet finishes with the connection, it must release it. This is done by calling the `ConnectionPool`'s `releaseConnection()` method:

```
// Release the connection
pool.releaseConnection(con);
```

That is all there is to it. After you are finished with the `ConnectionPool`, it still resides in the `ServletContext` waiting on future requests. You'll find the entire source for the `TitleListGlobalPooledServlet` in Listing 8.11.

LISTING 8.11   TITLELISTGLOBALPOOLEDSERVLET.JAVA

```
import javax.servlet.*;
import javax.servlet.http.*;
import java.io.*;
import java.util.*;
import java.sql.*;

import HTML.*;
import ConnectionPool.*;

public class TitleListGlobalPooledServlet extends HttpServlet {

  public void init(ServletConfig config)
    throws ServletException {
```

continues

8

SERVLETS AND THE
JDBC

LISTING 8.11   CONTINUED

```java
        super.init(config);
}

//Process the HTTP Get request
public void doGet(HttpServletRequest request,
  HttpServletResponse response)
    throws ServletException, IOException {

  // If we get a GET request, pass the request/response to
  // the doPost() method
  doPost(request, response);
}

//Process the HTTP Post request
public void doPost(HttpServletRequest request,
  HttpServletResponse response)
  throws ServletException, IOException {

  response.setContentType("text/html");
  PrintWriter out = response.getWriter();

  Connection con = null;
  ConnectionPool pool = null;

  // Create the HTML Document
  HTMLDocument document =
    new HTMLDocument("Title List Pooled Servlet");

  try {


    // Get a reference to the ConnectionPool from the Global
    // ServletContext
    pool =(ConnectionPool)
      getServletContext().getAttribute("CONNECTION_POOL");

    // Get a connection from the ConnectionPool
    con = pool.getConnection();

    if ( con != null ) {

      // Create the statement
      Statement statement = con.createStatement();
```

```
// Use the created statement to SELECT the DATA
// FROM the Titles Table.
ResultSet rs = statement.executeQuery("SELECT * " +
 "FROM Titles");

// Create the HTMLTable
HTMLTable table = new HTMLTable();
table.setBorder(1);

HTMLTableRow row = null;
HTMLTableCell cell = null;

// Create the Cell Headings
row = new HTMLTableRow();

cell = new HTMLTableCell(HTMLTableCell.HEADING);
cell.addObject(new HTMLText("ID"));
row.addObject(cell);

cell = new HTMLTableCell(HTMLTableCell.HEADING);
cell.addObject(new HTMLText("Name"));
row.addObject(cell);

cell = new HTMLTableCell(HTMLTableCell.HEADING);
cell.addObject(new HTMLText("Rating"));
row.addObject(cell);

cell = new HTMLTableCell(HTMLTableCell.HEADING);
cell.addObject(new HTMLText("Price"));
row.addObject(cell);

cell = new HTMLTableCell(HTMLTableCell.HEADING);
cell.addObject(new HTMLText("Quantity"));
row.addObject(cell);

cell = new HTMLTableCell(HTMLTableCell.HEADING);
cell.addObject(new HTMLText("Type ID"));
row.addObject(cell);

cell = new HTMLTableCell(HTMLTableCell.HEADING);
cell.addObject(new HTMLText("Category ID"));
row.addObject(cell);

table.addObject(row);
```

continues

LISTING 8.11   CONTINUED

```
// Iterate over the ResultSet
while ( rs.next() ) {

  row = new HTMLTableRow();

  // get the id, which is an int
  cell = new HTMLTableCell(HTMLTableCell.DATA);
  cell.addObject(new HTMLText(
    new Integer(rs.getInt("title_id")).toString()));
  row.addObject(cell);

  // get the name, which is a String
  cell = new HTMLTableCell(HTMLTableCell.DATA);
  cell.addObject(
    new HTMLText(rs.getString("title_name")));
  row.addObject(cell);

  // get the rating, which is a String
  cell = new HTMLTableCell(HTMLTableCell.DATA);
  cell.addObject(
    new HTMLText(rs.getString("rating")));
  row.addObject(cell);

  // get the price, which is a Float
  cell = new HTMLTableCell(HTMLTableCell.DATA);
  cell.addObject(new HTMLText(
    new Float(rs.getFloat("price")).toString()));
  row.addObject(cell);

  // get the Quantity, which is an Integer
  cell = new HTMLTableCell(HTMLTableCell.DATA);
  cell.addObject(new HTMLText(
    new Integer(rs.getInt("quantity")).toString()));
  row.addObject(cell);

  // get the Type, which is an Integer
  cell = new HTMLTableCell(HTMLTableCell.DATA);
  cell.addObject(new HTMLText(
    new Integer(rs.getInt("type_id")).toString()));
  row.addObject(cell);

  // get the Category, which is an Integer
  cell = new HTMLTableCell(HTMLTableCell.DATA);
  cell.addObject(new HTMLText(
    new Integer(rs.getInt("category_id")).toString()));
```

```
         row.addObject(cell);
         table.addObject(row);
       }
       // Close the ResultSet
       rs.close();
       document.addObject(table);
     }
   }
   catch (SQLException sqle) {

     System.err.println(sqle.getMessage());
   }
   catch (Exception e) {

     System.err.println(e.getMessage());
   }
   finally {

     // Release the connection
     pool.releaseConnection(con);
   }
   out.println(document.toHTML());
   out.close();
 }

 //Get Servlet information
 public String getServletInfo() {

   return "TitleListGlobalPooledServlet Information";
 }
}
```

SUMMARY

This chapter covers the basics of the JDBC. I discussed setting up the JDBC-ODBC Bridge and how to load JDBC drivers. You took a look at the most common SQL statements and how to execute them using the JDBC. You then merged the JDBC with the servlets and performed some basic queries.

Finally, you looked at some ways to optimize the use of JDBC in servlets. You did this by using a connection pool and inter-servlet communications.

At this point, you should be able to create your own servlet that can access a database using either a straight JDBC connection or a connection pool. You should understand how to create and execute basic SQL statements. You should also understand and be able to use the ServletContext for inter-servlet communications.

SERVLETS AND OBJECT DATABASES

IN THIS CHAPTER

WHAT IS AN OBJECT DATABASE?

An object database allows a developer of object-oriented software to extend his language to provide object persistence. When developing in an object-oriented language, your data is object-oriented and cannot easily be broken down into a tabular format. Relational databases require object-oriented developers to break down their objects into a tabular format (row/column format). This can be especially difficult with complex data types.

Object databases provide the ability to store these complex data types without the conversion step. An object database can provide the developer a means of storing an arbitrary number of complex data structures. In contrast, relational databases offer only a limited number of data types. The relational databases require complex structures to be converted into simplified table representations that can create problems with accessing the data. The data must be joined and presented back to the language before it can be manipulated.

In addition, object databases combine object properties with traditional database management system functions such as locking, protection, transactions querying, versioning, concurrency, and persistence. Instead of using Structured Query Language (SQL) to define, retrieve, and manipulate data, object databases use class definitions and traditional object-oriented languages such as C++, SmallTalk, and Java to define and access data. Thus the object database integrates the traditional relational database capabilities directly into the object-oriented language.

Some object databases that are currently in use in Java-based development are as follows:

- Versant Corporation's ODBMS (http://www.versant.com)
- Objectivity's ODBMS (http://www.objectivity.com/)
- Poet Software's ODBMS (http://www.poet.com)
- Object Design's ODBMS (http://www.objectdesign.com)

I have selected Object Design's ODBMS for the examples in this chapter. I have worked with this product in a professional capacity and Object Design is one of the leading companies in the ODBMS market.

WHAT IS OBJECTSTORE PSE PRO?

Object Design's ObjectStore Personal Storage Edition (PSE) for Java and ObjectStore PSE Pro for Java are pure Java, pure object databases for embedded database and mobile computing applications. PSE/PSE Pro are the only object databases written entirely in Java. I will be using PSE Pro for Java 3.0; you might use either the Windows or the UNIX version as you're executing the examples. In 1997, PSE Pro became the first DBMS to pass Sun Microsystems's 100 percent Pure Java certification tests. Thus, PSE Pro runs anywhere Java does.

I'm using the PSE Pro database for the chapter at the server level simply because it is free. Most objects stored on PSE Pro will work in the Enterprise Edition of ObjectStore.

SETTING UP OBJECTSTORE PSE PRO

Download the 20-day trial software from Object Design's Web site at `http://www.objectdesign.com`.

I'm going to explain how to configure your development environment for using PSE Pro for Java 3.0. I will assume that you already have a JDK 1.1 version installed on your machine, so the CLASSPATH and PATH changes in the chapter should actually be appended to your existing variables.

To avoid focusing on Windows or UNIX, I'll set up the shorthand notations shown in Table 9.1, which I'll use throughout this chapter.

TABLE 9.1 DIRECTORY SHORTHAND NOTATIONS ON WINDOWS AND UNIX

Notation	OS	Directory
`<odi_install>`	Windows	`e:\odi\pseproj`
	UNIX	`/usr/local/odi/pseproj`
`<odi_bin>`	Windows	`<odi_install>\bin`
	UNIX	`<odi_install>/bin`
`<odi_demo>`	Windows	`<odi_install>\COM\odi\demo`
	UNIX	`<odi_install>/COM/odi/demo`
`<osjcfpout>`	Windows	`<odi_demo>\osjcfpout`
	UNIX	`<odi_demo>/osjcfpout`

First, install PSE Pro for Java on your machine. Set your CLASSPATH variable as shown in Table 9.2.

TABLE 9.2 CLASSPATH FOR WINDOWS AND UNIX

OS	CLASSPATH
Windows	`".;<odi_install>\pro.zip;<odi_install>\tools.zip;<odi_install>".`
UNIX	`".:<odi_install>/pro.zip:<odi_install>/tools.zip:<odi_install>".`

These zip files must be explicitly in your class path. An entry for the directory that contains them is not sufficient. The entry for the installation directory is needed to build and run your programs. Alternatively, you might use the `jar` versions of these files. The period (`.`) in the CLASSPATH is needed because it includes your current working directory in the CLASSPATH. If you already have this in your CLASSPATH, it is not necessary to add it again.

9

SERVLETS AND OBJECT DATABASES

Set your PATH variable to include the `<odi_bin>` directory. The PSE Pro executables are located in this directory. You will need this to compile your classes and view the database with a command-line viewer that I will discuss later.

The PSE Pro documentation is included when you install the PSE Pro product (see Figure 9.1). It is accessed through a Bookshelf page located in the following directory:

- Windows—`<odi_install>/doc/index.html`
- UNIX—`<odi_install>\doc\index.html`

FIGURE 9.1

Bookshelf for ObjectStore PSE/PSE Pro Release 3.0 for Java.

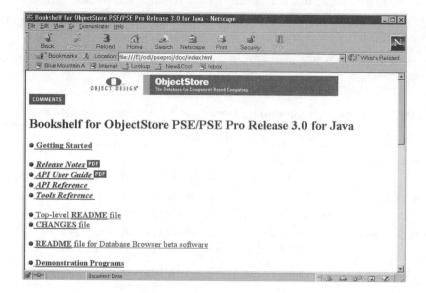

I reference documentation from the ObjectStore PSE/PSE Pro product throughout this chapter. One document is the *PSE/PSE Pro for Java API User Guide*, which is accessed by selecting the link for the *API User Guide*. This document will be subsequently referred to as the *API User Guide*. The second document is the *PSE/PSE Pro for Java API Reference*. This document will be subsequently referred to as the *API Reference*. You will probably want to bookmark these three documents.

A PERSON DEMO FOR OBJECTSTORE PSE PRO

You will start with a demo that I created from the ObjectStore Person demo to ensure that your environment is set up properly. The Person demo, which was part of your installation, uses deprecated methods, so I modified their demo to use the proper methods. Change directories to the `<odi_demo>` directory. Make a directory called `newpeople`. Change to that directory and place the file `Person.java`, shown in Listing 9.1, in the directory.

LISTING 9.1   PERSON.JAVA

```java
package COM.odi.demo.newpeople;

// Import the COM.odi package, which contains the API:
import COM.odi.*;

public
class Person {

  // Fields in the Person class:
  String name;
  int age;
  Person children[];

  // Main:
  public static void main(String argv[]) {
    try {
      String dbName = argv[0];

      // The following line starts a nonglobal session and joins
      // this thread to the new session.  This allows the thread
      // to use PSE Pro.
      Session.create(null, null).join();
      Database db = createDatabase(dbName);
      readDatabase(db);
      db.close();
    }
    finally {
      Session.getCurrent().terminate();
    }
  }

  static Database createDatabase(String dbName) {

    // Attempt to open and destroy the database specified on the
    // command line.  This ensures that that program creates a
    // new database each time the application is called.
    try {
      Database.open(dbName, ObjectStore.OPEN_UPDATE).destroy();
    } catch (DatabaseNotFoundException e) {
    }

    // Create a new database.
    Database db = Database.create(dbName,
      ObjectStore.ALL_READ | ObjectStore.ALL_WRITE);
```

continues

LISTING 9.1   CONTINUED

```java
// Start an update transaction.
Transaction tr = Transaction.begin(ObjectStore.UPDATE);

// Create instances of Person.
Person sophie = new Person("Sophie", 5, null);
Person joseph = new Person("Joseph", 1, null);
Person children[] = { sophie, joseph };
Person sally = new Person("Sally", 39, children);

// Create a database root and associate it with
// sally, which is a persistent-capable object.
// ObjectStore Java uses a database root as an entry
// point into a database.
db.createRoot("Sally", sally);

// End the transaction. This stores the three person objects,
// along with the String objects representing their names, and
// the array of children, into the database.  After this method
// call all Persistent object references are considered STALE.
tr.commit();

return db;
}

static void readDatabase(Database db) {

// Start a read-only transaction
Transaction tr = Transaction.begin(ObjectStore.READONLY);

// Use the "Sally" database root to access objects in the database.
// Because sally references sophie and joseph, obtaining the "Sally"
// database root allows the program to also reach sophie and joseph.
// In each transaction, an application must obtain a database root
// and use it to navigate to persistent objects. Be sure to write
// your application so that it does not hold on to references
// to persistent objects between transactions.
Person sally = (Person)db.getRoot("Sally");
Person children[] = sally.getChildren();
System.out.print("Sally is " + sally.getAge() + " and has " +
  children.length + " children: ");
for(int i=0; i<children.length; i++) {
  System.out.print(children[i].getName() + " ");
}
```

```
      System.out.println(" ");

      // End the read-only transaction. This ends the
      // accessibility of the persistent objects since the commit()
      // is of a RETAIN_STALE type.
      tr.commit();
  }

  // Constructor
  public Person(String nameValue, int ageValue,
    Person theChildren[]) {
    name = nameValue;
    age = ageValue;
    children = theChildren;
  }

  public String getName() {
    return name;
  }

  public void setName(String nameValue) {
    name = nameValue;
  }

  public int getAge() {
    return age;
  }

  public void setAge(int ageValue) {
    age = ageValue;
  }

  public Person[] getChildren() {
    return children;
  }

  public void setChildren(Person theChildren[]) {
    children = theChildren;
  }

  // This class is never used as a persistent hash key.
  // So using the Object's hashCode is ok.
  public int hashCode() {
    return super.hashCode();
  }
}
```

Compile the Java source code with the `javac *.java` command or the `javac Person.java` command. After compiling, observe the class size by performing a directory listing on the `Person.class` from the command line. This is the size of the Java formatted class file that is portable between Java Virtual Machines (JVMs). This class, which is derived from the `java.lang.Object`, is not an inherently persistent class after compilation. You must make it persistent capable by running the ObjectStore Java Class File PostProcesser utility (`osjcfp`).

The PostProcesser annotates the Java class file with instructions to ObjectStore PSE Pro on how to store and access the `Person` objects. The annotations make the `Person` objects persistent without writing mapping code and without forcing you to alter your object model with vendor-supplied access classes. Because you must run the PostProcessor on all class files in a batch at the same time, it takes an input file, which saves typing. The demo uses the input file `cfpargs`, shown in Listing 9.2, that was included in the `people` directory.

LISTING 9.2   CFPARGS

```
-dest . -inplace
Person.class
```

The `-dest .` option, which is a required option, tells the PostProcessor that the destination for the annotated class is the current directory. Because this is in the same directory as the `javac` generated class file, you must use the `-inplace Person.class` option to tell the PostProcessor that it is OK to overwrite the original class file. This is fine for this example. I will discuss later how to specify an output directory for the annotated classes.

To annotate the `Person` class, you must run the `osjcfp` utility as follows: `osjcfp @cfpargs`. If your PSE Pro environment is set up properly, you will receive no errors. Now, execute a directory listing on the `*.class` files to see what the PostProcessor has done. If you compare the size of the `Person.class` file before and after, you will see that the size has increased significantly. You will also see a new class file called `PersonClassInfo.class`. You will use the annotated `Person.class` file to run the demo and not the original class file. To execute the demo, change the current directory to `<odi_install>` and run the following command:

```
java COM.odi.demo.newpeople.Person person.odb
```

The expected output is

```
Sally is 39 and has 2 children: Sophie Joseph
```

If you tried to run the demo without annotating the `Person.class` file and you received an exception of type `COM.odi.ObjectNotPersistenceCapableException`, PSE Pro creates a directory entry `person.odx`. This is a lock file that PSE Pro uses to control access to the `person.odb` database. To rerun the demo, you must remove the `person.odx` directory.

After successful execution of the demo, the `<odi_install>` directory will contain three new files: `person.odb`, `person.odf`, and `person.odt`. These three files make the `person` object database from the demo program. You told the `Person.java` class to create a database `person.odb` by passing the parameter on the command line.

Overview of the Annotation Process

Your objects must be persistent-capable before they can be stored in the database, so the PostProcessor adds this code to your class file. This additional code consists of annotations to your class file. The annotation process does the following:

- Adds methods to implement the `COM.odi.IPersistent` interface
- Adds methods to provide initialization data from the database to instance fields
- Adds methods to write modified instance fields to the database
- Adds methods to reset instance fields to their default values

> **NOTE**
>
> The term *default values* refers to the values the class variables are assigned through initialization in your class or Java's initialized values for your variables (for example, a primitive `int` that isn't initialized is set to 0 by the JVM). Also, any variables that reference other persistent objects will be set to null.

- Modifies existing methods to retrieve the contents of persistent instances from the database (that is, makes a call to `ObjectStore.fetch()` before accessing the data)
- Modifies existing methods to mark persistent instances as "dirty" when they are changed, so their changes can be committed at the end of the transaction (that is, makes a call to `ObjectStore.dirty()`)
- Adds an additional class, which is a subclass of the `COM.odi.ClassInfo`, to provide schema information about the persistence-capable class

Yes, the PostProcesser does a lot for you. Yes, you can do all this yourself; however, ObjectDesign warns you to do it only in exceptional situations. If are interested, look at Chapter 9 of the *API User Guide* for details on how to manually generate persistence-capable classes.

Dissecting the Person Demo Code

Now that you have stored your first object, we will take a look at the code. I will walk through the tasks the `Person` demo performs.

Creating a Session

Line 22 of the demo makes a call to the static method to create a session:

```
Session.create(null, null).join();
```

In ObjectStore PSE Pro 3.0, a session is needed before any calls to the PSE Pro API can be made. This session remains active until your program terminates or you call the `terminate()` method for the current session. You cannot reuse sessions, but you can create new sessions. PSE Pro permits multiple concurrent sessions, thus each session gets a copy of the object and multiple sessions in a single JVM can manipulate the object. PSE Pro provides multiple read locks and one write lock to control updates to the persistent object. When using PSE Pro, the create call's host parameter should be `Null` and the `Properties` parameter can vary. It is beyond the scope of this chapter to explore the `Properties` options. Both of these parameters will be `Null` in all my examples.

> **NOTE**
>
> See the API documentation on `COM.odi.Session` for the details on multiple sessions. Suffice it to say that sessions become more apparent when you are trying to perform multiple reads and writes to the database at the same time within the same JVM.

Joining a Thread to the Session

Line 22 of the demo also makes a call to the `join()` method. This allows the current thread to join the existing session:

```
Session.create(null, null).join();
```

Calling the `join` method associates the session with the current thread within the JVM. Any number of threads might join a session. After they join a session they have, they share the same view of the database, transactions, persistent objects, and database locks. Any threads that join a session are operating asynchronously. Thus, synchronization issues apply when you use more than one thread in the same session. For brevity, I will not discuss this topic any more; for more information please consult Chapter 5, "Working with Transactions," and Chapter 6, "Storing, Retrieving, and Updating Objects," of the *PSE for Java User's Guide*.

Creating or Opening a Database

Line 38 of the demo calls the `open()` method to open a database specified by the application.

```
Database.open(dbName, ObjectStore.OPEN_UPDATE).destroy();
```

The signature of the `open()` method call is shown as follows:

```
public abstract Database open(String name, int openMode)
  throws AccessViolationExcpetion, DatabaseExcpetion,
  DatabaseLockedException, DatabaseNotFoundException,
  DatabaseOpenException, DatabaseUpgradeException,
  IllegalArgumentException, IncompatibleOpenModeException,
  ObjectStoreException
```

Notice from the *API Reference*, the `Database` class is an abstract class, and the `open()` method is a method that you are not expected to implement. PSE Pro does this automatically for you when you create or open a database, by creating a subclass instance of the `Database` class to represent your database. Through the `open()` or `create()` method call, you can maintain a handle to your database, which can be used to identify your database instance.

In the `Person` demo, I open the database in the `ObjectStore.OPEN_UPDATE` mode. This is because I'm not interested in using an existing database. Then I call the `destroy()` method so that the old database, if it exists, will be destroyed. This example is to illustrate the basics of PSE Pro database functionality. In later examples, I will use existing databases if they exist.

After destroying the database I create a new database in lines 43 and 44:

```
Database db = Database.create(dbName,
    ObjectStore.ALL_READ | ObjectStore.ALL_WRITE);
```

The database name must be of the form *database_name.odb*. I accept the `dbName` from the command-line `args` variable.

Starting and Committing Transactions

A *transaction* in ObjectStore is a unit of work that has a beginning and an end. Within the beginning and end of a transaction, any work on the database can be committed or aborted. You must be in a transaction to create a database, destroy a database, read a database, store persistent objects, and update persistent objects.

Although the transaction class is abstract, you need not implement it because when you call the `begin(int)` method to mark the start of the transaction, PSE Pro automatically creates a subclass instance to represent your transaction.

The `Person` demo uses two transactions. Line 47 is an `ObjectStore.UPDATE`:

```
Transaction tr = Transaction.begin(ObjectStore.UPDATE);
```

Line 73 is an `ObjectStore.READONLY`:

```
Transaction tr = Transaction.begin(ObjectStore.READONLY);
```

9

SERVLETS
AND OBJECT
DATABASES

Each transaction is marked with a beginning by calling the `begin()` method. What follows is the method signature of the `begin(int type)` method:

```
public static Transaction begin(int type)
  throws DatabaseLockedException, IllegalArgumentException,
  ObjectStoreException,TransactionInProgressException
```

The transaction is ended by either a call to commit or abort. There are two calls to commit in the `Person` demo. The first one is in the `createDatabase()` method on line 65:

```
// End the transaction. This stores the three person objects,
// along with the String objects representing their names, and
// the array of children, into the database.  After this method
// call all Persistent object references are considered STALE.
tr.commit();
```

The second is on line 95 in the `readDatabase()` method:

```
// End the read-only transaction. This ends the
// accessibility of the persistent objects since the commit()
// is of a RETAIN_STALE type.
tr.commit();
```

The `commit()` method is overloaded either to not take a parameter or to take an `int` parameter. The first method, which takes no parameter, is defined by

```
public abstract void commit()
  throws AbortException, NoTransactionInProgressException,
  ObjectStoreException
```

When this method is called, ObjectStore checks the transaction block to see whether any persistent objects have been updated; if so, it saves these changes to the database. It also checks to see whether these persistent objects have referenced any transient objects, or objects that are not stored in the database. If there were such references and these objects were defined as persistent-capable, ObjectStore stores them in the database. This is referred to as *transitive persistence*. Through their access by persistent objects, the transient objects can become persistent in the database. However, if persistent objects do not reference them, they are not stored in the database. For more information on transitive persistence, please consult Chapter 1, "Introducing PSE/PSE Pro," of the *API User Guide* under the link Transitive Persistence.

In addition, the `commit()` method changes the state of the persistent objects to `RETAIN_STALE` values.

These values are called the default values. If the persistent object references any other objects, these references are removed. Then if the application tries to read, update, or invoke a method on a stale object, PSE Pro throws an `ObjectException` error.

NOTE

A call to `commit()` is the same as calling `commit(ObjectStore.RETAIN_STALE)`.

The other `commit()` takes an `int` that specifies the disposition of the persistent objects after the transaction. The method signature is

```
public abstract void commit(int retain)
   throws AbortExecution, IllegalArgumentException,
   NoTransactionInProgressException,
   ObjectStoreException
```

The result of this commit differs only by the retain state of the persistent objects in the transaction. The acceptable retain parameters are

- `ObjectStore.RETAIN_STALE`—Marks the object as stale, sets the object to its default values and makes any references to other objects null, and throws an `ObjectException` if you try to read, update, or invoke a method on it. In addition, the entry of the stale object in the object table is reclaimed, and the stale object loses its persistent identity. The object must manually be read from the database on any subsequent transactions.

- `ObjectStore.RETAIN_HOLLOW`—Marks the object as stale and sets the object to its default values; however, the object entry in the object table is not reclaimed. Access of this type of object in the next transaction causes the object to be refreshed to match its persistent state in the database. The advantage of this is that the object does not need to be fetched by code, it is done automatically. Any access of a hollow object outside a transaction throws a `NoTransactionInProgressException`.

- `ObjectStore.RETAIN_READONLY`—Maintains the value of the object when it was written to the database so that your Java program can read these values without reading the database. However, the value of the object might be different from that in the database if another process has updated the object. If this occurs, your object does not change. However, within a transaction, if you access the persistent object it updates to reflect the persistent state of the object. Any access of a read-only persistent object outside a transaction throws a `NoTransactionInProgressException`.

- `ObjectStore.RETAIN_UPDATE`—Maintains the value of the object when it was written to the database so that your Java program can read and modify these values without fetching from the database. These type of values become "scratch" values that are reset with the current persistent values when accessed within a transaction. I can only imagine the trouble one could get into using a value like this, but I'm sure someone somewhere had a need for this.

Creating a Database Root

In line 59 of the demo, a database root is created to give access to the object in the database:

```
// Create a database root and associate it with
// sally, which is a persistent-capable object.
// ObjectStore Java uses a database root as an entry
// point into a database.
db.createRoot("Sally", sally);
```

This is a means for accessing your objects in the database because there are no tables like a relational database. All updates and reads are made from this root handle. The method signature is

```
public abstract void createRoot(String name, Object object)
  throws DatabaseNotOpenException, DatabaseRootAlreadyExistsException,
  IllegalArguementException, NoTransactionInProgressException,
  ObjectStoreException,
  UpdateReadOnlyException
```

The object specified as the root needs to be identified when you create a root or later before the transaction ends. The object that is assigned during the method call or later will be made persistent automatically if not already specified as such. A root can be associated with any object in the database. In the `Person` demo, `Sally` is the database root. Note, the root name that identifies the root object must be a unique name within the database; if not, the `DatabaseRootAlreadyExistsException` is thrown. In the example, it must be unique within the `person.odb`.

Storing Objects

To store objects in the database, the root object must reference them. In the example, the array of `Person` objects are contained within `Sally`'s object, so they are stored when the transaction performs the commit. This code is contained in the `createDatabase()` method. You construct the two children with null values for their children, and then create `Sally` with an array of the two children.

Retrieving Objects

To retrieve objects from the database, you must first access the database through the root. When you have the root, you can access all objects associated with the root. In the `Person` demo, the `readDatabase()` method gets the object that is associated with the root name. The `getRoot()` method returns an object, so you must cast this object to the `Person` class because you know what type of object was stored there. When the object that is identified as the root is fetched from the database, you have access to all associated objects. In the example, you retrieve the children that `Sally` has.

Ending the Session

In Line 28, you complete the example by ending the session with a call to the `terminate()` method:

```
Session.getCurrent().terminate();
```

The `terminate()` method has the following signature:

```
public void terminate()
```

Terminating the session disassociates the session with all `Database` and `Transaction` objects created within the session. Any thread belonging to the session might terminate the session, and if there is an open database, PSE Pro closes the database.

PERSISTENT-AWARE CLASSES

The `Person.java` example did not separate the database calls from the actual object. So if you're like me, you will want to encapsulate the database access into another class. When I attempted to do this, I learned a valuable lesson about persistent-aware classes. First I'll show the example and the error that occurs.

I took the `Person.java` class and broke it up into two classes. Under the `<odi_demo>` directory, create a directory named `newpeople2` and put in it `Person2.java`, `PersonManager.java`, and `cfpargs.first`—shown in Listings 9.3, 9.4, and 9.5.

LISTING 9.3   PERSON2.JAVA

```
package COM.odi.demo.newpeople2;

// Import the COM.odi package, which contains the API:
import COM.odi.*;

public
class Person2 {

  // Fields in the Person2 class:
  String name;
  int age;
  Person2 children[];

  // Constructor
  public Person2(String nameValue, int ageValue,
    Person2 theChildren[]) {
    name = nameValue;
    age = ageValue;
```

9

continues

LISTING 9.3   CONTINUED

```java
    children = theChildren;
  }

  public String getName() {
    return name;
  }

  public void setName(String nameValue) {
    name = nameValue;
  }

  public int getAge() {
    return age;
  }

  public void setAge(int ageValue) {
    age = ageValue;
  }

  public Person2[] getChildren() {
    return children;
  }

  public void setChildren(Person2 theChildren[]) {
    children = theChildren;
  }

  // This class is never used as a persistent hash key.
  // So using the Object's hashCode is ok.
  public int hashCode() {
    return super.hashCode();
  }
}
```

LISTING 9.4   PERSONMANAGER.JAVA

```java
package COM.odi.demo.newpeople2;

// Import the COM.odi package, which contains the API:
import COM.odi.*;

public
class PersonManager {
```

```
// Main:
public static void main(String argv[]) {
  try {
    String dbName = argv[0];

    // The following line starts a nonglobal session and joins
    // this thread to the new session.  This allows the thread
    // to use PSE Pro.
    Session.create(null, null).join();
    Database db = createDatabase(dbName);
    readDatabase(db);
    db.close();
  }
  finally {
      Session.getCurrent().terminate();
  }
}

static Database createDatabase(String dbName) {

  // Attempt to open and destroy the database specified on the
  // command line.  This ensures that that program creates a
  // new database each time the application is called.
  try {
    Database.open(dbName, ObjectStore.OPEN_UPDATE).destroy();
  } catch (DatabaseNotFoundException e) {
  }

  // Create a new database.
  Database db = Database.create(dbName,
      ObjectStore.ALL_READ | ObjectStore.ALL_WRITE);

  // Start an update transaction.
  Transaction tr = Transaction.begin(ObjectStore.UPDATE);

  // Create instances of Person2.
  Person2 sophie = new Person2("Sophie", 5, null);
  Person2 joseph = new Person2("Joseph", 1, null);
  Person2 children[] = { sophie, joseph };
  Person2 sally = new Person2("Sally", 39, children);

  // Create a database root and associate it with
  // sally, which is a persistent-capable object.
  // ObjectStore Java uses a database root as an entry
  // point into a database.
  db.createRoot("Sally", sally);
```

9

SERVLETS AND OBJECT DATABASES

continues

LISTING 9.4   CONTINUED

```
    // End the transaction.
    // This stores the three Person2 objects, along with
    // the String objects representing their names, and the array of
    // children, into the database.
    tr.commit();

    return db;
}

static void readDatabase(Database db) {

    // Start a read-only transaction
    Transaction tr = Transaction.begin(ObjectStore.READONLY);

    // Use the "Sally" database root to access objects in the database.
    // Because sally references sophie and joseph, obtaining the "Sally"
    // database root allows the program to also reach sophie and joseph.
    // In each transaction, an application must obtain a database root
    // and use it to navigate to persistent objects. Be sure to write
    // your application so that it does not hold on to references
    // to persistent objects between transactions.
    Person2 sally = (Person2)db.getRoot("Sally");
    Person2 children[] = sally.getChildren();
    System.out.print("Sally is " + sally.getAge() + " and has " +
      children.length + " children: ");
    for(int i=0; i<children.length; i++) {
      System.out.print(children[i].getName() + " ");
    }

    System.out.println(" ");

    // End the transaction. This ends the accessibility of the
    // persistent objects and abandons the transient objects.
    tr.commit();
  }
}
```

LISTING 9.5   CFPARGS.WRONG

```
-dest . -inplace
Person2.class
```

Compile the two `java` files using "`javac *.java`", and then annotate the `Person2.java` class by running "`osjcfp @cfpargs.wrong`". Change to the `<odi_install>` directory and execute the following command:

```
java COM.odi.demo.newpeople2.PersonManager person2.odb
```

When you execute this, you will get the following result:

```
>java COM.odi.demo.newpeople2.PersonManager person2.odb
Sally is 39 and has 2 children: java.lang.NullPointerException
    at COM.odi.demo.newpeople2.PersonManager.readDatabase
    (PersonManager.java:82)
    at COM.odi.demo.newpeople2.PersonManager.main(PersonManager.java:19)
```

The error message says that there was a null pointer encountered at line 82 of the `PersonManager.java` file. However, when you look at the line in question, there appears to be nothing wrong with the code:

```
System.out.print(children[i].getName() + " ");
```

If you notice from the previous printout, `Sally` does have a length of 2, but when you try to access the `children` array, you are acting upon a null pointer. This seems very strange because you are doing the same thing you did in the `Person.java` class, only you encapsulated the database access in the `PersonManager.java` class. So why the error?

Well, it turns out that the `PersonManager.java` class must be designated as persistence-aware because it is accessing persistent objects from the database. Basically, this means that the `PersonManager.java` class needs to know how the `Person2.java` class is stored in the database and how to retrieve a persistent object. So the lesson learned is that any class that deals with objects inside the database—but is itself not stored in the database—needs to be designated as persistence-aware (that is, aware of how to store persistent objects in the database and how to retrieve them from the database).

NOTE
See the definition of persistence aware in the glossary of the ObjectStore PSE/Pro for Java API Reference included in the documentation with PSE Pro.

It's not difficult to make the `PersonManager.java` class persistence-aware. In fact, it requires only a change to the annotation file. I have created an annotation file called `cfpargs.right`, shown in Listing 9.6, that contains the proper entries.

LISTING 9.6   CFPARGS.RIGHT

```
-dest . -inplace
Person2.class
-persistcapable Person2.class
-persistaware PersonManager.class
```

Notice that I have added additional parameters in the `cfpargs.right` file. These options designate `Person2.class` as persistent-capable and `PersonManager.class` as persistent-aware. Before you annotate the files, write down the size in bytes of the `PersonManager.class`. There is no need to recompile the Java code; all you have to do is reannotate both classes by running `osjcfp @cfpargs.right` from the `newpeople2` directory. When you do this, you will not see any new annotation files. However, the size of the `PersonManager.class` has increased.

> **NOTE**
>
> When I did the example, my `PersonManager.class`'s file size increased by 116 bytes.

The increase in size resulted from the `osjcfp` utility adding byte code to `PersonManager.class` to implement `ObjectStore.fetch()` and `ObjectStore.dirty()` to handle the persistent `Person2` class in the database.

Now, change to the `<odi_install>` directory and execute the following command:

```
java COM.odi.demo.newpeople2.PersonManager person2.odb
```

When you execute this, you will get the desired result:

```
Sally is 39 and has 2 children: Sophie Joseph
```

Using an Annotation Directory with osjcfp

The previous example illustrates a problem with annotating your class files in the same directory as your source files. As was the case with `PersonManager.class`, you can't tell whether the annotation process has taken place. Well, there is an option with the annotation file to relocate your annotation files. Listings 9.7 and 9.8 contain a modified annotation file to illustrate the point.

LISTING 9.7   CFPARGS.OSJCFPOUT.WINDOWS

```
-dest ..\osjcfpout
Person2.class
-persistcapable Person2.class
-persistaware PersonManager.class
```

LISTING 9.8   CFPARGS.OSJCFPOUT.UNIX

```
-dest ../osjcfpout
Person2.class
-persistcapable Person2.class
-persistaware PersonManager.class
```

Before you execute this annotation file, verify that the `<osjcfpout>` directory already exits. It should have been created when you installed PSE Pro; if not, create it now. To complete the relocation process, you must now place the `<osjcfpout>` directory in your CLASSPATH somewhere before the entry for the directory where the `Person2.class` and the `PersonManager.class` files are located (that is, before the period (.) in my example). Running the PostProcessor and specifying the `<osjcfpout>` directory as the destination will actually place the `Person2.class`, `Person2ClassInfo.class`, and `PersonManager.class` files in the following directory:

- Windows—`<osjcfpout>\COM\odi\demo\newpeople2`
- UNIX—`<osjcfpout>/COM/odi/demo/newpeople2`

To run the `Person2` example again, change to the `newpeople2` directory under the `<odi_demo>` directory. Delete all the `.class` files and recompile all the `java` files. Then run the command `osjcfp @cfpargs.osjcfpout`.

Now, verify the creation of the annotation files by executing a directory listing in the following directory:

- Windows—`<osjcfpout>\COM\odi\demo\newpeople`
- UNIX—`<osjcfpout>/COM/odi/demo/newpeople`

Now, run the example from the `<odi_install>` directory as before.

Why Do You Want an Annotation Directory?

Typically, when you are testing an application, you will use the `-inplace` option of `osjcfp` like the `Person` demo did. This isn't so bad if you have only one class. However, if you have more than one class, it can create a big headache trying to figure out which classes have been annotated and which have not. The other advantage you get is the classes that need to be shipped with the software. When you package your software for delivery to your customer, you must include all annotated files. By relocating your destination directory, you have these classes, so there is no hunt for the proper classes. In the `Person2` demo, you have `Person2.class`, `Person2ClassInfo.class`, and `PersonManager.class` as the annotated files. All persistent files will have two classes, and all persistent aware classes will have only one file.

USING SOME OBJECTSTORE COLLECTIONS

ObjectStore PSE Pro provides a package of persistence-capable utility collection classes called COM.odi.util. This package is consistent with the JDK1.2 package java.util. Although the JDK1.2 contains similar collections to ObjectStore PSE Pro's, there is no query or indexing possible on the JavaSoft classes. Of course, the ObjectStore products, as of the time of this writing, have not been upgraded to use the JDK1.2 classes. You can use the JDK1.2 compiler; however, you can't store the JavaSoft collections in the database. I discuss this in more detail later.

For now, I would like to focus on two collections, OSTreeSet and OSVectorList, that I will be using in my example to illustrate the power of the ObjectStore PSE Pro collection.

Description of an OSTreeSet

The OSTreeSet is the collection that ObjectDesign recommends when you are going to create a collection with a large number of objects.

> **NOTE**
>
> See Figure 9.5 in the section "Place a Persistent Catalog into a Servlet" for clarification on a large number of objects. A catalog would naturally have a large number of objects, even though my example does not contain that many.

That's because this class is designed for very large persistent collections. When you have large collections, the time to fetch objects from the database can sometimes be slower than for smaller collections. However, the OSTreeSet collection allows you to query the collection without fetching the objects from the database. The response of the query from the OSTreeSet collection is a "result collection" of objects that match the query.

Now, if you are like me, you might be wondering, "Why would I need to perform a query in an object-oriented database?" First of all, the query is not SQL-based, and second of all, it saves an immense amount of time retrieving objects. For a large collection, PSE Pro will need to navigate the collection looking for the requested object, so each object must be accessed to determine if there is a match. Given these reasons, the OSTreeSet provides a query function to speed up access of persistent objects in very large collections. And, yes, you can add an index to make the query return even faster! I will describe an example of each the section titled "Index and Query on an OSTreeSet."

Use the OSTreeSet with caution. First of all, it's unordered. So just because you put the objects into the collection one way, they might, and usually do, come out another way. Second, it doesn't allow duplicates.

> **NOTE**
>
> There are ordered collections that allow duplicate values, like any of the OSTreeMap*xxx* classes. See Chapter 7, "Working with Collections," in the *API User Guide*.

Additionally, OSTreeSet does not allow Null values, and the equals() and hashCode() methods are content-based, not reference-based. This means that you must define these methods for objects you store in the database. I'll illustrate this in my example.

Because OSTreeSet is a persistence-capable class, it does not need to be annotated. However, if you create persistent objects that extend from this class, they will need to be annotated or you must manually code these annotations.

> **NOTE**
>
> The classes in the COM.odi.util package do not need annotation because they are already persistence-capable. However, any classes that extend them must either be annotated or you must manually code the persistence-capable methods.

The OSTreeSet has a large inheritance structure, as illustrated in Figure 9.2.

Description of an OSVectorList

The OSVectorList is a collection that is a persistent expandable array. It's basically an OSVector that implements the List interface. The OSVector is similar to the API for a java.util.Vector in the Javasoft JDK. The OSVectorList associates each element with a numerical position based on insertion order. Thus, it is an ordered collection, unlike the OSTreeSet that I discussed earlier. OSVectorList does allow for duplicates, which is again different from the OSTreeSet.

The OSVectorList performs identity comparisons with the equals() and the hashCode() methods. This means that the objects must be of the same instance, or have the same reference, for them to be equal. It also means that an OSVectorList collection is not suitable for storage in a persistent hashtable or any other hashtable-based collection representation.

FIGURE 9.2

COM.odi.util. OSTreeSet object diagram.

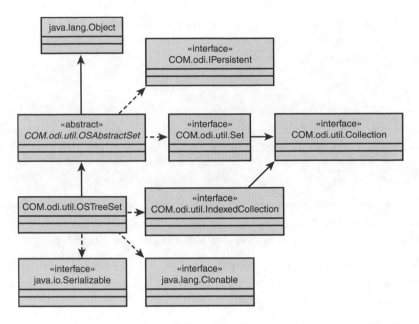

An `OSVectorList` contains less overhead code than other utility collections because `id` does not have quick lookup by object or key. Retrieval is performed by index or by iteration through the list.

The `OSVectorList` inheritance structure is illustrated in Figure 9.3.

A TreeCatalog Example

Given the background on two specific collection classes provided in PSE Pro, take a look at an example of a `treeCatalog` that I have put together, which uses both the `OSTreeSet` and the `OSVectorList`. This example, which uses the code found in Listings 9.9, 9.10, 9.11, and 9.12, is a persistent catalog, which has catalog items that can be any type of product. I have shown an example of books and movies. Figure 9.4 shows a high-level object diagram for the catalog item.

You must extend the abstract `Product` class for any additional classes that you would like to be catalog items. All catalog items can be stored in the persistent catalog.

FIGURE 9.3
COM.odi.util.OS-VectorList object diagram.

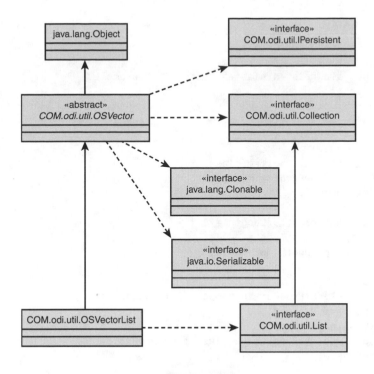

FIGURE 9.4
COM.odi.demo. treeCatalog. CatalogItem object diagram.

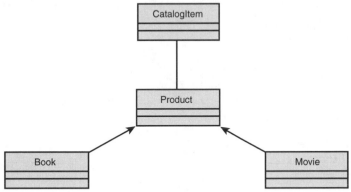

9

LISTING 9.9   CATALOGITEM.JAVA

```java
package COM.odi.demo.treeCatalog;

// Import the java related classes used in the example.
import java.io.*;
import java.util.*;

public class CatalogItem {

  // Fields in the CatalogItem class.
  private Product theProduct = null;
  private int quantity;

  private int initialBufferLength = 64;
  private String productType = null;
  private String productName = null;

  // Constructor
  public CatalogItem(Product inProduct, int inQuantity) {
    theProduct = inProduct;
    quantity = inQuantity;
    setProductType(theProduct.getClass().getName());
    setProductName();
  }

  public int getQuantity() {
    return quantity ;
  }

  public void setQuantity(int inQuantity) {
    quantity = inQuantity;
  }

  public Product getProduct() {
    return theProduct;
  }

  public String getName() {
    return theProduct.getName();
  }

  public void setProductName() {
    productName = getName();
  }
```

```java
public String getProductName() {
  return productName;
}

public void setProductType(String packageProductType) {
  String tmp = null;
  StringTokenizer strTokenizer =
    new StringTokenizer(packageProductType, ".");
  while(strTokenizer.hasMoreTokens()) {
    tmp = strTokenizer.nextToken();
  }
  productType = tmp;
}

public String getProductType() {
  return productType;
}

public String toString() {
  StringBuffer productBuffer = new StringBuffer(initialBufferLength);
  productBuffer.append("CatalogItem=[Product="+ productType +
    ", Value={" + theProduct.toString() + "}], Quantity={" +
    quantity + "}");
  return productBuffer.toString();
}
}
```

LISTING 9.10   PRODUCT.JAVA

```java
package COM.odi.demo.treeCatalog;

public abstract class Product {

  private String name;
  private String description;

  protected int initialBufferLength = 64;

  public Product(String inName, String inDescription) {
    name = inName;
    description = inDescription;
  }

  public String getName() {
    return name;
  }
```

9

SERVLETS
AND OBJECT
DATABASES

continues

LISTING 9.10   CONTINUED

```java
  public void setName(String inName) {
    name = inName;
  }

  public String getDescription() {
    return description;
  }

  public void setDescription(String inDescription) {
    description = inDescription;
  }

  public abstract String toString();
}
```

LISTING 9.11   BOOK.JAVA

```java
package COM.odi.demo.treeCatalog;

public class Book extends Product {

  private String publisher;    /* Publisher's name */
  private String[] authors;    /* Array of authors */

  public Book(String inName, String inDescription, String inPublisher,
    String[] inAuthors) {
    super(inName, inDescription);
    publisher = inPublisher;
    authors = inAuthors;
  }

  public String toString() {
    StringBuffer authorBuffer = new StringBuffer(initialBufferLength);
    authorBuffer.append("Authors=");
    for(int i=0; i<authors.length; i++) {
      authorBuffer.append(authors[i] + ",");
    }
    StringBuffer outputBuffer = new StringBuffer(initialBufferLength);
    outputBuffer.append("Name=" + getName() + ";" + "Description=" +
      getDescription() + ";" + "Publisher=" + publisher +
      authorBuffer.toString());
    return outputBuffer.toString();
  }
}
```

LISTING 9.12 MOVIE.JAVA

```java
public class Movie extends Product {

  private String genre;       /* Action Adventure, Comedy, Drama */
  private String formatType;  /* VHS, DVD, LaserDisk */
  private String rating;      /* Rating for the movie, G,PG,PG-13,R */
  private String[] talent;    /* Actress/Actor */

  public Movie(String inName, String inDescription, String inGenre,
    String inFormatType, String inRating, String[] inTalent) {
    super(inName, inDescription);
    genre = inGenre;
    formatType = inFormatType;
    rating = inRating;
    talent = inTalent;
  }

  public String getGenre() {
    return genre;
  }

  public String getFormatType() {
    return formatType;
  }

  public String getRating() {
    return rating;
  }

  public String getTalent() {
    StringBuffer talentBuffer = new StringBuffer(initialBufferLength);
    for(int i=0; i<talent.length; i++) {
      if(i!= 0) {
        talentBuffer.append(",");
      }
      talentBuffer.append(talent[i]);
    }
    return talentBuffer.toString();
  }

  public String toString() {
    StringBuffer outputBuffer = new StringBuffer(initialBufferLength);
    outputBuffer.append("Name=" + getName() + ";" +
      "Description=" + getDescription() + ";" + "Genre=" + genre +
      ";" + "FormatType=" + formatType + ";" + "Rating=" + rating +
```

9

SERVLETS
AND OBJECT
DATABASES

continues

LISTING 9.12   CONTINUED

```
      "Talent=" + getTalent());
    return outputBuffer.toString();
  }
}
```

A catalog item holds a product and retains a quantity of that product. The product can be either a book or a movie. The product generically defines the name of the product, a description of the product, and a toString() method for debugging.

I have created a catalog manager class that encapsulates all the database calls, as shown in Listing 9.13.

LISTING 9.13   CATALOGMANAGER.JAVA

```java
package COM.odi.demo.treeCatalog;
// Import the java related classes used in the example.
import java.io.*;
import java.util.*;

import COM.odi.*;
import COM.odi.util.*;
import COM.odi.util.query.*;

public class CatalogManager {
  private static String dbName = "treecatalog.odb";
  /* The database that this CatalogManager is operation against. */
  private static Database db = null;

  // Class storage for the HOLLOW roots.
  private static OSTreeSet catalogRoot = null;
  private static OSVectorList booksRoot = null;
  private static OSVectorList moviesRoot = null;

  private static String CATALOG_ROOT_NAME = "Catalog";
  private static String BOOKS_ROOT_NAME = "Books";
  private static String MOVIES_ROOT_NAME = "Movies";

  public CatalogManager() {
    try {
      // The following line starts a nonglobal session and joins
      // this thread to the new session.  This allows the thread
      // to use PSE Pro.
      Session.create(null, null).join();
```

```
    String threadName = Thread.currentThread().getName();
    String sessionName = Session.getCurrent().getName();
    System.out.println("threadName = " + threadName);
    System.out.println("sessionName = " + sessionName);
    createDatabase(dbName);
  } finally {
    // Insure shutdown is performed even if exception is caught.
    db.close();
    Session.getCurrent().terminate();
  }
}


// This method will create and open the database that is specified
//    on the command line when the Java application is invoked.
public static void createDatabase(String dbName) {
  System.out.println("Starting createDatabase("+dbName+")");

  // Attempt to open and destroy the database specified on the
  // command line.  This ensures that that program creates a
  // new database each time the application is called.
  try {
    Database.open(dbName, ObjectStore.OPEN_UPDATE).destroy();
  } catch (DatabaseNotFoundException e) {
  }

  // Create a new database.
  db = Database.create(dbName,
    ObjectStore.ALL_READ | ObjectStore.ALL_WRITE);

  // Build the data and store it in the OSTreeSet before
  //    a transaction is started.
  // Create books.
  String authors[] = {"James Goodwill", "Steven D. Wilkinson"};
  Book servletBook = new Book("Developing Java Servlets",
    "Cool book on Servlets", "Sams Publishing", authors);
  String authors2[] = {"Michael Morrison", "et. all"};
  Book javaBook = new Book("Java Unleashed, Second Edition",
    "Cool book on Java", "Sams Publishing", authors2);

  // Create movies.
  String talent[] = {"Will Smith", "Tommy Lee Jones",
    "Linda Fiorentino"};
  Movie menInBlack = new Movie("Men in Black",
    "Funny alien invasion move", "Sci-Fi/Horror",
    "VHS", "PG-13", talent);
  String talent2[] = {"Harrison Ford", "Gary Oldman"};
```

9

**SERVLETS
AND OBJECT
DATABASES**

continues

LISTING 9.13   CONTINUED

```java
Movie airForceOne = new Movie("Air Force One",
  "Thriller about hijacking of Air Force One", "Action/Adventure",
  "VHS", "PG-13", talent2);

// Create instances catalog items.
CatalogItem book1 = new CatalogItem(servletBook, 2);
CatalogItem book2 = new CatalogItem(javaBook, 1);
CatalogItem movie1 = new CatalogItem(menInBlack, 1);
CatalogItem movie2 = new CatalogItem(airForceOne, 3);

System.out.println("book1.getName()=" + book1.getName());
System.out.println("book2.getName()=" + book2.getName());
System.out.println("movie1.getName()=" + movie1.getName());
System.out.println("movie2.getName()=" + movie2.getName());

// Start an update transaction.
Transaction tr = Transaction.begin(ObjectStore.UPDATE);

catalogRoot = new OSTreeSet(db);
catalogRoot.add(book1);
catalogRoot.add(book2);
catalogRoot.add(movie1);
catalogRoot.add(movie2);
db.createRoot("Catalog", catalogRoot);

booksRoot = new OSVectorList(2);
booksRoot.addElement(book1);
booksRoot.addElement(book2);
db.createRoot("Books", booksRoot);

moviesRoot = new OSVectorList(2);
moviesRoot.addElement(movie1);
moviesRoot.addElement(movie2);
db.createRoot("Movies", moviesRoot);

// all database references will be STALE.
tr.commit();
System.out.println("Ending createDatabase("+dbName+")");
}

// Populate the HOLLOW Roots.
public static void getRoots() {
  // Start a read-only transaction:
  Transaction tr = Transaction.begin(ObjectStore.READONLY);
```

```
catalogRoot = (OSTreeSet)db.getRoot(CATALOG_ROOT_NAME);
booksRoot = (OSVectorList)db.getRoot(BOOKS_ROOT_NAME);
moviesRoot = (OSVectorList)db.getRoot(MOVIES_ROOT_NAME);

    // End the read-only transaction.  This makes the roots
    //  HOLLOW so later when used in a transaction, they don't
    //  have to be read from the database.
    tr.commit(ObjectStore.RETAIN_HOLLOW);
}

// This method reads the catalogItems out of the database.
public static void readDatabase(Database db) {
  System.out.println("Starting readDatabase("+dbName+")");

    // Start a read-only transaction:
    Transaction tr = Transaction.begin(ObjectStore.READONLY);

    // Use the HOLLOW root object.  The object will be refreshed
    //  in the transaction with this access.
    // Currently in COM.odi.util.* package, but will be in JDK1.2
    Iterator iterator = catalogRoot.iterator();

    CatalogItem item = null;
    int itemCount = 0;
    while(iterator.hasNext()) {
      item = (CatalogItem) iterator.next();
      itemCount++;
      System.out.println("item[" + itemCount + "]="+ item.toString());
    }

    // End the read-only transaction. This ends the
    // accessibility of the persistent objects and abandons
    // the transient objects.
    tr.commit(ObjectStore.RETAIN_HOLLOW);
    System.out.println("Ending readDatabase("+dbName+")");
}

public static void runProductQuery() {
    // Construct a query on all Book classes to find out how
    //  many books there are in the CatalogItems.
    Query productQuery = new Query(CatalogItem.class,
    "getProductType() == \"Book\"");

    long start = System.currentTimeMillis();
    // Start transaction.
    Transaction tr = Transaction.begin(ObjectStore.READONLY);
```

continues

LISTING 9.13   CONTINUED

```
    Collection result = productQuery.select(catalogRoot);
    System.out.println("Found " + result.size() + " Book.");

    long stop = System.currentTimeMillis();
    System.out.println("Time: " + (stop - start) + " milliseconds");

    Iterator iterator = result.iterator();
    while(iterator.hasNext()) {
      System.out.println("value="+iterator.next());
    }
    tr.commit(ObjectStore.RETAIN_HOLLOW);
  }

  public static void addIndexToCatalogItems() {

    // Start transaction.
    Transaction tr = Transaction.begin(ObjectStore.UPDATE);

    catalogRoot.addIndex(CatalogItem.class, "getProductType()");

    tr.commit(ObjectStore.RETAIN_HOLLOW);
    //db.close();
  }

  //Main
  public static void main(String argv[]) {
    CatalogManager catalogManager = new CatalogManager();

    try {
      Session.create(null, null).join();
      String threadName = Thread.currentThread().getName();
      String sessionName = Session.getCurrent().getName();
      System.out.println("threadName = " + threadName);
      System.out.println("sessionName = " + sessionName);
      try {
        db = Database.open(dbName, ObjectStore.OPEN_UPDATE);
      } catch (DatabaseNotFoundException e) {
        System.out.println("database("+dbName+") not found.");
      }

      getRoots();
      readDatabase(db);
      // Note a db.close make all persistent objects stale.
      System.out.println("Product Query before Index.");
```

```
    runProductQuery();
    addIndexToCatalogItems();
    System.out.println("Product Query after Index.");
    runProductQuery();
  } finally {
    // Insure shutdown is performed even if exception is caught.
    db.close();
    Session.getCurrent().terminate();
  }
 }
}
```

Along with the code listing, you need a `cfpargs` file for Windows and UNIX. These files are found in Listings 9.14 and 9.15.

LISTING 9.14   CFPARGS.WINDOWS

```
-dest ..\osjcfpout
CatalogItem.class
Product.class
Book.class
Movie.class
-persistcapable CatalogItem.class Book.class Movie.class
-persistaware CatalogManager.class
```

LISTING 9.15   CFPARGS.UNIX

```
-dest ../osjcfpout
CatalogItem.class
Product.class
Book.class
Movie.class
-persistcapable CatalogItem.class Book.class Movie.class
-persistaware CatalogManager.class
```

To run this example, create a treeCatalog directory under the <odi_demo> directory and place the previous files in the directory.

9

SERVLETS AND OBJECT DATABASES

NOTE

The case of the directory is important. The package name is case-sensitive, so the directory must contain the proper case.

Compile the java files using java *.java and annotate the files using osjcfp @cfpargs.*<OS>*, where *OS* is either Windows or UNIX. To execute the demo, change directories to <odi_install> and type

```
"java COM.odi.demo.treeCatalog.CatalogManager"
```

Proper execution should result in the following output:

```
threadName = main
sessionName = Session1
Starting createDatabase(treecatalog.odb)
book1.getName()=Developing Java Servlets
book2.getName()=Java Unleashed, Second Edition
movie1.getName()=Men in Black
movie2.getName()=Air Force One
Ending createDatabase(treecatalog.odb)
threadName = main
sessionName = Session2
Starting readDatabase(treecatalog.odb)
item[1]=CatalogItem=[Product=Book, Value={Name=Java Unleashed, Second
Edition;Description=Cool
book on Java;Publisher=Sams PublishingAuthors=Michael Morrison,et. all}],
 Quantity={1}
item[2]=CatalogItem=[Product=Movie, Value={Name=Air Force One;
Description=Thriller about
hijacking of Air Force One;Genre=Action/Adventure;FormatType=VHS;
Rating=PG-13Talent=Harrison
Ford, Gary Oldman}], Quantity={3}
item[3]=CatalogItem=[Product=Movie, Value={Name=Men in Black;
Description=Funny alien invasion
move;Genre=Sci-Fi/Horror;FormatType=VHS;Rating=PG-13Talent=Will Smith,
Tommy Lee Jones,Linda Fiorentino}], Quantity={1}
item[4]=CatalogItem=[Product=Book, Value={Name=Developing Java Servlets;
Description=Cool book
on Servlets;Publisher=Sams PublishingAuthors=James Goodwill,
Steven D. Wilkinson}], Quantity={2}
Ending readDatabase(treecatalog.odb)
Product Query before Index.
Found 2 Book.
Time: 681 milliseconds
value=CatalogItem=[Product=Book, Value={Name=Developing Java Servlets;
Description=Cool book
on Servlets;Publisher=Sams PublishingAuthors=James Goodwill,
Steven D. Wilkinson}], Quantity={2}
value=CatalogItem=[Product=Book, Value={Name=Java Unleashed,
Second Edition;Description=Cool
book on Java;Publisher=Sams PublishingAuthors=Michael Morrison,et.all}],
```

```
Quantity={1}
Product Query after Index.
Found 2 Book.
Time: 200 milliseconds
value=CatalogItem=[Product=Book, Value={Name=Developing Java Servlets;
Description=Cool book
on Servlets;Publisher=Sams PublishingAuthors=James Goodwill,
Steven D. Wilkinson}], Quantity={2}
value=CatalogItem=[Product=Book, Value={Name=Java Unleashed,
Second Edition;Description=Cool
book on Java;Publisher=Sams PublishingAuthors=Michael Morrison,et.all}],
Quantity={1}
```

The main() and CatalogManager() Methods

We will start with the `main()` method and trace through the important parts of the class. The `main()` method calls the `CatalogManager()` constructor. The constructor creates a session, joins its thread to the session, calls the `createDatabase()` method, closes the database, and terminates the session. The `main()` method continues by creating a session, opening the database, reading the roots, running a query, adding an index, and running the query again.

createDatabase() Method

Now examine the `createDatabase()` method. In this method, I create the objects to be stored in the catalog outside the `Transaction`. This is to reduce the amount of time spent in the `Transaction`. When you begin the `update` transaction on line 93 of the `CatalogManager.java class`

```
// Start an update transaction.
Transaction tr = Transaction.begin(ObjectStore.UPDATE);
```

the database is locked until line 113 when you commit the transaction:

```
// all database references will be STALE.
tr.commit();
System.out.println("Ending createDatabase("+dbName+")");
```

It might not seem like much of a time savings by creating the objects before entering the transaction, but your goal in developing PSE Pro applications should be to minimize the amount of time spent in a transaction, especially an `ObjectStore.UPDATE` transaction. In PSE Pro, there is only one write lock allowed per JVM on the database. When your code begins the transaction with a mode of `ObjectStore.UPDATE`, no other threads may access the database. This is because of a restriction imposed by PSE Pro.

NOTE

The next version of the Enterprise ObjectStore database with the Java Interface will allow multiple write locks on the database.

Transaction Types

That said, I would like to take a little more time to describe four different types of transactions, which are started by the following method, and the locks associated with them:

```
public static Transaction begin(int type)
  throws DatabaseLockedException, IllegalArgumentException,
  ObjectStoreException, TransactionInProgressException
```

- An `ObjectStore.UPDATE` transaction type, which is a blocking write lock, tries to obtain a write lock from the database if available. If a write lock is not available, the PSE Pro API call waits until it is available before returning to the calling application. If a write lock is available, PSE Pro grants a write lock and returns from the PSE Pro API call to the calling application. The write lock is in effect until the transaction is committed. The PSE Pro database can have only one write lock per JVM.

- An `ObjectStore.READONLY` transaction type, which is a blocking read lock, tries to obtain a read lock from the database if available. If a read lock is not available, the PSE Pro API call waits until it is available before returning to the calling application. If a read lock is available, PSE Pro grants a read lock and returns from the PSE Pro API call to the calling application. The read lock is granted until the transaction is committed. The PSE Pro database can have multiple read locks in the same or multiple JVMs.

- An `ObjectStore.UPDATE_NON_BLOCKING` transaction type, which is a nonblocking write lock, is just like the `ObjectStore.UPDATE` transaction type, except if a write lock is not available, PSE Pro API call throws a `COM.odi.DatabaseLockedException` and the `Transcation.begin(ObjectStore.UPDATE_NON_BLOCKING)` method call fails.

- An `ObjectStore.READONLY_NON_BLOCKING` transaction type, which is a nonblocking read lock, is just like the `ObjectStore.READONLY` transaction type, except if a read lock is not available, PSE Pro API call throws a `COM.odi.DatabaseLockedException` and the `Transcation.begin(ObjectStore.READONLY_NON_BLOCKING)` method call fails.

NOTE

In PSE Pro, there are multiple read locks available, but only one write lock per JVM.

Multiple Database Roots

In lines 95–100, I create an OSTreeSet, populate it with the previously created CatalogItems that are books and movies, and create a database root to access these objects:

```
catalogRoot = new OSTreeSet(db);
catalogRoot.add(book1);
catalogRoot.add(book2);
catalogRoot.add(movie1);
catalogRoot.add(movie2);
db.createRoot("Catalog", catalogRoot);
```

Now, because the OSTreeSet is unordered, I will not be able to maintain the order in which the objects were inserted into the collection. So, if I want to know all the books, I must traverse all the objects and retrieve only the books from the collection. Instead of doing this, I have created two additional database roots: a booksRoot and a moviesRoot. These roots will be used whenever I want to access only movies or only books out of the catalog, and these roots are ordered collections. The following listing, lines 102–110 of CatalogManager.java, illustrates the creation of the multiple roots:

```
booksRoot = new OSVectorList(2);
booksRoot.addElement(book1);
booksRoot.addElement(book2);
db.createRoot("Books", booksRoot);

moviesRoot = new OSVectorList(2);
moviesRoot.addElement(movie1);
moviesRoot.addElement(movie2);
db.createRoot("Movies", moviesRoot);
```

The multiple database root technique is common when developing database applications within ObjectStore. However, you should try to keep the number of roots as low as possible. You definitely don't need a root object for every object in the database; there would be more overhead than savings at this point. Some good rules of thumb regarding roots are as follows:

- If you have more than 100 roots, you have too many.
- If you have only one root and you have groups of similar objects, you might not have enough roots.

Finally, I end the createDatabase() with a commit. This inserts the objects into the database and marks them as STALE, which means that to access these persistent objects in the next transaction, I must retrieve them from the database.

After execution of the CatalogManager() constructor, you return to the main() method. Then you create another session and join your thread to it.

> **NOTE**
>
> This is done to illustrate that there are in fact two sessions, but only one thread of execution in the example.

The next method that main() executes is the getRoots() method. In this method, you start a READ_ONLY transaction and populate class level variables for each of the three database roots. Then you perform a RETAIN_HOLLOW commit. Thus, the class level roots will not need to be fetched when you access them in the next transaction. The database will automatically fetch them because you asked it to retain a hollow reference for these objects. The down side to this is that the garbage collector will not run on these objects until they are stale, but the upside is that you don't have to fetch them.

> **NOTE**
>
> Use this technique of retaining hollow references judiciously because it could cause your program to run out of memory in the JVM.

Because you retained a hollow reference to each of the roots, when you are in the readDatabase() method you ask the catalogRoot to return an iterator, the database refreshes the OSTreeSet root with a refreshed persistent value. This is done automatically when you access the root object.

Navigating Collections with Iterators

Because the OSTreeSet implements the Set interface as illustrated in Figure 9.2, you can obtain an iterator that will allow us to sequentially access the objects contained in the OSTreeSet. This is similar to an enumeration in the JDK1.1.x. In the JDK1.2, the enumeration is replaced with an iterator. The iterator also allows you to remove items in the collection without accessing those items.

Index and Query on an OSTreeSet

Now, I would like to illustrate a query without an index and a query with an index. In the main() method, I call the runProductQuery() method, which performs the query without the index. The query in PSE Pro is accomplished by creating a query object from the COM.odi.util.query package. I'm using the method with the following signature:

```
public Query(Class elementType, String queryExpression)
  throws IllegalArgumentException, QueryException
```

I have specified the `elementType` as the `CatalogItem.class` and the query expression is `"getProductName() == \""Book\""`. The element type must be public and the query string expression must return a Boolean value upon evaluation. The query is executed by calling the `select` method with the following signature:

```
public Set select(Collection coll)
   throws IllegalArgumentException, ClassCastException,
   InvalidPatternException, QueryIndexMismatchException, QueryException
```

The result of the select is a collection of objects that match the query expression. So PSE Pro queries the objects stored in the `catalogRoot` (that's the collection you are performing the query on in the example) and returns all objects whose `getProductName()` method returns a *Book* string. This is done without fetching the objects from the database. After the collection is returned, I create an iterator to extract the objects from the collection.

The *API User Guide* states that the query can also access public variables within the class and return the values that match the query expression. For example, if the `productType` class variable of the `CatalogItem` class were public, the query string would be `"productType == \""Book\""`. This does not seem like a good object-oriented practice in my estimation; I'm sure there are some developers who are grateful for this option. Another option is to use `FreeVariableBindings` that take their input from the user or variables that obtain their value within the program. Consult Chapter 7, "Working with Collections," in the *API User Guide* for an example.

In my example, on my platform, the first `productQuery` takes only 681 milliseconds. This is fast, but can be made even faster by creating an index before you do the query.

In the method `addIndexToCatalogItems()`, I do just that and the next query takes only 200 milliseconds. To create an index, call the `addIndex()` method on the `OSTreeSet` and give it the path or the expression to look for in the objects in the collection. Thus, the collection creates an index with the result of the query on every object in the specified database root. If you need to execute the query often, this will save the repeated lookups in the database. The index option is available to you because `OSTreeSet` implements the `IndexCollection` interface.

To summarize what was presented in the example: You created multiple database roots from which to access objects in the database, you created hollow class variables to save object retrieval time, and you performed a query without an index and a query with an index. I have tried in this limited amount of space to expose you to what I have found to be some of the most interesting things that a developer might need when using the PSE Pro product. In no way can I cover everything the PSE Pro product can do; maybe that will be another book some day!

9

Servlets and Object Databases

JDK 1.2 IMPACT

The JDK 1.2 has presented new interfaces that map directly with ObjectStore's PSE Pro interfaces, as shown in Table 9.3. This is no coincidence because ObjectDesign states that it patterned its collections after the JDK1.2 specification.

TABLE 9.3 JAVA.UTIL INTERFACES AND THEIR PSE PRO INTERFACE EQUIVALENTS

JDK1.2 Interface	*PSE Pro Interface*
java.util.Collection	COM.odi.util.Collection
java.util.Set	COM.odi.util.Set
java.util.List	COM.odi.util.List
java.util.Map	COM.odi.util.Map

These interfaces are used to create collection classes that implement the functionality defined in the Set, List, and Map interfaces. Table 9.4 illustrates the mapping between the JDK1.2 interfaces, the JDK1.2 implementation classes, and the PSE Pro implementation classes.

TABLE 9.4 JAVA.UTIL CLASSES AND THEIR PSE PRO CLASS EQUIVALENTS

Interface	*java.util Class*	*PSE Pro COM.odi.util Class*
Collection	Collection(abstract)	OSHashBag
Set	HashSet	OSHashSet
Set	ArraySet	OSTreeSet
List	Vector	OSVector
List	VectorList	OSVectorList
List	LinkedList	none
Map	Hashtable	OSHashtable
Map	HashMap	OSHashMap
Map	ArrayMap	none
Map	TreeMap	OSTreeMapxxx

Conversion to the JDK1.2 will require a new release of PSE Pro that supports the JDK1.2 collection classes. When this happens, you will probably import from the java.util package rather than the COM.odi.util package. Recompile your code with the new JDK1.2 compiler and upgrade your objects in your database with the osjhsh utility. For more information on this utility, see Chapter 11, "Tools Reference," in the *API User Guide*. The release data of the new PSE Pro product that supports the JDK 1.2 has not officially been announced as of the press time of this book. Contact ObjectDesign at support@odi.com to ascertain a release date if it has still not been released.

> **NOTE**
>
> Some classes will cause problems when compiling with the JDK1.2, including java.util.Collection and the java.util.Iterator. Although these classes have the same documented functionality as the COM.odi.util versions, they won't work with the PSE Pro 3.0. So, you must import the specific JDK1.2 classes rather than the wild-card imports like java.util.*. By importing with the wildcard *, you will receive compile errors for all Collection and Iterator uses within the source code. When the new version of PSE Pro for Java is modified to use the java.util classes rather than the COM.odi.util classes, you will have to revisit your code and change the import statements. I have not seen a beta on the JDK1.2 support, so things might change dramatically when the new version of PSE Pro is released.

HOW TO CHOOSE COLLECTIONS

In Chapter 7, "Working with Collections," in the *API User Guide*, there is a table that will assist you in selecting the appropriate collection for the application you are designing. Table 9.5 briefly shows the collections based on how many objects you envision storing in the database.

TABLE 9.5 COLLECTION CLASSES AND SIZE OF COLLECTION

Collection Class	Collection Size
OSHashBag	large
OSHashMap	large
OSHashSet	large
OSHashtable	large
OSTreeMap*xxx*	large
OSTreeSet	large
OSVector	small, medium
OSVectorList	small, medium

> **NOTE**
>
> `large` collections contain more 10,000 elements
>
> `medium` collections contain as many as 10,000 elements.
>
> `small` collections contain fewer than 100 elements.

ObjectStore designed these collections for speed relative to the collection size, so pay attention to these recommendations.

PLACE A PERSISTENT CATALOG INTO A SERVLET

Now, I'm going to use PSE Pro inside a servlet to illustrate that an object database can be used with servlets. I have taken the `BasicServlet` that was developed in Chapter 3, "Servlet Basics," and modified it to access the catalog of movies and books that I discussed previously. I have removed the package names from the `CatalogItem.java`, `Product.java`, `Movie.java`, and `Book.java` classes for `CLASSPATH` simplicity's sake. Listings 9.16–9.21 contain the classes used in the servlet catalog.

LISTING 9.16   CATALOGBASICSERVLET.JAVA

```java
import javax.servlet.*;
import javax.servlet.http.*;
import java.io.*;
// ODI class files.
import COM.odi.*;
import COM.odi.util.*;
import COM.odi.util.query.*;

public class CatalogBasicServlet extends HttpServlet {

    private static String dbName = "catalog.odb";
    /* The database that this CatalogManager is operation against. */
    private static Database db = null;

    // Class storage for the HOLLOW roots.
    private static OSTreeSet catalogRoot = null;
    private static OSVectorList booksRoot = null;
    private static OSVectorList moviesRoot = null;

    private static String CATALOG_ROOT_NAME = "Catalog";
    private static String BOOKS_ROOT_NAME = "Books";
```

```java
private static String MOVIES_ROOT_NAME = "Movies";

private static Session aSession = null;

public void init(ServletConfig config)
  throws ServletException {

  // Always pass the ServletConfig object to the super class
  super.init(config);
  System.out.println("Starting init.");
  aSession = Session.create(null, null);
  aSession.join();
  String threadName = Thread.currentThread().getName();
  String sessionName = Session.getCurrent().getName();
  System.out.println("threadName = " + threadName);
  System.out.println("sessionName = " + sessionName);
  createDatabase(dbName);
  getRoots();
  addIndexToCatalogItems();
  System.out.println("Exiting init.");
}

//Process the HTTP Get request
public void doGet(HttpServletRequest request,
  HttpServletResponse response)
  throws ServletException, IOException {
  doPost(request, response);
}

//Process the HTTP Post request
public void doPost(HttpServletRequest request,
  HttpServletResponse response)
  throws ServletException, IOException {

  // Construct a query on all Book classes to find out how
  //   many books there are in the CatalogItems.
  Query productQuery = new Query(CatalogItem.class,
    "getProductType() == \"Movie\"");

  // Start transaction.
  Transaction tr = Transaction.begin(ObjectStore.READONLY);

  Collection result = productQuery.select(catalogRoot);

  response.setContentType("text/html");
  PrintWriter out = response.getWriter();
```

9

SERVLETS
AND OBJECT
DATABASES

continues

LISTING 9.16   CONTINUED

```java
out.println("<html>");
out.println("<head><title>CatalogBasicServlet</title></head>");
out.println("<body>");

out.println("Query Found " + result.size() + " Movies." + "<BR>");
out.println("<BR>");
Iterator iterator = result.iterator();
int i = 0;
while(iterator.hasNext()) {
  i++;
  CatalogItem queryCatalogItem = (CatalogItem)iterator.next();
  Movie queryMovie = (Movie) queryCatalogItem.getProduct();
  out.println("Movie " + i + " is : " + queryMovie.getName()
    + "<BR>");
  out.println("description = " + queryMovie.getDescription()
    + "<BR>");
  out.println("category = " + queryMovie.getGenre()+ "<BR>");
  out.println("rating = " + queryMovie.getRating()+ "<BR>");
  out.println("format = " + queryMovie.getFormatType()+ "<BR>");
  out.println("actors = " + queryMovie.getTalent()+ "<BR>");
  out.println("quantity on hand = " +
    queryCatalogItem.getQuantity()+ "<BR>");
  out.println("<BR>");
}

out.println("</body></html>");
out.close();

tr.commit(ObjectStore.RETAIN_HOLLOW);
}

//Get Servlet information
public String getServletInfo() {

  return "BasicServlet Information";
}
// This method will create and open the database that is specified
//   on the command line when the Java application is invoked.
public static void createDatabase(String dbName) {
  System.out.println("Starting createDatabase("+dbName+")");

  // Attempt to open and destroy the database specified on the
  // command line.  This ensures that that program creates a
  // new database each time the application is called.
```

```
try {
  Database.open(dbName, ObjectStore.OPEN_UPDATE).destroy();
} catch (DatabaseNotFoundException e) {
}

// Create a new database.
db = Database.create(dbName,
  ObjectStore.ALL_READ | ObjectStore.ALL_WRITE);

// Build the data and store it in the OSTreeSet before
//   a transaction is started.
// Create books.
String authors[] = {"James Goodwill"};
Book servletBook = new Book("Developing Java Servlets",
  "Cool book on Servlets", "Sams Publishing", authors);
String authors2[] = {"Michael Morrison", "et. all"};
Book javaBook = new Book("Java Unleashed, Second Edition",
  "Cool book on Java", "Sams Publishing", authors2);

// Create movies.
String talent[] = {"Will Smith", "Tommy Lee Jones",
  "Linda Fiorentino"};
Movie menInBlack = new Movie("Men in Black",
  "Funny alien invasion movie", "Sci-Fi/Horror",
  "VHS", "PG-13", talent);
String talent2[] = {"Harrison Ford", "Gary Oldman"};
Movie airForceOne = new Movie("Air Force One",
  "Thriller about hijacking of Air Force One", "Action/Adventure",
  "VHS", "PG-13", talent2);

// Create instances catalog items.
CatalogItem book1 = new CatalogItem(servletBook, 2);
CatalogItem book2 = new CatalogItem(javaBook, 1);
CatalogItem movie1 = new CatalogItem(menInBlack, 1);
CatalogItem movie2 = new CatalogItem(airForceOne, 3);

// Start an update transaction.
Transaction tr = Transaction.begin(ObjectStore.UPDATE);

catalogRoot = new OSTreeSet(db);
catalogRoot.add(book1);
catalogRoot.add(book2);
catalogRoot.add(movie1);
catalogRoot.add(movie2);
db.createRoot("Catalog", catalogRoot);
```

9

SERVLETS
AND OBJECT
DATABASES

continues

LISTING 9.16   CONTINUED

```
    booksRoot = new OSVectorList(2);
    booksRoot.addElement(book1);
    booksRoot.addElement(book2);
    db.createRoot("Books", booksRoot);

    moviesRoot = new OSVectorList(2);
    moviesRoot.addElement(movie1);
    moviesRoot.addElement(movie2);
    db.createRoot("Movies", moviesRoot);

    // all database references will be STALE.
    tr.commit();
    System.out.println("Ending createDatabase("+dbName+")");
  }

// Populate the HOLLOW Roots.
public static void getRoots() {
  // Start a read-only transaction:
  Transaction tr = Transaction.begin(ObjectStore.READONLY);

  catalogRoot = (OSTreeSet)db.getRoot(CATALOG_ROOT_NAME);
  booksRoot = (OSVectorList)db.getRoot(BOOKS_ROOT_NAME);
  moviesRoot = (OSVectorList)db.getRoot(MOVIES_ROOT_NAME);

  // End the read-only transaction.  This makes the roots
  //  HOLLOW so later when used in a transaction, they don't
  //  have to be read from the database.
  tr.commit(ObjectStore.RETAIN_HOLLOW);
}

public static void addIndexToCatalogItems() {

  // Start transaction.
  Transaction tr = Transaction.begin(ObjectStore.UPDATE);

  catalogRoot.addIndex(CatalogItem.class, "getProductType()");

  tr.commit(ObjectStore.RETAIN_HOLLOW);
}
public void destroy() {
  super.destroy();
  // Insure shutdown is performed even if exception is caught.
  System.out.println("Closing database & terminating session.");
  db.close();
  aSession.terminate();
}
}
```

LISTING 9.17 CATALOGITEM.JAVA

```java
// Import the java related classes used in the example.
import java.io.*;
import java.util.*;

public class CatalogItem {

  // Fields in the CatalogItem class.
  private Product theProduct = null;
  private int quantity;

  private int initialBufferLength = 64;
  private String productType = null;
  private String productName = null;

  // Constructor
  public CatalogItem(Product inProduct, int inQuantity) {
    theProduct = inProduct;
    quantity = inQuantity;
    setProductType(theProduct.getClass().getName());
    setProductName();
}

  public int getQuantity() {
    return quantity ;
  }

  public void setQuantity(int inQuantity) {
    quantity = inQuantity;
  }

  public Product getProduct() {
    return theProduct;
  }

  public String getName() {
    return theProduct.getName();
  }

  public void setProductName() {
    productName = getName();
  }

  public String getProductName() {
    return productName;
  }
```

9

SERVLETS
AND OBJECT
DATABASES

continues

LISTING 9.17   CONTINUED

```java
public void setProductType(String packageProductType) {
  String tmp = null;
  StringTokenizer strTokenizer =
    new StringTokenizer(packageProductType, ".");
  while(strTokenizer.hasMoreTokens()) {
    tmp = strTokenizer.nextToken();
  }
  productType = tmp;
}

public String getProductType() {
  return productType;
}

public String toString() {
  StringBuffer productBuffer = new StringBuffer(initialBufferLength);
  productBuffer.append("CatalogItem=[Product="+ productType +
    ", Value={" + theProduct.toString() + "}], Quantity={" +
    quantity + "}");
  return productBuffer.toString();
}
}
```

LISTING 9.18   PRODUCT.JAVA

```java
public abstract class Product {

  private String name;
  private String description;

  protected int initialBufferLength = 64;

  public Product(String inName, String inDescription) {
    name = inName;
    description = inDescription;
  }

  public String getName() {
    return name;
  }

  public void setName(String inName) {
    name = inName;
  }
```

```
public String getDescription() {
  return description;
}

public void setDescription(String inDescription) {
  description = inDescription;
}

public abstract String toString();
}
```

LISTING 9.19   MOVIE.JAVA

```
public class Movie extends Product {
  private String genre;      /* Action Adventure, Comedy, Drama */
  private String formatType; /* VHS, DVD, LaserDisk */
  private String rating;     /* Rating for the movie, G,PG,PG-13,R */
  private String[] talent;   /* Actress/Actor */

  public Movie(String inName, String inDescription, String inGenre,
    String inFormatType, String inRating, String[] inTalent) {
    super(inName, inDescription);
    genre = inGenre;
    formatType = inFormatType;
    rating = inRating;
    talent = inTalent;
  }

  public String getGenre() {
    return genre;
  }

  public String getFormatType() {
    return formatType;
  }

  public String getRating() {
    return rating;
  }

  public String getTalent() {
    StringBuffer talentBuffer = new StringBuffer(initialBufferLength);
    for(int i=0; i<talent.length; i++) {
      if(i!= 0) {
        talentBuffer.append(",");
      }
```

9

continues

LISTING 9.19 CONTINUED

```java
        talentBuffer.append(talent[i]);
      }
    return talentBuffer.toString();
  }

  public String toString() {
    StringBuffer outputBuffer = new StringBuffer(initialBufferLength);
    outputBuffer.append("Name=" + getName() + ";" +
      "Description=" + getDescription() + ";" + "Genre=" + genre +
      ";" + "FormatType=" + formatType + ";" + "Rating=" + rating +
      "Talent=" + getTalent());
    return outputBuffer.toString();
  }
}
```

LISTING 9.20 BOOK.JAVA

```java
public class Book extends Product {

  private String publisher;    /* Publisher's name */
  private String[] authors;    /* Array of authors */

  public Book(String inName, String inDescription, String inPublisher,
    String[] inAuthors) {
    super(inName, inDescription);
    publisher = inPublisher;
    authors = inAuthors;
  }

  public String getAuthors() {
    StringBuffer authorBuffer = new StringBuffer(initialBufferLength);
    for(int i=0; i<authors.length; i++) {
      if(i!= 0) {
        authorBuffer.append(",");
      }
      authorBuffer.append(authors[i]);
    }
    return authorBuffer.toString();
  }
  public String toString() {
    StringBuffer outputBuffer = new StringBuffer(initialBufferLength);
    outputBuffer.append("Name=" + getName() + ";" + "Description=" +
      getDescription() + ";" + "Publisher=" + publisher +
      "Authors=" + getAuthors());
    return outputBuffer.toString();
  }
}
```

LISTING 9.21   CFPARGS.SERVLETS

```
-dest . -inplace
CatalogItem.class
Product.class
Book.class
Movie.class
-persistcapable CatalogItem.class Book.class Movie.class Product.class
-persistaware CatalogBasicServlet.class
```

Place all the files listed previously in the servlets directory. Compile the java files with the following command:

```
javac CatalogItem.java Book.java Product.java Movie.java
CatalogBasicServlet.java"
```

Then annotate the files by executing osjcfp @cfpargs.servlets in the same directory.

Because you are using the PSE Pro for Java libraries, you have to add an additional class path when you start the httpd process. Change to the directory where this executable is located and start the process with the following command:

- Windows—httpd -classpath
  <webserver_install>\servlets;<odi_install>\pro.zip;<odi_install>\tools.zip;

- UNIX—httpd -classpath
  <webserver_install>/servlets:<odi_install>/pro.zip:
  <odi_install>/tools.zip

Now you are ready to execute the CatalogBasicServlet. Enter the URL for the servlet in the browser as follows: http://localhost:8080/servlet/CatalogBasicServlet. If you have performed the steps properly, you should see output in your browser like Figure 9.5.

The CatalogBasicServlet.java is a persistent-aware class that deals with the PSE Pro catalog database. I set class-level variables much as I did in the CatalogManager.java class. Then in the init() method, I create a session, join it, createDatabase, store the roots (getRoots() method), and add an Index to the CatalogItems. These are essentially the same things that occurred in the CatalogManager.java class. I have moved the db.close() method and the session terminate() methods to the destroy() method of the servlet class. This is so that the database references will not be stale when I execute the query on the product name.

The doPost() method performs the query on product type Movie. The query returns a collection of CatalogItems in line 56:

```
Collection result = productQuery.select(catalogRoot);
```

Now I set up a PrintWriter to write the results back to the client in HTML. First I iterate over the collection and extract each CatalogItem. Because I know that I will get back only movies, I retrieve the Movie out of the CatalogItem and write the output to the client's page in HTML. Finally, I write out the quantity of the CatalogItem that is in the database.

FIGURE 9.5

Output from CatalogBasicServlet.

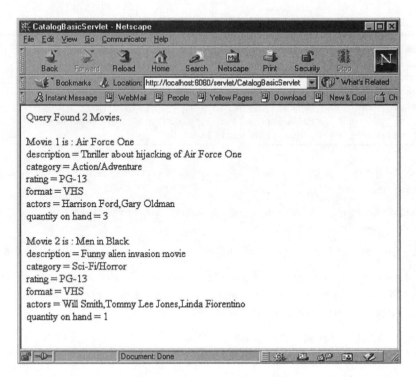

SUMMARY

In this chapter you learned the basics of a particular object-oriented database, ObjectStore's PSE Pro for Java 3.0. I have illustrated the following points in the chapter:

- How to make objects persistent
- How to make objects that deal with the database persistent aware
- How to create database roots to access objects in PSE Pro
- How to query objects in PSE Pro
- How to speed up the queries with an index
- How to use an object-oriented database in a servlet

Now, if I have succeeded, you should have enough information on ObjectDesign's products to effectively decide whether it is the appropriate persistent storage for a future project.

SERVLETBEANS

IN THIS CHAPTER

WHAT IS A JAVABEAN?

Before you can start learning about ServletBeans, you must take a look at what a bean is. A JavaBean is a 100 percent Java component that works on any Java Virtual Machine. The following is the minimum set of requirements that make a component a JavaBean:

- It must support the JDK 1.1 Serialization model.
- It must use get/set accessors to expose properties.

There is nothing magical about creating a JavaBean. You just create a Java class that implements a serializable interface and uses public get/set methods to expose its properties. Listing 10.1 contains a simple JavaBean.

LISTING 10.1   SIMPLEJAVABEAN.JAVA

```
import java.io.Serializable;

public class SimpleJavaBean implements java.io.Serializable{

  private String simpleProperty = new String("");

  public SimpleJavaBean() {

  }

  public String getSimpleProperty() {

    return simpleProperty;
  }

  public void setSimpleProperty(String value) {

    simpleProperty = value;
  }
}
```

This class is now a JavaBean. It satisfies the minimum requirements. You can now load the SimpleJavaBean into any JavaBeans aware program that uses introspection and change its properties. Its state can then be saved and reloaded any time because of its support of serialization.

I will show you an example that illustrates how to serialize the new bean. The example in Listing 10.2 creates an instance of our SimpleJavaBean, sets the simpleProperty to simple property value, serializes the bean to a file, reads the bean back in, and finally displays proof that its state was maintained.

LISTING 10.2 SIMPLEJAVABEANTESTER.JAVA

```java
import java.io.*;

public class SimpleJavaBeanTester {

  public SimpleJavaBeanTester() {

  }

  public void storeBean(SimpleJavaBean value) {

    try {

      // Create the ObjectOutputStream passing it the
      // FileOutputStream object that points to our
      // persistent storage.
      ObjectOutputStream os = new ObjectOutputStream(
        new FileOutputStream("file.dat"));
      // Write the SimpleJavaBean to the ObjectOutputStream
      os.writeObject(value);
      os.flush();
      os.close();
    }
    catch (IOException ioe) {

      System.err.println(ioe.getMessage());
    }
  }

  public SimpleJavaBean getBean() {

    SimpleJavaBean value = null;

    try {

      // Create the ObjectInputStream passing it the
      // FileInputStream object that points to our
      // persistent storage.
      ObjectInputStream is = new ObjectInputStream(
        new FileInputStream("file.dat"));
      // Read the stored object and downcast it back to
      // a SimpleJavaBean
      value = (SimpleJavaBean)is.readObject();
      is.close();
    }
```

10

SERVLETBEANS

continues

LISTING 10.2   CONTINUED

```java
    catch (IOException ioe) {

      System.err.println(ioe.getMessage());
    }
    catch (ClassNotFoundException cnfe) {

      System.err.println(cnfe.getMessage());
    }
    return value;
  }

  public void testBean() {

    // Create the Bean
    SimpleJavaBean simpleBean = new SimpleJavaBean();
    // Use accessor to set property
    simpleBean.setSimpleProperty("simple property value");
    // Serialize the Bean to a Persistent Store
    storeBean(simpleBean);

    // Get the Bean from the Persistent Store
    SimpleJavaBean newBean = getBean();

    System.out.println("The newBean's simpleProperty == " +
      newBean.getSimpleProperty());
  }

  public static void main(String[] args) {

    SimpleJavaBeanTester simpleJavaBeanTester =
      new SimpleJavaBeanTester();

    simpleJavaBeanTester.testBean();

    try {

      System.out.println("Press enter to continue...");
      System.in.read();
    }
    catch (IOException ioe) {

      System.err.println(ioe.getMessage());
    }
  }
}
```

If you build and run this application, the output should look similar to this:

```
The newBean's simpleProperty == simple property value
Press enter to continue...
```

WHAT IS A SERVLETBEAN?

A ServletBean is a serializable servlet that follows the JavaBeans architecture for getting and setting properties. In most cases, the only thing a servlet must do to satisfy these requirements is use get/set accessors when setting the servlet's properties. Because most servlets extend either the GenericServlet or HttpServlet objects, they are automatically satisfying the serializable requirement. This is because the GenericServlet implements the java.io.Serializable interface.

CREATING A SERVLETBEAN

Now that you understand what a ServletBean is, you can create a simple example. This ServletBean is going to expose a single property name. It does this by defining two public accessors setName() and getName(). When the servlet is executed, it prints the HTML message Hello : plus the value stored in the name attribute. Take a look at the source in Listing 10.3.

LISTING 10.3 SIMPLESERVLETBEAN.JAVA

```java
import javax.servlet.*;
import javax.servlet.http.*;
import java.io.*;
import java.util.*;

public class SimpleServletBean extends HttpServlet {

  // This value will be set by the Java Web Server
  private String name = "";

  // Public Accessors
  public void setName(String value) {

    if ( value != null ) {

      name = value;
    }
  }
```

continues

LISTING 10.3   CONTINUED

```java
public String getName() {

  return name;
}

public void init(ServletConfig config)
  throws ServletException {

  super.init(config);
}

//Process the HTTP Get request
public void doGet(HttpServletRequest request,
  HttpServletResponse response)
  throws ServletException, IOException {

  doPost(request, response);
}

//Process the HTTP Post request
public void doPost(HttpServletRequest request,
  HttpServletResponse response)
  throws ServletException, IOException {

  response.setContentType("text/html");
  PrintWriter out = response.getWriter();
  out.println("<html>");
  out.println("<head><title>SimpleServletBean</title></head>");
  out.println("<body>");

  out.println("Hello : " + getName() + "<BR>");

  out.println("</body></html>");
  out.close();
}

//Get Servlet information
public String getServletInfo() {

  return "SimpleServletBean Information";
}
}
```

PACKAGING, INSTALLING, AND EXECUTING A SERVLETBEAN

Before you can execute the `SimpleServletBean`, you must install it to the Java Web Server.

NOTE

Currently the only server that supports ServletBeans is the Java Web Server.

Jarring Your ServletBean

The first step in installing your ServletBean is to build and package it into a Java Archive File (JAR). To do this, you will need to use the `jar` utility that is part of the JDK. The following are the command-line parameters of the `jar` utility:

```
jar cvf targetfile.jar sourcefile.class
```

To `jar` the `SimpleServletBean`, you would type the following command:

```
jar cvf SimpleServletBean.jar SimpleServletBean.class
```

After you run this command, perform a directory listing. Make sure that you have the `SimpleServletBean.jar` file.

Installing the SimpleServletBean

Servlet beans can be installed to any one of the following directories:

- The `servlet/` directory
- The `servletbeans/` directory
- Any directory in the Java Web Server's CLASSPATH

It is best to install your servlet bean in the `servletbeans/` directory. This is the only ServletBean directory that will take advantage of the Java Web Server's automatic reloading feature, which reloads the servlet every time the `jar` file changes.

After you have the `jar` file in the appropriate directory, it's time to configure the ServletBean using the Java Web Server's servlet configuration screen. To do this you will need to follow these steps:

1. Open the servlet configuration screen as described in Chapter 2. You should see a screen similar to Figure 10.1.

10

SERVLETBEANS

FIGURE 10.1

The servlet configuration screen.

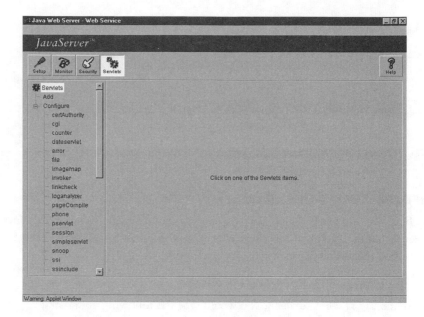

2. Select the Add option on the tree control. You should now see an Add a New Servlet screen similar to Figure 10.2.

FIGURE 10.2

The Add a New Servlet screen.

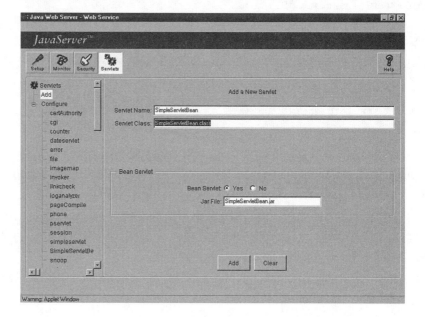

3. Enter the options found in Table 10.1.

TABLE 10.1 NEW SERVLET OPTIONS

Option	Value
Servlet Name	SimpleServletBean
Servlet Class	SimpleServletBean.class
Bean Servlet	Yes
Jar File	SimpleServletBean.jar

4. Press the Add button. You should now see the servlet configuration screen.

5. Select the Properties tab. The servlet properties screen should look similar to Figure 10.3.

FIGURE 10.3

The servlet properties screen.

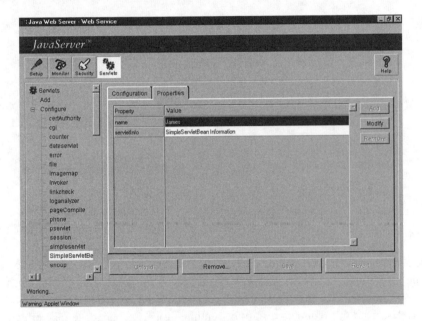

At this point the SimpleServletBean is installed. Notice that the servlet properties screen contains the name property from your servlet. Just like a GUI builder or the Bean Box, the Java Web Server can determine what the ServletBean's properties are through introspection. Now you are not forced to memorize the properties of a servlet. Instead, they are automatically available through the servlet properties screen. Go ahead and enter the string James (or any other name) as the value of the name property. Press the Modify and then Save buttons.

Executing the SimpleServletBean

You can invoke the ServletBean just like any other servlet. For this example, I am just going to use the URL that points to the servlet. The URL, on my local server, is listed as follows:

```
http://localhost:8080/servlet/SimpleServletBean
```

Open this URL using your Web browser. Notice that the URL still references the `servlet/` directory, and the Web server will automatically search the `servletbeans/` directory for the servlet. The output should look similar to Figure 10.4.

FIGURE 10.4

Output of the SimpleServletBean.

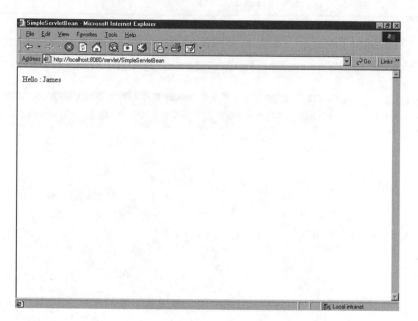

After you have executed it once, go back to the servlet properties screen and enter a different value for the name. After the property change has been saved, press the Refresh button on your browser. You will see that the results already reflect the property change. This is because ServletBeans don't require a restart for runtime property changes to take effect.

NOTE

You could have used `init` parameters to pass configuration parameters to the servlet in the `ServletConfig`, but there is no automatic mapping to properties and no automatic property updates.

CREATING A PRACTICAL SERVLETBEAN

In my final example, I am going to create a ServletBean that acts as a contacts page. It would be used to display a particular company's contact information. The reason I am making this particular servlet a bean is to show how this technology simplifies the packaging and distribution of servlets.

NOTE

You could easily embed this servlet as a server-side include.

The `ContactsServletBean` example exposes nine properties. These properties represent the contact information of the company. The properties I am going to use for my example can be found in Figure 10.5.

FIGURE 10.5

ContactsServletBean's servlet properties screen.

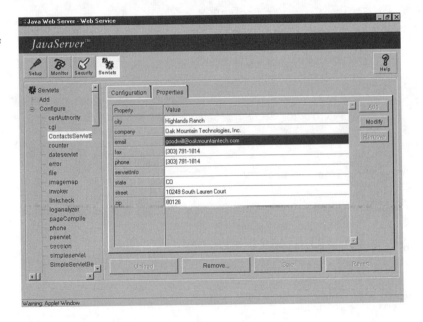

Because the company's contact information is exposed as properties in a ServletBean, any company could use the `ContactsServletBean` with changes only to the servlet properties screen. Listing 10.4 contains the source of the new ServletBean.

LISTING 10.4   CONTACTSSERVLETBEAN.JAVA

```java
import javax.servlet.*;
import javax.servlet.http.*;
import java.io.*;
import java.util.*;

public class ContactsServletBean extends HttpServlet {

  // contact attributes
  private String company = new String("");
  private String street = new String("");
  private String city = new String("");
  private String state = new String("");
  private String zip = new String("");
  private String email = new String("");
  private String phone = new String("");
  private String fax = new String("");

  // Accessors that make this a Bean
  public void setCompany(String value) {

    if ( value != null ) {

      company = value;
    }
  }

  public String getCompany() {

    return company;
  }

  public void setEmail(String value) {

    if ( value != null ) {

      email = value;
    }
  }

  public String getEmail() {

    return email;
  }

  public void setFax(String value) {
```

```
  if ( value != null ) {

    fax = value;
  }
}

public String getFax() {

  return fax;
}

public void setPhone(String value) {

  if ( value != null ) {

    phone = value;
  }
}

public String getPhone() {

  return phone;
}

public void setStreet(String value) {

  if ( value != null ) {

    street = value;
  }
}

public String getStreet() {

  return street;
}

public void setCity(String value) {

  if ( value != null ) {

    city = value;
  }
}

public String getCity() {
```

continues

LISTING 10.4   CONTINUED

```java
    return city;
  }

  public void setState(String value) {

    if ( value != null ) {

      state = value;
    }
  }

  public String getState() {

    return state;
  }

  public void setZip(String value) {

    if ( value != null ) {

      zip = value;
    }
  }

  public String getZip() {

    return zip;
  }


  public void init(ServletConfig config)
    throws ServletException {

    super.init(config);
  }

  //Process the HTTP Get request
  public void doGet(HttpServletRequest request,
    HttpServletResponse response)
    throws ServletException, IOException {
```

```
      doPost(request, response);
  }
//Process the HTTP Post request

  public void doPost(HttpServletRequest request,
    HttpServletResponse response)
    throws ServletException, IOException {

    response.setContentType("text/html");
    PrintWriter out = response.getWriter();

    // HTML Output
    out.println("<CENTER>");

    // Use the bean accessors to get data
    out.println(getCompany() + "<BR>");
    out.println(getStreet() + "<BR>");
    out.println(getCity() + "," + getState() + " " + getZip()
      + "<BR>");
    out.println(getEmail() + "<BR>");
    out.println(getPhone() + "<BR>");
    out.println(getFax() + "<BR>");
    out.println("</CENTER>");

    out.close();
  }
}
```

After you have built the ContactsServletBean, make sure that you "jar" it and move it to the servletbeans/ directory. You must then add and configure the ServletBean. You can then invoke it using the URL http://localhost:8080/servlet/ContactsServletBean. The output should look similar to Figure 10.6.

When you are comfortable with how the ContactsServletBean works, go into the servlet properties screen and change the values to represent your company's contact information. When the new properties are saved, press the Refresh button on your browser. You will see that the servlet is now customized for your company and no code change or recompilation was necessary.

FIGURE 10.6

Output from the ContactsServlet-Bean.

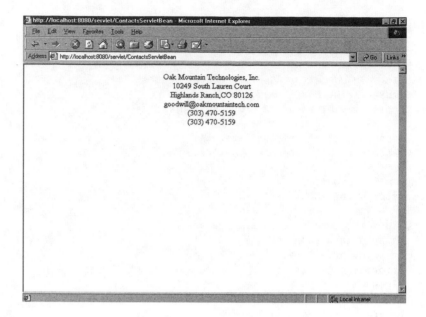

SUMMARY

In this chapter, I covered what a JavaBean is and how to create a servlet that follows the JavaBean architecture. I discussed how to package, install, and invoke a ServletBean. I also created a practical example that demonstrated how easy it is to reuse ServletBeans.

At this point, you should be able to create your own ServletBeans. You should know how to change the servlet's properties, using the servlet properties screen. You should also be able to package a ServletBean for distribution.

JAVASERVER PAGES

IN THIS CHAPTER

WHAT ARE JAVASERVER PAGES?

JavaServer Pages, also known as JSP, are a simple but powerful technology used to generate dynamic HTML on the server side. It provides a way to separate content generation from content presentation. The JSP engine is just another servlet that is mapped to the extension `*.jsp`. The following listing contains a simple example of a JSP file:

```
<HTML>
<BODY>

<%@ content_type="text/html" %>
<% out.println("HELLO JSP WORLD"); %>

</BODY>
</HTML>
```

Its output would look similar to Figure 11.1.

FIGURE 11.1

Output of the JSP example.

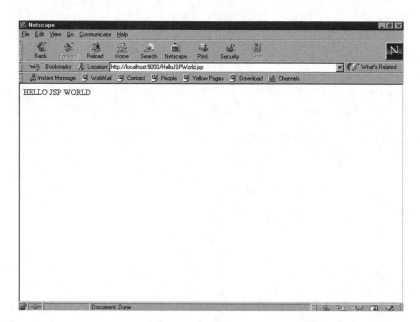

You can see that this document looks like any other HTML document with some added tags containing Java code. The previous listing is stored in a file called `HelloJSPWorld.jsp` and copied to the document directory of the Web server. When a request is made of this document, the server recognizes the `*.jsp` extension and realizes that special handling is required. The first time the file is requested, it is compiled into a servlet object and stored in memory, and the output is sent back to the requesting client. After the first request, the server checks to see whether the `*.jsp` file has changed. If it has not changed, the server invokes the previously compiled servlet object. Figure 11.2 shows these steps graphically.

FIGURE 11.2
Steps of a JSP request.

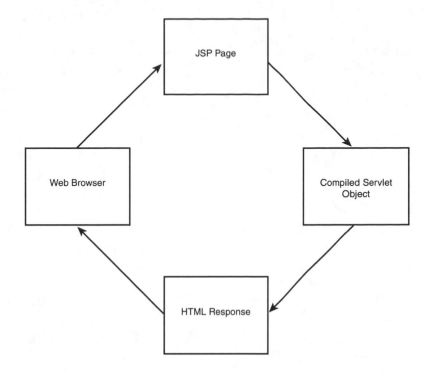

BEANS

JavaBeans play a very large role in JSP documents. The hierarchical naming convention used to reference a JavaBean inside a JSP document is as follows:

- Format: `beanname:propertyname`
- Example: `counter:count`

This example shows the name of the bean as `counter` and the property that is being addressed as `count`. Also notice that a colon (:) is used instead of a period (.) when referencing bean component properties.

Two types of JavaBeans are used in JSP documents: user-defined JavaBeans and implicit JavaBeans.

User-Defined JavaBeans

The tags I am going to describe in this section allow you to reference user-defined JavaBeans anywhere within a JSP file. These tags are defined in the following sections.

<USEBEAN></USEBEAN>

The <USEBEAN></USEBEAN> tags make a JavaBean available for use with the rest of the JSP document. When you include this tag in your JSP file, you have begun the life cycle of the referenced bean. The general format of the USEBEAN tags is listed in the following (note that each one of these attributes is required):

```
<USEBEAN
    NAME="nameofbeaninstance"
    TYPE="nameofbeanclass"
    LIFESPAN="page|session|application">
</USEBEAN>
```

- NAME—The value of this attribute is a case-sensitive name of a specific bean instance. To avoid conflicts, this value should not appear more than once in a single file.

- TYPE—The value of this attribute is the case-sensitive name of the bean class.

- LIFESPAN—This attribute defines the life span of a bean. Its values are defined in Table 11.1.

TABLE 11.1   LIFESPAN VALUES

Attribute Value	Description
page	The bean is available only to this request.
session	This bean exists throughout this HTTP session.
application	This bean lives for the entire life of the application.

<SETONCREATE>

This tag sets the initial values of a JavaBean's properties. It can only be used inside the <USEBEAN></USEBEAN> tags. The following is an example:

```
<SETONCREATE BEANPROPERTY="name" VALUE="Bob">
```

When using <SETONCREATE>, you must include both of its attributes to set the bean's property. The first attribute, BEANPROPERTY, names the actual bean property that is going to be set. The second attribute, VALUE, is the value that the property is being set to. My example sets the value of the name property to "Bob".

<SETFROMREQUEST>

This tag defines a request parameter to bean property mapping. It can also be used only inside the <USEBEAN></USEBEAN> tags. A sample use of this property is listed in the following:

```
<SETFROMREQUEST BEANPROPERTY="index" PARAMNAME="index_value">
```

The first attribute, BEANPROPERTY, names the bean property that is going to be set. The second attribute, PARAMNAME, is the name of the parameter in the incoming request. Its value will be stored in the previously named bean property.

The <SETFROMREQUEST>'s attributes can be formatted in the following three ways:

- <SETFROMREQUEST BEANPROPERTY="*">—When using the wildcard character, the BEAN-PARAMETER matches any property name. This means that all parameter/bean matches are set.

- <SETFROMREQUEST BEANPROPERTY="propertyname">—When the PARAMNAME attribute is not present, the value of the BEANPROPERTY is used for both attributes.

- <SETFROMREQUEST BEANPROPERTY="propertyname" PARANAME="request param name">—This is the fully qualified syntax of the <SETFROMREQUEST>'s attribute settings.

Property Display Tags

You can display two types of bean properties: single-value properties and multivalued properties. An instance in which you would display a combination of these occurs when a bean's property contains other beans with properties. These are nested properties. Take a look at the general syntax used to display a bean property:

```
<DISPLAY PROPERTY="beanname:property" PLACEHOLDER="defaultvalue">
```

The first DISPLAY attribute PROPERTY is the name of the bean and the bean's property to display, separated by a colon. The PLACEHOLDER attribute is an optional attribute that defines a value to display whether the bean's property value is missing or invalid.

NOTE

Inside the DISPLAY tag, Java native types will automatically be converted to a String. All other objects will have their toString() method called.

The easiest property type to display is the single-value property. This is when the bean's property holds a single value, like an integer. An example of the syntax used to display a single value is listed as follows:

```
<DISPLAY PROPERTY="hello:name">
```

This line displays the hello bean's property name. You could include this exact syntax anywhere in your HTML document, and it would display the name value.

NOTE

To display a bean's property value, the bean must first be created using the <USEBEAN></USEBEAN> tags.

The second type of bean property that can be displayed is a multivalue property. An example of this type would be a Vector or an array. The syntax for displaying multivalue properties is listed in the following:

```
<LOOP PROPERTY="beanname:indexedproperty" PROPERTYELEMENT="x">
<DISPLAY PROPERTY="x" PLACEHOLDER="substitutevalue">
</LOOP>
```

The two attributes you need to look at for the LOOP tag are the PROPERTY and PROPERTYELEMENT tags. The PROPERTY tag references the bean's indexed property. The PROPERTYELEMENT tag represents a single value of the multi-valued property. Take a look at an example bean that contains a multi-valued property and the JSP syntax used to display its values.

The bean I am going to display contains a list of names. The names are represented by a String type. For the JSP servlet to get access to the length of a multivalue property, the bean must expose a method that returns the number of elements in the property. The sample bean does this with the getListSize() method. It must also expose an accessor that takes an index value and returns the actual property value, which is accomplished by the getList() method of the sample bean. The sample bean can be found in Listing 11.1. Compile this bean and move it into your server's CLASSPATH.

LISTING 11.1   MULTIVALUEDBEAN.JAVA

```java
package Chapter11;

import java.util.*;

public class MultiValuedBean {

  // Multi-valued property
  private Vector list = new Vector(5);

  public MultiValuedBean() {

    // Build the list
    list.addElement(new String("Bob"));
    list.addElement(new String("Steve"));
    list.addElement(new String("Christy"));
    list.addElement(new String("Abby"));
    list.addElement(new String("Peyton"));
  }

  // This accessor returns a single property value
  // found at index.
  public String getList(int index) {

    return (String)list.elementAt(index);
  }

  // Returns the number of elements found in the
  // multi-valued property list.
  public int getListSize() {

    return list.size();
  }
}
```

NOTE

Other ways to expose the length and individual values of the property exist. You can find examples of them in the JSP 0.92 specification on the JavaSoft Web site.

The JSP file that displays this bean's values can be found in Listing 11.2. Make sure that you save this file in your server's <DOCUMENT_ROOT> directory.

LISTING 11.2 MULTIVALUEDBEAN.JSP

```
<HTML>
<BODY>

<USEBEAN NAME="listbean" TYPE="Chapter11.MultiValuedBean"
➥LIFESPAN="page">
</USEBEAN>

<LOOP PROPERTY="listbean:list" PROPERTYELEMENT="x">
<DISPLAY PROPERTY="x"><BR>
</LOOP>

</BODY>
</HTML>
```

Now load the JSP file into your browser. The output should look similar to Figure 11.3.

FIGURE 11.3

The output of JSP MutliValued-Bean.jsp.

Implicit JavaBeans

Two beans are provided to all JSP documents. They are the request and exception beans.

The request bean encapsulates the client's request. This bean provides the same information found in the HttpServletRequest.

The exception bean contains information about the most recent error. It can only be accessed from a JSP document defined by the errorpage directive, which will be discussed in the "Directives" section of this chapter. The exception bean is derived from java.lang.Throwable; therefore, you have access to all its methods.

CONDITIONS

The JSP 0.92 specification also provides the ability to include or exclude a section of a JSP document based on a JavaBean's property value. This functionality can be used only if the bean's property returns either a String or Java native type. The two JSP tags that provide this functionality are INCLUDEIF and EXCLUDEIF. The following code shows the syntax of these conditional tags:

```
<INCLUDEIF PROPERTY="bean:property" VALUE="valuetomatch"
CASE="sensitive¦insensitive" MATCH="null¦exact¦contains¦
startswith¦endswith">
```

This syntax can be interchanged between the INCLUDEIF and EXCLUDEIF tags. Each attribute is defined in the following:

- PROPERTY—The bean property you want to compare.
- VALUE—The value to compare to the value of the bean's property.
- CASE—This value determines whether the comparison should be case-sensitive or not case-sensitive. The default is not case-sensitive.
- MATCH—This attribute determines the type of comparison to perform. The comparison types are null, contains, exact, endswith, and startswith. The default is exact.

DIRECTIVES

Directives determine how the JSP servlet will interpret the code in a JSP file. Directives should always appear at the top of the document. The general syntax of a JSP directive is listed as follows:

```
<%@ variable="value" %>
```

Notice that directives are essentially tag/value pairs, where the tag equals the directive name and the value equals what you want to set the directive to. You should also notice that there must be a space on both sides of the tag/value pair. The three types of directives are listed in the following:

- language—The language directive defines the language that will be used inside scriptlets and expressions. Currently the default is Java, but soon there might be others. It would be a good idea to go ahead and always include the specific language. An example of setting the `language` directive is listed as follows:

```
<%@ language="java" %>
```

- `errorpage`—The `errorpage` directive defines an HTML or JSP page to display whether the current JSP document results in an error. An example of setting the `errorpage` directive is listed as follows:

```
<%@ errorpage="reporterrorpage.jsp" %>
```

- `import`—The `import` directive defines a comma-delimited list of packages to be imported for use by all scriptlets and expressions in a particular file. An example of setting the `import` directive is listed as follows:

```
<%@ import="java.util.*,java.sql.*" %>
```

DECLARATIONS

The JSP 0.92 provides a simple way to define page-wide variables. It does this by using the `<SCRIPT>` tag. The general syntax of the `<SCRIPT>` tag is listed in the following:

```
<SCRIPT RUNAT="location">

    declarations

</SCRIPT>
```

The only attribute available to the `<SCRIPT>` tag is the `RUNAT` attribute. The `RUNAT` attribute determines where the code between the opening and closing tags will be executed. The available values are `client` or `server`.

IMPLICIT VARIABLES

Four variables are automatically available to a JSP file. Each of these variables is described in the following:

- `request`—This is a reference to the `HttpServletRequest` object.
- `response`—This is a reference to the `HttpServletResponse` object.
- `in`—This is a reference to the `BufferedReader` object that is part of the client request.
- `out`—This is a reference to the `PrintWriter` object that will be sent back to the client.

SCRIPTLETS

Scriptlets provide the ability to directly insert code into an HTML document. Scriptlets can contain any code that is valid based on the language specified in the language directive. I will be concentrating only on Java code. The syntax of a JSP scriptlet is listed as follows:

```
<% "java code" %>
```

There must be a space on both sides of the Java code.

Scriptlets make heavy use of the implicit variables described previously. An example scriptlet, using the `request` and `out` variables, is listed in the following:

```
<HTML>
<BODY>

<%@ language="java" %>

<%

out.println("Your address is: " + request.getRemoteAddr() );

%>

</BODY>
</HTML>
```

This example calls the request's `getRemoteAddr()` method to get the address of the client and writes it to the variable `out`. Its output should look something like Figure 11.4.

FIGURE 11.4
Output of JSP Scriptlet-Example.jsp.

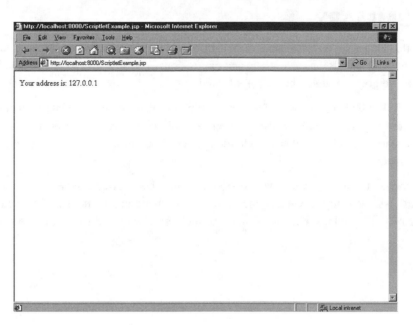

EXPRESSIONS

JSP expressions are like single-line scriptlets. You can think of an expression as a tag that will be replaced by the value of the evaluated expression. An example of an expression is listed in the following:

```
<HTML>
<BODY>

Your address is: <%= request.getRemoteAddr() %>

</BODY>
</HTML>
```

When this JSP file is requested by the client, the expression is evaluated by the JSP servlet, and the result is placed in the HTML response and sent back to the client. The resulting HTML will be similar to the following code snippet:

```
<HTML>
<BODY>

Your address is: 127.0.0.1

</BODY>
</HTML>
```

SUMMARY

In this chapter, I covered quite a bit of information. You should be able to create a JSP document using JavaBeans, scriptlets, and expressions. You should also understand the process a JSP file goes through when it is requested.

The JSP 0.92 specification, which at the time of this writing is the latest specification, is 54 printed pages and could easily be an entire book. I have tried to cover the main topics to get you started, but it would be a good idea to get a copy of the specification from the Javasoft Web site.

In the next chapter, I will cover session handling. I will discuss several different ways to maintain sessions using servlets. Some of the session-handling methods I will discuss are hidden forms field, cookies, URL rewriting, and the Servlet API's session handling functionality.

SERVLET SESSIONS

IN THIS CHAPTER

WHAT IS SESSION TRACKING?

Session tracking is the capability of a server to maintain the current state of a single client's sequential requests. The HTTP protocol used by Web servers is stateless. This means that every transaction is autonomous. This type of stateless transaction is not a problem unless you need to know the sequence of actions a client has performed while at your site.

For example, an online video store must be able to determine each visitor's sequence of actions. Suppose a customer goes to your site to order a movie. The first thing he does is look at the available titles. When he has found the title he is interested in, he makes his selection. The problem now is determining who made the selection. Because each one of the client's requests is independent of the previous requests, you have no idea who actually made the final selection.

> **NOTE**
>
> You could use HTTP authentication as a method of session tracking, but each of your customers would need an account on your site. This is fine for some businesses, but would be a hassle for a high-volume site. You probably could not get every user that simply wants to browse through the available videos to open an account.

In this chapter, you are going to look at several different ways to determine the actions that a particular client has taken. You will be examining hidden form fields, cookies, URL rewriting, and the built-in session tracking functionality found in the servlet API.

USING HIDDEN FORM FIELDS

Using hidden form fields is one of the simplest session-tracking techniques. Hidden form fields are HTML input types that are not displayed when read by a browser. A sample HTML listing that includes hidden form fields is listed in the following:

```
<HTML>
<BODY>

<FORM ACTION="someaction" METHOD="post">

<INPUT TYPE="hidden" NAME="tag1" VALUE="value1">
<INPUT TYPE="hidden" NAME="tag2" VALUE="value2">

<INPUT TYPE="submit">
```

```
</FORM>

</BODY>
</HTML>
```

When you open this HTML document in a browser, the input types marked as hidden will not be visible. They will, however, be transmitted in the request.

I will create a simple example that shows how this technique works. I am going to create a servlet that can service both POST and GET methods. In the doGet() method, I am going to build a form that contains hidden fields and an action that points to the servlet's doPost() method. The doPost() method will then parse the hidden values sent in the request and echo them back to the client. The example is found in Listing 12.1.

LISTING 12.1   HIDDENFIELDSERVLET.JAVA

```java
import javax.servlet.*;
import javax.servlet.http.*;
import java.io.*;
import java.util.*;

public class HiddenFieldServlet extends HttpServlet {

  public void init(ServletConfig config)
    throws ServletException {

    super.init(config);
  }

  //Process the HTTP Get request
  public void doGet(HttpServletRequest request,
    HttpServletResponse response)
    throws ServletException, IOException {

    response.setContentType("text/html");
    PrintWriter out = response.getWriter();
    out.println("<html>");
    out.println("<head><title>HiddenFieldServlet" +
      "</title></head>");
    out.println("<body>");

    // Create the Form with Hidden Fields
    out.println("<FORM ACTION=" +
      "\"/servlet/HiddenFieldServlet\" METHOD=\"POST\">");
```

continues

LISTING 12.1   CONTINUED

```java
    // These values would be uniquely generated
    out.println("<INPUT TYPE=\"hidden\" NAME=" +
      "\"user\" VALUE=\"James\">");

    out.println("<INPUT TYPE=\"hidden\" NAME=" +
      "\"session\" VALUE=\"12892\">");

    // These are the currently selected movies
    out.println("<INPUT TYPE=\"hidden\" NAME=" +
      "\"movie\" VALUE=\"Happy Gilmore\">");

    out.println("<INPUT TYPE=\"hidden\" NAME=" +
      "\"movie\" VALUE=\"So I Married an Axe Murderer\">");

    out.println("<INPUT TYPE=\"hidden\" NAME=" +
      "\"movie\" VALUE=\"Jaws\">");

    out.println("<INPUT TYPE=\"submit\" VALUE=" +
      "\"Finished Shopping\">");
    out.println("</FORM>");

    out.println("</body></html>");
    out.close();
  }

  //Process the HTTP Post request
  public void doPost(HttpServletRequest request,
    HttpServletResponse response)
    throws ServletException, IOException {

    response.setContentType("text/html");
    PrintWriter out = response.getWriter();
    out.println("<html>");
    out.println("<head><title>HiddenFieldServlet" +
      "</title></head>");
    out.println("<body>");

    // Get the hidden inputs and echo them
    String user = request.getParameter("user");
    String session = request.getParameter("session");

    out.println("<H3>" + user +
      ", the contents of your Shopping Basket are:</H3><BR>");
```

```
        String[] movies = request.getParameterValues("movie");

    if ( movies != null ) {

      for ( int x = 0; x < movies.length; x++ ) {

        out.println(movies[x] + "<BR>");
      }
    }

    out.println("</body></html>");
    out.close();
  }

  //Get Servlet information
  public String getServletInfo() {

    return "HiddenFieldServlet Information";
  }
}
```

When you have this servlet installed, open your browser to the servlet's URL. The URL on my local box is listed as follows:

```
http://localhost:8000/servlet/HiddenFieldServlet
```

When the servlet is loaded, you should only see a Finished Shopping button. If you view the current HTML source, you will see a listing similar to this snippet:

```
<html>
<head><title>HiddenFieldServlet</title></head>
<body>
<FORM ACTION="/servlet/HiddenFieldServlet" METHOD="POST">
<INPUT TYPE="hidden" NAME="user" VALUE="James">
<INPUT TYPE="hidden" NAME="session" VALUE="12892">
<INPUT TYPE="hidden" NAME="movie" VALUE="Happy Gilmore">
<INPUT TYPE="hidden" NAME="movie" VALUE="So I Married an Axe Murderer">
<INPUT TYPE="hidden" NAME="movie" VALUE="Jaws">
<INPUT TYPE="submit" VALUE="Finished Shopping">
</FORM>
</body></html>
```

Notice the hidden fields. Now press the Finished Shopping button.

The form invokes the doPost() method of the HiddenFieldServlet. This method parses the hidden fields out of the request and displays them in a "shopping cart" listing. Figure 12.1 shows the results of the HiddenFieldServlet's doPost() method.

FIGURE 12.1

Output of HiddenFieldServlet.

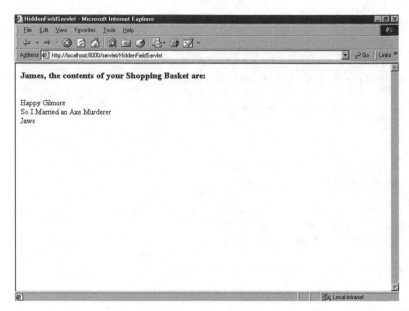

You can see that hidden form fields have their advantages. They are easy to implement and are supported by most browsers. This technique also has its disadvantages. The hidden fields must be created in a particular sequence. You are not able to press the Back button on your browser without losing the additional fields added to the current page. You are also restricted to dynamically generated documents.

WORKING WITH COOKIES

One of the more elegant solutions to session tracking is persistent cookies. Cookies were first introduced by Netscape in one of the company's first versions of Netscape Navigator.

A *cookie* is a keyed piece of data that is created by the server and stored by the client browser. Browsers maintain their own list of unique cookies. This makes cookies a very viable solution for session tracking.

The Servlet API provides built-in support for cookies. It does this through the use of the `Cookie` class and the `HttpServletResponse.addCookie()` and `HttpServletRequest.getCookies()` methods.

The `Cookie` class encapsulates persistent cookies as defined by RFC 2109. The prototype for the `Cookie`'s constructor takes a `String` representing the unique name of the cookie and a `String` representing the value of the cookie, and it is listed as follows:

```
public Cookie(String name, String value)
```

The Cookie class also provides accessors used to get and set the values of the cookie. Listing 12.2 contains an example of using cookies to perform session handling.

LISTING 12.2   COOKIESERVLET.JAVA

```java
import javax.servlet.*;
import javax.servlet.http.*;
import java.io.*;
import java.util.*;

public class CookieServlet extends HttpServlet {
//Initialize global variables

  public void init(ServletConfig config)
    throws ServletException {

    super.init(config);
  }

  private String getCurrentUser(String value) {

    String userName = new String("");

    // This would normally be a Select from a database or
    // other storage area.
    if ( value.equals("564XX892") ) {

      userName = new String("Bob");
    }
    return userName;
  }

  //Process the HTTP Get request
  public void doGet(HttpServletRequest request,
    HttpServletResponse response)
    throws ServletException, IOException {

    // Get the list of Cookies stored in the request
    Cookie[] cookieList = request.getCookies();
    String user = null;
    String responseString = null;

    if ( cookieList != null ) {

      // Cookies found, let's get the session id
      for ( int x = 0; x < cookieList.length; x++ ) {
```

continues

LISTING 12.2   CONTINUED

```
    String name = cookieList[x].getName();

    if ( name.equals("session_id") ) {

      // Get the user based on the session id
      user = getCurrentUser(cookieList[x].getValue());
      break;
    }
  }
}

if ( user == null ) {

  // Let's create a cookie that represents a unique
  // session id.
  response.addCookie(new Cookie("session_id", "564XX892"));
  responseString = new String("Welcome to our site, " +
    "we have created a session for you.");
}
else {

  responseString = new String("Hello : " + user);
}

response.setContentType("text/html");
PrintWriter out = response.getWriter();

out.println("<html>");
out.println("<head><title>CookieServlet</title></head>");

out.println("<body>");

out.println(responseString);

out.println("</body></html>");
out.close();
}

//Get Servlet information
public String getServletInfo() {

  return "CookieServlet Information";
}
}
```

Every time the `CookieServlet` services a request, it checks for cookies in the `HttpServletRequest`. It does this by calling the `HttpServletRequest.getCookies()` method. If the request does contain cookies, the servlet will iterate over the list of cookies looking for a cookie with the name `session_id`.

If the request contains no cookies or the list of cookies does not contain a cookie named `session_id`, we create one and add it to the response. The code snippet that does this is listed as follows:

```
response.addCookie(new Cookie("session_id", "564XX892"));
```

> **NOTE**
>
> Cookies are stored in the response as HTTP headers. Therefore, you must add cookies to the response before adding any other content.

The best way to test this functionality is to open your browser to the `CookieServlet`. The first time it runs, you should get a response that says "Welcome to our site, we have created a session for you." After you get this message, press your Refresh button. You should see a new response that says "Hello : Bob." The servlet can now identify the user "Bob" by the session ID stored as a cookie.

> **NOTE**
>
> If you have trouble running this example, make sure the use of cookies is enabled in your browser.

URL REWRITING

If your browser does not support cookies, URL rewriting provides you with another session tracking alternative. URL rewriting is a method in which the requested URL is modified to include a session ID. There are several ways to perform URL rewriting. You are going to look at one method that is provided by the Servlet API. Listing 12.3 shows an example of URL rewriting.

LISTING 12.3 URLREWRITINGSERVLET.JAVA

```
import javax.servlet.*;
import javax.servlet.http.*;
import java.io.*;
```

continues

LISTING 12.3   CONTINUED

```java
import java.util.*;

public class URLRewritingServlet extends HttpServlet {
//Initialize global variables

  public void init(ServletConfig config)
    throws ServletException {

    super.init(config);
  }

  //Process the HTTP Get request
  public void doGet(HttpServletRequest request,
    HttpServletResponse response)
    throws ServletException, IOException {

    response.setContentType("text/html");
    PrintWriter out = response.getWriter();
    out.println("<html>");
    out.println("<head><title>URL Rewriting</title></head>");
    out.println("<body>");

    // Encode a URL string with the session id appended
    // to it.
    String url = response.encodeRedirectURL(
      "http://localhost:8000/servlet/checkout?sid=5748");

    // Redirect the client to the new URL
    response.sendRedirect(url);

    out.println("</body></html>");
    out.close();
  }

  //Get Servlet information
  public String getServletInfo() {

    return "URLRewritingServlet Information";
  }
}
```

This servlet services a GET request and redirects the client to a new URL. This new URL has the string sid=5748 appended to it. This string represents a session ID. When the servlet that services the redirection receives the request, it will be able to determine the current user based on the appended value. At that point, the servlet can perform a database lookup on the user and her actions based on this ID.

Two methods are involved in this redirection. The first is the
`HttpServletResponse.encodeRedirectURL()`, which takes a `String` that represents a
redirection URL and encodes it for use in the second method. The second method used
is the `HttpServletRequest.sendRedirect()` method. It takes the `String` returned from
the `encodeRedirectString()` and sends it back to the client for redirection.

The advantage of URL rewriting over hidden form fields is the ability to include session-tracking
information without the use of forms. Even with this advantage, it is still a very arduous coding
process.

SESSION TRACKING WITH THE SERVLET API

The Servlet API has its own built-in support for session tracking. This functionality is provided
by the `HttpSession` object. In this section, I am going to focus on four of the `HttpSession`'s
session tracking methods.

The first method I am going to look at is the `putValue()` method. The `putValue()` method
binds a *name/value* pair to store in the current session. If the *name* already exists in the
session, it is replaced. The method signature for `putValue()` is listed as follows:

```
public void putValue(String name, Object value)
```

The next method I am going to look at is the `getValue()` method, which is used to get an
object that is stored in the session. The `getValue()` method takes a `String` representing the
name that the desired object is bound to. Its signature is listed as follows:

```
public Object getValue(String name)
```

The third session method returns an array of the current bound names stored in the session.
This method is convenient if you want to remove all the current bindings in a session. Its signature is listed as follows:

```
public String[] getValueNames()
```

The last session method I am going to discuss is the `removeValue()` method. As its name suggests,
it removes a binding from the current session. It takes a `String` parameter representing the *name*
associated with the binding. Its method signature is listed as follows:

```
public void removeValue(String name)
```

Now that I have discussed the `HttpSession` object, take a look at an example of how to use it.
In this example, you are going to service a request that contains a list of movies to add to a
user's account. You will then parse the submitted list, add it to the customer's session, and
redisplay it for approval. When the customer approves the list, they will press the Proceed to
Checkout button to commit the transaction. Listing 12.4 contains the source for this example.

Developing Java Servlets

LISTING 12.4 HttpSessionServlet.java

```java
import javax.servlet.*;
import javax.servlet.http.*;
import java.io.*;
import java.util.*;

public class HttpSessionServlet extends HttpServlet {

  public void init(ServletConfig config)
    throws ServletException {

    super.init(config);
  }

  //Process the HTTP Get request, this method
  // will handle the checkout
  public void doGet(HttpServletRequest request,
    HttpServletResponse response)
    throws ServletException, IOException {

    String[] movies = null;

    // Get a handle to the HttpSession Object
    // if there is no session create one
    HttpSession session = request.getSession(true);

    // Get the movies list object bound to the
    // name "Movies"
    if ( session != null ) {

      movies = (String[])session.getValue("Movies");
    }

    response.setContentType("text/html");
    PrintWriter out = response.getWriter();
    out.println("<html>");
    out.println("<head><title>Session Servlet</title></head>");
    out.println("<body>");

    // Iterate over the movies array, displaying the
    // current list of movies stored in the session
    out.println("<H2>Thank you for purchasing:</H2>");
    for ( int x = 0; x < movies.length; x++ ) {

      out.println(movies[x] + "<BR>");
```

```
    }
    out.println("</body></html>");
    out.close();
  }

  //Process the HTTP Post request
  public void doPost(HttpServletRequest request,
    HttpServletResponse response)
    throws ServletException, IOException {

    // Parse the movies selected
    String movies[] = request.getParameterValues("Movies");

    // Get a handle to the HttpSession Object
    // if there is no session create one
    HttpSession session = request.getSession(true);

    // add the list of movies to the session
    // binding it to the String "Movies"
    if ( session != null ) {

      session.putValue("Movies", movies);
    }

    response.setContentType("text/html");
    PrintWriter out = response.getWriter();
    out.println("<html>");
    out.println("<head><title>Session Servlet</title></head>");
    out.println("<body>");

    out.println("<H2>Contents of Shopping Cart</H2>");

    // Display the submitted movie array
    for ( int x = 0; x < movies.length; x++ ) {

      out.println(movies[x] + "<BR>");
    }
    // Create a form to submit an order
    out.println("<FORM action=/servlet/HttpSessionServlet " +
      "METHOD=GET>");
    out.println("<input type=\"Submit\" name=\"add\" value=" +
      "\"Proceed to Checkout\"></FORM>");

    out.println("</body></html>");
    out.close();
  }
```

continues

LISTING 12.4   CONTINUED

```
//Get Servlet information
public String getServletInfo() {

  return "HttpSessionServlet Information";
}
}
```

To invoke this servlet, you need to create an HTML file that will make a POST request containing a list of selected movies. The HTML file that contains this form is in Listing 12.5.

LISTING 12.5   HTMLSESSIONSERVLET.HTML

```
<HTML>
<HEAD>
<TITLE>
Movie List
</TITLE>
</HEAD>

<BODY>
<H2>Select From Available Movies</h2>

<FORM ACTION=/servlet/HttpSessionServlet method=POST>

  <SELECT NAME="Movies" SIZE="5" MULTIPLE>
    <OPTION SELECTED>Air Force One</OPTION>
    <OPTION>Happy Gilmore</OPTION>
    <OPTION>So I Married an Axe Murderer</OPTION>
    <OPTION>Austin Powers</OPTION>
    <OPTION>Pure Luck</OPTION>
  </SELECT><BR>
  <INPUT TYPE="Submit" NAME="add" VALUE="Add Movies">

</FORM>

</BODY>
</HTML>
```

To see how this example works, you must load this HTML page in a browser. You should see a screen similar to Figure 12.2.

When this page is loaded, select a couple of the movies in the list and press the Add Movies button. You should now see a screen containing the list of movies you selected. Figure 12.3 displays an example of this output.

FIGURE 12.2

The Movie Selection List screen.

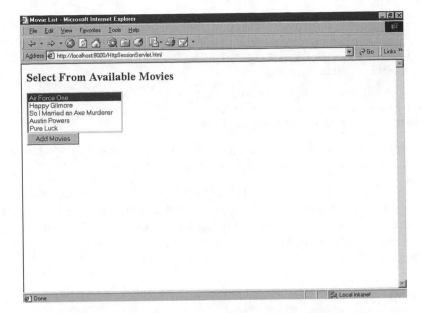

FIGURE 12.3

The Contents of Shopping Cart screen.

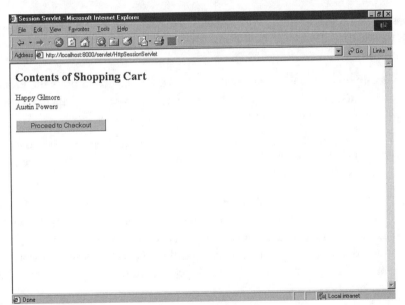

To understand how this first part works, you need to examine the doPost() method. This is the method that services the POST request sent by your HTML document.

The first thing the `doPost()` method does is get the list of submitted movies from the request. It then tries to get a reference to the `HttpSession` object stored in the `HttpServletRequest`. This is done by calling the `HttpServletRequest.getSession()` method. The code snippet that performs this is listed in the following:

```
// Get a handle to the HttpSession Object
// if there is no session create one
HttpSession session = request.getSession(true);
```

The `getSession()` method takes one parameter. This parameter is a Boolean value that, if true, tells the method to create a `HttpSession` if one doesn't exist.

When you have a reference to the `HttpSession` object, you can add our movie list to it. We do this by calling the `HttpSession.putValue()`, passing it the name `"Movies"` and the object to be bound to it: `movies`. The movie list is now stored in the client's session. The last thing you do in the `doPost()` method is redisplay the list of selected movies and ask the user to Proceed to Checkout.

NOTE

Sessions do expire. Therefore, you will need to consult your server's documentation to determine the length of time a session is valid.

Now you are going to look at the really cool part. Go ahead and press the Proceed to Checkout button. You should see a screen similar to Figure 12.4, which tells you "Thank you for purchasing:" and displays the movies you selected.

The request performed by this form simply called the same servlet using the GET method. If you look at the URL your browser is now pointing to, you will notice there is no movie data encoded in the URL string.

Take a look at the `doGet()` method and see exactly how this is done. The first thing you do is get a reference to the `HttpSession` object, which is done exactly as before with the `getSession()` method. When you have a reference to the session, you can get the list of movies stored in the session. You do this by calling the `HttpSession.getValue()` method, passing it the name bound to the `movies` object. The following code snippet shows how this is done:

```
// Get the movies list object bound to the
// name "Movies"
if ( session != null ) {

movies = (String[])session.getValue("Movies");
}
```

FIGURE 12.4

The Thank You screen.

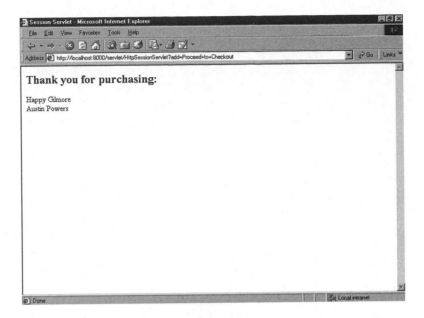

> **NOTE**
>
> Make sure that you downcast your stored object back to its original type. While in the HttpSession, it is stored as an object.

When you have the list of movies, thank the customer for the purchase and redisplay the list of ordered movies. That is all there is to it. As you have seen, the Servlet API provides you with a very elegant and simple-to-use method of maintaining persistent sessions.

SUMMARY

In this chapter, I covered several methods that you can integrate into your servlets to handle persistent sessions. I talked about the hidden form fields, persistent cookies, URL rewriting, and the Servlet API's built-in session-handling support. At this point, you should be able to examine your session-handling requirements and determine which method satisfies your needs. You should also be able to implement a session-handling solution based upon your decision.

In the next chapter, I am going to be looking at one of the more serious topics in Internet development: security. In my discussions, I will be examining different security methods and how each of them works.

SECURITY

IN THIS CHAPTER

INTRODUCTION TO SECURITY

The need for security has increased as the Internet's traffic has increased. Every day, more and more people are transferring their credit card numbers or other confidential information over the Internet. If these transfers are not secured, they are exposed to just about any evildoer with a network connection. In this chapter, I will cover some of the more common security methods from rolling your own to SSL.

One of the key benefits of servlets is that they inherit the security of the server, without any additional effort on your part. They are protected because they are resources of the server.

ROLL YOUR OWN

The first security method I will discuss is probably the worst method, but—at the same time— probably safe enough if you are protecting non-vital information.

In your homegrown version of security, you are going to use a basic form to query the user for an ID and password. When you have the request, parse off the ID/password combination and do a lookup to make sure that the user is approved for access. Once you have approval, add his ID to his HttpSession object as proof of his approval for future transactions. Listing 13.1 contains the servlet code for this example.

LISTING 13.1 ROLLYOUROWNSECURITYSERVLET

```
import javax.servlet.*;
import javax.servlet.http.*;
import java.io.*;
import java.util.*;

public class RollYourOwnSecurityServlet extends HttpServlet {

  public void init(ServletConfig config)
    throws ServletException {

    super.init(config);
  }

  private boolean validateUser(String id, String password) {

    // This is a dummy method.  If you really implement
    // a method like this, you will need to store id/password
    // combinations somewhere else
    return true;
  }
```

```java
//Process the HTTP Get request
public void doGet(HttpServletRequest request,
  HttpServletResponse response)
  throws ServletException, IOException {

  // Get the current session
  HttpSession session = request.getSession(true);
  // Get the id stored in the session after approval
  String id = (String)session.getValue("id");

  response.setContentType("text/html");
  PrintWriter out = response.getWriter();
  out.println("<html>");
  out.println("<head><title>Roll Your Own</title></head>");
  out.println("<body>");

  out.println("Hello " + id + " how can we help you today?");

  out.println("</body></html>");
  out.close();
}

//Process the HTTP Post request
public void doPost(HttpServletRequest request,
  HttpServletResponse response)
  throws ServletException, IOException {

  // Get the id/password combination from the request
  String id = request.getParameter("id");
  String password = request.getParameter("password");

  HttpSession session = null;

  // Check to see if this is a valid id/password combination.
  boolean valid = validateUser(id, password);

  // If it is valid, get the session
  // and add the id for future transactions
  if ( valid == true ) {

    session = request.getSession(true);
    session.putValue("id", id);
  }

  response.setContentType("text/html");
  PrintWriter out = response.getWriter();
```

continues

LISTING 13.1   CONTINUED

```
    out.println("<html>");
    out.println("<head><title>Roll Your Own</title></head>");
    out.println("<body>");


    if ( valid == true ) {

      // Successful validation, redirect the browser to
      // the GET method
      // of this servlet
      response.sendRedirect("/servlet/" +
        "RollYourOwnSecurityServlet");
    }
    else {

      out.println("We don't know who you are please leave!");
    }
    out.println("</body></html>");
    out.close();
  }

  //Get Servlet information
  public String getServletInfo() {

    return "RollYourOwnSecurityServlet Information";
  }
}
```

This is a really simple example of implementing your own security model. The first step is to display the login form when the user accesses the Web site. The HTML source for the login screen is in Listing 13.2.

LISTING 13.2   LOGINSCREEN.HTML

```
<HTML>
<HEAD>
<TITLE>
Login Screen
</TITLE>
</HEAD>
<BODY>

<CENTER>
<H2>Please Login</H2>
```

```
</CENTER>

<FORM ACTION="/servlet/RollYourOwnSecurityServlet" METHOD="POST">

  User Id:<INPUT TYPT="Text" NAME="id"><BR>
  Password:<INPUT TYPE="Password" NAME="password"><BR>
  <INPUT TYPE="Submit" NAME="login" VALUE="Login">

</FORM>

</BODY>
</HTML>
```

Go ahead and load the HTML file into your browser. You should see a screen similar to Figure 13.1.

FIGURE 13.1

The login screen.

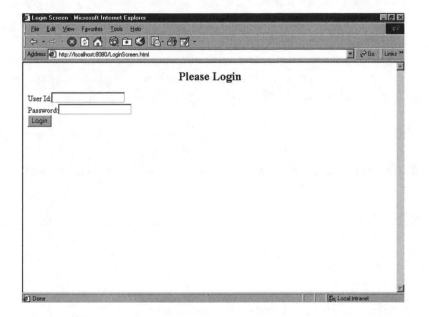

When the user submits her ID/password, it is parsed by the doPost() method of the servlet and checked against a database of valid users (in the example, everybody is approved). When the user is validated, her ID is added to her HttpSession object and she is redirected to the servlet's doGet() method. Now future requests only need to check for the user's ID in the session to verify that she has been properly validated.

BASIC AUTHENTICATION

Basic authentication is a challenge/response security model. It is based on the fact that the client must authenticate itself with a user ID/password combination for each resource it wants to access. A protected resource could be a directory, a servlet, or even a specific page. The steps involved in authenticating a client are listed in the following:

1. The client makes an unauthorized request for a protected resource.

2. The server responds with a challenge to authenticate.

3. The client sends a username/password combination (separated by a colon) within a base64 encoded string.

4. The server decodes the string containing the user ID/password combination and looks in its database for a match.

5. If the server finds a match, it grants access to the requested resource.

To get a better understanding of how this works, you are going to use the Java Web Server's Administration tool to protect a resource. The resource you are going to protect is a servlet called `AuthenticationServlet`. It services `GET` requests and responds with the remote username sent in the request. The name should be the same as the username used in the authentication process. The `AuthenticationServlet`'s source appears in Listing 13.3.

> **NOTE**
>
> You need to add the `AuthenticationServlet` to the Java Web Service list of servlets.

LISTING 13.3   AUTHENTICATIONSERVLET.JAVA

```java
import javax.servlet.*;
import javax.servlet.http.*;
import java.io.*;
import java.util.*;

public class AuthenticationServlet extends HttpServlet {

  public void init(ServletConfig config)
    throws ServletException {

    super.init(config);
  }

  //Process the HTTP Get request
```

```
public void doGet(HttpServletRequest request,
  HttpServletResponse response)
  throws ServletException, IOException {

  response.setContentType("text/html");
  PrintWriter out = response.getWriter();
  out.println("<html>");
  out.println("<head><title>Authentication" +
    "Servlet</title></head>");
  out.println("<body>");

  // Get the username used during authentication
  out.println("Hello " + request.getRemoteUser() +
    " I am glad to see you passed security.");

  out.println("</body></html>");
  out.close();
}

//Get Servlet information
public String getServletInfo() {

  return "AuthenticationServlet Information";
}
}
```

You must perform several tasks in order to protect a resource. Each of these steps is listed in the following:

1. Create a new user. To do this, you must go to the Java Web Service Security screen. Select the Users option on the tree control. Then choose defaultRealm from the Realm list. Figure 13.2 shows this screen.

   Now click the Add button and enter a username and password in the resulting Add User dialog box. Your dialog box should look something like Figure 13.3.

   Click the OK button to add the new user. You will see the new user name in the list if you were successful.

2. Add the new user to an access control list. Access control lists allow you to define a list of users and their permissions; you can apply this list to a resource. To do this, you need to select Access Control Lists from the tree control on the Web Service Security page. Make sure that you set the realm to defaultRealm and select defaultAcl. Your screen should look similar to Figure 13.4.

Developing Java Servlets

FIGURE 13.2

The Java Web Service Security screen.

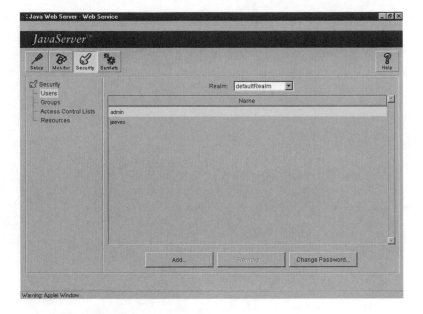

FIGURE 13.3

The Add User dialog box.

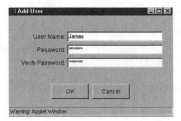

Now click the Add Permission button and select the new user you created. Table 13.1 shows the appropriate settings for this page.

TABLE 13.1 ADD PERMISSION SETTINGS

Field Name	Data Type
Add Permissions For	Files and Folders
Grant To	User
Permissions Are	Allowed
Permissions	Get

If everything has gone according to plan, your screen will look similar to Figure 13.5.

FIGURE 13.4

The Access Control Lists screen.

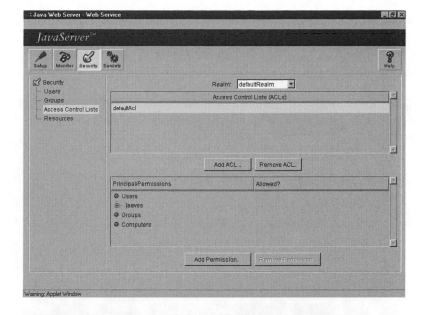

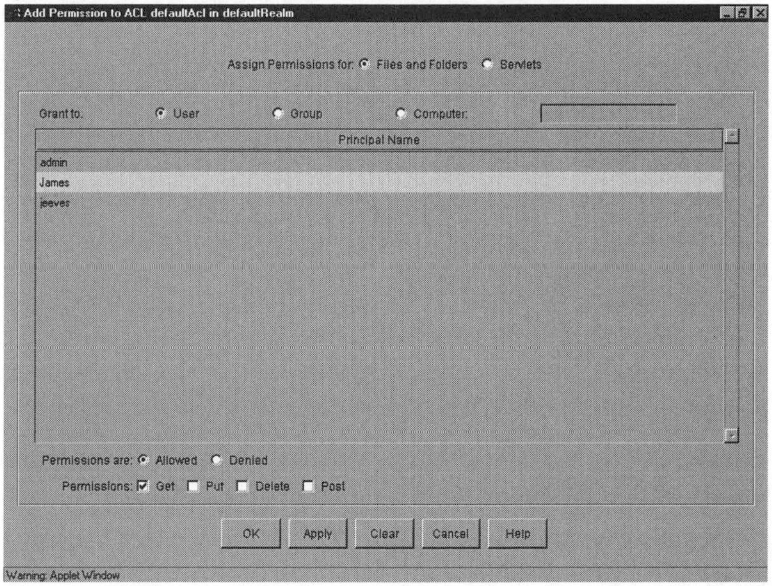

FIGURE 13.5

The Add Permission screen.

Now click the OK button. You should see the new user in the Users list.

3. Add a new resource. Select the Resources option from the tree control. This will bring up the Resources screen. Make sure the realm is set to defaultRealm and click the Add button. You should now see a screen similar to Figure 13.6.

FIGURE 13.6

The Protect a Resource screen.

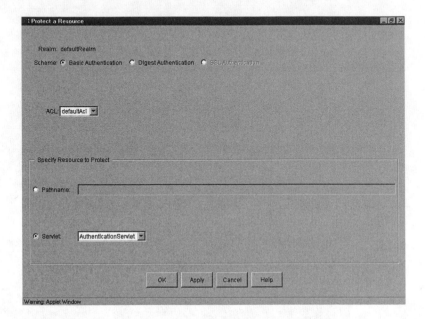

Several options appear on this page. Notice three options for the security scheme: Basic Authentication, Digest Authentication, and SSL Authentication. I am currently talking about Basic Authentication, so select that option. I will discuss the other two security schemes later in this chapter. Make sure your ACL list is set to defaultAcl and then select the Servlet option. If you added the AuthenticationServlet, you should see it in the list. Go ahead and select it and click the OK button. You should now see the AuthenticationServlet listed as a resource. It is now a protected resource.

Now that the resource is protected, open your browser to the AuthenticationServlet's URL. The URL is listed as follows for my local machine:

```
http://localhost:8080/servlet/AuthenticationServlet
```

You should be prompted with a dialog box querying you for a username/password. It should look something like Figure 13.7.

FIGURE 13.7

The Enter Network Password dialog box.

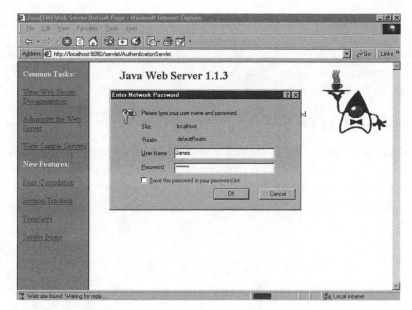

Enter your username/password combination for your new user and click the OK button. If everything goes well, you should get a response saying how glad we are that you made it past security. If you fail the challenge, you should see a response similar to Figure 13.8.

FIGURE 13.8

The 401 response.

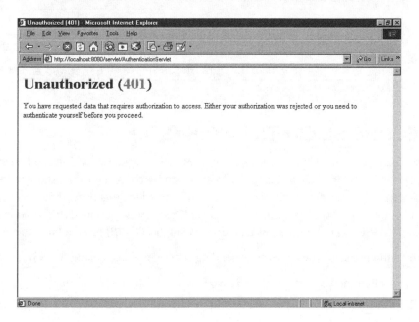

The problem with basic authentication is that the ID/password combination is transmitted in essentially clear text over the Internet. This is because the base64 encoding is very easily reversed, exposing the protected information to anyone listening. Because of this, basic authentication should not be used to protect sensitive material. If you choose to use basic authentication, do so for identification purposes only.

DIGEST AUTHENTICATION

Digest authentication, like basic authentication, is based on the challenge/response model. In fact, digest authentication was created as a direct result of basic authentication's shortcomings. The main difference between basic and digest authentication is that the digest scheme never sends the user's password across the network. It instead sends a digest representation of the password.

> **NOTE**
>
> Currently there is no support for digest authentication.

Two steps are involved in creating a digest value. The first is applying a mathematical formula to the ID/password combination. The second is to permute the mathematical calculation with a nonce. This makes each request more secure because the digest is unique to each request.

> **NOTE**
>
> A *nonce* is a server-specific data string that is uniquely generated each time a protected resource is requested.

SECURE SOCKETS LAYER (SSL)

The Secure Sockets Layer (SSL) is an authentication protocol used to send encrypted information over the Internet. It was originally developed by Netscape to transfer secure information between its Web browser and Web server products. Since this time, it has been widely adopted and is now one of the most popular methods for sending encrypted information over the Internet. SSL is implemented as a layer between the TCP/IP protocol and the application layer.

The following steps are involved in sending secure messages using the SSL protocol:

1. A client makes a request for a resource located on a secure site.
2. The server signs its public key with its private key and sends the public key back to the client.

3. The client takes the returned public key and makes sure it was signed by the appropriate owner.

4. The client then verifies that the key was signed by an approved certificate authority.

5. The client then creates a key that is encrypted with the public key of the server and sends the newly constructed key back to the server.

6. The server optionally compresses the information requested by the client.

7. The server encrypts the message using the key created in step 5.

8. The server then transmits the message to the client.

9. The client receives the message.

10. The message is then decrypted using the same key created in step 5.

11. The message is decompressed if necessary and delivered to the client.

12. All further requests restart at step 6, using the same public key.

These first five steps make the SSL protocol a very secure way to send information across the Internet. The only real drawback of the SSL protocol is the performance degradation taken during the public key encryption and decryption required during these first five steps.

The SSL protocol is very involved and is way beyond the scope of this book. If you have further interest, I would suggest getting the latest specification from the Netscape Web site at `http://www.netscape.com/eng/ssl3/3-SPEC.HTM#7-1`.

SUMMARY

In this chapter, I briefly discussed some of the more common security protocols. You saw how you could roll your own security, a technique that really isn't secure. I covered basic and digest authentication and their problems. Finally, I discussed the Secure Sockets Layer protocol, which is a very secure and widely used protocol.

In the next chapter, you will learn about the basics of RMI and CORBA. You will also see some ways to leverage these technologies in your servlets.

13

SECURITY

SERVLETS AS DISTRIBUTED OBJECT CLIENTS

IN THIS CHAPTER

DISTRIBUTED COMPUTING

In today's heterogeneous computing environment, many software packages solve business problems such as accounting, inventory, and billing systems.

> **NOTE**
>
> One popular example of a multifunction business package is SAP R/3, which is an Enterprise Resource Planning (ERP) package. See `http://www.sap.com/products/r3/index.htm`.

Some systems are custom developed by company resources. No single application—custom or packaged—solves all our business problems. The challenge then becomes sharing data between these applications or systems. Thus, an approach called *distributed computing* has been developed for object-oriented developers. In distributed computing, disparate systems use objects to share data and functionality to solve business problems. Sometimes these systems operate on different operating systems and are programmed in different languages.

Distributed computing is an outgrowth of the object-oriented development methods. Although there are many approaches to distributed computing, I am going to discuss only two, CORBA and RMI. I have chosen these two because of their popularity among Java developers. I'll introduce each subject and then illustrate—with a servlet—the distributed object clients that use CORBA and RMI to communicate with another application. My examples are simple, but the possibilities are endless.

The core of today's distributed computing is the concept of a *distributed object*. This permits objects that are implemented on one computer to share data and functionality with objects of other systems. This task would be considered a major undertaking without the assistance of some sort of communication standard.

> **NOTE**
>
> Although distributed computing is not purely an object-oriented paradigm, the latest trends in distributed computing are object-oriented. Thus, I'm approaching this discussion from an object perspective.

CORBA and RMI are two standards by which different applications can share data and functionality to solve different business problems. These two standards enable distributed computing and the sharing of distributed objects. Let's begin by looking at RMI.

RMI

Remote Method Invocation (RMI) is a Java-based Application Programming Interface (API) for distributed computing in a pure Java implementation. RMI, like other distributed computing paradigms, abstracts the socket layer communications. The abstraction permits a client and a server to communicate with objects over a network.

In RMI, the object is implemented on the server in Java and is accessed by a Java client. The client executes methods on a proxy object that in turn executes the same methods on the server. From the client perspective, it is as though the object is a local object in the same Java Virtual Machine (JVM). From the server perspective, the client is on the server in the same JVM as the server. This method of sharing objects over the network saves the large effort of establishing a data layer protocol that would require parsing on both the client and server machines.

The RMI implementation consists of three distinct layers: the stub/skeleton layer, the remote reference layer, and the transport layer. A *stub* is a client-side proxy for a remote object. The *skeleton* is an object interface for a server-side object. The *remote reference* layer (RRL) is an intermediate layer that transmits data through a stream-oriented connection between the client and the server objects. The *transport* layer handles the connection, tracking, and dispatching of remote objects. The transport might be implemented in different types of transports, such as TCP and UDP, to name a few. I will be discussing only the TCP transport.

In Figure 14.1, the client invokes a method on the stub. The stub forwards the request to the RRL. The RRL ushers or marshals the request to the transport layer. The transport layer carries the request from the client transport layer to the server's transport layer over the network. The request, once on the server, is forwarded to the RRL. The RRL forwards the request to the skeleton layer, where the request is unmarshaled, and the call on the server JVM object is accomplished. The process is reversed if a value is to be returned to the client.

NOTE

Marshaling is the serialization of the object to be transported. *Unmarshaling* is the reassembly of the serialized object. I discuss serialization in Chapter 7, "HTTP Tunneling."

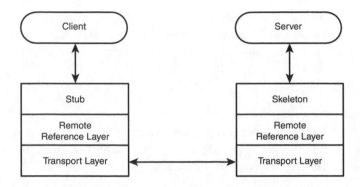

FIGURE 14.1
Java RMI layers.

RMI is used to share objects between a client computer running a JVM and a server computer running a JVM. However, RMI is typically implemented in the development phase on the same machine and then installed in a distributed network environment. The client is either a Java applet or a Java application. The server is a Java application usually with access to other systems. The client uses the server to access data and perform operations on the server.

RMI, like any other distributed communication system, also deals with destruction of distributed objects. RMI accomplishes this through the use of reference-counting garbage collection. The reference to a remote object is maintained by a weak reference. When the object on the client goes out of scope, the reference count on the server is decremented. When there are no other remote references to the object, it is marked for garbage collection on the server in the JVM.

A Catalog RMI Example

In the following example, I have implemented a catalog that can reside on a server. The catalog contains CD objects. The server constructs the catalog and registers with the RMI registry so that a client can interact with the catalog. This interface constitutes a contract of shared functionality between the client and the server in a distributed computing environment. Listing 14.1 contains the Inventory interface.

LISTING 14.1 INVENTORY.JAVA CLASS

```java
import java.rmi.*;
import java.util.*;

public interface Inventory extends Remote {
  public void addCatalogItem(CatalogItem inCatalogItem)
    throws RemoteException;
```

```
    public boolean inInventory(CatalogItem inCatalogItem)
      throws RemoteException;

    public Vector getCatalogItems() throws RemoteException;

    public int getQuantityInInventory(CatalogItem inCatalogItem)
      throws RemoteException;
}
```

In RMI, a contract is established between the client and the server via an interface. The first step in using RMI is creating an interface that extends the remote class.

We are going to share an inventory of catalog items over RMI. All methods and attributes in this interface must be public in order to be shared over RMI. Because we are object-oriented programmers, we share only methods and not attributes. We share methods by sharing objects that encapsulate functionality on the server side. By sharing objects, we can change the server-side implementation without changing the object interface of the shared object.

Notice that the Inventory interface extends the Remote interface in the java.rmi package. This code establishes the remote contract between the client and the server. It defines the methods available through the RMI API. The methods in the interface throw a RemoteException. The exceptions are passed via RMI to the remote client when there is an access error. This exception might be customized through extending the java.rmi. RemoteException class, just like any other exception. The actual throwing of the exception is on the server implementation of the object. The client must use the standard try-catch structure when calling these methods.

Before you look at the implementation of the Inventory object, take a look at the data that is passed via the Inventory interface. Figure 14.2 shows the UML diagram of the CatalogItem class and its relationship to the CD class. You can construct other classes that inherit the functionality of CatalogItem, such as book or movie. In this inventory, you will have only CD items, but they will be stored as CatalogItems in inventory.

Listings 14.2 and 14.3 contain the CatalogItem and CD classes.

LISTING 14.2 CATALOGITEM.JAVA CLASS

```
import java.io.*;

public abstract class CatalogItem
  implements Serializable {
```

continues

LISTING 14.2   CONTINUED

```java
private double price;
private int quantity;

public CatalogItem(double inPrice, int inQuantity) {
  price = inPrice;
  quantity = inQuantity;
}

public double getPrice() {
  return price;
}

public int checkQuantity() {
  return quantity;
}

public void decrementQuantity()
  throws Exception {

    if(quantity <= 0) {
      throw new Exception("Not enough in Inventory to decrement");
    }
    quantity--;
}

public void decrementQuantity(int amount)
  throws Exception {

    if(checkQuantity() < amount) {
      throw new Exception("Not enough in Inventory to decrement");
    } else {
      quantity -= amount;
    }
}

public void incrementQuantity(int amount) {
  quantity += amount;
}
}
```

FIGURE 14.2
UML diagram of CatalogItem and CD classes.

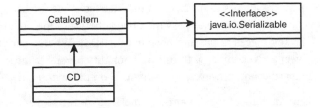

LISTING 14.3 CD.JAVA CLASS

```java
public class CD extends CatalogItem {
  private String title;
  private String artist;

  public CD(String inTitle, String inArtist, double inPrice,
    int inQuantity) {

    super(inPrice, inQuantity);
    title = inTitle;
    artist = inArtist;
  }

  public String getTitle() {
    return title;
  }

  public String getArtist() {
    return artist;
  }

  public String toString() {
    return ("CD " + title + " recorded by " + artist +
      " costs $" + getPrice() + " quantity in inventory is " +
      + checkQuantity());
  }
  public boolean equals(Object obj) {
    if(obj instanceof CD) {
      CD cd = (CD) obj;
      return (title.equals(cd.getTitle()) &&
        artist.equals(cd.getArtist()) );
    }
    return false;
  }
}
```

Any objects that are sent as arguments to methods in the interface must be serializable. RMI, as previously discussed, uses serialization to pass the objects between the client and the server. Serialization is one of the key pieces to passing objects over RMI. When a serialized object is passed over RMI, the object arrives intact with full functionality on either the client or the server. The object's reference count, however, is maintained on the server side.

The next step in RMI is to implement the `Inventory` interface on the server side. Listing 14.4 is the `InventoryImpl.java` class, which implements the `Inventory` interface.

LISTING 14.4 INVENTORYIMPL.JAVA

```java
import java.rmi.*;
import java.rmi.server.*;
import java.rmi.registry.*;
import java.util.*;

public class InventoryImpl extends UnicastRemoteObject
  implements Inventory {

  private Vector catalogItems = new Vector();

  public InventoryImpl() throws RemoteException {
    super();
  }

  public void addCatalogItem(CatalogItem inCatalogItem)
    throws RemoteException {

    if(!catalogItems.contains(inCatalogItem)) {
      catalogItems.addElement(inCatalogItem);
      System.out.println("Added item: " + inCatalogItem);
    } else {
      System.out.println("Store already contains: " + inCatalogItem);
    }
  }

  public boolean inInventory(CatalogItem inCatalogItem)
    throws RemoteException {

    return catalogItems.contains(inCatalogItem);
  }

  public int getQuantityInInventory(CatalogItem inCatalogItem)
    throws RemoteException {
```

```
    CatalogItem item = null;
    int quantity = -1;
    if(catalogItems.contains(inCatalogItem)) {
      int index = catalogItems.indexOf(inCatalogItem);
      item = (CatalogItem)catalogItems.elementAt(index);
      quantity = item.checkQuantity();
      System.out.println("quantity="+quantity);
    }
    return quantity;
  }

  public Vector getCatalogItems() throws RemoteException {
    return catalogItems;
  }

  public static void main(String args[]) throws Exception {
    int port = 2001;

    if(System.getSecurityManager() == null) {
      System.setSecurityManager(new RMISecurityManager());
    }

    Registry reg = LocateRegistry.createRegistry(port);
    System.out.println("Created registry on port: " + port);

    InventoryImpl inventory = new InventoryImpl();

    inventory.addCatalogItem(new CD("Under the Table and Dreaming",
      "Dave Matthews Band", 19, 2));
    inventory.addCatalogItem(new CD("Crash",
      "Dave Matthews Band", 15, 3));
    inventory.addCatalogItem(new CD("Don't Know How to Party",
      "The Mighty Mighty Boss Tones", 14.5, 1));

    reg.rebind("Inventory", inventory);
    System.out.println("Inventory created.");
  }
}
```

14

SERVLETS AS
DISTRIBUTED
OBJECT CLIENTS

It is traditional to call the class that implements the interface in RMI the XXXImpl class because it implements the interface; however, you may call it whatever you want. Take a look at the inheritance of InventoryImpl.java shown in Figure 14.3.

FIGURE 14.3
UML diagram of the InventoryImpl class.

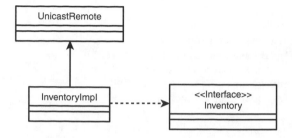

The `InventoryImpl.java` class extends the `java.rmi.server.UnicastRemote`, which has `RemoteObject` as its parent. All objects that are implemented on the server and intended for exporting to clients should extend `UnicastRemote`. `UnicastRemote` does the following things:

- Defines an object whose references are valid only while the server process is alive
- Provides support for invocations, parameters, and results using TCP streams
- Implements the functionality of the `hashCode`, `equals`, and `toString` methods that are inherited from the object class so that the class behaves appropriately for remote objects
- Provides the ability to export the object and allow it to accept calls from clients

If you choose to extend from `RemoteObject` or any other object, you must provide the same functionality as the `UnicastRemote` class. Lines 11–13 are the constructor for the `InventoryImpl.java` class.

```
public InventoryImpl() throws RemoteException {
  super();
}
```

This constructor is very basic, but essential. If you forget to implement it, you will receive a compiler error. The only method call in the constructor is to the constructor of the `UnicastRemoteObject` via the `super()` method.

NOTE

If you forget to include the call to `super()` method in the constructor, it still gets called.

The `main()` method of the class, lines 50–71, is where the object is constructed, registered for export, and bound in the RMI registry. This section could actually be separated from the `InventoryImpl.java` class:

```java
public static void main(String args[]) throws Exception {
    int port = 2001;

    if(System.getSecurityManager() == null) {
      System.setSecurityManager(new RMISecurityManager());
    }

    Registry reg = LocateRegistry.createRegistry(port);
    System.out.println("Creaded registry on port: " + port);

    InventoryImpl inventory = new InventoryImpl();

    inventory.addCatalogItem(new CD("Under the Table and Dreaming",
      "Dave Matthews Band", 19, 2));
    inventory.addCatalogItem(new CD("Crash",
      "Dave Matthews Band", 15, 3));
    inventory.addCatalogItem(new CD("Don't Know How to Party",
      "The Mighty Mighty Boss Tones", 14.5, 1));

    reg.rebind("Inventory", inventory);
    System.out.println("Inventory created.");
  }
```

In lines 53–55, I create an `RMISecurityManager`, if it does not already exist.

```java
if(System.getSecurityManager() == null) {
    System.setSecurityManager(new RMISecurityManager());
  }
```

The `RMISecurityManager` ensures that the classes, which get loaded, do not perform unauthorized operations. If no security manager is instantiated, class loading is limited to the `CLASSPATH`. You might define your own `SecurityManager` and grant access as dictated by your application. The `RMISecurityManager` applies only to applications and not to applets. In applets, the browser implements its own security manager.

In JDK1.1, the `SecurityManager` that `RMISecurityManager` extends is an abstract class. It provides only signatures for security methods and does not provide true functionality. For detailed information on security in the JDK1.1, see the following Web address:

`http://java.sun.com/docs/books/tutorial/security1.1/index.html`

In the JDK1.2 or the Java 2 platform, the `SecurityManager` is no longer abstract. It provides policy-based security and certificate interfaces that expand the security options available in the JDK1.2. For more information, visit the following Web sites:

`http://java.sun.com/products/jdk/1.2/docs/guide/security/`

`http://java.sun.com/security/index.html`

`http://java.sun.com/docs/books/tutorial/security1.2/index.html`

I will discuss security in another section and provide an introduction to security based on policies.

In line 57 of `main()`, I create a registry on `port=2001`:

`Registry reg = LocateRegistry.createRegistry(port);`

I have called the `createRegistry` method and specified the port number to be 2001. This creates a registry that is listening on port 2001. Typically, most examples on RMI have you manually start the registry from the command line by executing the `rmiregistry` executable. The registry starts on port 1099, unless you specify a port when starting it up from the command line. If I had not added the statement in line 57, you would need to execute the following command to start up the registry on port 2001:

`rmiregistry 2001`

Thus, the manual startup of the registry from the command line should be skipped for this example and the others in the chapter.

In line 60, I create the `InventoryImpl` instance:

`InventoryImpl inventory = new InventoryImpl();`

This code ends up calling the constructor for `UnicastRemoteObject` and makes the object available for export to clients. The object is ready to accept incoming calls from clients on an anonymous port, one chosen by RMI or the underlying operating system. Although the object is available for export, there is no means by which a client can obtain a reference. So, in line 69, I bind to the registry:

`reg.rebind("Inventory", inventory);`

This method rebinds or re-associates the inventory object with the name `Inventory`. If there was no binding before, this method creates a new binding. In the name `Inventory`, there is an implied format. The string needs to take on a URL format. In the example, the `Inventory` interface is assumed to be on the local machine. If it were on a remote machine at a different port, the name would look like this: `//host<:port>/Inventory`, where `host` would be the DNS hostname and `port` would be any port on which you want your client to connect. If the port is omitted, the default is 1099.

NOTE

An application can bind, unbind, or rebind remote object references only with a registry running on the same host. This limitation prevents a remote object from removing or overwriting objects already in the registry. A lookup, however, can be requested from any host, local or remote.

The assignment of a name to the object provides a gateway for the client to gain access to the server object. When this access has been established, the client can connect to other objects that are featured via the server object implementation.

So, you have created the interface and the implementation of the interface on the server. The next thing you need to do is create the client. Listing 14.5 contains `InventoryClient.java`.

LISTING 14.5 INVENTORYCLIENT.JAVA CLASS

```java
import java.util.*;
import java.rmi.*;

public class InventoryClient {

  public InventoryClient(String inHost) {

    if(System.getSecurityManager() == null) {
      System.setSecurityManager(new RMISecurityManager());
    }

    try {
      Inventory inventory = (Inventory)Naming.lookup("rmi://" +
        inHost + ":2001/Inventory");

      Vector catalogItems = inventory.getCatalogItems();
      CatalogItem item = null;
      for(int i=0, len=catalogItems.size(); i<len; i++) {
        item = (CatalogItem)catalogItems.elementAt(i);
```

continues

LISTING 14.5 CONTINUED

```
        System.out.println("CatalogItem = " + item);
      }
    } catch (Exception ex) {
      System.out.println("Caught exception = " + ex);
      ex.printStackTrace();
    }
  }

  public static void main(String args[]) {
    String host = "localhost";
    if(args.length >= 1) {
      host = args[0];
    }
    InventoryClient client = new InventoryClient(host);
  }
}
```

In lines 8–10, I set up a security manager for the client:

```
if(System.getSecurityManager() == null) {
  System.setSecurityManager(new RMISecurityManager());
}
```

In lines 13–14, I perform a lookup on the registry for the Inventory server object reference:

```
Inventory inventory = (Inventory)Naming.lookup("rmi://" +
  inHost + ":2001/Inventory");
```

The lookup() method takes a URL string to locate the registry that has the object reference.

In lines 16–21, I execute a method on the client stub, which in turn executes this method on the server skeleton to obtain a vector of catalogItems:

```
Vector catalogItems = inventory.getCatalogItems();
    CatalogItem item = null;
    for(int i=0, len=catalogItems.size(); i<len; i++) {
      item = (CatalogItem)catalogItems.elementAt(i);
      System.out.println("CatalogItem = " + item);
    }
```

Now, you are ready to compile and execute your first RMI application. Install the source code in a directory called rmi. Compile the source code by executing javac *.java. This example assumes that you have installed the JDK1.1 from the CD and set up a CLASSPATH that includes the current directory (.). Run the rmi compiler on the InventoryImpl class

```
rmic InventoryImpl
```

and you will obtain `InventoryImpl_Stub.class` and `InventoryImpl_Skel.class` in the same directory. Now, launch the `InventoryImpl` class by the following command:

```
java InventoryImpl
```

This command starts the `rmiregistry` on port 2001 and registers the `InventoryImpl` object as `"Inventory"` in the registry. You should receive output to the screen similar to this:

```
Created registry on port: 2001
Added item: CD Under the Table and Dreaming recorded by Dave Matthews
Band costs $19.0
quantity in inventory is 2
Added item: CD Crash recorded by Dave Matthews Band costs $15.0
quantity in inventory is 3
Added item: CD Don't Know How to Party recorded by The Mighty Mighty
Boss Tones costs $14.5
quantity in inventory is 1
Inventory created.
```

The `Inventory` server is up and stocked with three CDs waiting for clients to connect on port 2001.

In another window, execute `java InventoryClient`. This code attaches to the registry via a `lookup()` and gets a reference to the `Inventory` object from the registry. Then it will get a vector of `catalogItems` and perform a `toString()` on each one. Now, you have executed your first RMI program. The output listing of the client is listed as follows:

```
CatalogItem = CD Under the Table and Dreaming recorded by Dave Matthews
Band costs $19.0
quantity in inventory is 2
CatalogItem = CD Crash recorded by Dave Matthews Band costs $15.0
quantity in inventory is 3
CatalogItem = CD Don't Know How to Party recorded by The Mighty Mighty
Boss Tones costs $14.5
quantity in inventory is 1
```

Execution Errors

You might have problems when you run the `InventoryImpl.class` file on your computer. You might get the following error message:

```
java.rmi.AccessException: Registry.rebind
    at sun.rmi.registry.RegistryImpl.checkAccess(RegistryImpl.java:187)
    at sun.rmi.registry.RegistryImpl.rebind(RegistryImpl.java:146)
    at InventoryImpl.main(InventoryImpl.java:68)
```

If so, you probably do not have an IP address assigned to your machine. That's because most ISPs don't want you to assign an IP address to your machine. They want to assign these addresses when you log in. Thus, ISPs tell you not to set the Internet address before you connect to their sites. If you specify an IP address and use dial-up, you probably will not be able to run the application until after you connect with the ISP. So connect with your ISP and run the example again and it should work. If you continue to have problems, verify that you have an IP address assigned to your machine. If you are still having problems, look at the Java Network Programming FAQ at `http://java.sun.com/people/linden/index.html`.

Security

If you install the JDK1.2 or Java Platform 2 and try to execute a client and a server, your client and server will look for a security policy. If they don't find it, you will receive an error message similar to the one that follows:

```
Caught exception = java.security.AccessControlException:
access denied (java.net.SocketPermission
 127.0.0.1:2001 connect,resolve)
java.security.AccessControlException: access denied
(java.net.SocketPermission 127.0.0.1:2001
connect,resolve)
        at java.security.AccessControlContext.checkPermission
(Compiled Code)
        at java.security.AccessController.checkPermission(Compiled Code)
        at java.lang.SecurityManager.checkPermission(Compiled Code)
        at java.lang.SecurityManager.checkConnect
(SecurityManager.java:1006)
        at java.net.Socket.<init>(Socket.java:258)
        at java.net.Socket.<init>(Socket.java:98)
        at sun.rmi.transport.proxy.RMIDirectSocketFactory.createSocket
(RMIDirect
SocketFactory.java:29)
        at sun.rmi.transport.proxy.RMIMasterSocketFactory.createSocket
(CompiledCode)
        at sun.rmi.transport.tcp.TCPEndpoint.newSocket
(TCPEndpoint.java:462)
        at sun.rmi.transport.tcp.TCPChannel.createConnection
(TCPChannel.java:194)
        at sun.rmi.transport.tcp.TCPChannel.newConnection(Compiled Code)
        at sun.rmi.server.UnicastRef.newCall(UnicastRef.java:306)
        at sun.rmi.registry.RegistryImpl_Stub.lookup(Unknown Source)
        at java.rmi.Naming.lookup(Naming.java:89)
        at InventoryClient.<init>(Compiled Code)
        at InventoryClient.main(InventoryClient.java:33)
```

If you do receive an error like this, you will need to inform the registry of the security policy by passing a property parameter on the command line when you start the client and the server as shown in the following:

1. java -Djava.security.policy=java.policy InventoryImpl
2. java -Djava.security.policy=java.policy InventoryClient

Listing 14.6 shows a sample security policy.

LISTING 14.6   JAVA.POLICY

```
grant {
    permission java.net.SocketPermission "*:1024-65535", "connect,accept";
};
```

The `permission` line says that the socket has permission to connect or accept connections on unprivileged ports (ports greater than 1024) on any host.

In the example, passing the `parameter -Djava.security.policy=java.policy` to the client and the server should not make a difference. It would make a difference if you started the registry manually and in a different directory than the server code `InventoryImpl`.

Another means of restricting policy-based security would be to set properties within the server code. However, a detailed discussion on security in RMI is beyond the scope of this book. I have introduced the new policy-based security for the JDK1.2 simply to indicate that some of the examples will not run under the JDK1.2 unless you have a policy file. I have tried to provide notes for the examples that might have problems, but I will not be able to discuss security in detail. For more information on security in the JDK1.2, visit the previously mentioned Web sites.

RMI Development Summary

Here is a general list of steps for developing an RMI distributed application:

1. Design and implement the components of your distributed application. In this step, you will define the remote interfaces, implement remote objects on the server, and implement the clients.
2. Compile sources and generate stubs and skeletons. This is a two-step process: First compile the Java classes with `javac`, and then compile the remote interface files using the `rmic` compiler.

3. Make the classes network accessible. This involves grouping the interfaces, stubs, and other classes that need to be downloaded to clients into directories where they can be downloaded via a Web Server.

4. Start the application. This involves starting the `rmiregistry` unless the server implementation code calls the registry directly, like my example. It also involves starting the server implementation application, if not already started. Start the clients.

For more information on RMI, visit the following Web site:

`http://java.sun.com/docs/books/tutorial/rmi/index.html`

Servlets as Distributed RMI Clients

Now that I have explained RMI, I will take the client version of `InventoryClient.java` and put it into a servlet called `RMIInventoryServlet.java`. The servlet becomes a distributed RMI client to the `InventoryImpl.class` that could run on another server to provide inventory information to the servlet RMI client. Listing 14.7 contains the `RMIInventoryServlet` class.

LISTING 14.7   RMIINVENTORYSERVLET.JAVA CLASS

```java
import javax.servlet.*;
import javax.servlet.http.*;
import java.io.*;
import java.util.*;
import java.rmi.*;

public class RMIInventoryServlet extends HttpServlet {

  private Inventory rmiInventoryServer = null;
  private String rmiServerIP = "localhost";

  // Set up static connection to Security Manager.
  static {
    if(System.getSecurityManager() == null) {
      System.setSecurityManager(new RMISecurityManager());
    }
  }

  public void init(ServletConfig config) throws ServletException {

    // Always pass the ServletConfig object to the super class
    super.init(config);
```

```
    // Get a handle to the Inventory RMI Server.
    try {
      rmiInventoryServer = (Inventory)Naming.lookup("rmi://" +
        rmiServerIP + ":2001/Inventory");
    } catch (Exception ex) {
      System.out.println("Caught exception = " + ex);
      ex.printStackTrace();
    }

}

//Process the HTTP Get request
public void doGet(HttpServletRequest request,
  HttpServletResponse response)
  throws ServletException, IOException {

  doPost(request, response);
}

//Process the HTTP Post request
public void doPost(HttpServletRequest request,
  HttpServletResponse response)
  throws ServletException, IOException {

  response.setContentType("text/html");
  PrintWriter out = response.getWriter();
  out.println("<html>");
  out.println("<head><title>RMI Inventory</title></head>");
  out.println("<body>");

  // Get all the parameter names
  Enumeration parameters = request.getParameterNames();
  String param = null;

  // Iterate over the names, getting the parameters
  while(parameters.hasMoreElements()) {

    param = (String)parameters.nextElement();

    if(param.equals("Query Product Type") ) {
      String productType = request.getParameter(param);
      String title = request.getParameter("Title");
      String artist = request.getParameter("Artist-Author");
```

continues

LISTING **14.7** CONTINUED

```java
        out.println("<B>looking up product type: " + productType +
          "</B></BR>");

        // Only checking for Product Type of CD.
        if(productType.equalsIgnoreCase("CD")) {

          // rmi client stuff
          // Create a CD to lookup w/ bogus values for price, quantity.
          CD lookupCD = new CD(title, artist, -1, -1);

          // Write information to HTML client.
          String cd = "<B>CD information: Title=" +
            lookupCD.getTitle() +
            ", Artist=" + lookupCD.getArtist() + "</B><BR>";
          out.println(cd);

          System.out.println("Looking for cd Title=" +
          lookupCD.getTitle() + ", Artist=" + lookupCD.getArtist() +
            " in Inventory");

          // Execute method on RMI object.
          int qty = rmiInventoryServer.getQuantityInInventory(lookupCD);

          if(qty > 0) {
            // Debug for WebServer console.
            System.out.println("Found CD .");
            System.out.println("\t quantity in Inventory = " + qty);

            // Write HTML to client.
            out.println("<B> Quantity in Inventory is: " +
              qty + "</B><BR>");
          }
        } else {
          // Write error to HTML client.
          out.println("<B> Inventory does not exist for requested " +
            productType + ".</B><BR>");
        }
      }
    }

    out.println("</body></html>");
    out.close();
  }
```

```
//Get Servlet information

public String getServletInfo() {
    return "RMIInventoryServlet";
}
}
```

Now, look at how I insert the RMI client code into the servlet. In lines 13–17, I create a static instance of the RMISecurityManager and set it to the SecurityManager for the class:

```
// Set up static connection to Security Manager.
static {
    if(System.getSecurityManager() == null) {
        System.setSecurityManager(new RMISecurityManager());
    }
}
```

In lines 24–31, I get a reference to the InventoryImpl object by looking up the object in the registry:

```
// Get a handle to the Inventory RMI Server.
try {
    rmiInventoryServer = (Inventory)Naming.lookup("rmi://" +
        rmiServerIP + ":2001/Inventory");
} catch (Exception ex) {
    System.out.println("Caught exception = " + ex);
    ex.printStackTrace();
}
```

In lines 54–66 of the doPost() method, I get the request parameters and extract the information needed for looking up the CD in the remote Inventory:

```
// Get all the parameter names
    Enumeration parameters = request.getParameterNames();
    String param = null;

    // Iterate over the names, getting the parameters
    while(parameters.hasMoreElements()) {

        param = (String)parameters.nextElement();

        if(param.equals("Query Product Type") ) {
            String productType = request.getParameter(param);
            String title = request.getParameter("Title");
            String artist = request.getParameter("Artist-Author");
```

14

In lines 70–87, I check to make sure that the request is for a CD, create a CD item for comparison, and execute the method on the stub to getQuantityInInventory() for the CD that was requested by the HTML page. The request goes out over RMI to the InventoryImpl server and executes the method on the server, and a quantity is returned to the servlet client:

```
// Only checking for Product Type of CD.
if(productType.equals("CD") || productType.equals("cd")) {

// rmi client stuff
// Create a CD to look up w/ bogus values for price, quantity.
CD lookupCD = new CD(title, artist, -1, -1);

// Write information to HTML client.
String cd = "<B>CD information: Title=" + lookupCD.getTitle() +
  ", Artist=" + lookupCD.getArtist() + "</B><BR>";
out.println(cd);

System.out.println("Looking for cd Title=" +
lookupCD.getTitle() + ", Artist=" + lookupCD.getArtist() +
  " in Inventory");

// Execute method on RMI object.
int qty = rmiInventoryServer.getQuantityInInventory(lookupCD);
```

Compile and Execute the Servlet

First, copy the following classes into the servlets directory under the webserver directory: Inventory.java, InventoryImpl.java, and RMIInventoryServlet.java. Compile these classes using the javac compiler. Then run the rmic compiler against the InventoryImpl class to generate your InventoryImpl_Stub.class and InventoryImpl_Skel.class. Now run the InventoryImpl.class using java InventoryImpl to start up the server process and the registry with the registered server. Now, copy the RMIInventoryServlet.html file to the webserver's public_html directory. Start the webserver. Then access the RMIInventoryServlet by loading the RMIInventoryServlet.html file in the browser. Figure 14.4 illustrates the HTML page with a sample query.

To execute the RMI client, type the information shown in Figure 14.4 into the HTML page: the Product Type CD, the Title Crash, and the Artist/Author Dave Matthews Band. Then, click the Submit button. If everything works successfully, your browser should look like Figure 14.5.

So take a look at what happened. The servlet performed a lookup on the registry and executed the getQuantityInInventory(lookupCD) method on the stub. A CD object was sent via serialization to the server method getQuantityInInventory(CatalogItem inItem), and a lookup was done in the vector to get the quantity for the requested CD. Then the quantity was returned from the server to the stub and ultimately to the servlet. The `quantity` and the CD information were returned from the `doPost()` method and displayed on the HTML page.

FIGURE 14.4

The RMIInventory-Servlet.html.

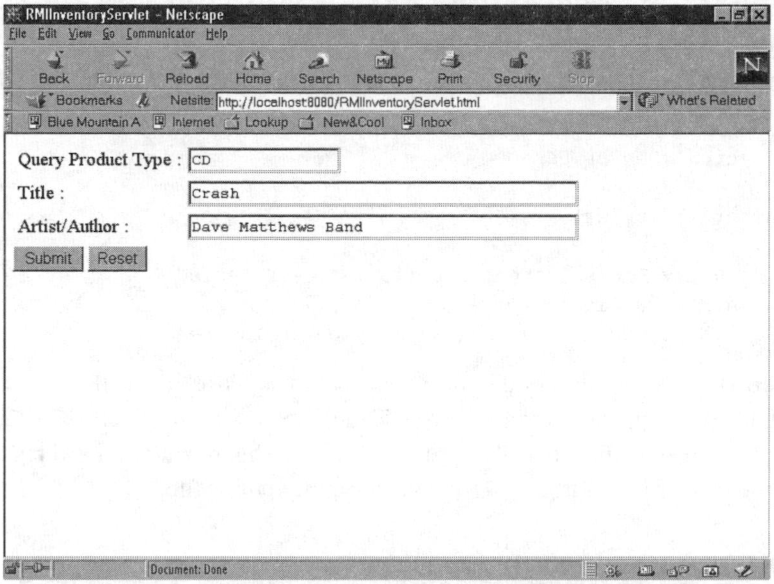

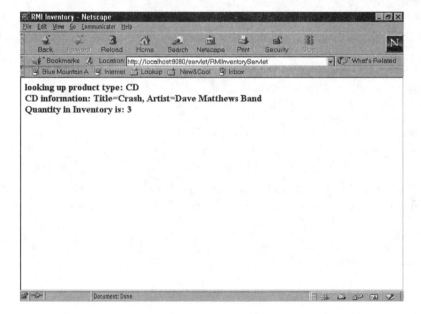

FIGURE 14.5

The response from the RMIInventory-Servlet.

Typically, the Inventory would be located on a remote machine at a fulfillment center and would have updates made by shipping. This is only one example of how servlets can be used as distributed object clients with RMI.

Running the RMIInventoryServlet with JRun Version 2.3

If you try to run the `RMIInventoryServlet` with JRun version 2.3, you will get a `java.-security.AccessControlException: access denied` error message that will look something like this:

```
500 Internal Server Error

RMIInventoryServlet:

java.security.AccessControlException: access denied
(java.io.FilePermission
F:\JRun\jsm-default\services\jse\logs\error.log read)
```

This error message indicates that the servlet could not write to the JRun `error.log` file. This is a JDK1.2 security access error message. To solve this, you must place a default security policy in your `user.home` directory. Then you will have to shut down JRun and restart it. Use the `.java.policy` file in Listing 14.8 for your security policy file.

LISTING 14.8   .JAVA.POLICY

```
grant {
  permission java.security.AllPermission;
};
```

The default security policy file is located at

```
user.home/.java.policy (Unix)
C:\Winnt\Profiles\<userName>\.java.policy
    (on multi-user Windows NT systems)
C:\Windows\Profiles\<userName>\.java.policy
    (on multi-user Windows 9x systems)
C:\Windows\.java.policy on single-user     (Windows 9x systems)
```

This security policy grants `AllPermissions` for JDK1.2 actions. For detailed information on setting up a specific security policy file, see the links at the end of the chapter.

RMI and Firewalls

RMI is a Java-centric, distributed computing facility. It requires that both the client and server be written in Java. It provides the Java developer a simplistic means of object distribution. However, many issues remain with communication through firewalls. There are two sides to the firewall problem. In one case, you have an application (not necessarily a Java application) behind a firewall and it attempts to get outside the firewall. In the other case, you have an application outside a firewall and it endeavors to get inside the firewall. The classic example is like this: a Java application as the server and a Java application as the client. The server will need to forward its request from inside the firewall to outside the firewall. This is accomplished by setting the `http.proxyHost` System property to the IP address of the proxy server.

The client is a totally different story. It will try to communicate directly to the server's port using sockets. If this fails, it will build a URL to the server's host and port and use an HTTP `POST` request on that URL, sending the information to the skeleton as the body of the post. If successful, the results of the post are the skeleton's response to the stub. If this also fails, RMI will build a URL to the server's host using port 80, the standard HTTP port, and you must use a CGI script that will forward the posted RMI request to the server. For more information on RMI and firewalls, visit the aforementioned Web sites and see the following FAQs:

- RMI and Object Serialization FAQ at
  `http://java.sun.com/products/jdk/rmi/faq.html`
- Java Distributed Computing FAQ at
  `http://java.sun.com/products/javaspaces/faqs/rmifaq.html`

For more information on distributed computing in Java-to-Java applications, read the following article at the Java Developer Connection:

`http://developer.java.sun.com/developer/technicalArticles/RMI/CreatingApps/index.html`

You will have to sign up to the Java Developer Connection before you can read it—but it's free—and if you're a Java developer, you should know about this site.

Well, in this short but action-packed section, I have touched upon distributed computing using RMI. Next I will investigate CORBA, another facility of distributed object computing that integrates well with Java.

CORBA

The Common Object Request Broker Architecture (CORBA) was created by the Object Management Group (OMG). CORBA is a language- and platform-independent specification for creating distributed computing frameworks that allow applications to communicate with one another no matter where they are located or what language they were written in. It's primarily used when communicating with legacy systems. It can also be used in heterogeneous environments where two systems must communicate over a network.

> **NOTE**
>
> The Object Management Group (OMG) is a non-profit corporation that was formed in 1989. Their mission was to establish CORBA as a middleware software product for the distribution of objects between heterogeneous systems. See the group's Web site for more information: http://www.omg.org.

This communication is accomplished by sharing objects and invoking methods on these objects to accomplish desired tasks, which in turn share data to solve problems in a distributed computing environment. The role of the OMG is to define specifications or interfaces for CORBA, but to not specify how the functionality is implemented.

The CORBA 1.1 specification was introduced in 1991 by the OMG. It defined the Interface Definition Language (IDL) and the Application Programming Interfaces (API) that enable interaction with an Object Request Broker (ORB). From this 1.1 specification, various vendors created commercial ORBs that became the core piece of their middleware products. Iona's Orbix and Inprise's VisiBroker are some of the more popular ORBS. The CORBA 2.0 specification introduced interoperability by specifying how ORBs from different vendors can interact.

IDL and ORB

IDL is a platform-independent language that allows the developer to define contracts of shared functionality, attributes, and combinations of both. I will cover some of the components in IDL later.

The ORB is the software—often referred to as *middleware*—that permits communication between two systems. The two systems operate in a client/server relationship through the ORB. The client invokes a method on the server object that is located across a network or on the same machine. As illustrated in Figure 14.6, the ORB accepts the request from the client on behalf of the server and ushers the request to the server object.

FIGURE 14.6
A request sent through the Object Request Broker.

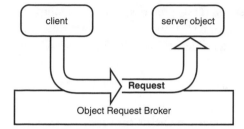

The client has no knowledge of where the server object is located or any knowledge of its implementation details, such as language or operating system. The ORB provides the communications infrastructure transparently to the client in order to access the server object.

CORBA Architecture

Next, I would like to explain the CORBA architecture, illustrated in Figure 14.7.

FIGURE 14.7
The CORBA architecture.

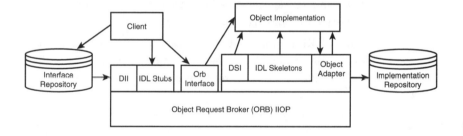

The definitions for each component in the figure are as follows:

- IDL stubs are static interfaces to object services. These stubs are generated from an IDL-type compiler. A stub acts like a proxy for a remote object. A stub includes necessary code to perform marshaling. The IDL stub functions similarly to an RMI stub.
- The Dynamic Invocation Interface (DII) lets you ascertain methods to be summoned at runtime. CORBA defines standards that permit dynamic discovery.
- The Interface Repository is a runtime distributed database repository of IDL method signatures. It can be thought of as a metadata repository.

- The ORB interface is actually an API to local services that might be of interest to an application. The API provides methods to store and communicate object references. This API exists for both the client and the object implementation side.

- The Dynamic Skeleton Interface (DSI) provides a runtime binding facility for servers to handle incoming method calls for components that do not have IDL-based compiled skeletons or stubs. The DSI determines the target object by viewing the parameter values in the incoming message.

- IDL skeletons are static interfaces to each service exported by the server and are created by an IDL compiler.

- The Object Adapter is a layer above the ORB's core communication services that accepts requests for service on behalf of the server's objects. It can be a vendor-specific implementation of the ORB's services called Basic Object Adapter (BOA), or it can be a vendor independent service called a Portable Object Adapter (POA). The CORBA 2.0 standard defines a BOA, and the CORBA 3.0 standard defines a POA. The POA was created to provide better vendor-to-vendor ORB compatibility.

- The Implementation Repository is a repository of server objects that are instantiated, along with their IDs. The ID is assigned by the BOA and is also referred to as an object reference ID. The repository supports runtime access of information about objects contained within the repository. Additional administrative information can be stored in the repository for debugging, audit trails, security, and so on.

- Internet Inter-ORB Protocol (IIOP) is a standard of communication based on TCP/IP that provides a common exchange of messages between ORBs. As of the CORBA 2.0 specification, all ORBs must implement this message interface.

NOTE

In this limited space, I will only be covering the static interface to the CORBA ORB using IDL. I'll leave the dynamic discussion to the books mentioned at the end of the chapter.

Now that I have provided a basic introduction to CORBA, take a look at a specific vendor ORB.

Inprise VisiBroker for Java

I am going to use VisiBroker 3.4 for Java as the middleware ORB that implements the CORBA specification. I recommend downloading the trial version of VisiBroker for Java at the following Web address: `http://www.inprise.com`. Look under free downloads for the latest VisiBroker for Java version.

> **NOTE**
>
> There is a bug in the version that I downloaded with the `java2iiop` and `java2idl` compilers. You need to add an empty `java` directory under whatever directory you are compiling in, or the utilities do not perform their code generation. I have only verified this bug on the Windows platform, and it occurs only if you install the product on a drive other than your C drive.

Setup for VisiBroker

The documentation for VisiBroker is located at the following address: `http://www.inprise.com/techpubs/visibroker`.

I suggest that you download the following documents for version 3.4:

- *Installation and Administration Guide*
- *Programmer's Guide*
- *Reference*

Chapter 3 of the *Installation and Administration Guide* leads you through the installation of the product for all platforms. If you choose to use command-line tools to compile your programs, you will need to add `vbjorb.jar` and `vbjapp.jar` to your CLASSPATH and include the `bin` directory in your PATH. Consult Chapter 4 of the *Installation and Administration Guide* for other environment variables that need to be added. I only added the following variables: VBROKER_ADM, OSAGENT_PORT, and OSAGENT_LOCAL_FILE. Consult the *Installation and Administration Guide* for instructions on setting these variables in your operating system.

java2iiop Code Generation

VisiBroker for Java incorporates features that enable Java to work more closely with the product. These products are collectively known as Caffeine. Their components and capabilities are

- java2iiop compiler—Allows you to use a Java interface to generate IIOP-compliant stubs and skeletons for Java. This tool uses a proprietary method of passing serialized objects called *extensible structs*.

- java2idl compiler—Allows you to turn your Java interface into IDL. Then you can implement your stubs and skeletons in any language.

- Web naming—Allows you to reference objects using a URL (uniform resource locator) name.

I will focus on the first feature, the java2iiop compiler. The java2iiop compiler requires a small modification to the Java interface. Set up a directory with the following files in it: CD.java, CatalogItem.java, Inventory.java, InventoryImpl.java, and CORBAInventoryServlet.java. You will start with the Inventory.java shown in Listing 14.9.

LISTING 14.9   INVENTORY.JAVA CLASS

```java
import java.util.*;

public interface Inventory extends org.omg.CORBA.Object {

    public void addCatalogItem(CatalogItem inCatalogItem);

    public boolean inInventory(CatalogItem inCatalogItem);

    public int getQuantityInInventory(CatalogItem inCatalogItem);

    public Vector getCatalogItems();
}
```

The only difference in this Inventory.java interface when compared to the RMI version is that it extends org.omg.CORBA.object rather than java.rmi.Remote.

The java2iiop reads the bytecodes from the Inventory.class to generate the stubs and skeletons for the CORBA/IIOP functionality, so we must first compile the Inventory.java class with the `javac` compiler. After this is complete, run the following command to generate the CORBA stubs and skeletons:

```
java2iiop –no_comments –no_tie Inventory
```

The `-no_comments` option leaves out the comments that the compiler normally puts in the `java` classes, and the `-no_tie` tells the compiler not to generate the code for the `tie` mechanism.

The tie Mechanism

In CORBA, there are two styles of programming: inheritance-based and delegation-based. The inheritance model means you inherit from the generated skeleton `_xxxImplBase.java`. In this case, it is called `_InventoryImplBase.java`. In the delegation model, you implement the `xxxOperations.java` file. The `xxxOperations.java` actually inherits from `_xxxImplBase.java`, but is only an interface that needs to be implemented. In this example, I'm using the inheritance model, so I specify the `-no_tie` option. I choose to not use the delegation-based or `tie` mechanism because it is slower than the inheritance model. The `tie` mechanism uses a delegate to which it passes all the work, so for every object you have a delegate. That's twice as many objects and twice as many method calls. A detailed discussion on the `tie` mechanism is beyond the scope of this chapter.

> **NOTE**
>
> The `java2iiop` compiler generates some files that are not used in this example. I will give a brief explanation of the purpose of each file and indicate the files that are used in the example. CORBA is such a broad topic that I will only be able to touch on some of the topics. Hopefully, I will cover some of the most important items for Java developers.

After running this command, you should have the following files in your directory:

- `CatalogItemHolder.java`
- `CatalogItemHelper.java`
- `InventoryHolder.java`
- `InventoryHelper.java`

- `_st_Inventory.java`
- `_InventoryImplBase.java`
- `_example_Inventory.java`

The `CatalogItemHolder.java` class, shown in Listing 14.10, is used to hold a public instance of the `CatalogItem`. It is used by clients and servers to pass objects of type `CatalogItem` as out and inout parameters inside method invocations. Because Java allows parameters to be passed only by value and not by reference, the `CatalogItemHolder` class is used to support the passing of out and inout parameters associated with operation requests. I don't use this class directly in my example.

LISTING 14.10   CATALOGITEMHOLDER.JAVA CLASS

```
final public class CatalogItemHolder implements
  org.omg.CORBA.portable.Streamable {
  public CatalogItem value;
  public CatalogItemHolder() {
  }
  public CatalogItemHolder(CatalogItem value) {
    this.value = value;
  }
  public void _read(org.omg.CORBA.portable.InputStream input) {
    value = CatalogItemHelper.read(input);
  }
  public void _write(org.omg.CORBA.portable.OutputStream output) {
    CatalogItemHelper.write(output, value);
  }
  public org.omg.CORBA.TypeCode _type() {
    return CatalogItemHelper.type();
  }
}
```

The `CatalogItemHelper.java` class, shown in Listing 14.11, is used to manipulate IDL types in various ways. Two of the main methods that this class provides are the `bind` method and the `narrow` method. The `bind` method allows you to retrieve the object from the server, and the `narrow` method provides a casting facility to go from an `omg.org.CORBA.object` to a `CatalogItem` type. I don't use this class in my example.

LISTING 14.11   CATALOGITEMHELPER.JAVA CLASS

```java
abstract public class CatalogItemHelper {
  private static org.omg.CORBA.ORB _orb() {
    return org.omg.CORBA.ORB.init();
  }
  public static CatalogItem read(org.omg.CORBA.portable.InputStream
    _input) {
    return (CatalogItem) ((com.visigenic.vbroker.orb.GiopInputStream)
      _input).read_estruct("CatalogItem");
  }
  public static void write(org.omg.CORBA.portable.OutputStream _
    output, CatalogItem value) {
    ((com.visigenic.vbroker.orb.GiopOutputStream)_output).
      write_estruct(value, "CatalogItem");
  }
  public static void insert(org.omg.CORBA.Any any, CatalogItem value) {
    org.omg.CORBA.portable.OutputStream output =
      any.create_output_stream();
    write(output, value);
    any.read_value(output.create_input_stream(), type());
  }
  public static CatalogItem extract(org.omg.CORBA.Any any) {
    if(!any.type().equal(type())) {
      throw new org.omg.CORBA.BAD_TYPECODE();
    }
    return read(any.create_input_stream());
  }
  private static org.omg.CORBA.TypeCode _type;
  public static org.omg.CORBA.TypeCode type() {
    if(_type -- null) {
      org.omg.CORBA.StructMember[] members =
        new org.omg.CORBA.StructMember[2];
      members[0] = new org.omg.CORBA.StructMember("price",
_orb().get_primitive_tc(org.omg.CORBA.TCKind.tk_double), null);
      members[1] = new org.omg.CORBA.StructMember("quantity",
_orb().get_primitive_tc(org.omg.CORBA.TCKind.tk_long), null);
      _type = ((com.visigenic.vbroker.orb.ORB)_orb()).
        create_estruct_tc(id(), "CatalogItem", null, members);
    }
```

continues

14

SERVLETS AS
DISTRIBUTED
OBJECT CLIENTS

LISTING 14.11   CONTINUED

```
    return _type;
  }
  public static java.lang.String id() {
    return "IDL:CatalogItem:1.0";
  }
}
```

The `InventoryHolder.java` class, shown in Listing 14.12, is similar to the `CatalogItemHolder` class except it's for the `Inventory` object. Notice the pattern: The `java2iiop` compiler provides a `<interface_name>Holder.java` file for the interface class and any objects referenced in the interface.

LISTING 14.12   INVENTORYHOLDER.JAVA CLASS

```
final public class InventoryHolder implements
  org.omg.CORBA.portable.Streamable {
  public Inventory value;
  public InventoryHolder() {
  }
  public InventoryHolder(Inventory value) {
    this.value = value;
  }
  public void _read(org.omg.CORBA.portable.InputStream input) {
    value = InventoryHelper.read(input);
  }
  public void _write(org.omg.CORBA.portable.OutputStream output) {
    InventoryHelper.write(output, value);
  }
  public org.omg.CORBA.TypeCode _type() {
    return InventoryHelper.type();
  }
}
```

The `InventoryHelper.java` class, shown in Listing 14.13, is similar to the `CatalogItemHelper` class. Notice yet another pattern: The `java2iiop` compiler provides a `<interface_name>Helper.java` file for the interface class and any objects referenced in the interface. I use this class in `InventoryClient.java` to obtain a copy of the `Inventory` class from the server.

LISTING 14.13 INVENTORYHELPER.JAVA

```java
abstract public class InventoryHelper {
  public static Inventory narrow(org.omg.CORBA.Object object) {
    return narrow(object, false);
  }
  private static Inventory narrow(org.omg.CORBA.Object object,
    boolean is_a) {
    if(object == null) {
      return null;
    }
    if(object instanceof Inventory) {
      return (Inventory) object;
    }
    if(is_a || object._is_a(id())) {
      _st_Inventory result = (_st_Inventory)new _st_Inventory();
      ((org.omg.CORBA.portable.ObjectImpl) result)._set_delegate
        (((org.omg.CORBA.portable.ObjectImpl) object)._get_delegate());
      ((org.omg.CORBA.portable.ObjectImpl) result._this())._set_delegate
        (((org.omg.CORBA.portable.ObjectImpl) object)._get_delegate());
      return (Inventory) result._this();
    }
    return null;
  }
  public static Inventory bind(org.omg.CORBA.ORB orb) {
    return bind(orb, null, null, null);
  }
  public static Inventory bind(org.omg.CORBA.ORB orb,
  java.lang.String name) {
    return bind(orb, name, null, null);
  }
  public static Inventory bind(org.omg.CORBA.ORB orb,
  java.lang.String name, java.lang.String host,
  org.omg.CORBA.BindOptions options) {
    if (orb instanceof com.visigenic.vbroker.orb.ORB) {
      return narrow(((com.visigenic.vbroker.orb.ORB)orb)
        .bind(id(), name, host, options), true);
    }
    else {
      throw new org.omg.CORBA.BAD_PARAM();
    }
  }
}
```

14

continues

LISTING 14.13   CONTINUED

```
private static org.omg.CORBA.ORB _orb() {
  return org.omg.CORBA.ORB.init();
}
public static Inventory read(org.omg.CORBA.portable.InputStream _
input) {
  return InventoryHelper.narrow(_input.read_Object(), true);
}
public static void write(org.omg.CORBA.portable.OutputStream _output,
Inventory value) {
  _output.write_Object(value);
}
public static void insert(org.omg.CORBA.Any any, Inventory value) {
  org.omg.CORBA.portable.OutputStream output =
    any.create_output_stream();
  write(output, value);
  any.read_value(output.create_input_stream(), type());
}
public static Inventory extract(org.omg.CORBA.Any any) {
  if(!any.type().equal(type())) {
    throw new org.omg.CORBA.BAD_TYPECODE();
  }
  return read(any.create_input_stream());
}
private static org.omg.CORBA.TypeCode _type;
public static org.omg.CORBA.TypeCode type() {
  if(_type == null) {
    _type = _orb().create_interface_tc(id(), "Inventory");
  }
  return _type;
}
public static java.lang.String id() {
  return "IDL:Inventory:1.0";
}
}
```

The _st_Inventory.java class, shown in Listing 14.14, is a sample stub class. I copy this file to the InventoryImpl.java class and implement the functionality of the server Inventory object. I will discuss implementation from this file later. For now, continue to look at the generated code.

Listing 14.14   _st_Inventory.java Class

```java
public class _st_Inventory extends
  com.inprise.vbroker.CORBA.portable.ObjectImpl
  implements Inventory {
  protected Inventory _wrapper = null;
  public Inventory _this() {
    return this;
  }
  public java.lang.String[] _ids() {
    return __ids;
  }
  private static java.lang.String[] __ids = {
    "IDL:Inventory:1.0"
  };
  public void addCatalogItem(
    CatalogItem arg0
  ) {
    org.omg.CORBA.portable.OutputStream _output;
    org.omg.CORBA.portable.InputStream _input;
    while(true) {
      _output = this._request("addCatalogItem", true);
      ((com.visigenic.vbroker.orb.GiopOutputStream)_output)
      .write_estruct(arg0, "CatalogItem");
      try {
        _input = this._invoke(_output, null);
      }
      catch(org.omg.CORBA.TRANSIENT _exception) {
        continue;
      }
      break;
    }
  }
  public boolean inInventory(
    CatalogItem arg0
  ) {
    org.omg.CORBA.portable.OutputStream _output;
    org.omg.CORBA.portable.InputStream _input;
    boolean _result;
    while(true) {
      _output = this._request("inInventory", true);
```

continues

14

LISTING 14.14   CONTINUED

```
      ((com.visigenic.vbroker.orb.GiopOutputStream)_output)
       .write_estruct(arg0, "CatalogItem");
      try {
        _input = this._invoke(_output, null);
        _result = _input.read_boolean();
      }
      catch(org.omg.CORBA.TRANSIENT _exception) {
        continue;
      }
      break;
    }
    return _result;
  }
  public int getQuantityInInventory(
    CatalogItem arg0
  ) {
    org.omg.CORBA.portable.OutputStream _output;
    org.omg.CORBA.portable.InputStream _input;
    int _result;
    while(true) {
      _output = this._request("getQuantityInInventory", true);
       ((com.visigenic.vbroker.orb.GiopOutputStream)_output)
       .write_estruct(arg0, "CatalogItem");
      try {
        _input = this._invoke(_output, null);
        _result = _input.read_long();
      }
      catch(org.omg.CORBA.TRANSIENT _exception) {
        continue;
      }
      break;
    }
    return _result;
  }
  public java.util.Vector getCatalogItems() {
    org.omg.CORBA.portable.OutputStream _output;
    org.omg.CORBA.portable.InputStream _input;
    java.util.Vector _result;
    while(true) {
      _output = this._request("getCatalogItems", true);
```

```
    try {
      _input = this._invoke(_output, null);
      _result = (java.util.Vector)
          ((com.visigenic.vbroker.orb.GiopInputStream)_input)
          .read_estruct("java.util.Vector");
    }
    catch(org.omg.CORBA.TRANSIENT _exception) {
      continue;
    }
    break;
  }
  return _result;
  }
}
```

This class provides the essentials for access of the objects through CORBA/IIOP. Notice that all the methods in the interface are present in this class. Do not add your code to this class because it will get regenerated every time you run the java2iiop compiler. You must copy this class and rename it before you add functionality. I do this later and show the implementation at that time.

NOTE

In the generated Java code with VisiBroker 3.4, notice a lot of casting with the com.visigenic.vbroker.orb object. These casts are present because the org.omg.CORBA package in the JDK1.2 differs from the org.omg.CORBA package in VisiBroker 3.4. This means that any java2iiop generated files are not compatible with the other release. This incompatibility will exist only if you are using the JDK1.2 with VisiBroker 3.4. However, the casting works under both JDK1.1.x and the JDK1.2.

If you intend to switch back and forth between VisiBroker version 3.4 and any previous version of VisiBroker, see the release notes for the Java 3.4 version for further information. These release notes are available when you download the trial version.

The next class, _InventoryImplBase.java, shown in Listing 14.15, is the skeleton code that provides access to the object from a CORBA/IIOP perspective. It permits access to methods of the server object via the org.omg.CORBA.portable.MethodPointer and provides an execute method to execute these methods. This class also handles the marshaling of the objects to the clients. To compare this to the RMI example earlier in the chapter, you don't get to see that actual code for the skeleton or the stub.

LISTING 14.15   _INVENTORYIMPLBASE.JAVA CLASS

```java
abstract public class _InventoryImplBase extends
  com.inprise.vbroker.CORBA.portable.Skeleton implements Inventory {
  protected Inventory _wrapper = null;
  public Inventory _this() {
    return this;
  }
  protected _InventoryImplBase(java.lang.String name) {
    super(name);
  }
  public _InventoryImplBase() {
  }
  public java.lang.String toString() {
    try {
      return super.toString();
    } catch (org.omg.CORBA.SystemException ex) {
      // delegate may not be set yet
      return "Unbound instance of Inventory";
    }
  }
  public java.lang.String[] _ids() {
    return _ _ids;
  }
  private static java.lang.String[] _ _ids = {
    "IDL:Inventory:1.0"
  };
  public org.omg.CORBA.portable.MethodPointer[] _methods() {
    org.omg.CORBA.portable.MethodPointer[] methods = {
      new org.omg.CORBA.portable.MethodPointer("addCatalogItem", 0, 0),
      new org.omg.CORBA.portable.MethodPointer("inInventory", 0, 1),
      new org.omg.CORBA.portable.MethodPointer(
        "getQuantityInInventory", 0, 2),
      new org.omg.CORBA.portable.MethodPointer("getCatalogItems", 0, 3),
    };
    return methods;
  }
  public boolean _execute(org.omg.CORBA.portable.MethodPointer method,
    org.omg.CORBA.portable.InputStream input,
    org.omg.CORBA.portable.OutputStream output) {
    switch(method.interface_id) {
    case 0: {
```

```
      return _InventoryImplBase._execute(_this(),
        method.method_id, input, output);
    }
  }
  throw new org.omg.CORBA.MARSHAL();
}
public static boolean _execute(Inventory _self, int _method_id,
  org.omg.CORBA.portable.InputStream _input,
  org.omg.CORBA.portable.OutputStream _output) {
  switch(_method_id) {
  case 0: {
    CatalogItem arg0;
    arg0 = (CatalogItem)
      ((com.visigenic.vbroker.orb.GiopInputStream)_input)
      .read_estruct("CatalogItem");
    _self.addCatalogItem(arg0);
    return false;
  }
  case 1: {
    CatalogItem arg0;
    arg0 = (CatalogItem)
      ((com.visigenic.vbroker.orb.GiopInputStream)_input)
      .read_estruct("CatalogItem");
    boolean _result = _self.inInventory(arg0);
    _output.write_boolean(_result);
    return false;
  }
  case 2: {
    CatalogItem arg0;
    arg0 = (CatalogItem)
      ((com.visigenic.vbroker.orb.GiopInputStream)_input)
      .read_estruct("CatalogItem");
    int _result = _self.getQuantityInInventory(arg0);
    _output.write_long(_result);
    return false;
  }
  case 3: {
    java.util.Vector _result = _self.getCatalogItems();
    ((com.visigenic.vbroker.orb.GiopOutputStream)_output)
    .write_estruct(_result, "java.util.Vector");
    return false;
  }
  }
  throw new org.omg.CORBA.MARSHAL();
}
}
```

The last class generated by the `java2iiop` compiler is the sample stub file, `_example_Inventory.java`, shown in Listing 14.16. Just as with the `_st_Inventory.java` file, don't add functionality to this class. Copy it and rename it before adding functionality.

LISTING 14.16   _EXAMPLE_INVENTORY.JAVA CLASS

```java
public class _example_Inventory extends _InventoryImplBase {
  public _example_Inventory(java.lang.String name) {
    super(name);
  }
  public _example_Inventory() {
    super();
  }
  public void addCatalogItem(
    CatalogItem arg0
  ) {
    // IMPLEMENT: Operation
  }
  public boolean inInventory(
    CatalogItem arg0
  ) {
    // IMPLEMENT: Operation
    return false;
  }
  public int getQuantityInInventory(
    CatalogItem arg0
  ) {
    // IMPLEMENT: Operation
    return 0;
  }
  public java.util.Vector getCatalogItems() {
    // IMPLEMENT: Operation
    return null;
  }
}
```

Notice the comments `IMPLEMENT: Operation`, which show you where you will need to add functionality. I do this in a class described later.

The `InventoryImpl.java` class, shown in Listing 14.17, is my server object copied from the skeleton example `_example_Inventory.java`. It is implemented with the same methods as the RMI server class `InventoryImpl.java` in my RMI example. The key differences are that it extends the generated class `_InventoryImplBase.java` class and that the `main()` method implements the CORBA functionality rather than the RMI functionality.

LISTING 14.17 INVENTORYIMPL.JAVA CLASS

```java
import java.util.*;

public class InventoryImpl extends _InventoryImplBase {

  private Vector catalogItems = new Vector();
  private static Properties properties;

  public InventoryImpl(java.lang.String name) {
    super(name);
    addCatalogItem(new CD("Under the Table and Dreaming",
      "Dave Matthews Band", 19, 2));
    addCatalogItem(new CD("Crash",
      "Dave Matthews Band", 15, 3));
    addCatalogItem(new CD("Don't Know How to Party",
      "The Mighty Mighty Boss Tones", 14.5, 1));
  }

  public void addCatalogItem(CatalogItem inCatalogItem) {
    if(!catalogItems.contains(inCatalogItem)) {
      catalogItems.addElement(inCatalogItem);
      System.out.println("Added item: " + inCatalogItem);
    } else {
      System.out.println("Store already contains: " + inCatalogItem);
    }
  }

  public boolean inInventory(CatalogItem inCatalogItem) {
    return catalogItems.contains(inCatalogItem);
  }

  public Vector getCatalogItems() {
    return catalogItems;
  }

  public int getQuantityInInventory(CatalogItem inCatalogItem) {

    CatalogItem item = null;
    int quantity = -1;
    if(catalogItems.contains(inCatalogItem)) {
      int index = catalogItems.indexOf(inCatalogItem);
      item = (CatalogItem)catalogItems.elementAt(index);
```

continues

LISTING 14.17   CONTINUED

```java
        quantity = item.checkQuantity();
        System.out.println("quantity="+quantity);
    }
    return quantity;
}

public static void main(String args[]) {
    // Properties needed for JDK1.2 compiling and execution.
    properties = System.getProperties();
    properties.put("org.omg.CORBA.ORBClass",
        "com.visigenic.vbroker.orb.ORB");
    properties.put("org.omg.CORBA.ORBSingletonClass",
        "com.visigenic.vbroker.orb.ORB");

    // Initialize the ORB.
    org.omg.CORBA.ORB orb = org.omg.CORBA.ORB.init(args,properties);
    // Initialize the BOA. if using Visibroker 3.3
    //org.omg.CORBA.BOA boa = orb.BOA_init();
    // Initialize the BOA. if using Visibroker 3.4
    org.omg.CORBA.BOA boa =
        ((com.visigenic.vbroker.orb.ORB)orb).BOA_init();
    // Create the Inventory object.
    InventoryImpl inventory = new InventoryImpl("Inventory");

    // Export the newly created object.
    boa.obj_is_ready(inventory);
    System.out.println(inventory + " is ready.");
    // Wait for incoming requests
    boa.impl_is_ready();
    System.out.println("Inventory created.");

}
}
```

The `main()` method, lines 47–72, provides the ORB setup, object creation, and object registration. First set up a `Properties` class so that you can run the sample code with the JDK1.2 and JRun 2.3. If you are not using the JDK1.2 product, this is not needed. Second, initialize the ORB with the call to the `init()` method and pass it the created `Properties` class. You can optionally provide runtime arguments and application-specific properties:

```java
// Properties needed for JDK1.2 compiling and execution.
    properties = System.getProperties();
    properties.put("org.omg.CORBA.ORBClass",
```

```
    "com.visigenic.vbroker.orb.ORB");
properties.put("org.omg.CORBA.ORBSingletonClass",
    "com.visigenic.vbroker.orb.ORB");

// Initialize the ORB.
org.omg.CORBA.ORB orb = org.omg.CORBA.ORB.init(args,properties);
```

The newly created ORB instance is returned for use in the application. I now use it to initialize the BOA. As I explained earlier, the BOA is a vendor-specific implementation of the ORB's services. It provides methods for instantiating server objects, passing requests to server objects, and registering server objects in the Implementation Repository.

In line 51 in the main method, I initialize the BOA and am returned an instance of the BOA from which I will call the services of the ORB:

```
// Initialize the BOA. if using Visibroker 3.3
//org.omg.CORBA.BOA boa = orb.BOA_init();
// Initialize the BOA. if using Visibroker 3.4
org.omg.CORBA.BOA boa = ((com.visigenic.vbroker.orb.ORB)orb).BOA_init();
```

> **NOTE**
>
> If you are using the JDK 1.1.x with either version of VisiBroker 3.3, you might use the code for VisiBroker 3.4 or the code for VisiBroker 3.3. Note, if you use the code for version 3.4, your code will not be backward compatible with other versions of VisiBroker. This difference and others are explained in the VisiBroker 3.4 release notes.

Next, create an instance of your server object. This is the object that will be registered into the Implementation Repository by the BOA:

```
InventoryImpl inventory = new InventoryImpl("Inventory");
```

After creating the server object, register the object with the BOA, which in turn registers the object in the Implementation Repository:

```
boa.obj_is_ready(inventory);
```

After you have registered the server object with the BOA, tell the BOA that your object is ready to service requests with the following method call:

```
boa.impl_is_ready();
```

14

SERVLETS AS
DISTRIBUTED
OBJECT CLIENTS

It took only five lines of code to set up the server object. If you refer to the RMI code, it took three lines of code to create the registry, instantiate the server object, and register the object with the registry. I think these two methods are both very easy and very similar.

Now take a look at the CORBA client class `CORBAInventoryServlet.java`, shown in Listing 14.18.

LISTING 14.18   CORBAINVENTORYSERVLET.JAVA CLASS

```java
import javax.servlet.*;
import javax.servlet.http.*;
import java.io.*;
import java.util.*;

public class CORBAInventoryServlet extends HttpServlet {

  private static Inventory inventory = null;
  private static Properties properties;

  public void init(ServletConfig config) throws ServletException {

    // Always pass the ServletConfig object to the super class
    super.init(config);

    try {
      System.out.println("started servlet init.");
      // Properties needed for JDK1.2 compiling and execution.
      properties = System.getProperties();
      properties.put("org.omg.CORBA.ORBClass",
        "com.visigenic.vbroker.orb.ORB");
      properties.put("org.omg.CORBA.ORBSingletonClass",
        "com.visigenic.vbroker.orb.ORB");

      // Initialize the ORB. Strange cast for null needed with vbj 3.4
      org.omg.CORBA.ORB orb = org.omg.CORBA.ORB.init((String[]) null,
                                                     properties);

      // Locate an Inventory Object and bind to it.
      inventory = InventoryHelper.bind(orb, "Inventory");
    } catch (Exception ex) {
      System.out.println("Exception ex.toString()="+ex.toString());
      ex.printStackTrace();
    }
  }
}
```

```java
//Process the HTTP Get request
public void doGet(HttpServletRequest request,
  HttpServletResponse response)
  throws ServletException, IOException {

  doPost(request, response);
}

//Process the HTTP Post request
public void doPost(HttpServletRequest request,
  HttpServletResponse response)
  throws ServletException, IOException {

  response.setContentType("text/html");
  PrintWriter out = response.getWriter();
  out.println("<html>");
  out.println("<head><title>RMI Inventory</title></head>");
  out.println("<body>");

  // Get all the parameter names
  Enumeration parameters = request.getParameterNames();
  String param = null;

  // Iterate over the names, getting the parameters
  while(parameters.hasMoreElements()) {

    param = (String)parameters.nextElement();

    if(param.equals("Query Product Type") ) {
      String productType = request.getParameter(param);
      String title = request.getParameter("Title");
      String artist = request.getParameter("Artist-Author");
      out.println("<B>looking up product type: " + productType +
        "</B></BR>");

      // Only checking for Product Type of CD.
      if(productType.equals("CD") || productType.equals("cd")) {

        // CORBA stuff
        // Create a CD to lookup w/ bogus values for price, quantity.
        CD lookupCD = new CD(title, artist, -1, -1);

        // Write information to HTML client.
        String cd = "<B>CD information: Title=" + lookupCD.getTitle() +
```

continues

LISTING 14.18   CONTINUED

```
                ", Artist=" + lookupCD.getArtist() + "</B><BR>";
            out.println(cd);

            // Debug for WebServer console.
            System.out.println("Looking for cd Title=" +
                lookupCD.getTitle() + ", Artist=" + lookupCD.getArtist() +
                " in Inventory");

            // Execute method on CORBA object.
            int qty = inventory.getQuantityInInventory(lookupCD);

            if(qty > 0) {
                // Debug for WebServer console.
                System.out.println("Found CD .");
                System.out.println("\t quantity in Inventory = " + qty);

                // Write HTML to client.
                out.println("<B> Quantity in Inventory is: " +
                    qty + "</B><BR>");
            }
        } else {
            // Write error to HTML client.
            out.println("<B> Inventory does not exist for requested " +
                productType + ".</B><BR>");
        }
      }
    }

    out.println("</body></html>");
    out.close();
  }

  //Get Servlet information

  public String getServletInfo() {
    return "CORBAInventoryServlet";
  }
}
```

There isn't much difference between this client and the RMI Servlet client, with the exception of some specific CORBA ORB-related code.

Execution of the CORBA Servlet Example

To execute the example, place the following files in a directory and compile them:

- `_InventoryImplBase.java`
- `CORBAInventoryServlet.java`
- `CatalogItem.java`
- `CatalogItemHelper.java`
- `CatalogItemHolder.java`
- `CD.java`
- `Inventory.java`
- `InventoryHelper.java`
- `InventoryHolder.java`
- `InventoryImpl.java`

After they are finished compiling, put the class files in the `<webserver>/servlets` directory. Next, put the `CORBAInventory.html` file in the `<webserver>/public_html` directory. Start the httpd process with the appropriate `CLASSPATH` from Table 14.1.

TABLE 14.1 CLASSPATH FOR THE HTTPD PROCESS BY OPERATING SYSTEM

OS	CLASSPATH
Windows	`httpd -classpath <vbroker_install_dir>\lib\vbjorb.jar;` `<vbroker_install_dir>\lib\vbjapp.jar`
UNIX	`httpd -classpath <vbroker_install_dir>/lib/vbjorb.jar:` `<vbroker_install_dir>/lib/vbjapp.jar`

Start the osagent from either the command line or from the icon in Windows. From the `<web-server>\servlets` directory, run the `java InventoryImpl` command. Remember, you must have the `vbjorb.jar` and `vbjapp.jar` files in your `CLASSPATH`. Open the following URL in your browser: `http://localhost:8080/CORBAInventoryServlet.html`. Then, input the CD information shown in Figure 14.8.

FIGURE 14.8

*The
CORBAInventory-
Servlet page.*

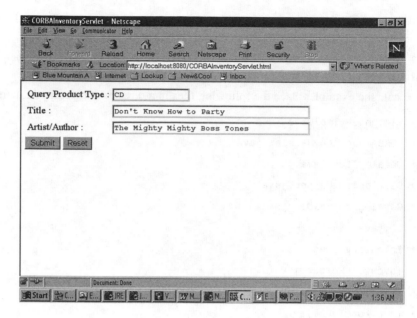

FIGURE 14.8

*The
CORBAInventory-
Servlet page.*

After you enter the CD information, press the Submit button, and you should receive output like Figure 14.9.

FIGURE 14.9

*The CORBA-
InventoryServlet
response page.*

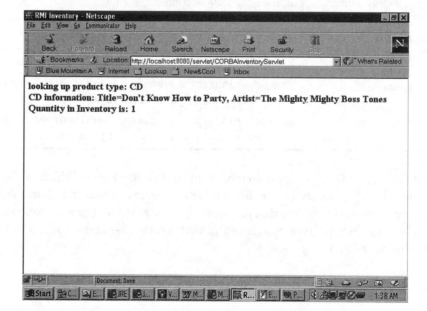

> **NOTE**
>
> If you are using the JDK1.2 and JRun version 2.3, you will need to add the `jar` files to the Java `CLASSPATH` setting under the jsm-default, General, Java tab. I have included the properties file `jsm.properties` with the source code, which is where the settings for the `CLASSPATH` are stored.

This example was relatively painless. You took the RMI `Inventory.java` interface file and generated the stubs and skeletons by running the `java2iiop` compiler. Then you implemented a `CORBAInventoryServlet.java` (client) from a sample file generated by the `java2iiop` compiler called `_example_Inventory.java`. Then you implemented the server object from the sample file `_st_Inventory.java`. Both the client and the server were very similar to the RMI servlet client and RMI server. The `java2iiop` compiler did all the work for you.

However, the `java2iiop` is a vendor-specific compiler. It implements extensible structs to provide the same pass-by-value functionality that Java has. This means that your implementation is not ORB neutral. Notice that you generated the stubs and skeletons without using IDL. All you did was change what object the `Inventory` interface extended and run the `java2iiop` compiler. If you would like to view the IDL file representation of the implementation, run the `java2idl` compiler on the `Inventory.class` file:

```
java2idl Inventory > Inventory.idl"
```

Listing 14.19 shows the output of this command.

LISTING 14.19 INVENTORY.IDL

```
extensible struct CatalogItem {
  double price;
  long quantity;
};
module java {
  module util {
    extensible struct Vector;
  };
};
interface Inventory {
  void addCatalogItem(
```

14

SERVLETS AS
DISTRIBUTED
OBJECT CLIENTS

continues

LISTING 14.19   CONTINUED

```
  in ::CatalogItem arg0
);
boolean inInventory(
  in ::CatalogItem arg0
);
long getQuantityInInventory(
  in ::CatalogItem arg0
);
::java::util::Vector getCatalogItems();
};
```

Here is where you see the use of the extensible struct for the `CatalogItem` class. The extensible struct permits the pass-by-value that Java needs. In the next example, I will begin with IDL and generate the CORBA stubs and skeletons. I'm not going to introduce IDL with the file; I'll create one for the inventory system and explain it.

USING IDL TO GENERATE CORBA STUBS AND SKELETONS

You have seen how easy it is to use the `java2iiop` compiler to create stubs and skeletons to implement your application. However, because the extensible struct is proprietary, I would like to illustrate another example where I specify the shared functionality via an IDL file and generate stubs and skeletons using the `idl2java` compiler. To do this, I will have to explain some IDL concepts. I'll start by illustrating, in Listing 14.20, the IDL for the inventory system. This inventory system example will be illustrated with a Java application client instead of a servlet.

LISTING 14.20   INVENTORY.IDL

```
module InventorySystem {

  struct CD {
    string title;
    string author;
  };

  struct CatalogItem {
    CD aCD;
    double price;
    long quantity;
  };
```

```
// Unbounded sequence of CatalogItems
typedef sequence<CatalogItem> CatalogItemArray;

interface Inventory {
  // set to readonly because want to define set methods
  readonly attribute CatalogItemArray catalogItemsArray;

  // other methods
  void addCatalogItem(in CatalogItem inItem);
  boolean inInventory(in CatalogItem inItem);
  CatalogItemArray getCatalogItems();
  long getQuantityInInventory(in CatalogItem inItem);
};
};
```

In line 1, a module maps the Java package. In lines 3–6 and 8–12, a struct maps to a Java class, but the Java class doesn't have `read` or `write` methods for the attributes. The attributes are set only through the constructor.

If you compare the attributes of the second struct, one noticeable IDL-to-Java mapping is the `int` in Java to the `long` in IDL. This mapping is based on the fact that an `int` in Java is 32 bits and IDL does not have an `int` with 32 bits. See Table 14.2 for a list of other basic IDL-to-Java mappings.

TABLE 14.2 BASIC IDL TYPE-TO-JAVA TYPE MAPPINGS

IDL Type	Java Type
boolean	boolean
char	char
wchar	char
octet	byte
string	java.lang.String
wstring	java.lang.String
short	short
unsigned short	short
long	int
unsigned long	int
long long	long
unsigned long long	long
float	float
double	double

The `CatalogItem` structure demonstrates that structures can be nested. In the RMI `Inventory.java` interface, I used a `Vector` to store the `CatalogItems`. In IDL, there is no native type that can be mapped to a Java `Vector`. This is the case with most of the collection type classes.

> **NOTE**
>
> The lack of collection classes such as the `Vector` class is a serious shortcoming of CORBA versus RMI, when viewed on the surface. However, when you remember that IDL is language and platform independent it's not as bad as initially thought. Typically, if you are using CORBA with Java, you are not sharing data in a pure Java implementation. Thus, you do need to represent the Java collection classes in IDL.

So, in IDL, the `Vector` is represented as an unbounded sequence of `CatalogItems`. This is shown in lines 14–15:

```
// Unbounded sequence of CatalogItems
  typedef sequence<CatalogItem> CatalogItemArray;
```

A bounded sequence with 10 items would look like this:

```
// Bounded sequence of CatalogItems
  typedef sequence<CatalogItem, 10> CatalogItemArray;
```

In IDL, all Java arrays will need to be mapped a similar way. Finally in the `Inventory.idl` file, you have an `Inventory` interface that—as you shall see later—maps to a Java class.

> **NOTE**
>
> For a complete listing of how to map IDL to Java, visit the following Web site: `http://www.omg.org/corba/cichpter.html#mijav`. This page is Chapter 24 for the CORBA/IIOP 2.2 Specification.

Now you need to generate the Java classes that will be used to implement this IDL file. To do this, execute the following command and the `idl2java` compiler will generate your classes:

```
idl2java -no_comments -no_tie Inventory.idl
```

After the compiler is done, you will see a directory `InventorySystem`. This is a Java package that corresponds to your module name. If you change to this directory, you will find the following files:

- `CD.java`
- `CDHolder.java`
- `CDHelper.java`
- `CatalogItem.java`
- `CatalogItemHolder.java`
- `CatalogItemHelper.java`
- `CatalogItemArrayHolder.java`
- `CatalogItemArrayHelper.java`
- `Inventory.java`
- `InventoryHolder.java`
- `InventoryHelper.java`
- `_st_Inventory.java`
- `_InventoryImplBase.java`
- `_example_Inventory.java`

I will briefly discuss the classes that are not `<attribute>Holder.java` and `<attribute>Helper.java`. Begin with `CD.java`, shown in Listing 14.21.

LISTING 14.21 CD.JAVA CLASS

```
package InventorySystem;
final public class CD {
  public java.lang.String title;
  public java.lang.String author;
  public CD() {
  }
  public CD(
    java.lang.String title,
    java.lang.String author
  ) {
    this.title = title;
    this.author = author;
  }
```

14

SERVLETS AS
DISTRIBUTED
OBJECT CLIENTS

continues

LISTING 14.21   CONTINUED

```java
public java.lang.String toString() {
  org.omg.CORBA.Any any = org.omg.CORBA.ORB.init().create_any();
  InventorySystem.CDHelper.insert(any, this);
  return any.toString();
}
}
```

The CD struct was mapped to a final public class named CD within the InventorySystem package. Notice that there are no read or write methods on the attributes. However, there is a constructor that takes the attributes upon instantiation. Also, notice the CORBA implementation of the toString() method.

The CatalogItem struct, shown in Listing 14.22, was mapped in a similar way. However, it contains a CD class within its own class.

LISTING 14.22   CATALOGITEM.JAVA CLASS

```java
package InventorySystem;
final public class CatalogItem {
  public InventorySystem.CD aCD;
  public double price;
  public int quantity;
  public CatalogItem() {
  }
  public CatalogItem(
    InventorySystem.CD aCD,
    double price,
    int quantity
  ) {
    this.aCD = aCD;
    this.price = price;
    this.quantity = quantity;
  }
  public java.lang.String toString() {
    org.omg.CORBA.Any any = org.omg.CORBA.ORB.init().create_any();
    InventorySystem.CatalogItemHelper.insert(any, this);
    return any.toString();
  }
}
```

The `Inventory.java` class, shown in Listing 14.23, was generated from the `Inventory` interface in the IDL file. There is no surprise here.

LISTING 14.23 INVENTORY.JAVA CLASS

```
package InventorySystem;
public interface Inventory extends com.inprise.vbroker.CORBA.Object {
  public InventorySystem.CatalogItem[] catalogItemsArray();
  public void addCatalogItem(
    InventorySystem.CatalogItem inItem
  );
  public boolean inInventory(
    InventorySystem.CatalogItem inItem
  );
  public InventorySystem.CatalogItem[] getCatalogItems();
  public int getQuantityInInventory(
    InventorySystem.CatalogItem inItem
  );
}
```

The next generated file is `_example_Inventory.java`. This is the sample code for the skeleton implementation. I have made a copy of this class and renamed it `InventoryImpl.java`. The implemented server object from the example is shown in Listing 14.24.

LISTING 14.24 INVENTORYIMPL.JAVA CLASS

```
package InventorySystem;
import java.util.Vector;

public class InventoryImpl
  extends InventorySystem._InventoryImplBase {

  // allocate storage for the Catalog Items.
  private Vector catalogItems = new Vector();

  public InventoryImpl(java.lang.String name) {
    super(name);

    CD cdUnderTable = new CD("Under the Table and Dreaming",
      "Dave Matthews Band");
    addCatalogItem(new CatalogItem(cdUnderTable, 19, 2));
```

14

SERVLETS AS
DISTRIBUTED
OBJECT CLIENTS

continues

LISTING 14.24   CONTINUED

```
    CD cdCrash = new CD("Crash", "Dave Matthews Band");
    addCatalogItem(new CatalogItem(cdCrash,15, 3));

    CD cdMMBT = new CD("Don't Know How to Party",
      "The Mighty Mighty Boss Tones");
    addCatalogItem(new CatalogItem(cdMMBT, 14.5, 1));
  }

  public InventoryImpl() {
    super();
  }

  public void addCatalogItem(InventorySystem.CatalogItem inItem) {
    // IMPLEMENT: Operation
    if(!catalogItems.contains(inItem)) {
      catalogItems.addElement(inItem);
      System.out.println("Added item: " + inItem);
    } else {
      System.out.println("Store already contains: " + inItem);
    }
  }

  public boolean inInventory(InventorySystem.CatalogItem inItem) {
    // IMPLEMENT: Operation
    return catalogItems.contains(inItem);
  }

  public InventorySystem.CatalogItem[] getCatalogItems() {
    // IMPLEMENT: Operation
    InventorySystem.CatalogItem[] catalogItemsArray =
      new InventorySystem.CatalogItem[catalogItems.size()];
    catalogItems.copyInto(catalogItemsArray);
    return catalogItemsArray;
  }

  public int getQuantityInInventory(
    InventorySystem.CatalogItem inItem
  ) {
    // IMPLEMENT: Operation
    CatalogItem item = null;
    if(catalogItems.contains(inItem)) {
      int index = catalogItems.indexOf(inItem);
```

```
        item = (CatalogItem)catalogItems.elementAt(index);
        System.out.println("quantity="+item.quantity);
    }
    return item.quantity;
}

public InventorySystem.CatalogItem[] catalogItemsArray() {
    // IMPLEMENT: Reader for attribute
    return getCatalogItems();
}

public static void main(String args[]) {
    // Initialize the ORB.
    org.omg.CORBA.ORB orb = org.omg.CORBA.ORB.init();
    // Initialize the BOA. use with VisiBroker 3.3
    //org.omg.CORBA.BOA boa = orb.BOA_init();
    // Initialize the BOA. use with VisiBroker 3.4
    org.omg.CORBA.BOA boa =
       ((com.visigenic.vbroker.orb.ORB)orb).BOA_init();
    // Create the MyRandom object.
    InventoryImpl inventory = new InventoryImpl("Inventory");

    // Export the newly created object.
    boa.obj_is_ready(inventory);
    System.out.println(inventory + " is ready.");
    // Wait for incoming requests
    boa.impl_is_ready();
    System.out.println("Inventory created.");
  }
}
```

The `InventoryImpl.java` class, just like the `_example_Inventory.java` class, extends the `_InventoryImplBase.java` class. I have added in the constructor the creation of CD items and added each one to the `Vector` inside the `InventoryImpl` class. Because this is the server object, you can use the Java collection classes within the class. In addition, I have provided the functionality for a `main()` method within the class. This method permits the object to be launched to initialize itself and perform the standard duties with the ORB. The additional added code is in each method where the comment is `// IMPLEMENT`.

Finally, Listing 14.25 contains the `InventoryClient.java` class that was created from a copy of the `_st_Inventory.java` class.

14

SERVLETS AS DISTRIBUTED OBJECT CLIENTS

LISTING 14.25   INVENTORYCLIENT.JAVA CLASS

```java
package InventorySystem;

public class InventoryClient extends
  com.inprise.vbroker.CORBA.portable.ObjectImpl
  implements InventorySystem.Inventory {

  protected InventorySystem.Inventory _wrapper = null;

  public InventorySystem.Inventory _this() {
    return this;
  }
  public java.lang.String[] _ids() {
    return __ids;
  }
  private static java.lang.String[] __ids = {
    "IDL:InventorySystem/Inventory:1.0"
  };
  public void addCatalogItem(
    InventorySystem.CatalogItem inItem
  ) {
    org.omg.CORBA.portable.OutputStream _output;
    org.omg.CORBA.portable.InputStream _input;
    while(true) {
      _output = this._request("addCatalogItem", true);
      InventorySystem.CatalogItemHelper.write(_output, inItem);
      try {
        _input = this._invoke(_output, null);
      }
      catch(org.omg.CORBA.TRANSIENT _exception) {
        continue;
      }
      break;
    }
  }
  public boolean inInventory(
    InventorySystem.CatalogItem inItem
  ) {
    org.omg.CORBA.portable.OutputStream _output;
    org.omg.CORBA.portable.InputStream _input;
    boolean _result;
    while(true) {
      _output = this._request("inInventory", true);
      InventorySystem.CatalogItemHelper.write(_output, inItem);
```

```
      try {
        _input = this._invoke(_output, null);
        _result = _input.read_boolean();
      }
      catch(org.omg.CORBA.TRANSIENT _exception) {
        continue;
      }
      break;
    }
    return _result;
  }
  public InventorySystem.CatalogItem[] getCatalogItems() {
    org.omg.CORBA.portable.OutputStream _output;
    org.omg.CORBA.portable.InputStream _input;
    InventorySystem.CatalogItem[] _result;
    while(true) {
      _output = this._request("getCatalogItems", true);
      try {
        _input = this._invoke(_output, null);
        _result = InventorySystem.CatalogItemArrayHelper.read(_input);
      }
      catch(org.omg.CORBA.TRANSIENT _exception) {
        continue;
      }
      break;
    }
    return _result;
  }
  public int getQuantityInInventory(
    InventorySystem.CatalogItem inItem
  ) {
    org.omg.CORBA.portable.OutputStream _output;
    org.omg.CORBA.portable.InputStream _input;
    int _result;
    while(true) {
      _output = this._request("getQuantityInInventory", true);
      InventorySystem.CatalogItemHelper.write(_output, inItem);
      try {
        _input = this._invoke(_output, null);
        _result = _input.read_long();
      }
      catch(org.omg.CORBA.TRANSIENT _exception) {
        continue;
```

continues

14

SERVLETS AS
DISTRIBUTED
OBJECT CLIENTS

LISTING 14.25   CONTINUED

```
      }
      break;
    }
    return _result;
  }
  public InventorySystem.CatalogItem[] catalogItemsArray() {
    org.omg.CORBA.portable.OutputStream _output;
    org.omg.CORBA.portable.InputStream _input;
    InventorySystem.CatalogItem[] _result;
    while(true) {
      _output = this._request("_get_catalogItemsArray", true);
      try {
        _input = this._invoke(_output, null);
        _result = InventorySystem.CatalogItemArrayHelper.read(_input);
      }
      catch(org.omg.CORBA.TRANSIENT _exception) {
        continue;
      }
      break;
    }
    return _result;
  }

  public static void main(String[] args) {
    // Initialize the ORB.
    org.omg.CORBA.ORB orb = org.omg.CORBA.ORB.init(args,null);

    // Locate an Inventory Object and bind to it.
    InventorySystem.Inventory inventory =
      InventorySystem.InventoryHelper.bind(orb, "Inventory");

    InventorySystem.CatalogItem[] rtnItems =
        inventory.getCatalogItems();

    CatalogItem item = null;

    for(int i=0, len=rtnItems.length; i<len; i++) {
      System.out.println("CatalogItem = " + rtnItems[i]);
    }

  }
}
```

The only added code to this class is the main() method to initialize the ORB, get an Inventory object reference from the ORB, execute the getCatalogItems() method on the stub, and have the skeleton on the server return the array of catalogItems. I have only printed out the items by calling the toString() method because this example was for giving the basics of the IDL to Java method.

To execute the example, perform the following tasks:

1. Run the javac *.java command in the InventorySystem directory.

2. Change to the parent directory of the InventorySystem directory.

3. Start the osagent.

4. Start the server with the following command:

   ```
   java InventorySystem.InventoryImpl
   ```

5. In another window, start the client with the following command:

   ```
   java InventorySystem.InventoryClient
   ```

The server will output the following message in its window:

```
Added item: struct CatalogItem{CD aCD=struct CD{string title=
"Under the Table and Dreaming";string author="Dave Matthews Band";};
double price=19.0;long quantity=2;}
Added item: struct CatalogItem{CD aCD=struct CD{string title=
"Crash";string author="Dave Matthews Band";};
double price=15.0;long quantity=3;}
Added item: struct CatalogItem{CD aCD=struct CD{string title=
"Don\'t Know How to Party";string author="The Mighty Mighty Boss
Tones";};double price=14.5;long quantity=1;}
InventorySystem.InventoryImpl[Server,oid=PersistentId
[repId=IDL:InventorySystem/Inventory:1.0,objectName=Inventory]] is ready.
```

The client will output the following message in its window:

```
CatalogItem = struct CatalogItem{CD aCD=struct CD{string title=
"Under the Table and Dreaming";string author="Dave Matthews Band";};
double price=19.0;long quantity=2;}
CatalogItem = struct CatalogItem{CD aCD=struct CD{string title=
"Crash";string author="Dave Matthews Band";};
double price=15.0;long quantity=3;}
CatalogItem = struct CatalogItem{CD aCD=struct CD{string title=
"Don\'t Know How to Party";string author="The Mighty Mighty Boss
Tones";};double price=14.5;long quantity=1;}
```

And thus, you have created a client/server CORBA solution using IDL and generating the Java stubs and skeletons.

14

SERVLETS AS
DISTRIBUTED
OBJECT CLIENTS

OTHER BOOKS THAT COVER CORBA AND RMI

If you would like additional information on using CORBA and RMI, you'll find any of the following books helpful:

- *The Official VisiBroker for Java Handbook* by Michael McCaffery. Publisher: Sams; ISBN: 0-672-31451-7.
- *Programming with VisiBroker: A Developer's Guide to VisiBroker for Java* by Doug Pedrick (Editor), Jonathan Weedon, Jon Goldberg, and Erik Bleifield. Publisher: John Wiley & Sons; ISBN: 0-471-23901-1.
- *CORBA Programming Unleashed* by Suhail Ahmed. Publisher: Sams; ISBN: 0-672-31026-0.
- *Sams Teach Yourself CORBA in 14 Days* by Jeremy Rosenberger; Publisher: Sams; ISBN: 0-672-31208-5.
- *Java Distributed Objects* by Bill McCarty. Publisher: Sams; ISBN: 0-672-31537-8.

SUMMARY

In this chapter, you have seen servlets as distributed object clients using both RMI and CORBA. It should be obvious to you that when using a pure Java client and server, the easiest distributed computing paradigm is RMI. However, you can use CORBA with relatively little work. The choice between the two relies more on the requirements of your problem domain. CORBA has firewall issues similar to RMI; however, firewall vendor companies are moving toward providing CORBA access to objects behind the firewall. The RMI firewall issue seems to have more difficulties. This, to me, seems to be the major reason someone would choose CORBA over RMI. If it were left solely to development issues, I would choose RMI. However, if you are going to have a distributed object solution, most likely you will have to deal with firewall issues.

I have not attempted to address speed comparisons between RMI and CORBA. If you are interested in speed, check out the following book: *Client/Server Programming with Java and CORBA*, Second Edition; authors, Robert Orfali and Dan Harkey; publisher, Wiley & Sons; ISBN, 047124578X. The authors use basic functionality examples to compare CORBA in many implementations.

THE ONLINE CATALOG

IN THIS CHAPTER

REQUIREMENTS

In this chapter, you are going to put your newly found knowledge to practical use by creating your very own movie catalog system. In this first section you will be looking at a simplified set of requirements for the Sams Online Catalog System, henceforth know as SOCS.

The SOCS's requirements can be broken down into three sections: the catalog, order processing, and database sections. Each of these sections is defined as follows.

> **NOTE**
>
> For this example, I will be using LiveSoftware's JRun 2.3. At the time of this writing, it is one of the few servers that support the JSDK 2.1.

Catalog Requirements

The catalog requirements define the display and selection of the movies in the catalog. These requirements are defined in the following sections.

Movie Presentation

The SOCS catalog interface must be able to present the user with two ways to display a list of movies. The first method is to select a category by which movies will be grouped. The second will be a list of movie titles displayed as the result of a title search. Both of these lists will be displayed in the same format.

Movie Selection

When the user has found the movie he is looking for, he should be able to select it and add it to the shopping cart. He can repeat these two steps as many times as he would like, until his order is complete.

Order Processing Requirements

The order processing section of the SOCS application comes into action when the user has selected all the movies he wants to order. At this point, he must be provided with a method to submit the order for processing. When the order has been submitted, it will then be transferred to the fulfillment department.

NOTE

For this example, the submitted order will not actually be submitted to fulfillment. It will only be acknowledged with a thank you message.

Database Requirements

This section of the requirements defines the database representation of the SOCS application. Only two objects in the SOCS application will be modeled in the database.

The first object that will be represented in the database is the Movie object itself. Each of the Movie object's attributes must be included in the table representation. Table 15.1 lists the required elements needed to store a Movie object.

TABLE 15.1 REQUIRED ATTRIBUTES TO MODEL A MOVIE

Attribute	Type
title_id	int
title_name	String
price	double
quantity	int
category	int

The second object that will be represented in the database is the Category object by which movies are grouped. Table 15.2 lists the required elements needed to store a Category object.

TABLE 15.2 REQUIRED ATTRIBUTES TO MODEL A CATEGORY

Attribute	Type
category_id	int
category_name	String

The category_id and category_name objects are directly mapped to the Titles and Categories tables, respectively. Figure 15.1 shows the relationship of these two tables.

NOTE

I will be using Microsoft Access and the JDBC-ODBC Bridge in this application.

FIGURE 15.1
The SOCS table relationships.

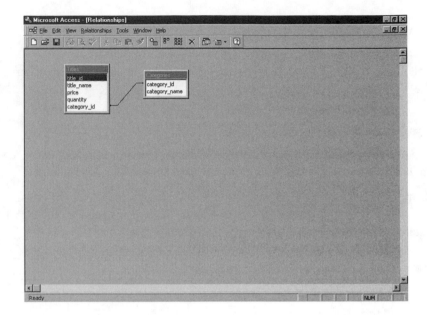

THE CATALOG OBJECTS

You will be using several objects in the SOCS application. These objects can be grouped into four categories. Each of these categories and their objects are described in detail in the following sections.

Database Connection Objects

The database connection objects provide the interface between your application and the persistent store of your catalog objects. It consists of the same three objects you used in Chapter 8, "Servlets and the JDBC." The object model in Figure 15.2 shows these objects and their relationships.

The ConnectionPoolServlet is the object that manages the ConnectionPool. It is derived from an HttpServlet and creates a ConnectionPool object. When it has created the ConnectionPool object, it places a reference to it in the ServletContext. The ConnectionPoolServlet should be compiled and added to the server as a preloaded Servlet Alias. Figure 15.3 shows the appropriate settings in the JRun Administration Tool.

The ConnectionPool object then creates a vector of PooledConnection objects. The PooledConnection objects actually encapsulate a JDBC connection. You can find the source for these objects in the ConnectionPool package, which is part of Chapter 8, "Servlets and the JDBC."

FIGURE 15.2

The database connection object model.

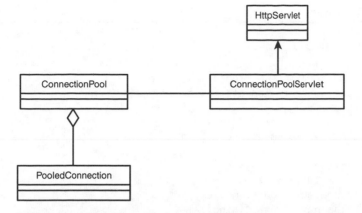

FIGURE 15.3

ConnectionPoolServlet alias setup.

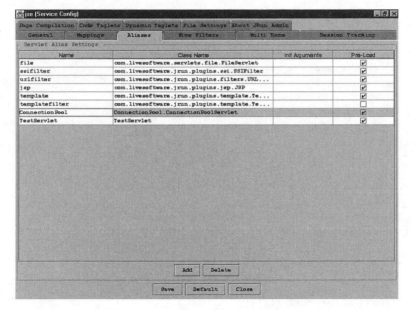

Catalog Objects

The catalog objects represent the movies and their categories. There are two main catalog objects. The first is the Movie object, which is a simple object that represents a single movie title. The Movie object is a one-to-one mapping to the database table Titles. The source for the Movie object is listed in Listing 15.1.

LISTING 15.1   MOVIE.JAVA

```java
import java.io.*;

/*
    This class represents a single movie from
    the database.  It implements the minimum requirements
    to be a bean.
*/
public class Movie implements Serializable {

  // Unique title_id
  private int title_id = -1;
  // String representation of movie
  private String name = new String("");
  // price of movie
  private double price = 0.0;
  // quantity in stock
  private int quantity = 0;
  // code that maps to the category table
  private int category = 0;

  // Method Name: Category()
  // Purpose: default constructor
  public Movie() {

  }

  // Method Name: setTitleId()
  // Purpose: Access used to set the title id
  public void setTitleId(int value) {

    title_id = value;
  }

  // Method Name: getTitleId()
  // Purpose: Access used to get the title id
  public int getTitleId() {

    return title_id;
  }

  // Method Name: setName()
  // Purpose: Access used to set the title name
  public void setName(String value) {
```

```
   if ( value != null ) {

     name = value;
   }
}

// Method Name: getName()
// Purpose: Access used to get the title name
public String getName() {

   return name;
}

// Method Name: setPrice()
// Purpose: Access used to set the price
public void setPrice(double value) {

   price = value;
}

// Method Name: getPrice()
// Purpose: Access used to get the price
public double getPrice() {

   return price;
}

// Method Name: setQuantity()
// Purpose: Access used to set the quantity
public void setQuantity(int value) {

   quantity = value;
}

// Method Name: getQuantity()
// Purpose: Access used to get the quantity
public int getQuantity() {

   return quantity;
}

// Method Name: setCategory()
// Purpose: Access used to set the category id
public void setCategory(int value) {
```

continues

15

THE ONLINE CATALOG

LISTING 15.1   CONTINUED

```java
    category = value;
  }

  // Method Name: getCategory()
  // Purpose: Access used to get the category id
  public int getCategory() {

    return category;
  }
}
```

The second catalog object is the `Category` object. It is also a simple object that represents a single movie category. The `Category` object is a one-to-one mapping to the database table Category. The source for the `Category` object is shown in Listing 15.2.

LISTING 15.2   CATEGORY.JAVA

```java
import java.io.Serializable;

/*
    This class represents a single category from
    the database.  It implements the minimum requirements
    to be a bean.
*/
public class Category implements Serializable {

  // Unique Id from database
  private int id = 0;
  // Name of Category
  private String name = new String("");

  // Method Name: Category()
  // Purpose: default constructor
  public Category() {

  }

  // Method Name: setId()
  // Purpose: Access used to set the category id
  public void setId(int value) {

    id = value;
  }
```

```
// Method Name: getId()
// Purpose: Access used to get the category id
public int getId() {

  return id;
}

// Method Name: setName()
// Purpose: Access used to set the category name
public void setName(String value) {

  if ( value != null ) {

    name = value;
  }
}

// Method Name: getName()
// Purpose: Access used to get the category name
public String getName() {

  return name;
}
}
```

HTML or Presentation Objects

The HTML objects you are going to use represent the presentation layer of the application. They are all derived from objects in the HTML package that you created in Chapter 4. Each of these HTML objects is created by the `CatalogServlet` and fitted together to create a default HTML page. An example of how these objects visually fit together is shown in Figure 15.4.

As you can see, there are three cells, a table, and a client area. This is the page layout used for most of the presentation. These objects are visually modeled in Figure 15.5.

NOTE

The client area from the previous figure is not modeled in the Object Model because it is only an instance of an `HTMLTable` object from the HTML package. You will see how it is created in the "Servlets" section of this chapter.

FIGURE 15.4

A visual layout of the SOCS HTML objects.

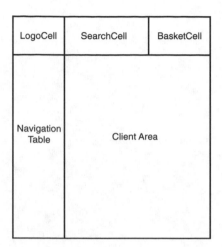

FIGURE 15.5

The object model of presentation objects.

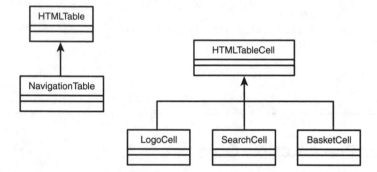

The LogoCell

The `LogoCell` object is the simplest of all the visual objects. It is derived from the `HTMLTableCell` object, and all its functionality is in the constructor. The `LogoCell`'s constructor performs two steps. It first passes the `HTMLTableCell.DATA` parameter to its parent, which defines the cell as a data cell. It then creates an `HTMLImage` containing a logo for the site. The source for the `LogoCell` object is in Listing 15.3.

LISTING 15.3   LOGOCELL.JAVA

```
import HTML.*;

/*
    This class represents a table cell that acts as a
    container for the Sams Logo
*/
```

```
public class LogoCell extends HTMLTableCell {

  // Method Name: Constructor()
  // Purpose: Creates an HTMLTableCell object and adds an
  // HTMLImage of the Sams logo.
  public LogoCell() {

    super(HTMLTableCell.DATA);
    // add the HTMLImage object to the HTMLTableCell
    addObject(new HTMLImage("/images/sams.gif", "Sams Logo"));
  }
}
```

The SearchCell

The SearchCell encapsulates the functionality to perform basic title searching. It is derived from the HTMLTableCell object and contains an HTMLForm object named SearchForm. The source for the SearchCell is in Listing 15.4.

LISTING 15.4   SEARCHCELL.JAVA

```
import HTML.*;

/*
    This class serves a container for the SearchForm.
    It creates a SearchForm object and adds it to itself.
    It is derived from HTMLTableCell.
*/

public class SearchCell extends HTMLTableCell {

  // Method Name: SearchCell() Constructor
  // Purpose : This is where all of the processing is done
  // in this class.  It creates an HTMLHeading and a SearchForm
  // object and adds it to its own list of HTMLObjects.
  public SearchCell() {

    super(HTMLTableCell.DATA);

    // Create an HTMLHeading
    HTMLHeading heading = new HTMLHeading("Title Search",
      HTMLHeading.H4);
    heading.setAlignment(CENTER);
    addObject(heading);
```

continues

LISTING 15.4   CONTINUED

```
    // Create a SearchForm
    addObject(new SearchForm());
  }
}
```

The `SearchForm` object contained by the `SearchCell` is a simple HTML form that contains an input box to enter a search string and a submit button to actually submit the action. The `ACTION` attribute of the `SearchForm` points to the `TitleListServlet`, which is described in the "Servlets" section of this chapter. The source for the `SearchForm` is in Listing 15.5.

LISTING 15.5   SEARCHFORM.JAVA

```
import HTML.*;

/*
    This class is an HTMLForm object used to perform
    title searches.  It is derived from HTMLForm.
*/

public class SearchForm extends HTMLForm {

  // Method Name: SearchForm() Constructor
  // Purpose : This is where all of the processing is done
  // in this class.  It creates the appropriate Input
  // objects that are necessary to perform a search.
  public SearchForm() {

    // Set the action to point to the TitleListServlet
    setAction("/servlet/TitleListServlet");
    setAlignment(CENTER);

    // Build the search string edit box
    HTMLTextInput text_input = new HTMLTextInput();
    text_input.setSize(30);
    text_input.setName("search_string");

    // Add the HTMLTextInput object to the Form
    addObject(text_input);

    // Create and add an HTMLSubmitButton
    HTMLSubmitButton submit_button = new HTMLSubmitButton();
    submit_button.setName("Submit");
    submit_button.setValue("GO");
```

```
        addObject(submit_button);
    }
}
```

The BasketCell

The `BasketCell` object is also derived from an `HTMLTableCell` object. It has quite a bit more functionality than the other display cells. It encapsulates the visual aspects of a shopping basket. Take a look at the `BasketCell`'s source in Listing 15.6.

LISTING 15.6   BASKETCELL.JAVA

```java
import javax.servlet.http.*;
import java.util.Vector;
import java.text.DecimalFormat;

import HTML.*;

/*
    This class serves as a container for the Shopping Basket.
    It gets a reference to the Shopping Basket in the
    HttpSession and iterates over it compiling the totals
    for immediate display.  It is derived from HTMLTableCell.
*/

public class BasketCell extends HTMLTableCell {

    // Method Name: BasketCell() Constructor
    // Purpose : This is where all of the processing is done
    // in this class.  It takes the current list of movies in
    // the HttpSession object and displays them in a table.
    public BasketCell(HttpServletRequest request) {

        super(HTMLTableCell.DATA);

        int items = 0;
        double total = 0;

        // Get a reference to the current session
        HttpSession session = request.getSession(true);

        // Try to get the current basket in the shopping cart
        Vector basket = (Vector)session.getValue("basket");

        if ( basket != null ) {
```

continues

LISTING 15.6   CONTINUED

```java
      // Get the total number of items.
      items = basket.size();

      // Total the price of all the items.
      for ( int x = 0; x < items; x++ ) {

        total = total + ((Movie)basket.elementAt(x)).getPrice();
      }
    }
    setHorizontalAlign(CENTER);

    // Create a Table to display the results in.
    HTMLTable table = new HTMLTable();
    HTMLTableRow row = new HTMLTableRow();

    HTMLTableCell cell = new HTMLTableCell(HTMLTableCell.DATA);
    cell.setHorizontalAlign(CENTER);

    // Add an image link to the Shopping Basket
    HTMLLink link =
      new HTMLLink("/servlet/ShoppingBasketServlet",
      new HTMLImage("/images/shopping_cart.gif",
      "ShoppingCart"));

    // Shopping Basket Image Link
    cell.addObject(link);
    // Add the cell to the row
    row.addObject(cell);
    // Add the row to the table
    table.addObject(row);

    // Number of items
    row = new HTMLTableRow();
    cell = new HTMLTableCell(HTMLTableCell.DATA);
    HTMLText text = new HTMLText("Items: " + items);
    cell.addObject(text);
    row.addObject(cell);
    table.addObject(row);

    // Total Prices
    // Format the Price textual display
    DecimalFormat form = new DecimalFormat("##0.00");

    row = new HTMLTableRow();
```

```
    cell = new HTMLTableCell(HTMLTableCell.DATA);
    text = new HTMLText("Total: $" + form.format(total));
    cell.addObject(text);
    row.addObject(cell);

    table.addObject(row);

    addObject(table);
  }
}
```

Notice that all its functionality is found in the constructor. Also notice that the constructor is passed a reference to an `HttpServletRequest` object. This is because it must have access to the current `HttpSession` object to get a reference to the basket `Vector` containing the currently selected movies.

The first thing the `BasketCell` does is get a reference to the current `HttpSession` object. When it has this reference, it looks in the session for a vector keyed by the string `basket`. This vector contains a list of movies that have been selected by the user. The `BasketCell` then iterates over the list of movies, totaling the price. It then takes this information and creates a table that contains an image link pointing to the `ShoppingBasketServlet` and the text displaying the total number of items and their total price.

The NavigationTable

The `NavigationTable` is used to perform basic navigation throughout the SOCS site. It provides three different navigational paths. It contains a link to the `WelcomeServlet`, which is the equivalent of most sites' `index.html` pages. It has a link to the `ShoppingBasketServlet`, which is where the user goes when she wants to see the current contents of her shopping basket. And, most importantly, it contains a dynamically generated list of movie categories.

The `NavigationTable`, like our other visual components, has all its functionality contained in the constructor. Notice that it receives only one parameter, a reference to the `ServletContext`.

The `NavigationTable` uses the `ServletContext` object to get a reference to the list of categories and their corresponding codes, which have been cached by the `CategoryDomainServlet`. It takes this vector of `Category` objects and constructs a list of encoded links that point to the `TitleListServlet`. These links contain a code that represents a category record in the database. The `TitleListServlet` uses these codes to perform database lookups on the selected categories. Take a look at the `NavigationTable`'s source in Listing 15.7.

LISTING 15.7   NAVIGATIONTABLE.JAVA

```java
import javax.servlet.*;
import java.util.Vector;

import HTML.*;

/*
    This class serves a container for the Navigation Table.
    It gets a reference to the DOMAIN_LIST in the
    ServletContext and iterates over it listing the Categories.
    It is derived from HTMLTable.
*/

public class NavigationTable extends HTMLTable {

  // Method Name: NavigationTable()
  // Purpose: This is the only constructor defined for the
  // NavigationTable.  All of this class's functionality
  // is defined in this method.
  public NavigationTable(ServletContext context) {

    // Define a fixed table width
    setWidthByPixel(150);
    //setWidth(15);

    setHorizontalAlign(LEFT);
    setVerticalAlign(TOP);
    HTMLText caption = new HTMLText("Categories");
    caption.setBold(true);
    setCaption(caption);

    // Get a reference to the Vector that contains the Category
    // objects.
    Vector categories =
      (Vector)context.getAttribute("DOMAIN_LIST");

    // Iterate over this Vector creating links to
    // the TitleListServlet including a category
    // id to perform a lookup on.
    for (int x = 0; x < categories.size(); x++ ) {

      Category category = (Category)categories.elementAt(x);

      HTMLTableRow row = new HTMLTableRow();
      HTMLTableCell cell
        = new HTMLTableCell(HTMLTableCell.DATA);
```

```
  // Create the link and add it to the cell
  cell.addObject(
    new HTMLLink("/servlet/TitleListServlet?category_id=" +
      category.getId(),
    new HTMLText(category.getName())));

  // add the cell to the row
  row.addObject(cell);
  // add the row to the table
  addObject(row);
}

// Create Other Navigation Items
HTMLTableRow row;
HTMLTableCell cell;

// Create a simple separator
row = new HTMLTableRow();
cell = new HTMLTableCell(HTMLTableCell.DATA);
cell.addObject(new HTMLHorizontalRule());
row.addObject(cell);
addObject(row);

// Link to the WelcomeServlet
row = new HTMLTableRow();
cell = new HTMLTableCell(HTMLTableCell.DATA);
cell.addObject(new HTMLLink("/servlet/WelcomeServlet",
  new HTMLText("Home")));
row.addObject(cell);
addObject(row);

// Link to the ShoppingBasketServlet
row = new HTMLTableRow();
cell = new HTMLTableCell(HTMLTableCell.DATA);
cell.addObject(new HTMLLink("/servlet/ShoppingBasketServlet",
  new HTMLText("Checkout")));
row.addObject(cell);
addObject(row);
  }
}
```

The Client Area

The client area depicted in Figure 15.4 is an HTMLTable object that is rendered differently by every servlet in the SOCS application. It is returned by the buildClientArea() method that is implemented by almost all the servlets. This area is described completely in the next section.

Servlets

The servlets defined in the SOCS application are the backbone of the site. A total of eight
servlets make up this system. Each one of these servlets is discussed in this section.

The CatalogDomainServlet

The CatalogDomainServlet is one of three utility servlets in the SOCS application. Its purpose
is to cache frequently used database information. In this case, you are caching the Category
objects from the database. Listing 15.8 contains the CatalogDomainServlet's source.

LISTING 15.8   CATALOGDOMAINSERVLET.JAVA

```java
import javax.servlet.*;
import javax.servlet.http.*;
import java.io.*;
import java.util.*;
import java.sql.*;

import ConnectionPool.*;

/*
    This servlet acts as a cache for domain values.  In our
    Catalog Example it caches the Category Names and Codes.
    Preventing excessive database queries.
*/
public class CatalogDomainServlet extends HttpServlet {

  // Method Name: init()
  // Purpose: This is the default init() method.
  public void init(ServletConfig config)
    throws ServletException {

    super.init(config);

    initializeDomains();
  }

  // Method Name: initializeDomains()
  // Purpose: This method gets a reference to the database
  // ConnectionPool from the ServletContext.  It then performs
  // a query getting all of the Category values in the
  // database.  These values are then stored in a Vector and
  // placed in the ServletContext keyed by the string
  // DOMAIN_LIST.
  private void initializeDomains() throws ServletException {
```

```
Connection con = null;
ConnectionPool pool = null;
Vector categories = new Vector(8);
Category category = null;

try {

  // Get a reference to the ConnectionPool from the Global
  // ServletContext
  ServletContext context = getServletContext();
  // Get a connection from the ConnectionPool
  if ( context == null ) {

    throw new ServletException("Could not get a reference" +
      " to the ServletContext");
  }
  pool =(ConnectionPool)
    context.getAttribute("CONNECTION_POOL");

  // Get a connection from the ConnectionPool
  if ( pool == null ) {

    // Sleep for 5 seconds and try again
    try {

      Thread.sleep(5000);
      pool =(ConnectionPool)
        context.getAttribute("CONNECTION_POOL");
    }
    catch (Exception e) {

      throw new ServletException(e.getMessage());
    }
    if ( pool == null ) {

      // Still could not get reference
      throw new ServletException("Could not get reference" +
        " to the CONNECTION_POOL");
    }
  }
  con = pool.getConnection();
  // Get a connection from the ConnectionPool
  if ( con == null ) {

    throw new ServletException("Could not get reference" +
      " Connection.");
```

continues

LISTING 15.8   CONTINUED

```java
    }
    if ( con != null ) {

      // Create the statement
      Statement statement = con.createStatement();

      // Use the created statement to SELECT the DATA
      // FROM the Categories Table.
      ResultSet rs = statement.executeQuery("SELECT * " +
       "FROM Categories");

      // Iterate over the ResultSet
      while ( rs.next() ) {

        category = new Category();

        category.setId(rs.getInt("category_id"));

        // get the name, which is a String
        category.setName(rs.getString("category_name"));

        // add the resulting category to the Vector
        categories.addElement(category);
      }
      // Close the ResultSet
      rs.close();

      // Once the domain list is Initialized, add it to the
      // Global ServletContext.  This makes it available
      // To other servlets using the same ServletContext.
      context.setAttribute("DOMAIN_LIST", categories);
    }
  }
  catch (SQLException sqle) {

    System.err.println(sqle.getMessage());
  }
  catch (Exception e) {

    System.err.println(e.getMessage());
  }
  finally {

    // Release the connection
```

```
      pool.releaseConnection(con);
   }
}

// Method Name: doGet()
// Purpose: This method services GET requests.  Its only
// purpose is to prove that the domain values are loading
// properly.
public void doGet(HttpServletRequest request,
  HttpServletResponse response)
  throws ServletException, IOException {

  response.setContentType("text/html");
  PrintWriter out = new PrintWriter (response.getOutputStream());
  out.println("<html>");
  out.println("<head><title>CatalogServlet</title></head>");
  out.println("<body>");

  // Get reference to ServletContext
  ServletContext context = getServletContext();
  // Get reference to the DOMAIN_LIST Vector
  Vector categories = (Vector)context.getAttribute("DOMAIN_LIST");

  // Iterate over the list of categories
  for (int x = 0; x < categories.size(); x++ ) {

    Category category = (Category)categories.elementAt(x);

   out.println(category.getId() + "-->" + category.getName() + "<BR>");
  }
  out.println("</body></html>");
  out.close();
}

// Method Name: destroy()
// Purpose: This method performs cleanup on the Vector
// and the ServletContext.
public void destroy() {

  // Access the ServletContext using the getAttribute()
  // method, which returns a reference to the Categories.
  ServletContext context = getServletContext();
  Vector categories =
    (Vector)context.getAttribute("DOMAIN_LIST");

  if ( categories != null ) {
```

continues

LISTING 15.8   CONTINUED

```
        // Empty List
        categories.removeAllElements();
        // Remove the Attribute from the ServletContext
        context.removeAttribute("DOMAIN_LIST");
    }
    else {

        System.err.println("Could not get a reference to DOMAIN_LIST!");
    }
}

//Get Servlet information
public String getServletInfo() {

    return "CatalogDomainServlet Information";
}
}
```

The initializeDomains() method is where most of the CatalogDomainSerlet's functionality is located. The first thing this method does is get a connection from the ConnectionPool stored in the ServletContext.

When the initializeDomains() method has the reference to the Connection object, it uses the reference to create a statement and perform a query that returns all the Category objects stored in the database. The results of this query are then used to create a vector of Category objects. The final step of the initializeDomains() method is to add the newly created vector to the ServletContext.

To install the CatalogDomainServlet, you must set it up as a preloaded alias. The appropriate settings using the JRun Administration tool are found in Figure 15.6.

The AddMovieServlet

The AddMovieServlet is another one of the SOCS application's utility servlets. Its only purpose is to take selected movie parameters and add them to the current shopping cart. It then redirects the browser back to the previous request. Its source code can be found in Listing 15.9.

FIGURE 15.6

CatalogDomainServlet alias settings.

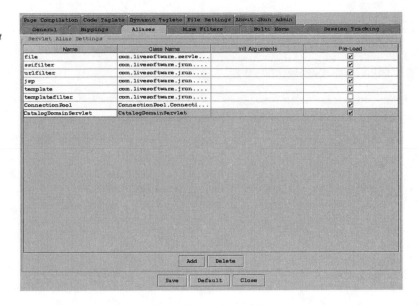

LISTING 15.9 ADDMOVIESERVLET.JAVA

```java
import javax.servlet.*;
import javax.servlet.http.*;
import java.io.*;
import java.util.*;

/*
    This servlet is used only to add a movie to the Shopping
    basket.
*/

public class AddMovieServlet extends HttpServlet {

  // Method Name: init()
  // Purpose: This is the default init() method.
  public void init(ServletConfig config)
    throws ServletException {

    super.init(config);
  }

  // Method Name: addToBasket()
  // Purpose : This method takes the Movie object passed
  // to it and adds it to the Shopping Basket Vector
```

continues

15

THE ONLINE
CATALOG

LISTING 15.9   CONTINUED

```java
// that is stored in the HttpSession Object
private void addToBasket(Movie movie,
  HttpServletRequest request) {

  // Get/Create the HttpSession
  HttpSession session = request.getSession(true);

  if ( session != null ) {

    // try to get a reference to the basket Vector.
    Vector basket = (Vector)session.getValue("basket");

    // If basket is null, create one
    if ( basket == null ) {

      basket = new Vector(5);
      session.putValue("basket", basket);
    }
    // Add the passed in movie to the basket.
    basket.addElement(movie);
  }
}

//Process the HTTP Get request
public void doGet(HttpServletRequest request,
  HttpServletResponse response)
  throws ServletException, IOException {

  response.setContentType("text/html");

  // Get the Movie parameters passed in the request.
  String id = request.getParameter("id");
  String price = request.getParameter("price");
  String redirect_url = request.getParameter("trans");

  // We are not checking out.  We are only adding an
  // item to the basket and redirecting to our previous
  // TitleListServlet response.
  if ( id != null ) {

    // Create the movie
    Movie movie = new Movie();
    movie.setTitleId((new Integer(id)).intValue());
    movie.setPrice((new Double(price)).doubleValue());
```

```
      // Add the movie to the basket.
      addToBasket(movie, request);
      // redirect the browser to the calling page.
      response.sendRedirect(redirect_url);
    }
  }

  //Get Servlet information
  public String getServletInfo() {

    return "AddMovieServlet Information";
  }
}
```

The AddMovieServlet begins its processing in the doGet() method. The first thing it does is parse parameters off the query string. It takes the received id and price values and creates a Movie object. It then passes this object to the addToBasket() method, which adds the movie to the basket vector in the current session. After the movie is added to the shopping basket, the servlet redirects the browser to the URL passed as the trans parameter in the request.

The EmptyBasketServlet

The last utility servlet in the SOCS application is the EmptyBasketServlet. It is simply used to remove the current contents of the shopping basket. It can be found in Listing 15.10.

LISTING 15.10 EMPTYBASKETSERVLET

```
import javax.servlet.*;
import javax.servlet.http.*;
import java.io.*;
import java.util.*;

/*
    This servlet is used only to handle requests to
    empty the contents of the Shopping Basket.
    Once the basket has been emptied, the servlet redirects
    the browser to the WelcomeServlet.
*/
public class EmptyBasketServlet extends HttpServlet {

  // Method Name: init()
  // Purpose: This is the default init() method.
  public void init(ServletConfig config)
    throws ServletException {
```

continues

15

LISTING 15.10 CONTINUED

```java
    super.init(config);
  }

  // Method Name: emptyBasket()
  // Purpose: This method gets a reference to the basket
  // Vector and calls the removeAllElements method, emptying
  // the entire contents of the shopping basket.
  private void emptyBasket(HttpServletRequest request) {

    // Get/Create a reference to the HttpSession object.
    HttpSession session = request.getSession(true);

    if ( session != null ) {

      // Get a reference to the basket Vector.
      Vector basket = (Vector)session.getValue("basket");

      // If basket is null, create one
      if ( basket != null ) {

        // Empty the basket.
        basket.removeAllElements();
      }
    }
  }

  // Method Name: doGet()
  // Purpose: Services requests to empty the current
  // contents of the shopping basket.  It then redirects
  // the browser to the WelcomeServlet.
  public void doGet(HttpServletRequest request,
    HttpServletResponse response)
    throws ServletException, IOException {

    emptyBasket(request);
    response.sendRedirect("/servlet/WelcomeServlet");
  }

  //Get Servlet information
  public String getServletInfo() {

    return "EmptyBasketServlet Information";
  }
}
```

The `EmptyBasketServlet` services only `GET` requests. When it receives a request, it calls the `emptyBasket()` method passing it the `HttpServletRequest` object.

The `emptyBasket()` method takes the passed-in `HttpServletRequest` object and gets the current `HttpSession` object from it. When it has a reference to the session, it gets the `Movie` vector from the session and removes all the elements stored in it.

When the `emptyBasket()` method returns, the `doGet()` method calls the `sendRedirect()` method with the URL of the `WelcomeServlet`.

The CatalogServlet

The `CatalogServlet` is probably the most important servlet in your application. It serves as the abstract base class of almost all your servlets. Its source code can be found in Listing 15.11.

LISTING 15.11   CATALOGSERVLET.JAVA

```java
import javax.servlet.*;
import javax.servlet.http.*;
import java.io.*;
import java.util.*;

import HTML.*;

/*
    This servlet is the base class for all of our servlets
    with visual responses.  It is an abstract class that
    defines a single abstract method called buildClientArea.
*/

public abstract class CatalogServlet extends HttpServlet {

  // Method Name: init()
  // Purpose: This is the default init() method.
  public void init(ServletConfig config)
    throws ServletException {

    super.init(config);
  }

  // Method Name: buildTopTable()
  // Purpose: This method builds a table that acts as a
  // container for the LogoCell, SearchCell and BasketCell
  // Objects.  All classes that inhereit from this class will
  // have this table included.
  private HTMLTable buildTopTable(HttpServletRequest request) {
```

continues

LISTING 15.11   CONTINUED

```java
HTMLTable table = new HTMLTable();
table.setWidth(100);

HTMLTableRow row = new HTMLTableRow();

// Create and add the LogoCell
LogoCell logo_cell = new LogoCell();
logo_cell.setAlignment(HTMLObject.CENTER);
row.addObject(logo_cell);

// Create and add the SearchCell
SearchCell search_cell = new SearchCell();
search_cell.setAlignment(HTMLObject.CENTER);
row.addObject(search_cell);

// Create and add the BasketCell
row.addObject(new BasketCell(request));
table.addObject(row);

return table;
}

// Method Name: buildBottomTable()
// Purpose: This method builds a table that acts as a
// container for the NavigationTable and Client Area
// Objects.  All classes that inherit from this class will
// have this table included.
private HTMLTable
  buildBottomTable(HttpServletRequest request)
  throws Exception {

  HTMLTable table = new HTMLTable();
  table.setVerticalAlign(HTMLObject.TOP);
  table.setHeight(500);
  HTMLTableRow row = new HTMLTableRow();

  // Create and add the NavigationTable
  HTMLTableCell cell = new HTMLTableCell(HTMLTableCell.DATA);
  cell.setVerticalAlign(HTMLObject.TOP);
  cell.setHorizontalAlign(HTMLObject.LEFT);
  cell.addObject(new NavigationTable(getServletContext()));

  // Call the child class's buildClientArea method, which
  // returns an HTMLTable object to be added to the
```

```
    // bottom table.
    cell.addObject(buildClientArea(request));
    row.addObject(cell);

    table.addObject(row);

    return table;
}

// Method Name: buildClientArea()
// Purpose: This is the abstract method that must be
// implemented by all children.  It represents the client
// area in the bottom table.
public abstract HTMLTable
  buildClientArea(HttpServletRequest request)
  throws Exception;

// Method Name: processRequest()
// Purpose: This method defines the framework for all child
// classes.
public final HTMLDocument
  processRequest(HttpServletRequest request)
  throws Exception {

  // Create the HTMLDocument
  HTMLDocument doc =
    new HTMLDocument("Sams Online Video Store");

  HTMLTable table = new HTMLTable();
  HTMLTableRow row = new HTMLTableRow();
  HTMLTableCell cell = new HTMLTableCell(HTMLTableCell.DATA);

  // build the Top Table
  cell.addObject(buildTopTable(request));
  row.addObject(cell);
  table.addObject(row);

  // build the Bottom Table
  row = new HTMLTableRow();
  cell = new HTMLTableCell(HTMLTableCell.DATA);
  cell.addObject(buildBottomTable(request));
  row.addObject(cell);
  table.addObject(row);

  doc.addObject(table);
```

15

continues

LISTING 15.11   CONTINUED

```
    return doc;
  }

// Method Name: doGet()
// Purpose: This is the doGet() method for all children.
// This method further defines the catalog servlet's
// framework.
public void doGet(HttpServletRequest request,
  HttpServletResponse response)
  throws ServletException, IOException {

  response.setContentType("text/html");
  PrintWriter out = response.getWriter();

  try {

    // Send the request through the processRequest()
    // method, which returns an HTMLDocument.  The
    // returned HTMLDocument.toHTML() method is then
    // called returning a String representing the HTML
    // text.
    out.println(processRequest(request).toHTML());
  }
  catch (Exception e) {

    throw new ServletException(e.getMessage());
  }
  out.close();
  }
}
```

The best place to start looking at the CatalogServlet is in the doGet() method. It is a very simple method, but it does service most of the servlet's GET requests. The first important thing the doGet() method does is call its processRequest() method, passing it a reference to the HttpServletRequest object. The processRequest() method returns an HTMLDocument object.

The processRequest() method is the heart of the CatalogServlet. It is declared as final, so no deriving objects can override it. The processRequest() method can be broken down into a four-step process:

1. It creates an HTMLDocument object to be used as a container for all the presentation objects described earlier.

2. Then it calls the `buildTopTable()` method. The `buildTopTable()` method creates an `HTMLTable` containing the three presentation `HTMLTableCell` objects: the `LogoCell`, `SearchCell`, and `BasketCell`. It returns this table object to `processRequest()`, which then adds it to the `HTMLDocument` object.

3. Next the `processRequest()` method calls the `buildBottomTable()` method. The `buildBottomTable()` method builds a table that acts as a container for the `NavigationTable` and the `HTMLTable` that is returned from the abstract `buildClientArea()` method. The `buildClientArea()` method must be implemented by all derived classes.

4. The final action of the `processRequest()` method is to return the `HTMLDocument` object to the `doGet()` method.

The framework, which is defined by the `CatalogServlet`, ensures that all its child servlets have the same look and feel. To gain these benefits, the derived servlets are only required to implement the abstract `buildClientArea()` method. This makes it very simple to plug new servlets into the SOCS application.

The WelcomeServlet

The `WelcomeServlet` is the very first servlet presented to the user in the SOCS application. It is the equivalent of most Web sites' `index.html` pages. It is derived from the `CatalogServlet` and therefore it must implement the `buildClientArea()` method.

The `WelcomeServlet`'s `buildClientArea()` is very simple. It returns an `HTMLTable` object with the message "Welcome to the Sams Online Video Store!" embedded in it. The source for the `WelcomeServlet` is in Listing 15.12.

LISTING 15.12   WELCOMESERVLET.JAVA

```
import javax.servlet.*;
import javax.servlet.http.*;
import java.io.*;
import java.util.*;

import HTML.*;

/*
    This servlet represents the first step in the order
    process.  It is the equivalent of an index.html page.
*/

public class WelcomeServlet extends CatalogServlet {
```

continues

LISTING 15.12   CONTINUED

```
// Method Name: init()
// Purpose: This is the default init() method.
public void init(ServletConfig config)
  throws ServletException {

  super.init(config);
}


// Method Name: buildClientArea()
// Purpose: This method implements its parent's abstract
// method.  It represents the client area of the browser
// window.
public HTMLTable
  buildClientArea(HttpServletRequest request)
  throws Exception {

  // Create the Table to return as the client area.
  HTMLTable table = new HTMLTable();
  table.setWidthByPixel(530);

  HTMLTableRow row = new HTMLTableRow();
  HTMLTableCell cell =
    new HTMLTableCell(HTMLTableCell.DATA);
  cell.setVerticalAlign(HTMLTableCell.TOP);
  cell.setHorizontalAlign(HTMLObject.LEFT);

  // Add a simple message welcoming customers to the
  // site.
  cell.addObject(
    new HTMLHeading("Welcome to the Sams Online Video Store!",
    HTMLHeading.H3));
  row.addObject(cell);
  table.addObject(row);

  return table;
}


//Get Servlet information
public String getServletInfo() {

  return "HTML.WelcomeServlet Information";
}
}
```

The TitleListServlet

The `TitleListServlet` is where most of the SOCS application's functionality is located. It is a servlet that is derived from the `CatalogServlet`, which forces it to implement the `buildClientArea()` method. But, more importantly, because of this derivation, it gains the same look and feel of all the servlets belonging to the framework created by the `CatalogServlet`. The source for the `TitleListServlet` is located in Listing 15.13.

LISTING 15.13   TITLELISTSERVLET.JAVA

```java
import javax.servlet.*;
import javax.servlet.http.*;
import java.io.*;
import java.util.*;
import java.sql.*;

import HTML.*;
import ConnectionPool.*;

/*
    This servlet displays a list of titles either from a
    category or title search.  Each of the titles in stock
    present the user with the option to order them.  This
    servlet inherits its doGet() method from CatalogServlet.
*/

public class TitleListServlet extends CatalogServlet {

  // Method Name: init()
  // Purpose: This is the default init() method.
  public void init(ServletConfig config)
    throws ServletException {

    super.init(config);
  }

  // Method Name: selectByCategory()
  // Purpose: This method takes the passed in category_id
  // and performs a database lookup returning the ResultSet
  // from the query.
  private ResultSet selectByCategory(int category_id) {

    Connection con = null;
    ConnectionPool pool = null;
    ResultSet rs = null;
```

continues

LISTING 15.13   CONTINUED

```
try {

  // Get a reference to the ConnectionPool from the Global
  // ServletContext
  ServletContext context = getServletContext();
  // Get a connection from the ConnectionPool
  if ( context == null ) {

    throw new ServletException("Could not get a " +
      "reference to the ServletContext");
  }
  pool =(ConnectionPool)
    context.getAttribute("CONNECTION_POOL");

  // Get a connection from the ConnectionPool
  if ( pool == null ) {

    throw new ServletException("Could not get reference" +
      " to the CONNECTION_POOL");
  }
  con = pool.getConnection();
  // Get a connection from the ConnectionPool
  if ( con == null ) {

    throw new ServletException("Could not get reference" +
      " Connection.");
  }
  if ( con != null ) {

    // Create the statement
    Statement statement = con.createStatement();

    // Use the created statement to SELECT the DATA
    // FROM the Titles Table.
    rs = statement.executeQuery("SELECT * " +
      "FROM Titles Where category_id = " + category_id);
  }
}
catch (SQLException sqle) {

  System.err.println(sqle.getMessage());
}
catch (Exception e) {
```

```
    System.err.println(e.getMessage());
  }
  finally {

    // Release the connection
    pool.releaseConnection(con);
  }
  return rs;
}

// Method Name: selectBySearchString()
// Purpose: This method takes the passed in search_string
// and performs a database lookup returning the ResultSet
// from the query.
private ResultSet
  selectBySearchString(String search_string) {

  Connection con = null;
  ConnectionPool pool = null;
  ResultSet rs = null;

  try {

    // Get a reference to the ConnectionPool from the Global
    // ServletContext
    ServletContext context = getServletContext();
    // Get a connection from the ConnectionPool
    if ( context == null ) {

      throw new ServletException("Could not get a " +
        "reference to the ServletContext");
    }
    pool =(ConnectionPool)
      context.getAttribute("CONNECTION_POOL");

    // Get a connection from the ConnectionPool
    if ( pool == null ) {

      throw new ServletException("Could not get reference" +
        " to the CONNECTION_POOL");
    }
    con = pool.getConnection();
    // Get a connection from the ConnectionPool
    if ( con == null ) {
```

continues

LISTING 15.13 CONTINUED

```java
        throw new ServletException("Could not get reference" +
          " Connection.");
    }
    if ( con != null ) {

      // Create the statement
      Statement statement = con.createStatement();

      // Use the created statement to SELECT the DATA
      // FROM the Titles Table.
      rs = statement.executeQuery("SELECT * " +
        "FROM Titles Where title_name = \'" +
        search_string + "\'");
    }
  }
  catch (SQLException sqle) {

    System.err.println(sqle.getMessage());
  }
  catch (Exception e) {

    System.err.println(e.getMessage());
  }
  finally {

    // Release the connection
    pool.releaseConnection(con);
  }
  return rs;
}


// Method Name: buildClientArea()
// Purpose: This method implements its parents abstract
// method.  It represents the client area of the browser
// window.
public HTMLTable
  buildClientArea(HttpServletRequest request)
  throws Exception {

  // Create the Table to return as the client area.
  HTMLTable table = new HTMLTable();
  ResultSet rs = null;
  table.setHorizontalAlign(HTMLObject.LEFT);
  table.setVerticalAlign(HTMLObject.TOP);
```

```
table.setWidthByPixel(650);

// Check for the parameter "category_id"
String category_id = request.getParameter("category_id");
if ( category_id != null ) {

  // If it is found perform the category_id select
  rs = selectByCategory(
    new Integer(category_id).intValue());
}
else {

  String search_string =
    request.getParameter("search_string");
  // If it is not found perform the title select
  rs = selectBySearchString(search_string);
}
// Iterate over the ResultSet
try {

  if ( rs != null ) {

    // This value is only used to switch the background
    // of the Title List.
    boolean flag = true;

    while ( rs.next() ) {

      HTMLTableRow row = new HTMLTableRow();

      // Switch every other row to lightgrey
      if ( flag ) {

        row.setBackgroundColor("lightgrey");
        flag = false;
      }
      else {

        flag = true;
      }

      // Get the values from the ResultSet
      String id = new Integer(
        rs.getInt("title_id")).toString();
```

continues

LISTING 15.13   CONTINUED

```java
String name = rs.getString("title_name");

String price = new Double(
  rs.getDouble("price")).toString();

int quantity = rs.getInt("quantity");

// Add the Name value to the table cell
HTMLTableCell cell =
  new HTMLTableCell(HTMLTableCell.DATA);
cell.addObject(new HTMLText(name));
row.addObject(cell);

// Add the price value to the table cell
cell =  new HTMLTableCell(HTMLTableCell.DATA);
cell.setWidth(55);
cell.addObject(new HTMLText(price));
row.addObject(cell);

if ( quantity == 0 ) {

  // If the quantity is 0, display the text
  // "Out of Stock"
  cell =  new HTMLTableCell(HTMLTableCell.DATA);
  cell.setWidth(145);
  cell.addObject(new HTMLText("Out of Stock"));
  row.addObject(cell);
}
else {

  // Otherwise create a link to the AddMovieServlet
  // with the id of the selected movie.
  // We are adding the extra parameter info in order
  // to redirect the browser to the List of Titles
  // before the selection.
  cell =  new HTMLTableCell(HTMLTableCell.DATA);
  cell.setWidth(145);

  String current_url =
    request.getServletPath() + "?" +
    request.getQueryString();

  cell.addObject(
    new HTMLLink("/servlet/AddMovieServlet?id=" +
```

```
                id + "&price=" + price + "&trans=" + current_url,
                new HTMLText("Buy")));
             row.addObject(cell);
          }
          table.addObject(row);
        }
      }
      else {

        HTMLTableRow row = new HTMLTableRow();
        HTMLTableCell cell =
          new HTMLTableCell(HTMLTableCell.DATA);

        // The result was empty, probably an error.
        cell.addObject(new HTMLText("The ResultSet was null," +
          " please contact technical support."));
        row.addObject(cell);
        table.addObject(row);
      }
    }
    finally {

      // Close the ResultSet
      if ( rs != null ) {

        rs.close();
      }
    }
    return table;
  }

  //Get Servlet information
  public String getServletInfo() {

    return "TitleListServlet Information";
  }
}
```

The TitleListServlet begins its processing in the buildClientArea() method. The first
thing it does is check to see whether the request was for a list of titles by category or title
search. It does this by checking the values passed in the request. If the parameter category_id
is in the request, it calls the selectByCategory() method, passing it the value of the cate-
gory_id parameter. If the category_id parameter is not found, it gets the value of the
search_string parameter and passes it to the selectBySearchString() method.

The selectByCategory() method first gets a reference to a Connection object from the ConnectionPool in the ServletContext. It then takes the resulting connection and creates a Statement object. When it has a reference to a Statement, it performs a database query requesting all the movie Title objects with a category_id matching the passed in ID. When it is finished with the connection, it calls the releaseConnection() method, which frees that connection for future use and returns the resultset returned from the query.

The selectBySearchString() method contains the same functionality as the selectByCategory() method, except for the type of query it performs. It takes the passed-in search_string and performs a query looking for movie titles with the same name as the search_string.

The last thing the buildClientArea() method does is take the ResultSet object, returned by either of the database queries, and iterate over it, creating a selectable list of movie titles. The links it creates point to the AddMovieServlet.

The ShoppingBasketServlet

The ShoppingBasketServlet is another servlet derived from CatalogServlet. Its purpose is to display the current contents of your shopping basket. The source for the ShoppingBasketServlet can be found in Listing 15.14.

LISTING 15.14   SHOPPINGBASKETSERVLET.JAVA

```
import javax.servlet.*;
import javax.servlet.http.*;
import java.io.*;
import java.util.*;
import java.sql.*;

import HTML.*;
import ConnectionPool.*;

/*
    This servlet displays a full list of the current items
    in the shopping basket.  It takes the current title ids
    found in the shopping basket and does a database lookup
    to complete the object.  It then displays the list of
    titles.  It also presents a button to complete the order
    or clear the contents of the shopping basket.  This
    servlet inherits its doGet() method from CatalogServlet.
*/

public class ShoppingBasketServlet extends CatalogServlet {
```

```
// Method Name: init()
// Purpose: This is the default init() method.
public void init(ServletConfig config)
  throws ServletException {

  super.init(config);
}

// Method Name: selectByTitleId()
// Purpose: This method takes the passed in title_id
// and performs a database lookup returning the ResultSet
// from the query.
private ResultSet selectByTitleId(int title_id)
  throws Exception {

  Connection con = null;
  ConnectionPool pool = null;
  ResultSet rs = null;

  try {

    // Get a reference to the ConnectionPool from the Global
    // ServletContext
    ServletContext context = getServletContext();
    if ( context == null ) {

      throw new ServletException("Could not get a reference" +
        " to the ServletContext");
    }
    pool =(ConnectionPool)
      context.getAttribute("CONNECTION_POOL");

    if ( pool == null ) {

      throw new ServletException("Could not get reference" +
        " to the CONNECTION_POOL");
    }
    // Get a connection from the ConnectionPool
    con = pool.getConnection();
    if ( con == null ) {

      throw new ServletException("Could not get reference" +
        " Connection.");
    }
    if ( con != null ) {
```

continues

LISTING 15.14   CONTINUED

```java
        // Create the statement
        Statement statement = con.createStatement();

        // Use the created statement to SELECT the DATA
        // FROM the Titles Table.
        rs = statement.executeQuery("SELECT * " +
          "FROM Titles Where title_id = " + title_id);
      }
    }
    finally {

      // Release the connection
      pool.releaseConnection(con);
    }
    return rs;
}


// Method Name: buildClientArea()
// Purpose: This method implements its parents abstract
// method.  It represents the client area of the browser
// window.
public HTMLTable
  buildClientArea(HttpServletRequest request)
  throws Exception {

  // We are now getting ready to checkout.
  // get a reference to the HttpSession object
  HttpSession session = request.getSession(true);
  Vector basket = null;

  // Create the Table to return as the client area.
  HTMLTable table = new HTMLTable();
  table.setWidthByPixel(400);
  table.setAlignment(HTMLObject.CENTER);
  table.setCaption(new HTMLHeading("Shopping Basket Contents",
    HTMLHeading.H3));
  HTMLTableRow row = new HTMLTableRow();
  HTMLTableCell cell = new HTMLTableCell(HTMLTableCell.DATA);

  if ( session != null ) {

    // Get the Shopping Basket's current contents.
    basket = (Vector)session.getValue("basket");
```

```
// Iterate over the basket's contents
if ( basket != null ) {

  for ( int x = 0; x < basket.size(); x++ ) {

    row = new HTMLTableRow();

    Movie movie = (Movie)basket.elementAt(x);

    // Get the complete database representation of the
    // Movie based on title_id
    ResultSet rs = selectByTitleId(movie.getTitleId());

    if ( rs.next() ) {

      // Set the name attribute of the movie
      // to the result of the database query.
      movie.setName(rs.getString("title_name"));
    }

    // Add the name to the table cell for display
    cell = new HTMLTableCell(HTMLTableCell.DATA);
    cell.addObject(new HTMLText(movie.getName()));
    row.addObject(cell);

    // Add the price to the table cell for display
    cell =  new HTMLTableCell(HTMLTableCell.DATA);
    cell.addObject(new HTMLText(new Double(
      movie.getPrice()).toString()));
    row.addObject(cell);

    table.addObject(row);
  }

  // Add a row containing a link to empty the basket
  row = new HTMLTableRow();
  cell = new HTMLTableCell(HTMLTableCell.DATA);
  cell.addObject(
    new HTMLLink("/servlet/EmptyBasketServlet",
    new HTMLText("Empty Basket")));
  row.addObject(cell);

  // Add a row containing a link to complete the order
  cell = new HTMLTableCell(HTMLTableCell.DATA);
  cell.addObject(
```

continues

LISTING 15.14   CONTINUED

```
            new HTMLLink("/servlet/ProcessOrderServlet",
            new HTMLText("Submit Order")));
        row.addObject(cell);

        table.addObject(row);
    }
    else {

        // If the basket was empty, say so.
        row = new HTMLTableRow();
        cell.addObject(new HTMLText("No items in basket!"));
        row.addObject(cell);
        table.addObject(row);
    }
  }
  return table;
}

//Get Servlet information
public String getServletInfo() {

    return "ShoppingBasketServlet Information";
  }
}
```

The ShoppingBasketServlet, like the other servlets derived from CatalogServlet, starts its processing in the buildClientArea() method. It starts by taking the current list of title IDs stored in the HttpSession and performing a database query to complete the attributes of the Movie object.

NOTE

The contents of the Movie objects stored in the basket vector is limited to only the title_id and price until they are completed by the ShoppingBasketServlet.

When the buildClientArea() method has the completed list of Movie objects, it iterates over them, displaying the attributes each movie currently in the basket vector. It then presents the user with two options: either empty his shopping basket or submit the order.

The ProcessOrderServlet

This servlet represents the final step in the order process (see Listing 15.15). It takes a request, empties the contents of the shopping basket, and responds with a simple thank you message.

This is where you would add the appropriate functionality to handle your orders. You could be sending a message to fulfillment or just logging the order to a database for later processing. This servlet inherits its doGet() method from CatalogServlet; therefore its processing begins in the buildClientArea() method.

LISTING 15.15   PROCESSORDERSERVLET.JAVA

```java
import javax.servlet.*;
import javax.servlet.http.*;
import java.io.*;
import java.util.*;

import HTML.*;

/*
    This servlet represents the final step in the order
    process.  It takes a request, empties the contents of
    the shopping basket and responds with a simple
    thank you message.  This is where you would add the
    appropriate functionality to handle your orders.
    This could be sending a message to fulfillment or just
    logging it in a database for later processing.  This
    servlet inherits its doGet() method from CatalogServlet.
*/

public class ProcessOrderServlet extends CatalogServlet {

  // Method Name: init()
  // Purpose: This is the default init() method.
  public void init(ServletConfig config)
    throws ServletException {

    super.init(config);
  }

  // Method Name: emptyBasket()
  // Purpose: This method gets a reference to the basket
  // Vector and calls the removeAllElements method, emptying
  // the entire contents of the shopping basket.
  private void emptyBasket(HttpServletRequest request) {

    // Get/Create a reference to the HttpSession object.
    HttpSession session = request.getSession(true);

    if ( session != null ) {
```

15

continues

LISTING 15.15   CONTINUED

```java
    // Get a reference to the basket Vector.
    Vector basket = (Vector)session.getValue("basket");

    // If basket is null, create one
    if ( basket != null ) {

      // Empty the basket.
      basket.removeAllElements();
    }
  }
}


// Method Name: buildClientArea()
// Purpose: This method implements its parent's abstract
// method.  It represents the client area of the browser
// window.
public HTMLTable buildClientArea(HttpServletRequest request)
  throws Exception {

  // empty the shopping basket, so future requests will
  // begin with an empty basket
  emptyBasket(request);

  // We are now getting ready to checkout.
  HttpSession session = request.getSession(true);
  Vector basket = null;

  // Create a table container for the client area.
  HTMLTable table = new HTMLTable();
  // Set a fixed width.
  table.setWidthByPixel(400);
  table.setAlignment(HTMLObject.CENTER);

  HTMLTableRow row = new HTMLTableRow();
  HTMLTableCell cell = new HTMLTableCell(HTMLTableCell.DATA);
  // Create and add a simple thank you message
  cell.addObject(new HTMLHeading("Thank you for shopping" +
    " with Sams!", HTMLHeading.H3));

  row.addObject(cell);
  table.addObject(row);

  return table;
}
```

```
//Get Servlet information
public String getServletInfo() {

    return "ProcessOrderServlet Information";
}
}
```

USING THE ONLINE CATALOG

Now that you have seen what the SOCS application does and how it does it, take a look at it in action. The following steps will guide you through placing an order using the SOCS application:

1. Make sure that you have compiled all your objects, and the appropriate servlets are pre-loaded. You must make sure that the ODBC data source is set up according to the steps in Chapter 8. To use the new database for this chapter, change the ODBC data source settings to point to the moviecatalog.mdb file found in the \Chapter 15\Source\ directory.

2. Open your browser to the URL pointing to the WelcomeServlet. On my local machine it is http://localhost:8000/servlet/WelcomeServlet. You should see an image similar to Figure 15.7.

FIGURE 15.7

The WelcomeServlet page.

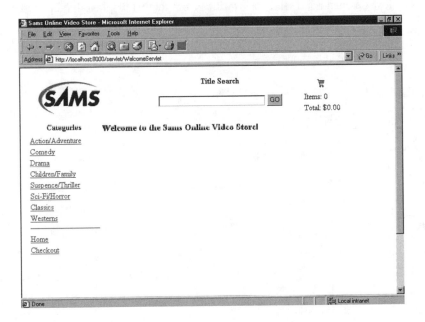

3. From this step, you can take two paths. For this example, select a category from the Categories list on the left of the page. Based on the category you choose, the result should be similar to Figure 15.8.

FIGURE **15.8**

The TitleListServlet page.

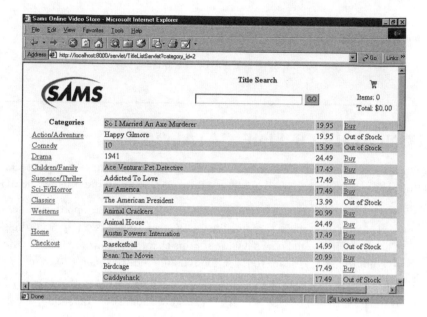

4. Now go ahead and select a few titles from the list displayed. Notice that each time you select a title, the shopping basket displays a new total and price. These values reflect each new selection you make. Figure 15.9 shows the `TitleListPage` after you have made some selections.

FIGURE **15.9**

The TitleListServlet Page after movie selections.

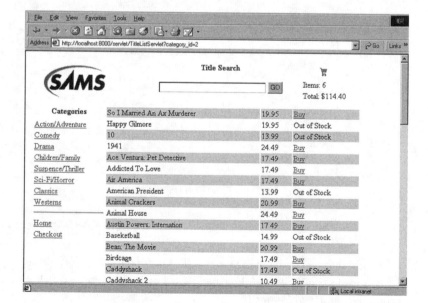

5. After you have completed your selections, select either the Checkout link on the left or the Shopping Basket image. This invokes the `ShoppingBasketServlet`, which displays the current contents of your shopping basket. The output of the `ShoppingBasketServlet` should be similar to Figure 15.10.

FIGURE 15.10

The ShoppingBasket-Servlet page.

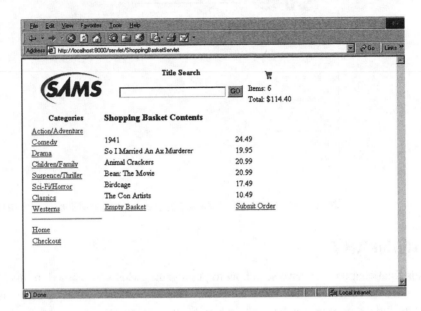

6. At this point, you have two choices. You can either empty the shopping cart or submit your order. Go ahead and select the Submit Order link and invoke the `ProcessOrderServlet`. This is where you would normally have functionality in place to really process the order. For this example, the servlet simply responds with a thank you message. The output should look like Figure 15.11.

FIGURE 15.11
The ProcessOrderServlet page.

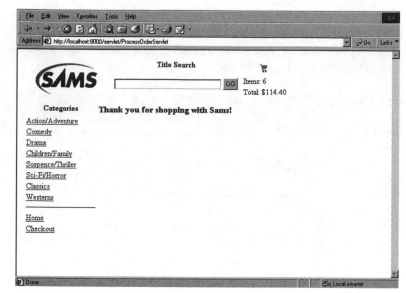

SUMMARY

In this final chapter, you have seen how to put together what you learned in this book into a practical application. You have seen how you can create an entire Web application using servlets and a database. You have also seen how you can use the object-oriented nature of servlets to create a hierarchy of servlet objects, giving you the ability to simply "plug" new servlets into a reusable framework.

At this point, you should feel very comfortable with what servlets are and how they work. You should understand how to create and integrate a servlet application. You should also be able to look at a given problem or set of requirements and determine where servlets fit into the equation.

THE JAVAX.SERVLET PACKAGE

IN THIS APPENDIX

The `javax.servlet` package is at the core of all servlet development. It contains the generic interfaces and classes that are implemented and extended by all servlets. Figure A.1 contains the `javax.servlet` object model.

FIGURE A.1

The javax.servlet object model.

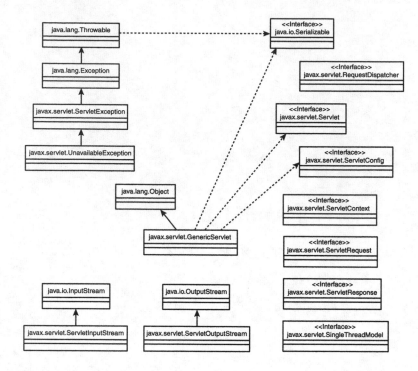

INTERFACES

The RequestDispatcher Interface

`public interface RequestDispatcher`

The `RequestDispatcher` interface defines an object that can serve as a wrapper around another resource on the server. It is most often used to forward requests to other server resources. It defines two methods.

The forward() Method

```
public void forward(ServletRequest request,
  ServletResponse response)
  throws ServletException,
  java.io.IOException
```

The forward() method is used to forward a request from one servlet to another. It allows the first servlet to perform some initial tasks on the request before forwarding it to another resource on the server.

forward() has two parameters:

- ServletRequest
- ServletResponse

It does not return a value.

It throws these exceptions:

- ServletException
- java.io.IOException

The include() Method

```
public void include(ServletRequest request,
  ServletResponse response)
  throws ServletException,
  java.io.IOException
```

The include() method is used to merge content from another server resource in the response of the final servlet.

include() has two parameters:

- ServletRequest
- ServletResponse

It does not return a value.

It throws these exceptions:

- ServletException
- java.io.IOException

The Servlet Interface

```
public abstract interface Servlet
```

The Servlet interface is implemented by all servlets either through direct implementation or inheritance. It defines five methods, including the three life cycle methods, to be implemented by all servlets.

The init() Method

```
public void init(ServletConfig config)
  throws ServletException
```

The init() method, the first life cycle method, marks the beginning of a servlet's life. It is called only when the servlet is first loaded, and it must execute successfully before the servlet can service requests. The init() method should contain all initialization code for the servlet.

init() has one parameter:

- ServletConfig—Encapsulates the servlet's startup configuration and initialization parameters

It does not return a value.

It throws this exception:

- ServletException

The getServletConfig() Method

```
public ServletConfig getServletConfig()
```

The getServletConfig() method returns the servlet's ServletConfig object, which contains the servlet's startup configuration and initialization parameters.

getServletConfig() has no parameters.

It returns this value:

- ServletConfig

It does not throw any exceptions.

The service() Method

```
public void service(ServletRequest request,
  ServletResponse response)
  throws ServletException,
  java.io.IOException
```

The service() method defines the servlet's entry point for servicing requests. It can only be executed after the servlet's init() method has executed successfully. The service() method is the life cycle method that is executed for every incoming request.

service() has two parameters:

- ServletRequest
- ServletResponse

It does not return a value.

It throws these exceptions:

- `ServletException`
- `java.io.IOException`

The getServletInfo() Method

`public java.lang.String getServletInfo()`

The `getServletInfo()` method is used to provide the servlet user with information about the servlet itself. You will usually include information copyright or versioning.

`getServletInfo()` takes no parameters.

It returns this value:

- `String`

It doesn't throw any exceptions.

The destroy() Method

`public void destroy()`

The `destroy()` method is the life cycle method that marks the end of a servlet's life. It is executed only once, when the servlet is removed from the service. This is where you should place all your clean-up functionality.

`destroy()` has no parameters.

It does not return a value.

It doesn't throw any exceptions.

The ServletConfig Interface

The `ServletConfig` interface defines an object, to be generated by a servlet engine, used to pass configuration information to a servlet during startup. It contains name/value pairs of initialization parameters for the servlet. It also contains a reference to the `ServletContext` object, which is described in the next section. The `ServletConfig` interface defines three methods for accessing this information.

The getServletContext() Method

`public ServletContext getServletContext()`

The `getServletContext()` method returns a reference to the current `ServletContext` object.

getServletContext() has no parameters.

It returns this value:

- ServletContext

It throws no exceptions.

The getInitParameter() Method

public java.lang.String getInitParameter(java.lang.String)

The getInitParameter() method returns a string containing the value of the initialization parameter's name/value pair referenced by the passed-in string representing the name.

getInitParameter() has this parameter:

- java.lang.String

It returns these values:

- java.lang.String
- null if the parameter does not exist

It throws no exceptions.

The getInitParameterNames() Method

public java.util.Enumeration getInitParameterNames()

The getInitParameterNames() method returns an enumeration of strings representing all the initialization parameters names, or an empty Enumeration if there are no init parameters.

getInitParameterNames() has one parameter:

- java.lang.String

It returns this value:

- java.util.Enumeration

It throws no exceptions.

The ServletContext Interface

public interface ServletContext

The ServletContext interface defines an object, to be created by a servlet engine, that contains information about the servlet's environment. This interface provides several methods to access this information.

The getContext() Method

```
public ServletContext getContext(java.lang.String uripath)
```

The `getContext()` method returns a reference to a `ServletContext` object belonging to a particular URI path.

`getContext()` has one parameter:

- `java.lang.String`

It returns these values:

- ServletContext
- It could return `null` in a security-conscious environment.

It throws no exceptions.

The getMajorVersion() Method

```
public int getMajorVersion()
```

The `getMajorVersion()` method returns an integer representing the major version of the servlet API that the servlet engine supports. If the servlet engine supported the servlet API 2.1, the result would be 2.

`getMajorVersion()` has no parameters.

It returns this value:

- int

It throws no exceptions.

The getMinorVersion() Method

```
public int getMinorVersion()
```

The `getMinorVersion()` method returns an integer representing the minor version of the servlet API that the servlet engine supports. If the servlet engine supported the servlet API 2.1, the result would be 1.

`getMinorVersion()` has no parameters.

It returns this value:

- int

It throws no exceptions.

The getMimeType() Method

`public java.lang.String getMimeType(java.lang.String file)`

The `getMimeType()` method returns a string representing the MIME type of the passed-in filename, or `null` if the MIME type of the file is not known.

`getMimeType()` has one parameter:

- `java.lang.String`

It returns this value:

- `java.lang.String`

It throws no exceptions.

The getResource() Method

```
public java.net.URL getResource(java.land.String path)
  throws MalformedURLException
```

The `getResource()` method returns an URL object of a resource matching the passed-in path parameter, permitting a servlet to access content from the servlet engine's document space without system dependencies.

`getResource()` has one parameter:

- `java.lang.String`

It returns these values:

- java.net.URL
- `Null` if there is no resource mapped to the given URL.

It throws this exception:

- `java.net.MalformedURLException`

The getResourceAsStream() Method

```
public java.io.InputStream
  getResourceAsStream(java.land.String path)
```

The `getResourceAsStream()` method returns an `InputStream` object, which allows access to the resource matching the passed in the URL path.

`getResourceAsStream()` has one parameter:

- `java.lang.String`

The javax.servlet Package

APPENDIX A

435

A

THE
JAVAX.SERVLET
PAGCKAGE

It returns this value:

- java.io.InputStream
- Null if no resource is mapped to the given URL.

It throws no exceptions.

The getRequestDispatcher() Method

```
public RequestDispatcher
  getRequestDispatcher(java.land.String urlpath)
```

The getRequestDispatcher() method returns a RequestDispatcher object based on the passed-in URL path.

getRequestDispatcher() has one parameter:

- java.lang.String

It returns these values:

- RequestDispatcher
- Null if the context cannot provide a dispatcher for the provided path

It throws no exceptions.

The log() Method

```
public void log(java.lang.String msg)
```

This log() method writes the passed-in message to the context's log. The location of the log is servlet engine-specific.

log() has one parameter:

- java.lang.String

It returns no value.

It throws no exceptions.

A Second log() Method

```
public void log(java.lang.String msg,
  java.lang.Throwable throwable)
```

This log() method writes the passed-in message and the stack trace of the passed-in Throwable object to the context's log. The location of the log is servlet engine-specific.

log() has two parameters:

- java.lang.String
- java.lang.Throwable

It returns no value.

It throws no exceptions.

The getRealPath() Method

```
public java.lang.String getRealPath(java.lang.String path)
```

The getRealPath() method returns a string representing the passed-in virtual path converted to the real path, based on the operating system on which the servlet engine is running.

getRealPath() has one parameter:

- java.lang.String

It returns these values:

- java.lang.String
- Null if the conversion failed

It throws no exceptions.

The getServerInfo() Method

```
public java.lang.String getServerInfo()
```

The getServerInfo() method returns a string representing the name and version of the server that the servlet is running under. If the servlet was running under the Java Web Server 1.1.3, the returned string would be "Java Web Server/1.1.3".

getServerInfo() has no parameters.

It returns this value:

- java.lang.String

It throws no exceptions.

The getAttribute() Method

```
public java.lang.Object getAttribute(java.lang.String name)
```

The getAttribute() method returns an object stored in the ServletContext and keyed by the name value passed in. This is one of the methods used to share resources between servlets. The returning object must be downcast to its original type before use.

The javax.servlet Package

APPENDIX A

437

A

THE
JAVAX.SERVLET
PAGCKAGE

getAttribute() has one parameter:

- java.lang.String

It returns these values:

- java.lang.Object
- Null if no object is associated with the passed-in string

It throws no exceptions.

The getAttributeNames() Method

```
public java.util.Enumeration getAttributeNames()
```

The getAttributeNames() method returns an enumeration of strings representing the names of the attributes currently stored in the ServletContext or an empty Enumeration if there are no attributes.

getAttributeNames() has no parameters.

It returns this value:

- java.util.Enumeration

It throws no exceptions.

The setAttribute() Method

```
public void setAttribute(java.lang.String name,
  java.lang.Object object)
```

The setAttribute() method stores an object in the ServletContext and binds the object to the given name. If the name already exists in the ServletContext, it is replaced.

setAttribute() has two parameters:

- java.lang.String
- java.lang.Object

It returns no value.

It throws no exceptions.

The removeAttribute() Method

```
public void removeAttribute(java.lang.String name)
```

The removeAttribute() method removes from the ServletContext the object that is bound to the passed-in name.

`removeAttribute()` has one parameter:

- `java.lang.String`

It returns no value.

It throws no exceptions.

The ServletRequest Interface

`public interface ServletRequest`

The `ServletRequest` interface defines an object used to encapsulate information about the client's request. Information included in the `ServletRequest` object includes parameter name/value pairs, attributes, and an input stream. The `ServletRequest` interface defines the `getAttribute()` method to access this information.

The getAttribute() Method

`public java.lang.Object getAttribute(java.lang.String name)`

The `getAttribute()` method returns the value of the object keyed by the `name` string for the current request.

`getAttribute()` has one parameter:

- `java.lang.String`

It returns these values:

- java.lang.Object
- `Null` if the attribute does not exist

It throws no exceptions.

The getAttributeNames() Method

`public java.util.Enumeration getAttributeNames()`

The `getAttributeNames()` method returns an enumeration containing the names of all the attributes in the current request, or an empty Enumeration if there are no attributes.

`getAttributeNames()` has no parameters.

It returns this value:

- `java.util.Enumeration`

It throws no exceptions.

The getCharacterEncoding() Method

`public java.lang.String getCharacterEncoding()`

The `getCharacterEncoding()` method returns a string representing the character set encoding for this request, or `Null` if there is no character encoding defined for this request.

`getCharacterEncoding()` has no parameters.

It returns this value:

- `java.lang.String`

It throws no exceptions.

The getContentLength() Method

`public int getContentLength()`

The `getContentLength()` method returns an `int` value equal to the length of the request's data or `-1` if the content length is unknown. It is equivalent to the CGI variable `CONTENT_LENGTH`.

`getContentLength()` has no parameters.

It returns this value:

- `int`

It throws no exceptions.

The getContentType() Method

`public java.lang.String getContentType()`

The `getContentType()` method returns a string representing the MIME type of the request's data or `Null` if the content type was not specified by the browser. It is equivalent to the CGI variable `CONTENT_TYPE`.

`getContentType()` has no parameters.

It returns this value:

- `java.lang.String`

It throws no exceptions.

The getInputStream() Method

`public ServletInputStream getInputStream()`
`  throws java.io.IOException`

The getInputStream() method returns an input stream for reading binary data from the request's body.

getInputStream() has no parameters.

It returns this value:

- ServletInputStream

It throws these exceptions:

- IllegalStateException
- java.io.IOException

The getParameter() Method

```
public java.lang.String getParameter(java.lang.String name)
```

The getParameter() method returns the value of the requested parameter. If the parameter has or could have more than one value, use the getParameterValues() method.

getParameter() has one parameter:

- java.lang.String

It returns this value:

- java.lang.String

It throws no exceptions.

The getParameterNames() Method

```
public java.util.Enumeration getParameterNames()
```

The getParameterNames() method returns an enumeration of strings representing the parameter names for this request or an empty enumeration if there are no parameter names.

getParameterNames() has no parameters.

It returns this value:

- java.util.Enumeration

It throws no exceptions.

The getParameterValues() Method

```
public java.lang.String[] getParameterValues(java.lang.String name)
```

The javax.servlet Package

APPENDIX A

441

A

THE
JAVAX.SERVLET
PAGCKAGE

The getParameterValues() method returns an array of strings representing all the values for the named parameter in the current request, or Null if there are no parameters.

getParameterValues() has one parameter:

- java.lang.String

It returns this value:

- java.lang.String[]

It throws no exceptions.

The getProtocol() Method

```
public java.lang.String getProtocol()
```

The getProtocol() method returns a string representing the protocol and version of the request. It is the same as the CGI variable SERVER_PROTOCOL.

getProtocol() has no parameters.

It returns this value:

- java.lang.String

It throws no exceptions.

The getScheme() Method

```
public java.lang.String getScheme()
```

The getScheme() method returns a string representing the scheme of the URL used in the request. Example schemes include "http", "httpc", and "ftp".

getScheme() has no parameters.

It returns this value:

- java.lang.String

It throws no exceptions.

The getServerName() Method

```
public java.lang.String getServerName()
```

The getServerName() method returns a string representing the host name of the server that received the request. It is the same as the CGI variable SERVER_NAME.

getServerName() has no parameters.

It returns this value:

- `java.lang.String`

It throws no exceptions.

The getServerPort() Method

`public int getServerPort()`

The `getServerPort()` method returns an `int` representing the port number that the request was received on. It is the same as the CGI variable `SERVER_PORT`.

`getServerPort()` has no parameters.

It returns this value:

- `int`

It throws no exceptions.

The getReader() Method

```
public java.io.BufferedReader getReader()
  throws java.io.IOException
```

The `getReader()` method returns a `BufferedReader` for reading text input from the request body.

`getReader()` has no parameters.

It returns this value:

- `java.io.BufferedReader`

It throws these exceptions:

- `java.io.UnsupportedEncodingException`
- `IllegalStateException`
- `java.io.IOException`

The getRemoteAddress() Method

`public java.lang.String getRemoteAddress()`

The `getRemoteAddress()` method returns a string representing the IP address of the client sending the request. It is the same as the CGI variable `REMOTE_ADDR`.

`getRemoteAddress()` has no parameters.

It returns this value:

- java.lang.String

It throws no exceptions.

The getRemoteHost() Method

`public java.lang.String getRemoteHost()`

The getRemoteHost() method returns a string representing the qualified host name of the client sending the request. It is the same as the CGI variable REMOTE_HOST.

getRemoteHost() has no parameters.

It returns this value:

- java.lang.String

It throws no exceptions.

The setAttribute() Method

```
public void setAttribute(java.lang.String key,
  java.lang.Object object)
```

The setAttribute() method adds an attribute to the request's context keyed by the passed-in key string. It throws an IllegalStateException if the key already exists.

setAttribute() has two parameters:

- java.lang.String
- java.lang.Object

It returns no value.

It throws this exception:

- IllegalStateException

The ServletResponse Interface

`public interface ServletResponse`

The ServletResponse interface defines an object for sending MIME data back to the client from the servlet's service method. The ServletResponse object is a parameter of the servlet's service method. The ServletResponse interface defines several methods for implementing objects.

The getCharacterEncoding() Method

```
public java.lang.String getCharacterEncoding()
```

The `getCharacterEncoding()` method returns the character set encoding used for this request's body. If there has been no content type assigned, it is by default set to text/plain.

`getCharacterEncoding()` has no parameters.

It returns this value:

- `java.lang.String`

It throws no exceptions.

The getOutputStream() Method

```
public ServletOutputStream getOutputStream()
  throws java.io.IOException
```

The `getOutputStream()` method returns an output stream used for writing binary data to the response.

`getOutputStream()` has no parameters.

It returns this value:

- `ServletOutputStream`

It throws these exceptions:

- `IllegalStateException`
- `java.io.IOException`

The getWriter() Method

```
public java.io.PrintWriter getWriter()
  throws java.io.IOException
```

The `getWriter()` method returns a print writer used for writing formatted text to the response object.

`getWriter()` has no parameters.

It returns this value:

- `java.io.PrintWriter`

It throws these exceptions:

- `java.io.UnsupportedEncodingException`
- `IllegalStateException`
- `java.io.IOException`

The setContentLength() Method

```
public void setContentLength(int len)
```

The `setContentLength()` method sets the content length of the current response.

`setContentLength()` has one parameter:

- `int`

It returns no value.

It throws no exceptions.

The setContentType() Method

```
public void setContentType(java.lang.String type)
```

The `setContentType()` method sets the content type of the current response. You can set this property only once for the current response. This method must be called before calling the `getWriter` or `getOuputStream` methods.

`setContentType()` has one parameter:

- `java.lang.String`

It returns no value.

It throws no exceptions.

The SingleThreadModel Interface

```
public interface SingleThreadModel
```

The `SingleThreadModel` interface defines a single-threaded model for implementing the servlet's execution. Implementing this interface makes the servlet thread safe. This guarantees that the implementing servlet's `service` method will not be executed concurrently by more than one thread.

CLASSES

The GenericServlet Class

The `GenericServlet` class was created to provide a basic foundation of new servlets. It provides default life cycle methods and default implementations of the `ServletConfig`'s methods.

The GenericServlet() Method

```
public GenericServlet()
```

The `GenericServlet()` method is an empty default constructor.

`GenericServlet()` has no parameters.

It returns no value.

It throws no exceptions.

The destroy() Method

```
public void destroy()
```

The `destroy()` method is executed when the servlet is removed from the running service. It performs any cleanup of resources that were allocated in the `init()` method.

`destroy()` has no parameters.

It returns no value.

It throws no exceptions.

The getInitParameter() Method

```
public java.lang.String getInitParameter(
  java.lang.String name)
```

The `getInitParameter()` method returns a string containing the value of the initialization parameter keyed by the passed in name, or `Null` if there is no matching `init` parameter.

`getInitParameter()` has one parameter:

- `java.lang.String`

It returns this value:

- `java.lang.String`

It throws no exceptions.

The getInitParameterNames() Method

`public java.lang.Enumeration getInitParameterNames()`

The `getInitParameterNames()` method returns an enumeration containing all the names for each initialization parameter, or an empty enumeration if there are no `init` parameters.

`getInitParameterNames()` has no parameters.

It returns this value:

- `java.util.Enumeration`

It throws no exceptions.

The getServletConfig() Method

`public ServletConfig getServletConfig()`

The `getServletConfig()` method returns a `ServletConfig` object containing any startup configuration information for this servlet.

`getServletConfig()` has no parameters.

It returns this value:

- `ServletConfig`

It throws no exceptions.

The getServletContext() Method

`public ServletContext getServletContext()`

The `getServletContext()` method returns a `ServletContext` object containing information about the servlet's network service.

`getServletContext()` has no parameters.

It returns this value:

- `ServletContext`

It throws no exceptions.

The getServletInfo() Method

`public java.lang.String getServletInfo()`

The `getServletInfo()` method returns a string containing servlet-specific information about the implementing servlet.

`getServletInfo()` has no parameters.

It returns this value:

- `java.lang.String`

It throws no exceptions.

The init() Method

```
public void init(ServletConfig config)
  throws ServletException
```

The `init()` method marks the beginning of a servlet's life. It is called only when the servlet is first loaded, and it must execute successfully before the servlet can service requests. The `init()` method should contain all initialization code for the servlet.

`init()` has one parameter:

- `ServletConfig`—Encapsulates the servlet's startup configuration and initialization parameters.

It returns no value.

It throws this exception:

- `ServletException`

A Second init() Method

```
public void init()
  throws ServletException
```

This parameterless implementation of the `init()` method is provided only for convenience. It prevents derived servlets from having to store the `ServletConfig` object.

`init()` has no parameters.

It returns no value.

It throws this exception:

- `ServletException`

The log() Method

```
public void log(java.lang.String message)
```

The `log()` method takes the passed-in message and the name of the servlet and writes them to a log file. The location of the log is server-specific.

log() has one parameter:

- java.lang.String

It returns no value.

It throws no exceptions.

A Second log() Method

```
public void log(java.lang.String message,
  java.lang.Throwable t)
```

This log() method takes the passed-in message and throwable object and logs the message with a stack trace from the throwable object.

log() has two parameters:

- java.lang.String
- java.lang.Throwable

It returns no value.

It throws no exceptions.

The service() Method

```
public void service(ServletRequest request,
  ServletResponse response)
  throws ServletException,
  java.io.IOException
```

The service() method defines the servlet's entry point for servicing requests. It can only be executed after the servlet's init() method has executed successfully. The service() method is the life cycle method that is executed for every incoming request.

service() has two parameters:

- ServletRequest
- ServletResponse

It returns no value.

It throws these exceptions:

- ServletException
- java.io.IOException

The ServletInputStream Class

The `ServletInputStream` is an abstract class defined for servlet writers to get data from the client. It is meant to be implemented by a network services writer.

The ServletInputStream() Method

```
protected ServletInputStream()
```

This is the empty default constructor.

`ServletInputStream()` has no parameters.

It returns no value.

It throws no exceptions.

The readLine() Method

```
public void readLine(byte[] b,
  int off,
  int len)
  throws java.io.IOException
```

The `readLine()` method reads the `len` of bytes into the passed in byte array `b` starting at position `off`. If the character `\n` is encountered, no more bytes are read in.

`readLine()` has three parameters:

- `byte[]`
- `int`
- `int`

It returns no value.

It throws this exception:

- `java.io.IOException`

The ServletOutputStream Class

The `ServletOutputStream` is used to write responses back to the client. It is an abstract class that is implemented by the network services implementor. To access the `ServletOutputStream`, you must call the `ServletResponse`'s `getOutputStream()` method.

The ServletOutputStream() Method

```
public ServletOutputStream()
```

This is the empty default constructor.

`ServletOutputStream()` has no parameters.

It returns no value.

It throws this exception:

- `java.io.IOException`

The print() Method

```
public void print(boolean value)
    throws java.io.IOException
```

This version of the `print()` method prints the passed-in `boolean` value to the output stream.

`print()` has one parameter:

- `boolean`

It returns no value.

It throws this exception:

- `java.io.IOException`

A Second print() Method

```
public void print(char value)
    throws java.io.IOException
```

This version of the `print()` method prints the passed-in `char` value to the output stream.

`print()` has one parameter:

- `char`

It returns no value.

It throws this exception:

- `java.io.IOException`

A Third print() Method

```
public void print(double value)
  throws java.io.IOException
```

This version of the `print()` method prints the passed-in `double` value to the output stream.

`print()` has one parameter:

- `double`

It returns no value.

It throws this exception:

- `java.io.IOException`

A Fourth print() Method

```
public void print(float value)
  throws java.io.IOException
```

This version of the `print()` method prints the passed-in `float` value to the output stream.

`print()` has one parameter:

- `print()`

It returns no value.

It throws this exception:

- `java.io.IOException`

A Fifth print() Method

```
public void print(int value)
  throws java.io.IOException
```

This version of the `print()` method prints the passed-in `int` value to the output stream.

`print()` has one parameter:

- `int`

It returns no value.

It throws this exception:

- `java.io.IOException`

The javax.servlet Package

APPENDIX A

453

A

THE
JAVAX.SERVLET
PAGCKAGE

A Sixth print() Method

```
public void print(long value)
    throws java.io.IOException
```

This version of the print() method prints the passed-in long value to the output stream.

print() has one parameter:

- long

It returns no value.

It throws this exception:

- java.io.IOException

A Seventh print() Method

```
public void print(java.lang.String value)
    throws java.io.IOException
```

This version of the print() method prints the passed-in String value to the output stream.

print() has one parameter:

- java.lang.String

It returns no value.

It throws this exception:

- java.io.IOException

A println() Method

```
public void println()
    throws java.io.IOException
```

This version of the println() method prints CRLF to the output stream.

println() has no parameters.

It returns no value.

It throws this exception:

- java.io.IOException

A Second println() Method

```
public void println(java.lang.String value)
    throws java.io.IOException
```

This version of the `println()` method prints the passed-in `String` value to the output stream, followed by a CRLF.

`println()` has one parameter:

- `java.lang.String`

It returns no value.

It throws this exception:

- `java.io.IOException`

A Third println() Method

```
public void println(boolean value)
  throws java.io.IOException
```

This version of the `println()` method prints the passed-in `boolean` value to the output stream, followed by a CRLF.

`println()` has one parameter:

- `boolean`

It returns no value.

It throws this exception:

- `java.io.IOException`

A Fourth println() Method

```
public void println(char value)
  throws java.io.IOException
```

This version of the `println()` method prints the passed-in `char` value to the output stream, followed by a CRLF.

`println()` has one parameter:

- `char`

It returns no value.

It throws this exception:

- `java.io.IOException`

A Fifth println() Method

```
public void println(int value)
    throws java.io.IOException
```

This version of the println() method prints the passed-in int value to the output stream, followed by a CRLF.

println() has one parameter:

- int

It returns no value.

It throws this exception:

- java.io.IOException

A Sixth println() Method

```
public void println(long value)
    throws java.io.IOException
```

This version of the println() method prints the passed-in long value to the output stream, followed by a CRLF.

println() has one parameter:

- long

It returns no value.

It throws this exception:

- java.io.IOException

A Seventh println() Method

```
public void println(float value)
    throws java.io.IOException
```

This version of the println() method prints the passed-in float value to the output stream, followed by a CRLF.

println() has one parameter:

- float

It returns no value.

It throws this exception:

- `java.io.IOException`

An Eighth println() Method

```
public void println(double value)
  throws java.io.IOException
```

This version of the `println()` method prints the passed-in `double` value to the output stream, followed by a CRLF.

`println()` has one parameter:

- `double`

It returns no value.

It throws this exception:

- `java.io.IOException`

EXCEPTIONS

ServletException

A `ServletException` object is thrown when a problem is encountered within a servlet.

The ServletException() Method

```
public ServletException()
```

This is the default constructor.

`ServletException()` has no parameters.

It returns no value.

It throws no exceptions.

A Second ServletException() Method

```
public ServletException(java.lang.String message)
```

Creates a new `ServletException` object with the passed-in string as the message.

`ServletException()` has one parameter:

- `java.lang.String`

It returns no value.

It throws no exceptions.

A Third ServletException() Method

```
public ServletException(java.lang.String message,
  java.lang.Throwable rootCause)
```

Creates a ServletException object with a message and a Throwable object representing the cause of the exception.

ServletException() has two parameters:

- java.lang.String
- java.lang.Throwable

It returns no value.

It throws no exceptions.

A Fourth ServletException() Method

```
public ServletException(java.lang.Throwable rootCause)
```

Creates a new ServletException object with a Throwable object representing the cause of the exception.

ServletException() has one parameter:

- java.lang.Throwable

It returns no value.

It throws no exceptions.

The getRootCause() Method

```
public java.lang.Throwable getRootCause()
```

The getRootCause() method returns a Throwable object representing the cause of the exception or Null if no root cause is available.

getRootCause() has no parameters.

It returns this value:

- java.lang.Throwable

It throws no exceptions.

UnavailableException

An UnavailableException is thrown when a servlet is not available to service a request. There are two types of UnavailableExceptions: permanent and temporary.

When a servlet is permanently unavailable, the servlet will not be able to service requests until some administrative task is completed. When a servlet is temporarily unavailable, the servlet is expected to be able to service requests within a given period of time.

The UnavailableException() Method

```
public UnavailableException(Servlet servlet,

  java.lang.String msg)
```

This constructor creates an UnavailableException with a reference to the servlet that is unavailable and a string representing the error message. This constructor creates an UnavailableException denoting permanent unavailability.

UnavailableException() has two parameters:

- Servlet
- java.lang.String

It returns no value.

It throws no exceptions.

A Second UnavailableException() Method

```
public UnavailableException(int seconds
  Servlet servlet,
  java.lang.String msg)
```

This constructor creates an UnavailableException with an int value representing an estimated time of unavailability. It also receives a reference to the servlet that is unavailable and a string representing the error message.

UnavailableException() has three parameters:

- int
- Servlet
- java.lang.String

It returns no value.

It throws no exceptions.

The isPermanent() Method

```
public boolean isPermanent()
```

The isPermanent() method returns True if the servlet is permanently unavailable, otherwise it returns False.

isPermanent() has no parameters.

It returns this value:

- boolean

It throws no exceptions.

The getServlet() Method

```
public Servlet getServlet()
```

The getServlet() method returns a reference to the servlet that is reported as unavailable.

getServlet() has no parameters.

It returns this value:

- Servlet

It throws no exceptions.

The getUnavailableSeconds() Method

```
public int getUnavailableSeconds()
```

The getUnavailableSeconds() method returns an int representing the number of seconds a servlet is expected to be temporarily unavailable.

getUnavailableSeconds() has no parameters.

It returns this value:

- int

It throws no exceptions.

THE JAVAX.SERVLET.HTTP PACKAGE

IN THIS APPENDIX

The `java.servlet.http` package contains the interfaces and classes that are implemented and extended respectively to create HTTP-specific servlets. Figure B.1 contains the `javax.servlet.http` object model.

FIGURE B.1
The javax.servlet.http object model.

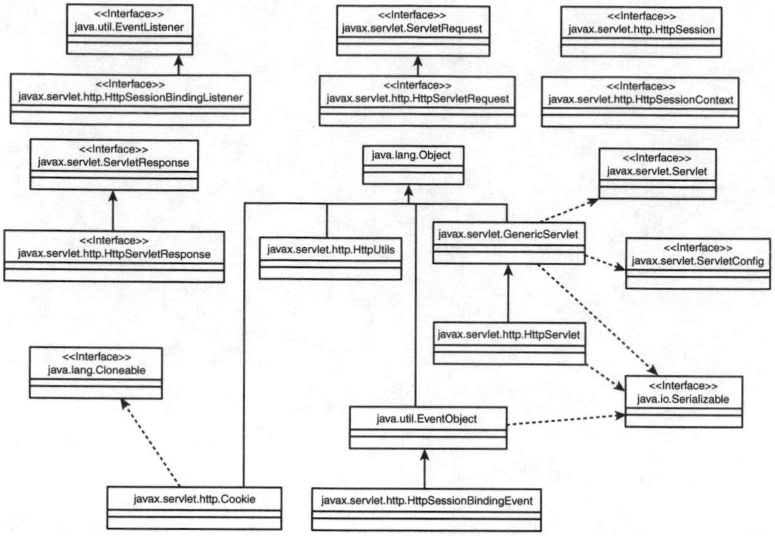

INTERFACES

The HttpServletRequest Interface

```
public interface HttpServletRequest
  extends ServletRequest
```

The `HttpServletRequest` interface defines an object that provides the `HttpServlet.service()` method with access to HTTP-protocol specific header information sent by the client.

The getAuthType() Method

```
public java.lang.String getAuthType()
```

The `getAuthType()` method returns the authentication scheme used in this request, or `Null` if none. It is the same as the `AUTH_TYPE CGI` variable.

`getAuthType()` has no parameters.

It returns this value:

- `java.lang.String`

It throws no exceptions.

The getCookies() Method

```
public Cookie[] getCookies()
```

The getCookies() method returns an array of Cookie objects found in the client request, or a zero-length array if there are no existing cookies.

getCookies() has no parameters.

It returns this value:

- Cookie[]

It throws no exceptions.

The getDateHeader() Method

```
public long getDateHeader(java.lang.String name)
```

The getDateHeader() method returns the value of the requested date header field found in the client request, or –1 if the date was not found.

getDateHeader() has one parameter:

- java.lang.String

It returns this value:

- long

It throws no exceptions.

The getHeader() Method

```
public java.lang.String getHeader(java.lang.String name)
```

The getHeader() method returns the value of the requested header field found in the client request. The name of the header is not case-sensitive.

getHeader() has one parameter:

- java.lang.String

It returns this value:

- java.lang.String

It throws no exceptions.

The getHeaderNames() Method

`public Enumeration getHeaderNames()`

The `getHeaderNames()` method returns an `Enumeration` containing all the header names found in the client request, or `Null` if the server does not allow this type of access to the header names.

`getHeaderNames()` has no parameters.

It returns this value:

- `java.lang.String`

It throws no exceptions.

The getIntHeader() Method

`public int getIntHeader(java.lang.String name)`

The `getIntHeader()` method returns the `int` value of the named header field, found in the client request. If the header cannot be converted to an `int`, a `NumberFormatException` is thrown.

`getIntHeader()` has one parameter:

- `java.lang.String`

It returns this value:

- `int`

It throws no exceptions.

The getMethod() Method

`public java.lang.String getMethod()`

The `getMethod()` method returns the `HTTP` method used by the client request. It is the same as the CGI variable `REQUEST_METHOD`.

`getMethod()` has no parameters.

It returns this value:

- `java.lang.String`

It throws no exceptions.

The getPathInfo() Method

`public java.lang.String getPathInfo()`

The `getPathInfo()` method returns a String containing any additional path information following the servlet path, but preceding the query string, or `Null` if there is no additional path information. It is the same as the CGI variable `PATH_INFO`.

`getPathInfo()` has no parameters.

It returns this value:

- `java.lang.String`

It throws no exceptions.

The getPathTranslated() Method

`public java.lang.String getPathTranslated()`

The `getPathTranslated()` method returns the same information as the `getPathInfo()` method, but translates the path to its real path name before returning it, or `Null` if there is no additional path information. It is the same as the CGI variable `PATH_TRANSLATED`.

`getPathTranslated()` has no parameters.

It returns this value:

- `java.lang.String`

It throws no exceptions.

The getQueryString() Method

`public java.lang.String getQueryString()`

The `getQueryString()` method returns the query string from the request or `Null` if there is no query string. It is the same as the CGI variable `QUERY_STRING`.

`getQueryString()` has no parameters.

It returns this value:

- `java.lang.String`

It throws no exceptions.

The getRemoteUser() Method

`public java.lang.String getRemoteUser()`

The getRemoteUser() method returns the name of the user making the request. If the name is not available, Null is returned. It is the same as the CGI variable REMOTE_USER.

getRemoteUser() has no parameters.

It returns this value:

- java.lang.String

It throws no exceptions.

The getRequestedSessionId() Method

public java.lang.String getRequestedSessionId()

The getRequestedSessionId() method returns the session ID associated with the request.

getRequestedSessionId() has no parameters.

It returns this value:

- java.lang.String

It throws no exceptions.

The getRequestURI() Method

public java.lang.String getRequestURI()

The getRequestURI() method returns the first line of the request's URI. This is the part of the URI that is found to the left of the query string.

getRequestURI() has no parameters.

It returns this value:

- java.lang.String

It throws no exceptions.

The getServletPath() Method

public java.lang.String getServletPath()

The getServletPath() method returns the part of the URI that refers to the servlet being invoked.

getServletPath() has no parameters.

It returns this value:

- `java.lang.String`

It throws no exceptions.

The getSession() Method

`public HttpSession getSession(boolean create)`

The `getSession()` method returns the session associated with the request. If there is no valid session and the `boolean` parameter passed in is `True`, the method will create a new session. If the passed-in Boolean value is `False` and there is no session, `Null` is returned.

`getSession()` has one parameter:

- `boolean`

It returns this value:

- `HttpSession`

It throws no exceptions.

A Second getSession() Method

`public HttpSession getSession()`

This `getSession()` method performs the same as the previous `getSession()` method; it just performs as if it were always passed a `True` value.

`getSession()` has no parameters.

It returns this value.

- `HttpSession`

It throws no exceptions.

The isRequestedSessionValid() Method

`public boolean isRequestedSessionValid()`

The `isRequestedSessionValid()` method returns `True` if the session is valid in the current context, otherwise it returns `False`.

`isRequestedSessionValid()` has no parameters.

It returns this value:

- `boolean`

It throws no exceptions.

The isRequestedSessionFromCookie() Method

`public boolean isRequestedSessionFromCookie()`

The `isRequestedSessionFromCookie()` method returns `True` if the session ID from the request came in as a cookie, otherwise it returns `False`.

`isRequestedSessionFromCookie()` has no parameters.

It returns this value:

- `boolean`

It throws no exceptions.

The isRequestedSessionFromURL() Method

`public boolean isRequestedSessionFromURL()`

The `isRequestedSessionFromURL()` method returns `True` if the session ID from the request came in as part of the URL, otherwise it returns `False`.

`isRequestedSessionFromURL()` has no parameters.

It returns this value:

- `boolean`

It throws no exceptions.

The HttpServletResponse Interface

```
public interface HttpServletRequest
  extends ServletRequest
```

The `HttpServletResponse` interface defines an object that provides the `HttpServlet.service()` method with the ability to manipulate HTTP-protocol–specific header information and return data to the client.

SC_CONTINUE

`public static final int SC_CONTINUE`

Represents a status code of (100), indicating that the client can continue.

SC_SWITCHING_PROTOCOLS

```
public static final int SC_SWITCHING_PROTOCOLS
```

Represents a status code of (101), indicating the server is switching protocols according to the upgrade header.

SC_OK

```
public static final int SC_OK
```

Represents a status code of (200), indicating the request succeeded normally.

SC_CREATED

```
public static final int SC_CREATED
```

Represents a status code of (201), indicating the request succeeded and created a new resource on the server.

SC_ACCEPTED

```
public static final int SC_ACCEPTED
```

Represents a status code of (202), indicating that a request was accepted for processing, but was not completed.

SC_NON_AUTHORITATIVE_INFORMATION

```
public static final int SC_NON_AUTHORITATIVE_INFORMATION
```

Represents a status code of (203), indicating that the meta information presented by the client did not originate from the server.

SC_NO_CONTENT

```
public static final int SC_NO_CONTENT
```

Represents a status code of (204), indicating that the request succeeded but that there was no new information to return.

SC_RESET_CONTENT

```
public static final int SC_RESET_CONTENT
```

Represents a status code of (205), indicating that the agent SHOULD reset the document view that caused the request to be sent.

SC_PARTIAL_CONTENT

```
public static final int SC_PARTIAL_CONTENT
```

Represents a status code of (206), indicating that the server has fulfilled the partial GET request for the resource.

SC_MULTIPLE_CHOICES

```
public static final int SC_MULTIPLE_CHOICES
```

Represents a status code of (300), indicating that the requested resource corresponds to any one of a set of representations, each with its own specific location.

SC_MOVED_PERMANENTLY

```
public static final int SC_MOVED_PERMANENTLY
```

Represents a status code of (301), indicating that the resource has permanently moved to a new location and that future references should use a new URI with their requests.

SC_MOVED_TEMPORARILY

```
public static final int SC_MOVED_TEMPORARILY
```

Represents a status code of (302), indicating that the resource has temporarily moved to another location, but future references should still use the original URI to access the resource.

SC_SEE_OTHER

```
public static final int SC_SEE_OTHER
```

Represents a status code of (303), indicating that the response to the request can be found under a different URI.

SC_NOT_MODIFIED

```
public static final int SC_NOT_MODIFIED
```

Represents a status code of (304), indicating that a conditional GET operation discovered that the resource was available and not modified.

SC_USE_PROXY

```
public static final int SC_USE_PROXY
```

Represents a status code of (305), indicating that the requested resource MUST be accessed through the proxy given by the Location field.

SC_BAD_REQUEST

`public static final int SC_BAD_REQUEST`

Represents a status code of (400), indicating the request sent by the client was syntactically incorrect.

SC_UNAUTHORIZED

`public static final int SC_UNAUTHORIZED`

Represents a status code of (401), indicating that the request requires HTTP authentication.

SC_PAYMENT_REQUIRED

`public static final int SC_PAYMENT_REQUIRED`

Represents a status code of (402) for future use.

SC_FORBIDDEN

`public static final int SC_FORBIDDEN`

Represents a status code of (403), indicating the server understood the request but refused to fulfill it.

SC_NOT_FOUND

`public static final int SC_NOT _FOUND`

Represents a status code of (404), indicating that the requested resource is not available.

SC_METHOD_NOT_ALLOWED

`public static final int SC_METHOD_NOT_ALLOWED`

Represents a status code of (405), indicating that the method specified in the `Request-Line` is not allowed for the resource identified by the `Request-URI`.

SC_NOT_ACCEPTABLE

`public static final int SC_NOT_ACCEPTABLE`

Represents a status code of (406), indicating that the resource identified by the request is only capable of generating response entities—which have content characteristics not acceptable, according to the accept headers sent in the request.

SC_PROXY_AUTHENTICATION_REQUIRED

`public static final int SC_PROXY_AUTHENTICATION_REQUIRED`

Represents a status code of (407), indicating that the client MUST first authenticate itself with the proxy.

SC_REQUEST_TIMEOUT

`public static final int SC_REQUEST_TIMEOUT`

Represents a status code of (408), indicating that the client did not produce a request within the time that the server was prepared to wait.

SC_CONFLICT

`public static final int SC_CONFLICT`

Represents a status code of (409), indicating that the request could not be completed because of a conflict with the current state of the resource.

SC_GONE

`public static final int SC_GONE`

Represents a status code of (410), indicating that the resource is no longer available at the server and no forwarding address is known. This condition SHOULD be considered permanent.

SC_LENGTH_REQUIRED

`public static final int SC_LENGTH_REQUIRED`

Represents a status code of (411), indicating that the request cannot be handled without a defined `Content-Length`.

SC_PRECONDITION_FAILED

`public static final int SC_PRECONDITION_FAILED`

Represents a status code of (412), indicating that the precondition given in one or more of the request-header fields evaluated to `False` when it was tested on the server.

SC_REQUEST_ENTITY_TOO_LARGE

`public static final int SC_REQUEST_ENTITY_TOO_LARGE`

Represents a status code of (413), indicating that the server is refusing to process the request because the request entity is larger than the server is willing or able to process.

SC_REQUEST_URI_TOO_LONG

```
public static final int SC_REQUEST_URI_TOO_LONG
```

Represents a status code of (414), indicating that the server is refusing to service the request because the Request-URI is longer than the server is willing to interpret.

SC_UNSUPPORTED_MEDIA_TYPE

```
public static final int SC_UNSUPPORTED_MEDIA_TYPE
```

Represents a status code of (415), indicating that the server is refusing to service the request because the entity of the request is in a format not supported by the requested resource for the requested method.

SC_INTERNAL_SERVER_ERROR

```
public static final int SC_INTERNAL_SERVER_ERROR
```

Represents a status code of (500), indicating an error inside the HTTP server that prevented it from fulfilling the request.

SC_NOT_IMPLEMENTED

```
public static final int SC_NOT_IMPLEMENTED
```

Represents a status code of (501), indicating the HTTP server does not support the functionality needed to fulfill the request.

SC_BAD_GATEWAY

```
public static final int SC_BAD_GATEWAY
```

Represents a status code of (502), indicating that the HTTP server received an invalid response from a server it consulted when acting as a proxy or gateway.

SC_SERVICE_UNAVAILABLE

```
public static final int SC_SERVICE_UNAVAILABLE
```

Represents a status code of (503), indicating that the HTTP server is temporarily overloaded and unable to handle the request.

SC_GATEWAY_TIMEOUT

```
public static final int SC_GATEWAY_TIMEOUT
```

Represents a status code of (504), indicating that the server did not receive a timely response from the upstream server while acting as a gateway or proxy.

SC_HTTP_VERSION_NOT_SUPPORTED

`public static final int SC_HTTP_VERSION_NOT_SUPPORTED`

Represents a status code of (505), indicating that the server does not support or refuses to support the HTTP version found in the request.

The addCookie() Method

`public void addCookie(Cookie cookie)`

The `addCookie()` method adds a Cookie to the `HttpServletResponse` object.

`addCookie()` has one parameter:

- Cookie

It returns this value:

- void

It throws no exceptions.

The containsHeader() Method

`public boolean containsHeader(java.lang.String name)`

The `containsHeader()` method returns `True` if the named header exists in the response.

`containsHeader()` has one parameter:

- java.lang.String

It returns this value:

- boolean

It throws no exceptions.

The encodeURL() Method

`public java.lang.String encodeURL(java.lang.String url)`

The `encodeURL()` method URL encodes the passed in `String` and returns it. If no changes are necessary, it simply returns the `String`.

`encodeURL()` has one parameter:

- java.lang.String

It returns this value:

- `java.lang.String`

It throws no exceptions.

The encodeRedirectURL() Method

`public java.lang.String encodeRedirectURL(java.lang.String url)`

The `encodeRedirectURL()` method encodes the passed in `String` for use in the `sendRedirect()` method. If no changes are necessary, it simply returns the `String`.

`encodeRedirectURL()` has one parameter:

- `java.lang.String`

It returns this value:

- `java.lang.String`

It throws no exceptions.

The sendError() Method

```
public void sendError(int sc,
  java.lang.String message)
throws java.io.IOException
```

The `sendError()` method sends an error to the client in the response object. The error consists of the `int` status code and a `String` message.

`sendError()` has two parameters:

- `int`
- `java.lang.String`

It returns no value.

It throws this exception:

- `java.io.IOException`

The sendError() Method

```
public void sendError(int sc)
throws java.io.IOException
```

This `sendError()` method sends an error to the client in the response object. The error consists of only the `int` status code.

`sendError()` has one parameter:

- `int`

It returns no value.

It throws this exception:

- `java.io.IOException`

The sendRedirect() Method

```
public void sendRedirect(java.lang.String url)
throws java.io.IOException
```

The `sendRedirect()` method redirects the client to the passed in URL, which must be an absolute URL.

`sendRedirect()` has one parameter:

- `java.lang.String`

It returns no value.

It throws this exception:

- `java.io.IOException`

The setDateHeader() Method

```
public void setDateHeader(java.lang.String name,
  long date)
```

The `setDateHeader()` method adds a name/date-value field to the response header. The date value is a long parameter representing milliseconds since the epoch.

`setDateHeader()` has two parameters:

- `java.lang.String`
- `long`

It returns no value.

It throws no exceptions.

The setHeader() Method

```
public void setHeader(java.lang.Sting name,
  java.lang.String value)
```

The `setHeader()` method adds a name/value field to the response header. If the field is already present in the request, it is replaced.

`setIntHeader()` has two parameters:

- `java.lang.String`
- `java.lang.String`

It returns no value.

It throws no exceptions.

The setIntHeader() Method

```
public void setIntHeader(java.lang.String name,
   int value)
```

The `setIntHeader()` method adds a name/int-value field to the response header. If the field is already present in the request, it is replaced.

`setIntHeader()` has two parameters:

- `java.lang.String`
- `int`

It returns no value.

It throws no exceptions.

The setStatus() Method

```
public void setStatus(int sc)
```

The `setStatus()` method sets the status code for the response.

`setStatus()` has one parameter:

- `int`

It returns no value.

It throws no exceptions.

The HttpSession Interface

```
public interface HttpSession
```

The `HttpSession` interface defines an object that provides an association between a client and server persisting over multiple connections. Using `HttpSessions` gives you the ability to maintain state between transactions.

The getCreationTime() Method

```
public long getCreationTime()
```

The getCreationTime() method returns the time in which the session was created. This time value is a long value representing the milliseconds elapsed since January 1, 1970 UTC.

getCreationTime() has no parameters.

It returns this value:

- long

It throws this exception:

- IllegalStateException

The getId() Method

```
public java.lang.String getId()
```

The getId() method returns a String containing a unique identifier for the current HttpSession.

getId() has no parameters.

It returns this value:

- java.lang.String

It throws this exception:

- IllegalStateException

The getLastAccessedTime() Method

```
public long getLastAccessedTime()
```

The getLastAccessedTime() method returns the last time, in milliseconds, the client sent a request with HttpSession.

getLastAccessedTime() has no parameters.

It returns this value:

- long

It throws this exception:

- IllegalStateException

The getMaxInactiveInterval() Method

```
public int getMaxInactiveInterval()
```

The getMaxInactiveInterval() method returns the maximum interval between requests that the server will keep the session valid.

getMaxInactiveInterval() has no parameters.

It returns this value:

- int

It throws no exceptions.

The getSessionContext() Method

```
public HttpSessionContext getSessionContext()
```

The getSessionContext() method returns a reference to an HttpSessionContext object bound to the current session.

getSessionContext() has no parameters.

It returns this value:

- HttpSessionContext

It throws this exception:

- IllegalStateException

The getValue() Method

```
public java.lang.Object getValue(java.lang.String name)
```

The getValue() method returns a reference to the named object in the current session, or Null if there is no such bound object. The object must be downcasted to its original type.

getValue() has one parameter:

- java.lang.String

It returns this value:

- java.lang.Object

It throws this exception:

- IllegalStateException

The getValueNames() Method

```
public java.lang.String[] getValueNames()
```

The getValueNames() method returns an array of Strings representing all the data objects bound to this session, or a zero-length array if no objects are in the session.

getValueNames() has no parameters.

It returns this value:

- `java.lang.String[]`

It throws this exception:

- `IllegalStateException`

The invalidate() Method

```
public void invalidate()
```

The invalidate() method forces the session to be invalidated and removed from the context.

invalidate() has no parameters.

It returns no value.

It throws this exception:

- `IllegalStateException`

The isNew() Method

```
public boolean isNew()
```

The isNew() method returns True if the server has just created the session, and the session has not been acknowledged by the client.

isNew() has no parameters.

It returns this value:

- `boolean`

It throws this exception:

- `IllegalStateException`

The putValue() Method

```
public void putValue(java.lang.String name)
  java.lang.Object value)
```

The putValue() method binds the passed in object to the passed in String and puts the object into the session. If there is an object in the session already bound to the name, that object is replaced.

putValue() has two parameters:

- java.lang.String
- java.lang.Object

It returns no value.

It throws this exception:

- IllegalStateException

The removeValue() Method

`public void removeValue(java.lang.String name)`

The removeValue() method removes the object from the current session that is bound to the passed in name. All objects implementing the HttpSessionBindingListener interface will have their valueUnbound() methods called.

removeValue() has one parameter:

- java.lang.String

It returns no value.

It throws this exception:

- IllegalStateException

The setMaxInactiveInterval() Method

`public void setMaxInactiveInterval(int interval)`

The setMaxInactiveInterval() method sets the maximum interval between requests before a server invalidates the session.

setMaxInactiveInterval() has one parameter:

- int

It returns no value.

It throws no exceptions.

The HttpSessionBindingListener Interface

```
public interface HttpSessionBindingListener
  extends java.util.EventListener
```

The HttpSessionBindingListener interface defines methods that an object can implement if it wants to be notified of an object in the session being bound or unbound.

The valueBound() Method

```
public void valueBound(HttpSessionBindingEvent event)
```

The valueBound() method notifies a listener that the object is being bound into a session.

valueBound() has one parameter:

* HttpSessionBindingEvent

It returns no value.

It throws no exceptions.

The valueUnbound() Method

```
public void valueUnbound(HttpSessionBindingEvent event)
```

The valueUnbound() method notifies a listener that the object is being unbound from a session.

valueUnbound() has one parameter:

* HttpSessionBindingEvent

It returns no value.

It throws no exceptions.

CLASSES

The Cookie Class

```
public class Cookie
  extends java.lang.Object
  implements java.lang.Cloneable
```

The Cookie class represents a "cookie" used for session management in HTTP protocols. Cookies are name/value pairs that are created by the server and stored in the client.

The Cookie() Method

```
public Cookie(java.lang.String name,
  java.lang.String value)
```

The `Cookie()` constructor initializes a `Cookie` object with the passed in name/value pair. Names cannot contain whitespace, commas, or semicolons, and they should only contain ASCII alphanumeric characters.

`Cookie()` has two parameters:

- `java.lang.String`
- `java.lang.String`

It returns no value.

It throws this exception:

- `IllegalArgumentException`

The setComment() Method

`public void setComment(java.lang.String purpose)`

The `setComment()` method is used to describe the cookie's purpose, when requested by the client.

`setComment()` has one parameter:

- `java.lang.String`

It returns no value.

It throws no exceptions.

The getComment() Method

`public java.lang.String getComment()`

The `getComment()` method returns the comment used to describe the cookie's purpose, or `Null` if no comment is defined.

`getComment()` has no parameters.

It returns this value:

- `java.lang.String`

It throws no exceptions.

The setDomain() Method

`public void setDomain(java.lang.String pattern)`

The `setDomain()` method sets the pattern to which to match the host domain. If the host does not match, the cookie will not be presented to the host.

`setDomain()` has one parameter:

- `java.lang.String`

It returns no value.

It throws no exceptions.

The getDomain() Method

`public java.lang.String getDomain()`

The `getDomain()` method returns the domain pattern of this cookie.

`getDomain()` has no parameters.

It returns this value:

- `java.lang.String`

It throws no exceptions.

The setMaxAge() Method

`public void setMaxAge(int value)`

The `setMaxAge()` method sets the maximum age of the cookie. The cookie will expire after the passed in number of seconds. If the passed-in age is 0, the cookie is deleted immediately. If a negative number is passed, the cookie will exist until the browser exits.

`setMaxAge()` has one parameter:

- `int`

It returns no value.

It throws no exceptions.

The getMaxAge() Method

`public int getMaxAge()`

The `getMaxAge()` method returns the maximum age of the cookie in seconds.

`getMaxAge()` has no parameters.

It returns this value:

- `int`

It throws no exceptions.

The setPath() Method

```
public void setPath(java.lang.String uri)
```

The setPath() method sets the valid path for the cookie. If the URL does not begin with the passed in value, it is not a valid path.

setPath() has one parameter:

- `java.lang.String`

It returns no value.

It throws no exceptions.

The getPath() Method

```
public java.lang.String getPath()
```

The getPath() method returns the URL prefix for which this cookie is targeted.

getPath() has no parameters.

It returns this value:

- `java.lang.String`

It throws no exceptions.

The setSecure() Method

```
public void setSecure(boolean flag)
```

The setSecure() method indicates to the user agent that the cookie should only be transmitted using a secure protocol.

setSecure() has one parameter:

- `boolean`

It returns no value.

It throws no exceptions.

The getSecure() Method

```
public boolean getSecure()
```

The getSecure() method returns True if the cookie can only be transmitted using a secure protocol.

getSecure() has no parameters.

It returns this value:

- `boolean`

It throws no exceptions.

The getName() Method

`public java.lang.String getName()`

The `getName()` method returns the name of the cookie.

`getName()` has no parameters.

It returns this value:

- `java.lang.String`

It throws no exceptions.

The setValue() Method

`public void setValue(java.lang.String value)`

The `setValue()` method sets the value of the cookie.

`setValue()` has one parameter:

- `java.lang.String`

It returns no value.

It throws no exceptions.

The getValue() Method

`public java.lang.String getValue()`

The `getValue()` method returns the value of the cookie.

`getValue()` has no parameters.

It returns this value:

- `java.lang.String`

It throws no exceptions.

The getVersion() Method

```
public int getVersion()
```

The getVersion() method returns the version number of the cookie. A 0 indicates the cookie is based on the original specification developed by Netscape. A 1 indicates the cookie is based on the RFC 2109.

getVersion() has no parameters.

It returns this value:

- int

It throws no exceptions.

The setVersion() Method

```
public void setVersion(int value)
```

The setVersion() method sets the cookie protocol used when the cookie saves itself.

setVersion() has one parameter:

- int

It returns no value.

It throws no exceptions.

The clone() Method

```
public java.lang.Object clone()
```

The clone() method returns a copy of this object.

clone() has no parameters.

It returns this value:

- java.lang.Object

It throws no exceptions.

The HttpServlet Class

```
public class HttpServlet
    extends javax.servlet.GenericServlet
    implements java.io.Serializable
```

The `HttpServlet` class is meant to simplify the writing of HTTP servlets. It extends the `GenericServlet` class and implements the `java.io.Serializable` interface. The `HttpServlet` class is an abstract class; therefore it cannot be instantiated directly.

The HttpServlet() Method

```
public HttpServlet()
```

The `HttpServlet()` constructor is a default empty constructor.

`HttpServlet()` has no parameters.

It returns no value.

It throws no exceptions.

The getLastModifiedTime() Method

```
protected long getLastModifiedTime(HttpServletRequest request)
```

The `getLastModifiedTime()` method returns the last time the requested entity was modified. The value returned is measured in milliseconds since January 1, 1970.

`getLastModifiedTime()` has one parameter:

- `HttpServletRequest`

It returns this value:

- `long`

It throws no exceptions.

The doPost() Method

```
protected void doPost(HttpServletRequest request,
  HttpServletResponse response)
  throws ServletException
  java.io.Exception
```

The `doPost()` method services all POST requests for the servlet. The `doPost()` method receives two parameters: an `HttpServletRequest` object, which encapsulates the client's request, and an `HttpServletResponse` object, which contains the response that is sent back to the client. The `doPost()` method throws a `ServletException` if it cannot service the request and throws a `java.io.IOException` if there was an I/O error.

`doPost()` has two parameters:

- `HttpServletRequest`
- `HttpServletResponse`

It returns no value.

It throws these exceptions:

- `ServletException`
- `java.io.IOException`

The doPut( ) Method

```
protected void doPut(HttpServletRequest request,
  HttpServletResponse response)
  throws ServletException
  java.io.Exception
```

The `doPut()` method services all PUT requests for the servlet. The `doPut()` method receives two parameters: an `HttpServletRequest` object, which encapsulates the client's request, and an `HttpServletResponse` object, which contains the response that is sent back to the client. The `doPut()` method throws a `ServletException` if it cannot service the request and throws a `java.io.IOException` if there was an I/O error.

`doPut()` has two parameters:

- `HttpServletRequest`
- `HttpServletResponse`

It returns no value.

It throws these exceptions:

- `ServletException`
- `java.io.IOException`

The doGet( ) Method

```
protected void doGet(HttpServletRequest request,
  HttpServletResponse response)
  throws ServletException
  java.io.Exception
```

The `doGet()` method services all GET requests for the servlet. The `doGet()` method receives two parameters: an `HttpServletRequest` object, which encapsulates the client's request, and an `HttpServletResponse` object, which contains the response that is sent back to the client. The `doGet()` method throws a `ServletException` if it cannot service the request, and throws a `java.io.IOException` if there was an I/O error.

doGet() has two parameters:

- HttpServletRequest
- HttpServletResponse

It returns no value.

It throws these exceptions:

- ServletException
- java.io.IOException

The doDelete() Method

```
protected void doDelete(HttpServletRequest request,
  HttpServletResponse response)
  throws ServletException
  java.io.Exception
```

The doDelete() method services all DELETE requests for the servlet. The doDelete() method receives two parameters: an HttpServletRequest object, which encapsulates the client's request, and an HttpServletResponse object, which contains the response that is sent back to the client. The doDelete() method throws a ServletException if it cannot service the request and throws a java.io.IOException if there was an I/O error.

doDelete() has two parameters:

- HttpServletRequest
- HttpServletResponse

It returns no value.

It throws these exceptions:

- ServletException
- java.io.IOException

The doOptions() Method

```
protected void doOptions(HttpServletRequest request,
  HttpServletResponse response)
  throws ServletException
  java.io.Exception
```

The doOptions() method services all OPTIONS requests for the servlet. The default implementation automatically determines what HTTP options are supported. The doOptions() method throws a ServletException if it cannot service the request and throws a java.io.IOException if there was an I/O error.

doOptions() has two parameters:

- HttpServletRequest
- HttpServletResponse

It returns no value.

It throws these exceptions:

- ServletException
- java.io.IOException

The doTrace() Method

```
protected void doTrace(HttpServletRequest request,
  HttpServletResponse response)
  throws ServletException
  java.io.Exception
```

The doTrace() method services all TRACE requests for the servlet. The doTrace() method receives two parameters: an HttpServletRequest object, which encapsulates the client's request, and an HttpServletResponse object, which contains the response that is sent back to the client. The default implementation copies all the headers from the request into the response to be sent back to the client. The doTrace() method throws a ServletException if it cannot service the request and throws a java.io.IOException if there was an I/O error.

doTrace() has two parameters:

- HttpServletRequest
- HttpServletResponse

It returns no value.

It throws these exceptions:

- ServletException
- java.io.IOException

The service() Method

```
protected void service(HttpServletRequest request,
  HttpServletResponse response)
  throws ServletException
  java.io.Exception
```

This is an HTTP-specific implementation of the `Servlet.service()` method. It handles standard HTTP requests by dispatching them to the appropriately implemented methods. The `service()` method throws a `ServletException` if it cannot service the request and throws a `java.io.IOException` if there was an I/O error.

`service()` has two parameters:

- `HttpServletRequest`
- `HttpServletResponse`

It returns no value.

It throws these exceptions:

- `ServletException`
- `java.io.IOException`

A Second service() Method

```
public void service(ServletRequest request,
  ServletResponse response)
  throws ServletException
  java.io.Exception
```

This method implements the `Servlet.service()` method by delegating requests to the appropriate HTTP-specific `service()` method. The `service()` method throws a `ServletException` if it cannot service the request and throws a `java.io.IOException` if there was an I/O error.

`service()` has two parameters:

- `ServletRequest`
- `ServletResponse`

It returns no value.

It throws these exceptions:

- `ServletException`
- `java.io.IOException`

The HttpSessionBindingEvent Class

```
public class HttpSessionBindingEvent
  extends java.util.EventObject
```

The `HttpSessionBindingEvent` object is sent to all objects that implement the `HttpSessionBindingListener`, when a listener is bound or unbound from an `HttpSession`.

The HttpSessionBindingEvent() Method

```
public HttpSessionBindingEvent(HttpSession session,
   java.lang.String name)
```

The `HttpSessionBindingEvent()` constructor initializes the object with the session acting as the source of the event and the name of the object being bound or unbound.

`HttpSessionBindingEvent()` has two parameters:

- `HttpSession`
- `java.lang.String`

It returns no value.

It throws no exceptions.

The getName() Method

```
public java.lang.String getName()
```

The `getName()` method returns the name of the object that is being bound or unbound.

`getName()` has no parameters.

It returns this value:

- `java.lang.String`

It throws no exceptions.

The getSession() Method

```
public HttpSession getSession()
```

The `getSession()` method returns the session from which the listener is being bound or unbound.

`getSession()` has no parameters.

It returns this value:

- `HttpSession`

It throws no exceptions.

The HttpUtils Class

```
public class HttpUtils
   extends java.util.EventObject
```

The `HttpUtils` class contains a collection of static utility methods that are useful to HTTP servlets.

The HttpUtils() Method

`public HttpUtils()`

The `HttpUtils()` constructor creates an empty `HttpUtility` object.

`HttpUtils()` has no parameters.

It returns no value.

It throws no exceptions.

The parseQueryString() Method

```
public static java.util.Hashtable
  parseQueryString(java.lang.String s)
```

The `parseQueryString()` method takes the passed in query string and parses it into a hash table of key-value pairs, where the values are arrays of strings.

`parseQueryString()` has one parameter:

- `java.lang.String`

It returns this value:

- `java.util.Hashtable`

It throws this exception:

- `IllegalArgumentException`

The parsePostData() Method

```
public static java.util.Hashtable
  parsePostData(int len,
  ServletInputStream in)
```

The `parsePostData()` method takes HTML form data that is sent to the server as a POST request, parses it, and returns a hash table of key/value pairs. If keys have multiple values, their values are stored as an array of Strings.

`parsePostData()` has two parameters:

- `int`
- `ServletInputStream`

It returns this value:

- `java.util.Hashtable`

It throws this exception:

- IllegalArgumentException

The getRequestURL() Method

```
public static java.lang.StringBuffer
  getRequestURL(HttpServletRequest request)
```

The getRequestURL() method takes a request object and reconstructs the URL used by the client to make the request.

getRequestURL() has one parameter:

- HttpServletRequest

It returns this value:

- java.lang.StringBuffer

It throws no exceptions.

INDEX

Get **FREE** books and more...when you register this book online for our Personal Bookshelf Program

http://register.samspublishing.com/

 Register online and you can sign up for our *FREE Personal Bookshelf Program...*unlimited access to the electronic version of more than 200 complete computer books—immediately! That means you'll have 100,000 pages of valuable information onscreen, at your fingertips!

 Plus, you can access product support, including complimentary downloads, technical support files, book-focused links, companion Web sites, author sites, and more!

 And you'll be automatically registered to receive a *FREE subscription to a weekly email newsletter* to help you stay current with news, announcements, sample book chapters, and special events, including sweepstakes, contests, and various product giveaways!

 We value your comments! Best of all, the entire registration process takes only a few minutes to complete, so go online and get the greatest value going—absolutely FREE!

Don't Miss Out On This Great Opportunity!

Sams® is a brand of Macmillan Computer Publishing USA.

For more information, please visit *www.mcp.com.*

Other Related Titles

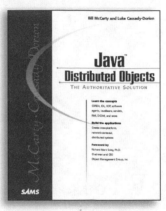

Java Distributed Obects
Bill McCarty
Luke Cassady-Dorion
ISBN: 0-672-31537-8
$49.99 US/$74.95 CAN

Pure JFC Swing
Satyaraj Pantham
ISBN: 0-672-31423-1
$34.99 US/$52.95 CAN

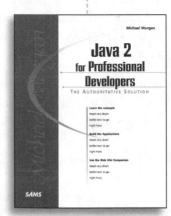

Java 2 for Professional Developers
Michael Morgan
ISBN: 0-672-31697-8
$34.99 US/$52.95 CAN

All prices are subject to change.